THE AUTOBIOGRAPHY OF
MARTIN VAN BUREN

A Da Capo Press Reprint Series

THE AMERICAN SCENE
Comments and Commentators

GENERAL EDITOR: WALLACE D. FARNHAM
University of Illinois

THE AUTOBIOGRAPHY OF MARTIN VAN BUREN

Edited By John C. Fitzpatrick

Volume I

DA CAPO PRESS • NEW YORK • 1973

Library of Congress Cataloging in Publication Data

Van Buren, Martin, Pres. U.S., 1782-1862.
   The autobiography of Martin Van Buren.

   (The American scene: comments and commentators)
   Reprint of the 1920 ed., which was issued as v. 2
of the Annual report of the American Historical
Association for the year 1918.
   Includes bibliographical references.
   1. Van Buren, Martin, Pres. U.S., 1782-1862.
I. Fitzpatrick, John Clement, 1876-1940, ed.
II. Series: American Historical Association. Annual
report, 1918, v. 2.
E387.A32   1973   973.5'7'0924 [B]   72-75314
ISBN 0-306-71275-X

This Da Capo Press edition of *The Autobiography of Martin Van
Buren* is an unabridged republication in two volumes of the one-
volume first edition published in Washington, D.C., in 1920 as
Volume II of the *Annual Report of the American Historical
Association for the Year 1918.*

Published by Da Capo Press, Inc.
A Subsidiary of Plenum Publishing Corporation
227 W. 17th Street, New York, New York 10011

THE AUTOBIOGRAPHY OF
MARTIN VAN BUREN

ANNUAL REPORT

OF THE

AMERICAN HISTORICAL ASSOCIATION

FOR

THE YEAR 1918

IN TWO VOLUMES

VOL. II

THE AUTOBIOGRAPHY OF MARTIN VAN BUREN

EDITED BY JOHN C. FITZPATRICK

WASHINGTON
GOVERNMENT PRINTING OFFICE
1920

WASHINGTON, D. C., *June 9, 1919.*
To the Executive Council of the American Historical Association.

GENTLEMEN : In recommending to you for publication the Autobiography of Martin Van Buren, the Historical Manuscripts Commission begs leave to acknowledge the public spirit of Mrs. Smith Thompson Van Buren, of Fishkill, N. Y., who placed this valuable document in the Library of Congress, and the courteous assistance of the Library, which offers a typewritten copy of it supplemented with an introduction and notes prepared by a member of the staff.

Very respectfully yours,

JUSTIN H. SMITH, *Chairman*

PREFATORY NOTE.

The autobiography of Martin Van Buren was presented to the Library of Congress by Mrs. Smith Thompson Van Buren, of Fishkill, New York, in 1905. At the same time the Van Buren Papers were presented to the Library by Mrs. Smith Thompson Van Buren and Dr. and Mrs. Stuyvesant Fish Morris, of New York City. A Calendar of the Papers was published by the Library in 1910.

The Autobiography is the manuscript copy, in seven folio volumes (1247 pages), made by Smith Thompson Van Buren, the son and literary executor of the President, from Van Buren's original draft. Portions of Volumes VI and VII are in another hand, and the last fifteen pages of the manuscript have many changes and corrections by Van Buren himself.

The first two hundred and fifty-nine pages of this copy were edited by Mr. Worthington C. Ford, formerly Chief of the Manuscript Division, Library of Congress. The lettered footnotes are Van Buren's own; the chapter divisions and numbered notes are the editor's.

The Autobiography is written with engaging frankness, and the insight it affords to the mental processes of a master politician is deeply interesting. Van Buren's desire to be scrupulously fair in his estimates is evident, and, if he did not always succeed, his failures are not discreditable. Though the Autobiography does not compel the revision of established historical judgments, it yet presents authority for much in our political history hitherto somewhat conjectural and records political motives and activities of the period in an illuminating and suggestive manner.

In analyzing men and measures, Van Buren all unconsciously paints a picture of himself and it is a truthful and worthy portrait. It is impossible to read the Autobiography through without greatly regretting that it was not carried beyond the point it reaches.

As a contribution to the political history of the United States, its presentation of facts is too valuable to be ignored safely by the conscientious investigator.

J. C. FITZPATRICK,
Assistant Chief, Manuscript Division,
Library of Congress.

3

FOURTEENTH REPORT OF THE HISTORICAL MANUSCRIPTS COMMISSION

June 4, 1919

THE AUTOBIOGRAPHY OF MARTIN VAN BUREN

Edited by JOHN C. FITZPATRICK

AUTOBIOGRAPHY OF MARTIN VAN BUREN.

CHAPTER I.

VILLA FALANGOLA,
Sorrento, June 21, 1854.

°At the age of seventy one, and in a foreign land, I commence a sketch of the principal events of my life. I enter upon this work in the hope of being yet able to redeem promises exacted from me by friends on whose judgments and sagacity I have been accustomed to rely. I need not now speak of the extent to which an earlier compliance with their wishes has been prevented by an unaffected diffidence to assume that the scenes, of which they desire to perpetuate the memory, will be found to possess sufficient interest to justify such a notice. That their opinions in regard to that question have not been biased by the partiality of their ardent friendship is hardly to be supposed, yet it ought not, perhaps, to surprise any that they should have thought that not a few of our contemporaries and successors would be interested, and, possibly, the young men of the country benefited, by a true and frank account of the rise and progress of one, who, without the aid of powerful family connexions, and with but few of the adventitious facilities for the acquisition of political power had been elevated by his Countrymen to a succession of official trusts, not exceeded, perhaps, either in number, in dignity or in responsibility by any that have ever been committed to the hands of one man—consisting of the respective offices of Surrogate of his County, State Senator, Attorney General of the State of New York, Regent of the University, Member of a Convention to revise the Constitution of the State, Governor of the State, Senator in Congress for two terms, Secretary of State of the United States, Minister to England, Vice President, and President of the United States.

As it is not improbable that much of the solicitude manifested by my friends, in connection with this work, has grown out of their feelings and opinions in regard to transactions of 1840 and 1844, in which my interests were supposed to be deeply involved, it may not be amiss that I should say a few words on those subjects in advance.

° MS. Book I, p. 1.

The Presidential Canvass of 1840, and its attending occurrences, are at this moment, without reasonable doubt, subjects of regret with ninety-nine hundredths of the sober minded and well informed people of the United States. No one of that number can now hesitate in believing that the scenes thro' which the Country passed in that great political whirlwind were discreditable to our Institutions and could not fail, if often repeated, to lead to their subversion. Indeed nothing could have better served to justify and strengthen our reliance upon the sober second-thought of our People, than the sense so widely entertained of those transactions as soon as the passions that produced them had subsided, and the fact that no attempt has been since made to revive them. It is the duty of every sincere friend to those Institutions to regard with forbearance whatever took place at a period & under circumstances to so great a degree unfavorable to the diffusion of truth & to a correct appreciation of public measures.

The defeat of my nomination for re-election in 1844, after it had been demanded by Constituencies represented by ―― out of ―― (the whole number of Electors of President and Vice President) was the result of an intrigue that had its origin exclusively in the Presidential aspirations of individuals, aided at its inception by prejudices, unjust I hope, but such as the long continued exercise of political power seldom, if ever, fails to generate, and only finally made successful by the co-operation of the slave power, subsequently & adroitly brought to the assistance of designs already matured.

Upon both of these topicks I shall of course have more to say hereafter. For the present, it is sufficient to declare, as I do with entire sincerity that I have never entertained the thought that a majority of the People designed to deal unjustly with me on either occasion. Errors were doubtless committed on all sides, delusions set on foot which there was not time to dissipate and means, designed for good ends, perverted to bad purposes. But neither of these events, important as they were have ever planted in my breast a single root of bitterness against the People at large, and it affords me equal satisfaction to say that the reconciling influence of Time, with the consciousness that I had already enjoyed a larger share of popular favor than I could think myself entitled to, have brought me to look with complacency, at least, upon the conduct of the individual actors in those stirring scenes.

My feelings towards a People, with whom I have had so many and such interesting relations are consequently, now, & I trust will continue to be those of gratitude and respect. What I may write will not therefore proceed, as is often the case with those whose public career has been abruptly closed, from a wounded spirit, seeking self-vindication, but will, on the contrary be under the control of a judgment which satisfies me that I ought to be, as my feelings lead me to be, at peace with all the world. I have besides imbibed a large share of Mr. Jefferson's repugnance to "provings & fendings of personal character." So strong has this feeling been that it has induced me, over and over again, to wait for the tardy but certain effects of time to vindicate me from unjust censure, when I had the means at my command for the prompt & effectual refutation.

After abandoning a direct attempt to go on with this work, commenced more than a year ago, I employed some of my leisure moments in the collection of materials. These from the irresolution under which I laboured did not seem to promise results of much value, beyond a temporary relief from the self reproach which was caused by past neglect. Hoping to arrive at a better mood on the course of my travels, I have brought these with me & to them has fortunately been added a complete analysis of the Political History of New York by Judge Hammond, made for me by my much beloved & lamented son Martin, who had, as I find from his papers, with the affectionate forethought that characterized him, devoted much of °his time to similar occupations in anticipation of my possible wants & wishes. This supplies me with the chronological order of early events, which I have found to be, at this distance from my papers, an indispensable requisite.

With these scanty preparations, but under the stimulus imparted by high health, the exhilaration of this beautiful situation and salubrious climate in the mountains of Sorrento, and the thought-stirring vicinage of Vesuvius, the promontory of Misenum, the classic Bay of Baiae, the island of Capri, and the exhumed cities of Pompeii and Herculaneum, I have once more determined to overcome that disinclination to mental efforts which has thro' life been my besetting infirmity, and to enter with spirit upon the accomplishment of a task, the performance of which I have hitherto had too much reason to regard with feelings of despair.

My family was from Holland, without a single intermarriage with one of different extraction from the time of the arrival of the first emigrant to that of the marriage of my eldest son, embracing a period of over two centuries and including six generations.[1] I spent a few weeks in Holland, after the abrupt close of my brief mission to England in 1832, and was very kindly received by the King, William I. He informed me that a gentleman of my name was at

---

° MS. I, p. 5.

[1] The record of the family of Martin Van Buren has been traced by Frank J. Conkling, who published it in the New York Genealogical and Biographical Record, vol. xxviii, pp. 121 and 207.—W. C. F.

one time Minister of Foreign Affairs under one of his ancestors; that the name was derived from the town of Buren, in the neighbourhood of Utrecht,[1] which was formerly an Earldom, and from which by the marriage of one of his forefathers, he derived one of his present titles—that of Count Buren. Of the fact which he suggested that my family was from the same stock I have neither knowledge or belief, or, I may add concern, nor do I feel any temptation to claim family relationship with a branch of the Van Burens of Holland as the family is literally extinct, even though its head had the honor of connecting her name with that of Nassau.[a]

All I know of my ancestors commences with the first emigrant from Holland who came over in 1633, and settled in what is now called Rensselaer County in the State of New York. His son, [Marten], my great Grandfather, moved to Kinderhook and settled on lands conveyed to him in 1669, by a Deed in my possession, given pursuant to his father's will by Derick Wessels, of Albany, a distinguished man in his day, as his father's part of a patent granted nominally to Wessels, but for the benefit of his co-proprietors.[2] He and his son Martin and grand-son Abraham (my father) lived and died—the latter at the advanced age of 82—on the lands thus acquired. They were all farmers, cultivating the soil themselves for a livelihood, holding respectable positions in society and sustaining throughout unblemished characters. My mother's maiden name was Goes,[3] a name also favorably known in Dutch annals, and she was regarded by all who knew her as liberally endowed with the qualities & virtues that adorn the female character. My father was an unassuming amiable man who was never known to have an enemy. Utterly devoid of the spirit of

---

[1] The village of Buren is in the Province of Gelderland.—W. C. F.

[a] Finding it in my way on my second visit to Holland in 1854, I paid a visit to the ancient town of Buren. I found it a pleasant little place containing a population of about seven hundred souls. On inquiry I found that there were yet three of the name left & I sent for the eldest. He took me to the place where Castle Buren, as represented on the map, had stood, and showed the ground yet bearing traces of a fortified place & of its appropriate environs. He pointed out the lands & houses which had belonged to the Earldom, but which had all been sold by the French during their dominion in Holland, and were now occupied, doubtless to their great improvement, by the owners of the soil. The grounds belonging to the Castle were purchased & are now owned by the Corporation. The family had become extinct & their bones had been within a year, for reasons he assigned, removed from a previous place of interment and reburied within a small yard near the spot where the Castle stood, surrounded by an evergreen hedge, and shaded by a weeping willow in the centre, to the expense of which, he said, the King had contributed liberally. A spot had been reserved for my guide, not he said, as a relation, but as the oldest of the name in the town.

[2] Cornelis Maessen, the first of the line, sailed for America in the vessel *Renssalaerswyck* in the summer of 1631, bringing his wife, Catalyntje Martense, and a son, Marten. They settled on the Van Rensslaer property at a place called Papsknee, on the east side of the Hudson River, near Greenbush. A generation appears to have been omitted in this account, for the son of Maessen, Marten, did not remove to Kinderhook. The son of Marten, Pieter Martense, removed to that place, and his son, Marten, was the grandfather of the President.—W. C. F.

[3] Maria Goes [Hoes] widow of Johannes Van Alen.—W. C. F.

accumulation, his property, originally moderate, was gradually reduced until he could but illy afford to bestow the necessary means
upon the education of his children. My advantages, in that respect, were therefore limited to those afforded by the village academy
& I was at a very early age (I believe not more than fifteen or
sixteen), placed in a lawyers office where I remained for several
years. It has thro' life been to me a source of regret that I had not
pursued the course so often successfully adopted by our New England young men under like circumstances,—that is to spend a portion of their time in teaching the lower branches of learning, and,
with the means thus obtained, to acquire access for themselves to
the highest.

My mind might have lost a portion of its vivacity, in the plodding
habits formed by such a course, but it could not have failed to acquire
in the elements of strength supplied by a good education much
more than it lost. In place of the studies by which I would thus
have given employment to an uncommonly active mind I adopted
at a very early age the practice of appearing as Counsel before
Arbitrators and inferior tribunals and my success was such as
to give rise to exaggerated impressions that were brought before
the public in the course of my after political career. Altho' my
mind was in this way severely and usefully disciplined for the
examination and discussion of facts, & the practice in that respect
was eminently useful, yet the tendency of the course of training was
adverse to deep study, and gave an early direction and character
to my reading that I was never able to change. Instead of laying
up stores of useful knowledge, I read for amusement and trusted
to my facility for acquiring necessary information when occasions
for its use presented themselves. I was born with a sanguine temperament, the mental features of which as described by Dr. Mayo
(the well known English Surgeon and author) "are a disposition
ardent, hasty and impetuous; the spirits high and buoyant, a capacity for intellectual exertions of the strongest kind or highest
flight, but often capricious and ill sustained," in contradistinction
from those of the "mixed or equal temperament" which is, he says,
"well disposed towards great and continually renewed exertions."
I feel free to say that I have never been able to overcome the tendencies ascribed to the former.

How often have I felt the necessity of a regular course of reading
to enable me to maintain the reputation I had acquired and to sustain me in my conflicts with able and better educated men, and resolved to enter upon it without further delay! But ever in a whirl
of excitement, and absorbed by the cares attached to the new public
stations to which I was successively elevated I was sure to fall back,

after a few spasmodic efforts, to my old habit of reading light matters° to relieve the mind and to raise it out of the ruts in which long thinking on one class of subjects is so apt to sink it, leaving the weightier matters of the law, as well as those that appertained to public affairs to the period when it became indispensable to grapple with them. I am now amazed that with such disadvantages I should have been able to pass through such contests as it has been my lot to encounter with so few discomfitures. Much adroitness was often necessary to avoid appearing in debate until I had been able to make myself master of the subject under discussion. That remarkable man John Randolph, in one of his morbid moods, wrote a series of letters to General Jackson in which he assailed Mr. Calhoun with great severity and at the same time laboured to divert the General from a purpose he attributed to him—that of making me his successor. These General Jackson, as was his habit in regard to all private letters designed to sow tares between us, sent to me for my perusal: Among many curious and characteristic observations in regard to myself he said that in his long experience in public life he had scarcely ever met with a single prominent man less informed than myself upon great questions when they were first presented, or who understood them better when I came to their discussion. I remember well the General's hearty laugh when he heard me subscribe to the justice of the description. Few can have been more entirely indebted for whatever success may at any time have crowned intellectual efforts to uncultivated nature than myself, yet I do not remember the occasion when I succeeded in satisfying my friends that I did not feel that I could have done much better if I had possessed better advantages of Education and study. Hence my resolutions revived at almost every period of my life to become a severe student—resolutions which were frustrated, if not, as the Apostle says of sin, by a war in my members, certainly by one in my unconquerable mental habits.

I cannot pass from the subject of my early professional career in inferior tribunals without a caution to my young friends, the circumstances of whose start in life may resemble my own, against the adoption of a similar course. The temptation to anticipate professional fame is a strong one, and my success, humble as it has been, is well calculated to mislead young men of genius and ambition. Whatever the degree of that success may have been they may be assured that it would have been much greater and more substantial if like many others, who may not have succeeded as well, I had first acquired a sound education and stored my mind with useful knowledge. After those invaluable objects are substantially accomplished, many advantages may be derived from the practice I pursued; but if those acquisitions do not precede its adoption they will in all probability never be made.

I was admitted to the Bar of the Supreme Court in the Fall of 1803, and gave my first vote in the ensuing spring in the celebrated Gubernatorial election between Aaron Burr, and Morgan Lewis. Altho' I had for some time before been entrusted with professional business, and, as a zealous politician, represented my county at the age of nineteen in a District Convention held at Troy, which nominated John P. Van Ness for Congress, yet both my professional and political career can only be considered as commenced at this period. The families which had hitherto taken the lead in the politics of my native town were the Van Ness on the Republican, and the Van Schaack and the Silvester on the Federal side. They had been opposed to each other, as Whigs and Tories in the Revolution, and they imbibed the prejudices and resentments engendered by Civil War; they had also been arrayed in adverse ranks in all the political divisions that had subsequently arisen, but by a remarkable combination of circumstances I was, at my first appearance on the political stage, placed in direct opposition to those influential families and their friends as a united body, and experienced a full share in the intolerance that characterized the times.

Mr. Silvester,[1] in whose office I had been placed as a student, was a just and honorable man. Such was also the character of his venerable father, and indeed of all the members of his family. ° His Uncles, the Van Schaacks, and their numerous connexions, including the widely known and justly respected Peter Van Schaack, were persons of much reputation and distinction. But they were all ardent politicians, and some of them very violent in their feelings. Efforts to divert me from my determined course were not wanting. I will refer to but one of them. After the election of 1798 or '9, when I was between sixteen and seventeen years of age, Elisha Williams, who in the sequel became my principal professional competitor, arrived in the village, and announced the success of the federal candidates, of whom Peter Silvester, the father of my instructor and one of the purest men I ever knew, was one. There followed, of course, a gathering of the faithful—a firing of cannon and all the usual methods of rejoicing over political success, continuing until night. It was noticed that I did not participate in these expressions, and whilst a collection of choice spirits, (of whom an elder half-brother of mine was one) were drinking their wine and singing "Hail Columbia!" and other patriotic songs in an

---

[1] Francis Silvester. ° MS. I, p. 15.

upper room, Cornelius Silvester, a brother of my instructor, a merchant, and a generous, noble hearted man, having observed the state of my feelings, came out and pressed me earnestly to join them. Having declined his invitation, which was given with delicacy and kindness, I retired to his store, where I slept in the absence of his clerk. Some time after midnight I heard a knocking at the door, and on opening it, admitted Mr. Silvester himself. At his instance I returned to my bed, and he placed himself by its side, and for more than an hour occupied himself in presenting the reasons which ought to induce me to adopt the politicks of the Federal party, and solicited me to do so with a degree of earnestness and obvious concern for my welfare which I could not but respect.

After hearing him out, I replied calmly that I appreciated thoroughly the kindness of his feelings, and was well satisfied of the purity of his motives, but that my course had been settled after much reflection, and could not be changed. He paused a moment, and then took my hand and said he would never trouble me again on the subject, and would always remain my friend. As was quite natural my insensibility to repeated remonstrances and solicitations and the active part which I thus early took against them in party politics engendered heart burning with all and occasional tho' slight bickerings between Mr. Silvester and myself which rendered my situation disagreeable, and determined me to seek another place to complete my studies. Mr. Van Ness succeeded in his election to Congress, married an heiress at Washington, and returned to Kinderhook in high feather. His father, altho' a man of wealth had been disappointed in his son's first progress in life and, being withal a very severe man, had withheld from him all advances not indispensable to his support. So poor were both of us, that when I went to Troy to sustain his nomination, I had to borrow the amount necessary to defray my expences. Being now in very affluent circumstances, and conscious of the increasing embarrassment of my situation in Mr. Silvester's office, he pressed me to enter one of the prominent law offices in the city of New York, and offered to loan me the necessary funds, to be repaid when I was able. I accepted the offer, went to New York, and entered temporarily, the office of his brother William P. Van Ness, intending to look about me before selecting an office of the character we contemplated. Mr. W. P. Van Ness treated me kindly, and altho' he had but little business, as I found so much the more opportunity for study I remained with him to the end of my Clerkship. It becoming necessary for Mr. Van Ness to advance large sums to relieve estates on which his wife owned mortgages from prior incumbrances he was only able to fulfill his promise to me to the trifling extent of Forty dollars, but tendered his pledge to re-imburse any temporary accommodation I might obtain from other sources; but at this juncture my half brother stepped forward and loaned me all I wanted. The prompt return of the forty dollars to Mr. Van Ness closed our pecuniary relations in advance of the change that soon after took place in those of a personal and political character.

The war between Colonel Burr, and the Clintonians was then raging·with its greatest severity, and the contest which closed the political career of the former took place in the ensuing spring. Mr. William P. Van Ness carried me occasionally to visit Colonel Burr at Richmond Hill, and I met him sometimes at Mr. Van Ness's house. He treated me with much attention, and my sympathies were excited by his subsequent position. Having entered upon the practice of my profession in my native town, under very favorable circumstances and already acquired the reputation of an active politician, the course I would take in the election became a question of considerable local interest. The relation in which I had stood to the Van Ness family, with my known personal partiality for Colonel Burr, created so strong an impression that I would support him, that my friends have often in later years been called upon to defend me against the charge of having been a Burrite. In reply to a friendly and very proper letter from William P. Van Ness I stated to him the grounds upon which I had decided to support the Republican candidate Morgan Lewis. These letters are still among my papers.[1] Notwithstanding this, Mr. John P. Van Ness came from Washington to attend the election, and re-opened the matter to me. I explained to him at our first interview the stand I had taken, and the grounds of it. He however continued the discussion for several days, until not finding me disposed to yield, he stopped abruptly in the street, and said, with emphasis, "I see, Sir, that you are determined upon your course." I replied, "Yes, Sir! I told you so at the beginning." He immediately said " Good morning, Sir! " with a very grave look and tone, turned on his heel, and walked off. From that moment our friendship terminated, and our social relations even were suspended for nearly twenty years. We encountered each other in the newspapers and at the polls, and when I offered my vote, the first I ever gave, his father, Peter Van Ness, and Peter Van Schaack, who had been, as I have already said, at variance since the Revolution, but were now both ardent supporters of Col. Burr, came forward, arm in arm, accompanied by the son of the latter, who, with their approbation, challenged my vote. Altho' the inspectors declared themselves satisfied, I was compelled to take the oath prescribed by law—an indignity which at the

---

[1] *William P. Van Ness to Van Buren,* 22 February, 1804, and Van Buren's reply, 13 March, 1804.

next election I retaliated upon young Van Schaack in a way as technically lawful as his own, but which stung him and his friends too deeply to be soon forgotten.

Peter Van Ness and Peter Van Schaack, whose combined influence frowned so harshly upon the commencement of my political career were men of no common mark. Judge Van Ness commenced life in the humble but respectable trade of a wheelwright, with very little education, and yet by the force of a strong intellect and an indomitable spirit, he raised himself to high positions as well in the government as in the society in which he lived. As early as the French War in 1756, and at the age of nineteen, he commanded a company, by their own choice, and served with them in Canada. He afterwards commanded a Regiment at the capture of Burgoyne in 1777. He was a prominent member, perhaps the most so, of the Committee of Public Safety for his County, during the Revolutionary War, State Senator, Member of the Council of Appointment, Member of the Convention for the Adoption of the Constitution, and First Judge of his County, which office he held at the time of his death. He was intolerant in his political opinion and arbitrary in his disposition. The traditions of the neighbourhood, in which he lived and died, abound with anecdotes of his fiery temper and personal courage, and in the epitaph on his tombstone, erected at Lindenwald, forty years after his death, and after the place had been some time mine, he is described by his eldest son, General John P. Van Ness, as "an honest brave man, who feared nothing but his God." My opposition to° his views, which he regarded as a species of treason in a stripling and a member of a family with whom he had been connected at marriage and had been always intimate, produced during the canvass unpleasant collisions between us that made it difficult to treat him with the respect due to his years and position, and his death occurred too soon after those exciting scenes to give his anger time to subside. In that interval I had but one meeting with him, and that under circumstances that I had reason to believe did not aggravate his prejudice. His son William, having been the second of Col. Burr in his duel with Gen. Hamilton, which took place soon after the election, finding it prudent to leave the city of New York after the result was known came to his father's house at Kinderhook.

He informed me by a friendly note, of his desire to go to Albany, and to consult with me, before going, in regard to his right to be bailed if he should be arrested there, and for that purpose asked me to call on him at his father's house. Happy in the opportunity thus afforded to shew him that our differences in regard to the election

---

° MS. I, p. 20.

had made none in my friendly feelings towards him I started at once for his father's residence without a thought of the existing relations between the old gentleman and myself. As I approached the porch of the house built and then owned and occupied by Judge Van Ness, I perceived that the lower half of the old-fashioned front door which was divided through the middle (a style greatly favored by our Dutch ancestors) was closed, and the upper open, at which the Judge was seated close to and with his back against the lower door, for the benefit of the light, reading a newspaper. Hearing my steps he looked around and perceiving me, instantly resumed his reading in a manner that precluded me from addressing him. The door for explanation, as well as that for entrance, being thus closed upon me, and not feeling disposed to retreat, I seized the knocker which was hanging near his head, and gave it a somewhat emphasized rap, and as I did so I saw a smile upon his countenance of which my position afforded me a profile view. His son answered the summons immediately, spoke to his father, (who passed into the drawing room without looking behind him) and opened the door for me. He proposed a walk to the neighboring bank of the creek to prevent interruption from visitors. We passed thro' the Hall, and, as we left the house by the back door, he apologized to me for having forgotten the relations between his father and myself, which would have made it more proper for him to come to me. I told him he was not to blame, for, in the pre-occupation of the moment, I had forgotten them myself, but thought the circumstances bid fair to improve our intercourse, and then described the old gentleman's irrepressible amusement at the free use I had made of the knocker. He laughed and said that he had no doubt his father was pleased with the way, so much in character with his own decisive temper, in which I had extricated myself from the embarrassment in which he had placed me. The Judge died in the succeeding month of December, possessed of considerable wealth. The estate on which he had long resided, and on which he was buried, was originally settled by a family who were relations of my father. It was sold at the close of the Revolutionary War to pay the debts of the then head of the family, and purchased by the Judge. He devised it to his son William, in whose hands it went thro' a similar process, and was purchased by one of his creditors who sold it to me. In the many alterations and improvements I have made in the house I have preserved the old double-door, and its knocker, as interesting memorials of my last interview with its orignal owner.

During my long official residence at Washington, very courteous relations were maintained with my old friend Gen. John P. Van

Ness, but he by no means liked my political principles. My course in regard to the currency and particularly in respect to the Banks of the District of Columbia, in one of which he was deeply interested, displeased him so much, as to induce him to come to our county in 1840, to speak and electioneer against my re-election. Having, at an early day, obtained my permission to erect a monument over his father's grave, he came up for that purpose, not a great while before his death, but with an evident resolution that our intercourse should be of the most reserved character. Altho' the business he had in hand would detain him some days, he declined my invitation to stay with me, and, at first, every other advance on my part to facilitate his operations. I notwithstanding directed my people to give him all the assistance he needed, and on the second day he consented to dine with me. He did the same on each succeeding day, and left me when his work was finished with feelings as kind as those which existed at the commencement of our acquaintance. We visited the tomb together on the last day of his stay and he read aloud the inscription on the monument, and when he came to the words commemorating his father's bravery, which I have elsewhere quoted, he turned to me and said emphatically "You, Sir, know that this is true;" to which I very heartily and sincerely assented. The General died shortly afterwards. I did not see him again. I have thought this brief notice due to a gentleman with whom I was at the commencement of my career so closely connected, and who was in every sense a remarkable man.

Peter Van Schaack was a native of Kinderhook. His family was among its first settlers, and generally independent in their circumstances. He was a graduate of Columbia College and had every facility afforded him for improvement. Of these he did not fail to avail himself and came to be extensively and justly regarded as a finished scholar as well as a learned Counsellor. Having studied the Common law thoroughly as a science and made himself master of its general principles, their application to particular cases was to him always a matter of pleasant entertainment rather than of labour. A diffidence which he could not overcome prevented him from becoming a successful advocate, but his legal opinions were generally respected. He was through life, excepting the period of the War of the Revolution, the friend and close companion of Jay, Benson, and Sedgwick, but those ties were suspended by the course he took in that great struggle. They became prominent and efficient Whigs, while his principles made him a Tory. The correspondence between Mr. Jay and himself, while they stood in that position of antagonism, which is published in a very creditable life of Mr. Van Schaack, written by his son, does high and enduring honor to both parties. He was banished, and resided in England until the close of the War. When he returned Mr. Jay met him at the wharf and gave him a cordial and generous reception. He resumed the practice of his profession and in the progress of time became once more united in political principle with Gov. Jay and the other friends I have named in the ranks of the federal party. Altho' he occupied an eminent position at the Bar and in Society for half a century following he was never elected to any public office, nor was he to my knowledge ever a candidate for one. He lived in times and in locations which would have been favorable to his election, if he had desired it, but his sight became gradually impaired, ending in total blindness. That circumstance and feelings of delicacy connected with his course in the Revolution kept him out of the Arena, as a candidate, but did not prevent him from being a thorough partisan.

His prejudices against me in early life were of the rankest kind, but being frequently associated as counsel in important professional business, in which our feelings were deeply enlisted, we came to understand and to like each other better. For a series of years before his death our relations were of a friendly character—politics always excepted. In respect to the latter we never made an approach toward accord, and but a few years before his death, he went, old and blind as he was, to the Polls to vote against me, in my canvass for the office of Governor of New York, and in favor of a gentleman whom I knew he did not like, personally, half as well as he liked me.[1] My faith in the capacity of the masses of the People of our Country to govern themselves, and in their general integrity in the exercise of that function, was very decided and was more and more strengthened as my intercourse with them extended.° Of this he had, to use the mildest term, very little. The limited extent to which his nature would allow him to entertain it was, at an early and critical period, overthrown, and the severe penalties inflicted upon his unbelief, doubtless gave to his feelings in this regard a character of harshness. Differing so widely at the starting point, our views became more divergent at every step we took in politics, as well in regard to men as to measures. On my first return from England I visited Kinderhook, and hearing that he was lying hopelessly ill, I was on the point of starting to see him, when his son came with an invitation from him that I should do so; and I was deeply impressed with the solemnity of the interview. I found him lying on a temporary bed in his library, where he desired to die, and where I had so often seen him in the full possession and exercise of his powerful mental faculties. As soon

---

[1] Van Buren's opponents were Smith Thompson and Solomon Southwick, the latter running on the anti-Masonic ticket.—W. C. F.

° MS. I, p. 25.

as I entered he had himself raised in his bed, extended his hand to me and expressed his satisfaction at seeing me. He said that he was going through his last change, and on my expressing a hope that such might not prove to be the case, he stopped me, and said "No!" he had lived out the full measure of his days, and could not be too thankful that his mental faculties had been preserved till his last moments. It so happened that I had made myself familiar with the place of his residence during his exile in London, and he listened with interest to my description of its present condition. He spoke kindly and considerately of the relations that had existed between us, and I was struck with his evident desire to make the civil things his gentlemanly disposition induced him to say conform strictly to the fact, without reviving unpleasant recollections. In bidding me farewell forever he said "I am happy, Sir, to think that we have always been"—*friends* he seemed about to add, but, pausing a moment, he continued—"*that you always came to see me when you visited Kinderhook.*" In a day or two I heard that this distinguished man had ceased to live.

CHAPTER II.

I remained in the practice of the law twenty five years, and until I entered upon the duties of the office of Governor, since which I have never appeared in a professional capacity before any judicial tribunal, comprising from my admission to the present time a period of fifty one years. For my business I was to a marked extent indebted to the publick at large, having received but little from the Mercantile interest or from Corporations, and none from the great landed aristocracies of the country. It was notwithstanding fully equal to my desires and far beyond my most sanguine expectations. I was not worth a shilling when I commenced my professional career. I have never since owed a debt that I could not pay on demand nor known what it is to want money, and I retired from the practice of my profession with means adequate to my own support, and to leave to my children, not large estates, but as much as I think it for their advantage to receive. The cases in which I was employed embraced not only the ordinary subjects of litigation between man and man in communities like that in which I resided but extended to the most intricate and important causes that arose during the last fifteen or twenty years of my practice. In the management of these I was repeatedly associated with and opposed to such men as Richard Harrison, Aaron Burr, Thomas Addis Emmett, Daniel Webster, John Wells, John V. Henry, Peter Van Schaack, Abraham Van Vechten, David B. Ogden, Samuel A. Talcott and Elisha Williams— a galaxy of great lawyers scarcely equalled in the professional ranks of any country.

Elisha Williams, altho' ten years my senior was my professional antagonist thro' the whole of my professional career. We were for a long succession of years employed in almost every cause that was tried at the Bar of Columbia County, where we both resided, and almost always on opposite sides. We were at the same time prominent leaders in our respective political parties, and both warm partisans. To the danger of imbibing personal prejudice from these prolific sources was added that which threatened the discharge of adverse duties in cases embittered by the strong personal antipathies of the parties to the litigation; and yet, with a constant indulgence in what is called loose, and means liberal practice, we never had, to my recollection, a motion before the Court for relief against technical or formal advantages taken on either side. I invariably encountered him with more apprehension at the Circuits than any of

21

the great men I have named, and I am sure I speak but the opinion of his professional contemporaries when I say that he was the greatest *nisi-prius* lawyer of the New York Bar. It seemed scarcely possible to excel his skill in the examination of witnesses or his addresses to the Jury, but with these his ambition seemed satisfied; for arguments at the Term he was seldom well prepared and far less successful. On closing our last professional concern after my retirement he expressed to me by letter his great satisfaction that in a practice so peculiarly exciting as ours had been we had never any cause for personal complaint in our professional proceedings and tendered me assurances of his respect and esteem, feelings which were very cordially reciprocated on my part.

The briefest sketch of the incidents of such a professional career as mine has been would yet be too long for insertion here, assuming that they would be of sufficient interest so long after their occurence, to justify it. They must therefore, with one or two exceptions, be left to the judicial reports, and to the traditions of the times. The exceptions, as will be seen, have more than professional relations.

My employment as Counsel to contest the title of the Livingston family to the Manor which bears their name, has been a fruitful scource of misrepresentation of both my professional and political conduct, and I will therefore be excused for placing that matter upon its true ground. Did the subject possess no other interest than my own vindication from unmerited aspersions I would, on the principle by which I am governed in the preparation of this Memoir, pass it by. But a brief and true statement of a matter which has, at intervals for nearly a century produced bitter litigation and violence, making repeated appeals to military aid necessary to the preservation of the public order, and in regard to which the acts of distinguished individuals have been brought in question, cannot be without interest.

Robert Livingston, in the year 1684, obtained a Patent from the Crown for a strip of Land on the Eastern shore of the North (or Hudson) River, stretching from the Northern to the Southern Boundary of the Manor, as it is now held, and extending into the woods so far as to contain Eighteen Hundred acres, with a reference to monuments at each end of the strip, which are now the North and South bounds of the Patent. A short time afterwards he obtained another Patent for what was then and has ever since been known as Tackkanic (Taghkanie?) Flats lying East of the first Tract, and supposed to contain eight hundred Morghens of land. Both grants contained definite bounds and distinct quantities. In 1686 he obtained a Patent of Confirmation, which recites the two previous Patents, and states that the tracts described in them *lie adjacent to each other.* This Patent contains apt words granting and confirming to him and to his heirs the said Tracts of land, therein represented to have been previously granted and now described by exterior bounds, referring to natural objects, which bounds included the present Manor. In point of fact the lands embraced in the two first Patents lay from eighteen to twenty miles apart from each other, and the intermediate lands constitute the principal part of the present Manor, amounting to some   acres, whilst the tracts contained in the original Patents amount to between three and four thousand. That this representation was the act of the applicant for the Patent and that it was grossly untrue are undeniable facts. They have never been controverted because they could not be denied, and there is not the slightest doubt that if the Government at °Home had, become apprised of the glaring falsity upon which the Patent of Confirmation was granted, and had, within a proper time, instituted proceedings to vacate it, the Patent would have been declared void. Why it was not done, and why this indirect course was originally pursued by Mr. Livingston, and why he did not afterwards apply for and obtain an original Patent not referring to and wholly independent of those which were tainted with the fraud, are questions which will probably never be solved. The regulations in force in regard to the quantity for which grants to individuals were authorized when the first Patents were granted, the footing on which he stood with the Government at the different periods when they were issued, and a natural repugnance to an acknowledgment of the original Error may each have had their influence in controlling his course, and there may have been inducements of which we have no knowledge or suspicion. But instead of adopting the course I have referred to, Mr. Livingston made it the business of his life, as it has been that of his heirs, to uphold the tainted title by a succession of acts on the part of the Crown, by its Colonial Government, and on the part of the State Authority after the Revolution, to strengthen the Patent of Confirmation, and his claim under it.

The fact of the misrepresentation and the fraud involved in it was open to the tenants, and the ground readily taken that no after acts, bottomed on that original fraud could render the title valid. This state of things gave rise to periodical agitations and repeated outbreakings among the tenants from about the year 1760 to the present time; one or more arose before I was born, one whilst I was a student at law, one whilst I was at the Bar, and one after I left it. When I was retained by the Committee who represented the Tenants, I gave the main opinion in writing in which I held,

---

° MS. I, p. 30.

First, that the Patent of 1686 (the first which covered the Manor) was void on account of the fraudulent misrepresentation it contained and on which it was founded, and was not made valid by the subsequent Patents which recited it, and were, in that respect, avowedly designed as Patents of Confirmation only; and *Secondly*, That the effect of the possession of the claimants under it and of the statutes of limitation in barring the rights of the State was a question of greater difficulty, in regard to which I must not be understood as encouraging them with a prospect of a favorable result. A suit to try titles was brought by Thomas Addis Emmett as Attorney General on behalf of the State, but before it could be brought to trial, he was displaced from office by a political change, and succeeded by Abraham Van Vechten. The Committee not believing that they could be properly prepared at the first Circuit for which the cause was noticed for trial, in which opinion their counsel, including Mr. Emmett, (whom they had retained after his removal) concurred, and assuming that their wishes for a postponement until the next Circuit would, under the circumstances, be respected, took no preparatory steps. These views and wishes were communicated to Mr. Van Vechten, on his arrival at Hudson, who declined to comply with them, and decided to proceed in the trial. The Committee protested against this decision, and refused to take any part in the investigation. The trial, virtually an *ex-parte* proceeding, resulted in a verdict for the defendants. No farther steps were taken whilst I was at the Bar, but the matter was, as is well known, subsequently revived and bitterly contested.

Whilst the proceedings first referred to were going on, I was called upon by Gen. Jacob R. Van Rensselaer, accompanied by Mr. Williams, and informed that a report was in circulation on the Manor, that he had said on the floor of the House of Assembly, in a debate on a petition of the tenants, "that the tenants were not fit to govern themselves, and deserved to have a Master"—that this report was doing him great injury in the matter of his re-election, and that, as I could not believe that he had said so, he wished me to authorize the Newspaper to contradict the report in my name as the most effectual way of putting it down. I asked him whether he had any suspicion that the report had been in any degree countenanced by me. He replied,—"not the slightest"—that he had fully satisfied himself upon that point. I then told him that he had done me but justice in that regard, that I had never heard of the report before, and had no hesitation in saying to him and to Mr. Williams that I believed him to be a man of too much good sense to make such a remark, and this I thought would be the general opinion. But I added that their press had been for a long time and was at that very moment teeming with the most outrageous calumnies against me on the same general subject charging me with things which he could not but be satisfied were false, but that I heard of no attempts on his part or that of his friends to check their course; that I would point out the libels to which I alluded, shew him their falsity, if that were necessary, and that the moment I found him interfering in my behalf, as he wished me to do for him, I would with pleasure comply with his wishes;—until then I must decline to do so. He refused to connect other matters with his request and was as persistent in making it as I was in declining it. He then gave me notice that he would call a meeting of the People of the Manor towns, on a day and at a place he named, at which meeting he would charge me with writing a letter during the preceding winter (as he had been credibly informed was the case), to a member of the Legislature—Mr. Whallon advising him to stave off action on the Tenant's petition until after the Spring elections, with a view to securing the favourable effect on those elections of the pendency of the matter. I assured him that his information was entirely false, and offered to give him a letter, authorizing Mr. Whallon to furnish him with copies of any letters I had written to him, or to obtain copies for him myself. He declined the offer and called his meeting. I sent a messenger to the place with a letter, addressed to the Chairman of the meeting narrating what had taken place between the General and myself—giving the fullest contradiction to the revelation he proposed to make, and requesting to have my letter read to the meeting. The Chairman put my communication in his pocket, and allowed Gen. Van Rensselaer to make his statement—without saying one word to the meeeting about its receipt or contents.

When informed of this I published a card in the Newspapers and in Hand bills, denouncing in the strongest terms the falsity of the General's accusations, and called a meeting at the same place for the purpose of making the same denial in person. I gave the General notice of the time, place, and object of the meeting with an invitation to attend. When my friend Mr. Morell, and myself arrived at the place of meeting we found a very large assemblage of people, and among them General Van Rensselaer, Mr. Williams and several members of the Livingston family and their Agents. As soon as the meeting was organized I rose and stated my object in calling it—submitted to it certified copies of the only letters I had written to Mr. Whallon—denied the charge upon which the General had arraigned me before them and called upon him to maintain it if he could. He stood in a remote part of the room, but did not then speak or shew any disposition to do so. After a pause I rose again, and, repeating what had transpired, claimed that his continued silence must under the circumstances be regarded by the meeting as a confession that his charge was untrue. He then came forward, greatly agitated, and made an earnest appeal to the meeting, which he concluded by pledging himself that if I would commence a suit against him, he would, as the words were not actionable, deposit in Court five hundred dollars, as stipulated damages, to be forfeited if he did not prove the charge. I promised to comply with the suggestion, and contented myself with asking the meeting to remember my prediction that the Deposit would never be made. After the close of the Election I called upon him to redeem his promise, when he replied that he had, at the time, limited the period within which the call was to be made, and as that had expired he now declined to make the Deposit; a declaration which the whole assembly before whom his pledge had been given knew to be unfounded. The publication of our correspondence closed the affair between the General and myself. I also brought a libel suit against the Editor [1] of the federal newspaper for a still broader [o] and libelous impeachment of my conduct and motives in the Manor controversy. This I ceased to prosecute on the application of Mr. Williams made by a letter in which he disclaimed for the Editor a design to accuse me of anything beyond or inconsistent with my professional rights and duties, claiming only that my opinions were wrong and led to injurious results.

I make these explanations in view of the extent to which these questions between Landlord and Tenant have in later times been made the subject of political agitation—leading to such debauchery of the publick mind as to enable it to hear without apparent shock, of the extension of Executive pardon to persons convicted of the darkest crimes growing out of such agitations, under circumstances justifying deep suspicion of being designed to operate upon their suffrages and the suffrages of their friends. The time has I hope never been when my mind would not have revolted at the mere contemplation of such dealings with such subjects, and I am quite unwilling to have any acts of mine confounded with those we have witnessed in more recent times.

I am induced to speak of another matter connected with my professional life because it relates to the only personal dispute I ever had which led to the extremity to which it was pursued. At the Columbia Circuit in the year 181 [?] we brought to a final and favorable decision, so far as related to the Courts of law, the long existing controversy in regard to the effect of a Patent, in which many of the Dutch families (and mine among them) w re inter-

---

ested, and which Mr. Van Schaack had had under his professional care and management since the year 1772. Being very much dissatisfied with the testimony of a surveyor, who had formerly been on our side but was now against us, I thought it but fair, as I was entitled to the closing speech, to give him notice of the attack I intended to make upon his credibility and the grounds of it, to afford the opposing Counsel an opportunity of sustaining him. Among the latter was John Suydam, a young gentleman from another county and then rapidly rising in professional fame, and also high in the confidence and esteem of the federal party. When I came to that part of the case he interrupted me and used offensive expressions, to which I replied hastily and still more offensively. No farther notice was taken of the matter on that or the next day, but on the third a dinner was given by General Van Rensselaer, at Claverack, to a large party of distinguished gentlemen of the federal party, including Mr. Suydam and also General Harry Livingston, a valorous old gentleman, who owed me much ill will and acknowledged the debt with no more reserve than that with which he strove to pay it. I am far from saying or even believing that the affair between Mr. Suydam and myself was made the subject of particular action at that dinner; but it gave Mr. Suydam a better opportunity than he had yet had to see to what extent I was an eye-sore to the Magnates of the County, and exposed him to the temptation of raising himself in their estimation by becoming the instrument of my humiliation. On the succeeding morning I was called from my seat in Court by Thomas P. Grosvenor (who had been one of the guests at the entertainment referred to) and by him presented with a challenge from Mr. Suydam. Mr. Grosvenor was the brother-in-law of Mr. Williams and a man of decided talent and distinction in publick life: he became afterwards a prominent member of Congress, had a personal affair with Mr. Calhoun, and died at Baltimore. He expressed his desire to accommodate the matter in which I believe he was sincere, as, altho' a man of extreme violence in politics, he was not wanting in generous impulses, and proceeded to state how he thought the affair might be arranged without discredit on either side. I thanked him for his good disposition, but had no difficulty in showing him that the reciprocal declarations he suggested would be directly inconsistent with what I had said of Mr. Suydam, and concluded by telling him that I had no course but to accept the invitation, and would give him a formal answer, through my friend Mr. Morell, after the adjournment of the Court. No one entertains a more contemptuous opinion of the bravery of the Duel field than myself, or holds the practice in less respect, but I deemed it indispensable to the maintenance of my position to follow the bad examples which publick opinion had sanctioned if not required. I therefore delivered my acceptance to Mr. Morell on my returning from Court. He reported to me the next morning that Mr. Grosvenor irritated by the incessant remonstrances of his friends against his agency in the affair, had refused to have any intercourse with him upon the subject, and had tendered to him any responsibility that he chose to demand; that he had then called on Mr. Suydam and offered him my reply which he refused to receive unless it came thro' Mr. Grosvenor. I requested him to see Mr. Suydam immediately and to propose to him, in my name, that we should agree to dispense with the farther action of both of our friends and appoint others as the only way in which the difficulty that had arisen could be obviated. He executed the commission and returned with a verbal answer from Mr. Suydam that he could not, under the circumstances, consent to dispense with Mr. Grosvenor's services. I went immediately to his hotel and posted him, and the affair finally evaporated in newspaper publications and recognizances to keep the peace.[1] For some years there was no intercourse between us, tho' a disposition to restore friendly relations was quite apparent on his part, and at length meeting at dinner, while attending Court in a neighbouring county, and sitting opposite to each other, he asked me to pass the wine which stood before me, and I met the overture with an invitation to take a glass with me which he accepted " with pleasure ", and we walked arm-in-arm to the Court house to our mutual gratification and the astonishment of our friends. He soon after joined our side in politicks, was elected to the [State] Senate as a Democrat, became my zealous friend and supporter and remained so till he died, sincerely lamented by all who knew him, and by none more than myself, as a man of noble impulses, honorable character and decided talent.

Earnestly engaged in a successful and lucrative practice, I had no desire to be a candidate for an elective office, nor did I become one until the Spring of 1812, when I was forced into that position by circumstances with which I could not deal differently. But from my boyhood I had been a zealous partisan, supporting with all my power the administrations of Jefferson and Madison—including the Embargo and other restrictive measures,—had acted with the great body of the Republican party in supporting the election of Morgan Lewis against Aaron Burr for Governor, and subsequently that of Daniel D. Tompkins against Governor Lewis[2] for the same office, sustained the prorogation of the Legislature by Governor Tompkins on the ground of the use of corrupt means to obtain the charter of the bank of America, and had exerted myself, as far as I could,

[1] Two notes of this affair are in the Van Buren Papers, November 25, 1811, and February 17, 1812.—W. C. F.

[2] In 1807.—W. C. F.

to arrest the bank mania of the times by which the State was dishonored and its best interests impaired. It is a curious coincidence in my publick career that notwithstanding my devotion to politicks, my first nomination for an elective office as well as that for the last I held, should both have been brought about by the unfriendly acts of those who chose to regard themselves as rivals without being, at the moment, anticipated by myself. There were several highly respectable citizens who aspired to the nomination to fill the vacancy in the office of State Senator which occurred in my District in 1812, but I was not of the number. I was unwilling to permit the possession of such an office or any other cause to interfere with the prosecution of my profession, to which I was warmly attached, and the circumstance that there had not then been so young a man as myself elected to the Senate prevented me from even thinking of it. William P. Van Ness, in whose office I had studied law, was one of the aspirants. He had succeeded to the title and possession of his father's place at Kinderhook and Mr. John C. Hogeboom and myself had prevailed upon Governor Tompkins to relieve him, by pardon, from the disfranchisement to which he had become liable as a second of Colonel Burr in the duel with General Hamilton. He had solicited my support but received for answer that I considered Mr. °Hogeboom best entitled to the place. To this he assented and assured me that he should do nothing to prevent his selection.

Not long afterwards and while Mr. Hogeboom and myself were spending a few days at Albany, we accidentally discovered that Mr. Van Ness (who had accompanied us to the city) was at that moment prosecuting a complicated intrigue to defeat our wishes in the matter—whatever they might be. Indignant at the information we had received, and mortified that in a matter in regard to which, as it proved, neither of us had any personal desires, we should have been thus treated, we immediately started for home determined to defeat the machinations that had been set on foot with so much secrecy and had already been in part executed. On our way from Albany Mr. Hogeboom, for the first time, informed me that the state of his private business would not admit of his being a candidate,—that he had consulted with our friends at Albany,—that they all thought it important that I should be in the Senate, and that Mr. De Witt Clinton was particularly desirous that I should be sent. I objected to the proposition for reasons already referred to, with sincerity and earnestness. He entreated me not to come to a final conclusion until he could have a full opportunity to place the subject in all its bearings before me, and prevailed upon me to stop at his house for the night that we might talk the matter over more fully.   In the course of the evening he informed me more particularly of the views taken of the matter by Mr. Clinton, and remonstrated earnestly against a refusal to comply with the wishes of my friends.   I agreed to give him a final answer in the morning when, satisfied that there was but one ground on which I could with propriety decline, I informed him that altho' I had not heard so I thought it very probable that Mr. Robert Jenkins, a highly respected citizen of Hudson, might, if the nomination was to come from that city, desire to have it; that if he did so desire, as I had but recently become a resident of Hudson I could not think of entering into competition with him; that I should on reaching home communicate to Mr. Jenkins' friends without reserve all that had passed between us, and that if they did not desire the nomination for Mr. Jenkins I would not oppose the wises of my friends, but if they did I must insist on being excused.   To this he consented and we parted. On my arrival I found that there also the city delegates had already been chosen and that I had been placed at their head, with three other gentlemen, the particular friends of Mr. R. Jenkins, of whom his brother, Mr. Seth Jenkins, was one.   I immediately asked an interview with those gentlemen at my own house, in which I stated to them all that had passed between Mr. Hogeboom and myself— my own disinclination to be a candidate—and my determination to refuse the nomination if they desired to bring Mr. Jenkins forward, and I begged them to inform me frankly of their wishes.   From their conversation I inferred that I was mistaken in supposing they entertained the views I had anticipated, and that they concurred in the opinion of Mr. Hogeboom that I could not refuse to run.   Finding myself thus committed as I supposed to a contest with Mr. Van Ness only for the nomination, I thought it important in view of the transaction at Kinderhook to have the attention of the Party immediately directed to the subject by a call of the Convention.

Some days after the publication of the Call, Judge Wager, a political friend from the country called at my office and said, " I learn that you intend to have the Senator taken from Hudson "—to which I replied, in a tone which under such circumstances gentlemen who suppose themselves referred to usually employ.   He responded that I need not speak so modestly as it was not to me but to Robert Jenkins that he referred.   I told him that he was mistaken upon that point, as Mr. Jenkins did not wish the nomination, on hearing which he informed me, to my amazement, that my co-delegate Seth Jenkins had within the hour applied to him to support his brother, and had, in reply to a suggestion from him about me, referred to my youth and recent settlement in the city as reasons why I ought not to be selected.   Satisfied from the character of my informant that there could be no mistake on his part I immediately addressed notes to the three gentlemen of the Committee inviting them to meet me in the evening. They came to my house at the time appointed and I repeated to them what had passed at our previous interview, as I have stated it here, and then asked whether my statement was correct. Mr. Seth Jenkins (who was the spokesman throughout) answered affirmatively, but added that they had not at any time expressed themselves to the effect I had inferred, altho' he freely admitted that my inference from what had been said was, under the circumstances, as right and fair as if they had expressed themselves to that effect in terms. I then mentioned his conversation on that day with Judge Wager, my account of which he admitted to be correct. I then asked him with much feeling on what possible ground he could justify himself in treating me in so ungenerous a manner. He replied promptly that he would not attempt to deny that their course had in appearance been both disingenuous and unkind, but he affirmed solemnly that it had not proceeded from unfriendly motives, but that they had been controlled by circumstances which he might some day explain to me, and placed in a situation that put it out of their power to act otherwise and that they would have no reason to complain of any course I thought proper to take. I replied that they had left me no other choice than to obtain the nomination if in my power, which I should assuredly do, and we parted. The remaining members of the Committee were both honorable and upright men, incapable of an unworthy design. Mr. Jenkins had many of the good qualities of his race, but had besides an innate passion for political intrigue, and as I have almost always found to be the case with men subject to that infirmity, was neither skillful in his schemes or successful in their execution. His subsequent explanation was that he had entered into an arrangement with Mr. Van Ness that they would combine their strength against me, assuming that I would be a candidate, and leave it to the convention to decide between his brother and Van Ness, and that he had been obliged to promise the latter that he would hold no communication with me upon the subject until they met again. But why such an understanding precluded him from saying what would certainly exclude me from the canvass he could never explain without conceding that they were certain of their game, and that they had a farther object, viz; to break down my influence in the county, which he was not willing to admit.

The contest excited great interest, and the Convention was the most imposing in numbers and character that had ever been held in the county. The republican portion of the Livingston family sup-

ported Edward [P.] Livingston, and combined their opposition to
me with the supporters of Jenkins and Van Ness, each willing that
the convention should nominate either of them so that I should be
excluded. I was chosen by a majority over all of them on the first
ballot. The election was severely contested. The federalists supported Mr. Livingston, who had also a spurious republican nomination. Against me were arrayed the entire federal party, the Lewisites, the Burrites, and the supporters of the Bank of America, who
had obtained its charter at a previous session of the Legislature, but
designed to procure from the next a reduction of the *bonus* they had
been obliged to promise to the State—a project they were well satisfied would be opposed by me. Our Senatorial district then embraced
a quarter of the State. Mr. Livingston and myself were the only
candidates in the field, and I was successful by a majority of less
than two hundred, the whole number of votes given being about
Forty thousand. Altho' this was the actual result, much delay and
many unfavorable reports and contradictions preceded the final an-
nunciation of my political birth and baptism.

The annual election under the old Constitution took place in the
last week of April, and the Supreme Court of the State commenced
its spring session at the city of New York in the first week of May.
Thither flocked all the leading lawyers of the State, who were, in those
days more even than now, also its prominent politicians, bringing
with them the results of the elections in their several counties; we
had then neither railroads, nor electric telegraphs, and the first week
or two of the Term was generally spent in anxious expectation and
digestion of election reports. My district was mainly° composed
of River Counties, lying on both sides of the North River, and therefore among the first to be heard from; still, when I left Hudson to
attend the Term, it was generally conceded that I had been defeated.
Whilst I was arranging my luggage and my papers, my opponents,
headed by the leading men of my county, were celebrating their
supposed victory at the Hotel on the opposite side of the street,
and when I left my door the most jubilant among them appeared
on the piazza and shed upon me, at parting, the light of their beam-
ing countenances. On the steamboat I met the well known Ebenezer
Foot, an able lawyer and remarkable man of the day, always before
that time a Democrat, but then seduced from my side thro' the influence of the Bank, who professed to sympathize with me in my
defeat. While passing Catskill I perceived the tall figure of my
brother-in-law, Judge Cantine,[1] towering above the crowd, and pointing his finger at a small boat that was making towards us. When it

---

° MS. I, p. 45.   [1] Moses J. Cantine.—W. C. F.

reached us a letter was brought to me containing a canvass of the old republican county of Delaware which shewed that my majority in that county had been understated, and was in fact sufficient to render my election certain. I handed the letter to my sympathizing friend Counsellor Foot, whose countenance, notoriously not handsome, supplied an amusing commentary upon his recent condolences. When the steamer arrived at New York, early on Sunday morning, Judge William W. Van Ness of the Supreme Court, a very distinguished man, of whom I will have to speak hereafter, and Barent Gardinier, a famous federal member of Congress during the War of 1812, were standing arm in arm, on the wharf, and recognizing Thomas J. Oakley on the boat, they hailed him, and demanded to know the result of the election for Senator in the Middle District. His characteristic reply was that " Van Buren was on board, and they should ask him." The Judge only said " Come Gardinier, let us go," and they walked off without farther question, but meeting afterwards with a citizen of Rockland County, who gave him a canvass of its election different from the one theretofore conceded to be correct, he came to my lodgings, and asked me what would be the result if Rockland had given the vote he named, to which I replied that in that case Mr. Livingston was certainly elected. He gave me the name of his informant and kindly assured me that the information might be relied on. Having received the official Canvass from the county of Rockland, the next morning, I reciprocated Judge Van Ness' polite attention, by enclosing it in a note which was delivered to him, whilst seated on the Bench, by that great man, in his way, High Constable Hays, and this ended all question on the subject.

From this period to the expiration of my Presidential Term I occupied, without the intermission of a year, responsible official positions either in the state or federal governments, two thirds of the time in the latter,—positions which made it my duty to take active part in the discussion and settlement of almost every public question, in conjunction with or in opposition to many of the distinguished public men of the day.

It is of those questions, and of the measures produced by them,—of the parts taken in regard to them by myself and by my contemporaries, with my views of their characters and dispositions, that I propose to speak. I design to state as well how those subjects presented themselves to me at the time, as how far my first impressions have been changed or modified by subsequent experience or reflection.

I would shew myself unfit for the performance of this task if I were not deeply sensible of the obstacles to its satisfactory execution. To check the indulgence in egotism, to which human nature is so prone, especially when it has the temptation and the excuse of an auto-biography, so far as to make what is said endurable; to pronounce justly and impartially on matters in which we have been ourselves implicated and to speak with equal truth and candour of contemporaries, whether they have been bound to us by political agreement and personal ties, or separated from us by the lines and perhaps by the asperities of party—are difficult things. My best efforts will however not be wanting to accomplish these objects, and my confidence in my ability to do so is founded on qualifications of the heart rather than of the mind. My political opponents, at every stage of my public life, have with great unanimity, and with no more than justice, conceded to me a rare exemption from that personal ill will which party differences are apt to engender, nor is my breast now the abiding place of those morbid feelings and adhesive prejudices so often cherished by public men who have been thwarted in their career. I feel that I have made efforts in support of right principles which have failed, at times, either of being rightly understood or justly appreciated: a thing that has happened to every man who has aspired to an influence in the State. Yet it would be unjust in me not to admit, as I have elsewhere and always done, that my share of public honors has been greater than I could think myself entitled to by public services. The excess must be credited to the generosity of political friends, seldom very accurately proportioned to the merits of their favorites.

My confidence in the integrity of public opinion is at this moment as strong as it ever was, and my heart assures me that there lives not now and has not lived in our country a public man to whom I am not disposed to do justice. I may be mistaken as to facts and conclusions and I may overrate my ability to be impartial, but no ingenuous mind shall read what I write without acknowledging the purity of my intentions. I claim to be tolerably well acquainted with the workings of the human heart, and if I am not satisfied at the conclusion that the fruits of my present labours will bear this test, I will destroy them.

Accounts of personal transactions with delineations of individual peculiarities of mind and manners constitute the usual staple of works of this description. It might seem on first view that in regard to political Memoirs it would afford more interest to explain the nature of the great questions that occupied the public mind, and to re-examine the discussions that grew out of them, during the period embraced by the writer. But such an impression must I think lose its force when it is considered that at the time when such memoirs are usually prepared those questions have generally been finally settled in public opinion, have lost their importance or have been exhausted of their interest by re-iterated argumentation. The apathy and indifference which in such cases succeed to great interest, almost in proportion to its previous intensity, must be familiar to all observing minds. But whilst our concern in public questions is thus, in the nature of things, doomed to die away, it is very different in regard to the conduct and motives of distinguished individuals who took part in them. These seem never to lose their fascination, and hence our curiosity is seldom wearied by recitals of events of even little importance, before unknown, in the lives of men who acquired notoriety in their day. Hence also a great part of our interest in accounts of stirring scenes which we know to be fictitious. The most attractive as well as the proper study of mankind is man—not only to gratify our curiosity but by instructing us in the nature and dispositions of our fellow men, to increase our ability to perform well and successfully our own parts in the great drama of life.

CHAPTER III.

My Senatorial term commenced at a most critical period both of the State and Nation. War had been declared against Great Britain shortly after my election, and New York, as a frontier State, was destined to bear the brunt of the contest. Her extended frontier, as well by land as by sea, and the defenceless condition of both, cast a heavy responsibility on her Legislature. The Presidential election was close at hand, and the State had, with great unanimity put one of her most distinguished citizens in nomination for that high office. In addition to these grave matters, the Bank mania was at its highest point, and the State violently excited by the employment of the most profligate means for its gratification.

Neither the first nor the last of these subjects could cause me the slightest embarrassment. I had, as a citizen, given my ardent support to the preventive measures recommended by Jefferson and Madison, and regarded the declaration of war as a step indispensable to the maintenance of our National honor. No consideration, personal or political, could therefore withhold me from giving my aid to its vigorous prosecution. I was always opposed to the multiplication of banks, and throughout my eight years' service in the State Senate, voted against every application for a bank charter, save one at Buffalo, the object of which was to aid in repairing the losses sustained by the destruction of that town by the enemy, and justified as being in some sense a war measure.

Still more hostile to the bank corruptions so prevalent at the time, and against which I had successfully struggled in my election, nothing could be more congenial to my feelings and opinions than a cordial co-operation with all efforts to arrest the increase of banks, and to expose the guilty authors of those corruptions to the execration of the People.

My course in respect to the Presidential Question was, on the other hand, beset with serious difficulties. Mr. Madison had been nominated for re-election by a majority of the members of Congress —(then the usual method of making such nominations) and he was admitted by the Republicans, of every sort, to be an honest man and an accomplished Statesman. The Republican members of the New York Legislature had, however, before I became a member of that body, as I have already said, with great unanimity, presented Mr. Clinton as the opposing candidate, and had asked and obtained his

36

assent to the proceeding. The impending danger of War,° and a supposed superior capacity on the part of Mr. Clinton to meet such a Crisis were among the reasons assigned for his nomination. To New Yorkers it was urged that the Legislature having placed him in his then position, and no change having taken place save the actual declaration of War, the anticipation of which was one of the main reasons for his nomination, they owed it to their own and his honor to give him the vote of the State. I took my seat in the Senate for the first time at the Extra-session of the Legislature, held for the choice of Presidential Electors, and it was claimed that I stood in a position to which these considerations applied. I yielded to their influence, but did so with undisguised reluctance, and with a determination, understood by all, that nothing should prevent me from giving my votes and influence in favor of a vigorous prosecution of the War. Judge Hammond, in his Political History of New York, places my motives upon the true ground.[1] That I acted in strict conformity to the wishes of my immediate constituents there was no doubt, and it is equally true that I conscientiously believed that I was acting in the line of my duty. But now, when the excitements of the day have passed away, and personal predilections have lost their influence upon the question, I am free to say that·we all committed a great error. The rejection by the People of the President who had recommended the War, in the absence of any act to show his incompetency, would have done more injury to the public service than could have been counter-balanced by the alleged superior qualifications of Mr. Clinton for the crisis. This consideration should have induced Governor Clinton to decline the State nomination, after the declaration of War, notwithstanding the ground upon which he had been put forward, and to unite with his friends in the support of Mr. Madison. His failure to do so was fatal to his national aspirations, and many of his friends destroyed their political influence by adding disparagements of the War to their opposition to the candidate by whom its declaration had been recommended. But I reasoned differently then, or I might perhaps say more correctly, felt differently, for my personal attachment to Mr. Clinton was strong and probably too much influenced my judgment. My course however, although wrong, was thus far entitled to the merit of disinterestedness of motive, that I embarked in his support without a hope of success. Having heard of some remarks of mine indicative of this state of mind, addressed to a mutual and ardent friend at that very session, he called on me and said: "I hear that you despair of the election." I admitted that I had made the observation to which he alluded, and proceeded to explain my views upon the subject, which were in substance, that after what had taken place in the spring, we had no other course to pursue than to give the vote of the State to him, but that I fully believed it would be unavailing. He then shewed me a calculation very favorable to his election, made by a noted politician, that did not change my opinion though it had evidently produced a strong impression on him.

Mr. Clinton had not on account of particular circumstances expected my support. These I will briefly state as they afford an illustration of the danger of acting upon inferences be they ever so plausible and the propriety of prompt explanations between political friends.

Whilst Judge Ambrose Spencer and myself were sitting together, one evening, in the porch of Judge Richardson's house, in Auburn, Cayuga County, (at which place the former was holding a Circuit Court which I was attending as Counsel), our letters were brought to us containing news of the death of Attorney General Hildreth.[1] The Judge after a moments reflection, turned to me and said—" You ought to be Hildreth's successor "—and at once tendered me his support. I thanked him cordially, but expressed an apprehension that there were older members of the profession among our political friends who would think themselves slighted by the appointment of so young a man. He controverted the supposition with his usual earnestness, and I promised to think of the matter. The Judge and myself were at the time upon very good terms, but in the then scarcely perceptible but still existing division in our party, between himself and the friends of Clinton I ranked among the latter, and I did not like to take a step in the matter suggested by Judge Spencer without consulting Mr. Clinton. On my return home I wrote to Mr. Richard Riker, then a confidential friend of Mr. Clinton, informing him of what had passed between the Judge and myself, and requesting him to converse with Mr. Clinton and to let me know his opinion upon the subject. I also asked him to say to Mr. Clinton that if he thought I was too young or if he desired the appointment of some other friend he should have no embarrassment about saying so, and might rest assured that I would be perfectly satisfied. Mr. Riker informed me at once that Mr. Clinton was anxiously desirous of my appointment, and asked me to make no objections to having my name placed before the Council of Appointment. An Extra-meeting of that body was called to fill the vacancy in the summer of 1812, and a friend, [Richard Riker] with my consent, called on and broached the subject to Alderman Gilbert, a leading member of the Council, and a particular friend of Mr. Clin-

---

[1] Matthias B. Hildreth, of Johnstown.—W. C. F.

ton.[1] My friend found him reserved and indisposed to converse farther on the subject than courtesy required. Inferring from the report of this conversation that Mr. Clinton had changed his views, I requested my friend to return at once and inform Mr. Gilbert that I wished my name to be considered as withdrawn.

When I saw the appointment of Thomas Addis Emmet announced I was confirmed in the correctness of my inference, and from that moment to the meeting of the Legislature for the choice of Electors I received no explanation either from Mr. Clinton or Mr. Riker. Knowing the friendly relations existing between Mr. Clinton and Mr. Emmet, and sensible of the partiality for him on the part of our Irish citizens, I would at the latest moment have consented to the appointment of Mr. Emmet if Mr. Clinton had informed me of his wishes, but I felt injured by his silence.

After the Electors were chosen, in a manner and with a result very gratifying to him, Mr. Clinton asked me to spend the evening with him. Other visitors were denied admission, and whilst we were at tea he introduced the subject of the appointment to the office of Attorney General, and said he feared that I had thought hardly of him in regard to it. I explained my feelings to him as I have done above, and he then assured me in a very solemn manner that he had no agency, direct or indirect, in causing the appointment of Mr. Emmet. He admitted that from Mr. Gilbert's conduct and from the fact that the Council were all his particular friends, I had a right to draw the inferences I had drawn, but that they were nevertheless entirely unfounded. Although bound to believe from this explanation that Mr. Clinton had not himself taken any part in the matter, I could not yet dismiss from my mind the impression that the affair had been so managed by some of his friends as to produce the result without connecting him with it. This subject will again be noticed by me.

A brief relation of the interior history of a contest which excited great attention and effort at the time, and has never been forgotten in the States may even now, not be without interest. The friends of Mr. Clinton, in whom I confided and with whom I consulted, decided at the beginning to avoid throughout any intercourse or arrangement with the federalists in regard to their course. If we could get the vote of the state for him, without entering into or sanctioning a concerted coalition with them he

---

[1] The members of the Council of Appointment were William W. Gilbert, of the southern ; Johannes Bruyn, of the middle ; Henry Yates, Jun, of the eastern ; and Francis A. Bloodgood, of the western districts. " This council was decidedly Clintonian ; but the party decrees having been carried into effect by the preceding council, little remained to be done by this. Such appointments, however as were made, were made in accordance with the wishes and views of Mr. Clinton." Hammond History of Political Parties in the State of New York, I, 304.—W. C. F.

should have it. If not, the matter should be allowed to shape its own course. All we desired therefore was to place a ticket of Electors before the joint Convention of the two houses of the Legislature, in whole or in part (according° to the action of the Madisonians) favorable to Mr. Clinton, and to leave it to the option of the Federalists, without explanation or solicitation, either to vote for it, or to elect their own, if they could, by the aid of the Madisonians, or to make themselves a Madisonian ticket and elect that by combining their votes with those of the friends of Mr. Madison. One of these courses they would be obliged to pursue. We had a majority in the Senate over both Federalists and Madisonians, and of course the power of forming as we pleased one of the tickets to be submitted to the joint convention. The Federalists had a similar preponderance in the lower house, with, of course, like power.

The question between us and the Madisonians in regard to the composition of the Republican Ticket could only be settled in Caucus, where we had a decided majority over them. The venerable Judge Taylor, always before and soon after again a Clintonian, though now warmly opposed to him, was, on my motion, made Chairman of the Caucus. We offered at once to give them a portion of the ticket equal to their proportion of representatives in the Legislature compared with ours, and to elect the Ticket by our joint vote. This offer was peremptorily and perseveringly refused, and no proposition made in lieu of it that had even a shew of fairness to support it. After a very protracted discussion, and when it had become evident that no equitable compromise could be effected, I moved that an entire Clintonian ticket should be nominated. The Chairman called me to him and asked under great excitement whether I intended to persist in that motion. I replied " Certainly! unless the Madisonians will accept of a reasonable portion of the ticket." Upon this the Veteran put his large brimmed hat that was lying by his side, on his head, rose from the chair without another word to the meeting, called out " Lew! Boy! " to his servant, and in a few moments the jingling of his sleigh bells notified us that he was on his way home. Judge Humphreys, of Onandaga, was, after a brief pause, called to the chair, and my motion was adopted by a decided majority—after which matters proceeded quietly to their consummation. Two tickets only were before the joint meeting of the two houses, to wit, the Clintonian from the Senate, and the Federal from the House of Assembly; the Madisonian being driven to a choice between them. Many of them voted blank ballots, and some thirty six out of sixty

° MS. I, p. 55.

one (the whole number of their members) voted for our ticket and elected it.[1]

Whatever objection may have existed against our support of Mr. Clinton, none can, I think, be made against the manner in which our determined course was carried out. We acted upon a principle that we believed to be sound, avowed it openly and sustained it firmly. So free were we from intriguing with the Federalists, that no charge or insinuation to that effect has ever been made even against me, whose whole life has been since so closely canvassed for matters of accusation by an untiring throng of opponents.

The session having been called for the purpose of appointing Electors only, no other business was done. Altho' the youngest man, and one of the youngest members of the body, I was placed at the head of the Committee to report the answer of the Senate to the Governor's Speech, which having been adopted and presented, the Legislature adjourned to the 1st day of January 1813.

There were occurrences prior in date, but connected with these transactions, which from their relation to distinguished individuals and the light they shed upon the private history of the times, are not without interest. A short time before the Extra session, William King, of Maine, an enterprising and not over-scrupulous politician, visited Albany to prevail upon the friends of Mr. Clinton, to withdraw his name from the Canvass. He very naturally addressed himself to Judge Ambrose Spencer, the brother-in-law of Mr. Clinton, and to Judge Taylor, an ancient friend and adherent of his family. These gentlemen addressed a letter to Mr. Riker, advising a compliance with the suggestion of Mr. King. The advice was good but badly received by Mr. Clinton who regarded King as an emissary of the Administration at Washington, sent to tamper with his friends, and became indignant at this evidence of his success. It is quite certain that Mr. Madison knew nothing of the affair, and the mission, most probably, had its origin in Mr. King's passion for intrigue, stimulated by the hope of increasing his influence with the Administration.

The "American Citizen" a newspaper then edited by William Lucius Rose, and previously by the more famous James Cheetham, after the letter to Riker, commenced a series of pungent and well written attacks upon Judge Spencer, entitled the "Ambrosiad." In these the Judge's early life on his father's farm at Ancram, was, with other matters, lampooned in Mr. Clinton's happiest style. I happened to be at the time attending a Term of the Supreme Court

---

[1] See Hammond, History of Political Parties in the State of New York, I, 321.—
W. C. F.

at New York, and lodged at the same house[a] with the Judge and General John Armstrong, then Secretary of War under Madison, who had been Judge Spencer's early and constant friend, and was supposed to have been instrumental in inducing him to secede from the Federal ranks. The General had been quite as constant in his enmity to Mr. Clinton, and was the conceded author of a pamphlet attacking his private character, in which he referred to the " rubric of his countenance " as " indicating the Deity he adored ! " and to his friends as the " Brotherhood of hope "—; a pamphlet that shewed by its talent and bitterness that the pen that had indited the " Newburgh letters " at the close of the Revolutionary War, had lost none of its pungency or venom. His disposition was eminently pugnacious, and he did not attempt to conceal either his satisfaction at the rupture between the distinguished brothers-in-law, or his indisposition to appease the quarrel.

The fourth number of the "Ambrosiad " was announced for the next day. Seeing the extent to which the Judge was annoyed by these provoking Articles, and regretting, in common with most of our political friends, the schism that had arisen between two of our strongest men, I visited Mr. Clinton in the evening in the hope of being able to prevent its appearance. He received me kindly, but was at first very reserved in his conversation. I found no difficulty in attributing this unusual circumstance to an apprehension that he had offended me in the affair of the Attorney Generalship, and a consequent belief that I was no longer his friend—an impression doubtless greatly strengthened by the fact of my intimacy with Spencer and Armstrong. I introduced the subject of the Presidential election first; assigned the reasons by which I was influenced, as I have done here, expressed my regret that the Republican members had placed him in the position he occupied, but closed with an avowal of my determination to sustain him in the contest, and to vote for Electors favourable to him. He was evidently both disappointed and gratified by my communication, listened readily to what I had to say upon the subject that occasioned my visit and spoke of it without reserve, save only that he professed entire ignorance of the Author of the "Ambrosiad." This I was satisfied he did not expect me to believe. He assured me that I was mistaken as to Judge Spencer's regret at the separation,—that he had with his eye open and to subserve his own personal ends gone into the support of Mr. Madison, and had it not in his power to return. I did not concur in that opinion, but urged strongly the inutility of these attacks upon either supposition, and earnestly invoked his interference for their

---

[a] A popular boarding house kept by Mrs. Keese, on the north corner of Broadway and Wall Streets.

suppression. At this stage of our conversation his friend Preserved Fish, entered, remained a short time, and left us under the impression that we desired to be alone; Mr. Clinton followed him out of the room, and remained out some minutes. On his return I rose to depart when he referred again to the subject, repeating much of what he had said in regard to the state of Judge Spencer's mind, but expressed a hope that Mr. Rose might be induced to suspend the publication of the "Ambrosiad " at least long enough to satisfy me that there was no use in forbearance. He said this in a way that convinced me that he had commissioned Mr. Fish to procure such a suspension. On the following morning there was of course much curiosity to see the "Citizen," and Mr. Ross[1] of Newburgh, a State Senator, and a friend to both Clinton and Spencer went to the Barber's shop—that immemorial news market—for that purpose. We were all assembled at breakfast when he returned ° and he was immediately interrogated as to the contents of the "Citizen." He replied that the promised number was not in it, or alluded to. Armstrong promptly demanded " What is in it ? " and on being told that the paper contained Riker's answer to Judges Spencer and Taylor, which was very severe, exclaimed "Ah! only a change of dish! Good policy that! Tomorrow we shall have the " Ambrosiad " again!" Upon this Judge Spencer said with emphasis and considerable formality that it was quite immaterial whether the abusive article did or did not appear, as Mr. Clinton had already gone too far to make his future course of any consequence in regard to their personal relations. It never occurred to me to speak to Mr. Clinton upon the subject during the short period of our subsequent intimacy but I never doubted that some one of the company at the table, which was numerous, informed him of Judge Spencer's observation. The suspended number appeared a few days afterwards and was followed by articles from the same pen, published at Albany as well as New York, in which the Judge's feelings were cruelly lacerated. These were in turn resented by him in verbal denunciations of unequaled harshness. In this way a furious warfare between them was kept up for about three years disgraceful to their personal relations and in the highest degree discreditable to political controversy.

Mr. Madison was elected to the Presidency by a large majority; a result well calculated to call into vigorous action the energies of the country and to show to the enemy that the War was national. The dispositions of nearly all the Republican members of the Legislature were in favor of aiding the Federal Government in support of the War by all the means in their power. The course of the federal

---

[1] William Ross.   ° MS. I, p. 60.

majority in the House of Assembly was, on the other hand, one of uncompromising, and, it is not too much to say, of reckless opposition. All hopes of peace had disappeared, and the National Government was in want of means. State co-operation was the readiest aid that presented itself, and a resolution was offered in the Senate, proposing a loan by the State to the National Treasury of half a million of Dollars, which I supported. After a violent debate, in which Morgan Lewis and Erastus Root took active and honorable parts, it passed the Senate by a party vote, but was rejected by a similar division in the lower House. The same course was pursued by the latter body in respect to every measure of the Senate designed for the support of the War. These differences led to repeated public conferences between the two Houses, in which their respective views were presented by Committees, chosen by the majorities in each, in the presence of multitudes of the People. I was on every occasion a member of the Committee on the part of the Senate; and although these debates in no instance produced the change of a vote in either House, they exerted a very salutary influence upon the public mind. The feelings of the members, as also of the audience, frequently became highly excited. On one occasion Judge Hager,[1] an honest German and Republican Senator from Schoharie, stepped forward, at the close of my speech, and carried away by his feelings, embraced and kissed me, and thanked me in the presence of the two Houses. A Committee of the Republicans of Albany called on me, by appointment the same evening for a copy of my speech for publication, which I could not give them as I had spoken from a few hasty notes and had not time to write it out.

The Bank of America, which had obtained its charter at the previous session, now applied for a reduction of the *bonus* it had stipulated to pay to the State. This had purposely been made larger than they could afford to pay to screen the members who voted for the Charter, from the resentments of their constituents. The subject produced a violent debate, and the failure of the project in the Senate was, for a time, probable. Whilst I was speaking on a motion I had made for its rejection, the Chairman, Mr. Parris,[2] fell back on his seat from an attack of vertigo, and the Senate was forced to adjourn. On the following morning the Senate received information of the death of Chancellor Livingston, with an invitation to attend his funeral. This caused an adjournment for two days, during which time the lobby succeeded in securing votes enough to make the passage of the bill certain.[3]

---

[1] Henry Hager.—W. C. F.

[2] Daniel Parris.—W. C. F.

[3] See Hammond, History of Political Parties in the State of New York, I, 306.—W. C. F.

The election of United States Senator, which caused a final political separation between Mr. Clinton and myself was made at this session. I was alarmed by the confidence shewn by the Federalists in the election of Rufus King, notwithstanding the Republican majority in the Legislature, and was induced to suspect an intrigue between them and a portion of Mr. Clinton's friends to secure the votes of the latter for Mr. King. These gentlemen had voted for the Bank of America, and, to divert public attention from their delinquency in that regard, were, on all occasions, the loudest in their devotion to Mr. Clinton. Finding them reserved in conversation on the Senatorial question, I called on Mr. Clinton, apprised him of my suspicions and remonstrated earnestly against what I feared would be their course. I urged that the election of Mr. King by their votes would expose his (Mr. C's) friends to the suspicion of having intrigued with the Federalists, and having promised them the Senatorship as a consideration for their votes in his favor for the Presidency, and insisted that we had a right to ask his active interference to protect us against such a result. He concurred with me entirely as to the great impropriety of such a step on the part of any of his friends, assured me in so earnest a manner that my suspicions were unfounded, and promised his attention to the subject so readily, that I returned to my room not only satisfied of my error, but under no small degree of self reproach. To increase the certainty of our getting the votes of all his friends, I made myself instrumental in securing the nomination of James W. Wilkin as our Candidate, an old friend of Mr. Clinton and the Chairman of the Legislative Convention by which he had been nominated for the Presidency. At the *viva-voce* nomination in each House every Republican member then acting with the party named Mr. Wilkin, and he received a majority of the entire Legislature. The House having a majority of Federalists nominated Mr. King and the Senate Mr. Wilkin. When the balloting commenced in joint-meeting, Ruggles Hubbard a Senator, and always an enthusiastic friend of Mr. Clinton, asked me to write his ballot and to accompany him to the Chair to see him deposit it in the box. Supposing him to be influenced by the suspicions entertained by myself, I assured him that they were groundless, and that all would be right. He shook his head, and said " I ask you but a small favor and I hope you will not refuse to grant it."

Moved by the earnestness of his manner I wrote his ballot and saw him put it in the box. When the ballots were counted it appeared that Gen. Wilkin was defeated. There was immediately a report put in circulation that the few Lewisites in the Legislature (who put in blank ballots) had voted for King. Knowing the in-

timacy that had existed between Mr. Hubbard and the men I originally suspected I was morally certain that they had acted as I
feared they would act. When we returned to the Senate chamber,
Mr. Clinton approached me and said "I hope you no longer entertain the suspicion you spoke of." My reply was "No!" at which
he expressed his satisfaction. I then said gravely, "Mr. Clinton,
you must not misunderstand me. My suspicions have become convictions. I know that the men I pointed out to you have done this
deed." He replied, under evident excitement, that he believed I did
them great injustice; and at that moment the Secretary apprised
him that they were waiting for him to organize the Senate. He took
the chair, made his Report, and adjourned the body.[1]

Nothing further passed between us until the day the evening of
which had been appointed for holding the Republican caucus for
the nomination of candidates for the offices of Governor and Lieutenant Governor, when at a brief interview, held at my request, I
referred to the business of the evening. He asked what I supposed
would be done. I told him an attempt would be made to nominate
Judge Taylor in his place as Lieut. Governor. In reply to his enquiry as to my opinion of the result of such an attempt, I told him
that it was my intention, if he did not object, to propose his name
for a re-nomination, but that I thought there was reason to fear,
from the prevalent feeling in the party, that it would be rejected,
upon which he asked quickly whether I would submit to the nomination of Taylor. I answered, as promptly, "Certainly![o] if it is
fairly made." After a moment's pause he bowed respectfully, left
me, and resumed the Chair. From that day we never met as political friends, altho' our personal relations afterwards became familiar
and kind and continued so till his death. In the caucus there was a
great deal of feeling exhibited; an apparent determination on the
part of the majority to vote against his nomination, but, so far as
I could see, a general disposition to bring the question to that result
without giving unnecessary offense. For some time no one seemed
inclined to move in the matter. At length a motion was made for
the joint nomination of Tompkins and Taylor, the first for Governor and the last for Lieut-Governor. As the motion was not accompanied by any remarks I was obliged to introduce the subject
myself, which I did in a speech of considerable length which was
listened to with interest and received with kindness. I referred to
the dissatisfaction that prevailed in our ranks in consequence of the
recent appointment of Senator, admitted that from all I knew on
the subject I felt obliged to concur in that sentiment; that I had
notwithstanding brought my own mind to the conclusion that it

---

[1] See Life and Correspondence of Rufus King, V, 291.—W. C. F.   [o] MS. I, p. 65.

would be expedient in view of the condition of the country and of the honorable position that Mr. Clinton had long occupied in the party to tender him a renomination; that I would do this under a full conviction that Mr. Clinton would not accept the nomination unless he was sincerely desirous to act with us in the future; that our party was powerful and had always been magnanimous; that I would be gratified if a majority of the meeting should concur with me in these sentiments, but that if I was so unfortunate as to fail in this, I would support cheerfully and heartily the candidate of their choice. I then moved to substitute the name of Mr. Clinton for that of Judge Taylor. I was followed by the gallant Gen. Leavenworth, of the Assembly, who, tho' a law-partner and warm friend of Gen. Root, who was at that time a leader of the opposition to Clinton, supported my motion in a very impressive speech. He appreciated and applauded the grounds on which I had proposed the re-nomination, and sustained them with a zeal and earnestness that obtained for him credit and a kind reception from all present. My recollection is very distinct of the favorable impression made upon me by the absence of anything like violent attack upon Mr. Clinton. Upon the ballot Mr. Clinton received sixteen votes, and Taylor thirty two. Tompkins and Taylor were then nominated, and a Committee having been appointed to prepare an Address to the People, I was made Chairman and wrote the Address.[1] It contained a full review of the matters in controversy between Great Britain and ourselves, and was extensively published at the time and afterwards and very well received by the public. Judge Spencer in the warmth and I should add in the excess of his admiration called it a second Declaration of Independence.

The Federalists nominated Stephen Van Rensselaer for Governor and James Huntington for Lieut. Governor. A number of Mr. Clinton's prominent friends, including such names as those of Generals German and Van Courtlandt came out with an address in which they severely censured the administration of Mr. Madison, and protested against the support of Tompkins. My course on the occasion caused a final political separation between my early friend John C. Hogeboom and myself. He was a clear headed and strong minded man, and always an ardent friend of Mr. Clinton, who cordially reciprocated his regard. He had taken an early interest in my success, and I fortunately had it in my power to make him ample returns for his friendly offices before his death. We had a warm correspondence upon the subject of supporting Tompkins which ended in a settled difference of opinion. When he saw that I was designated to write the Address, he came to Albany to dissuade me

---

[1] The autograph draft of this Address is in the Van Buren Papers in the Library of Congress under date of 1813, March.

from doing so. He insisted that the prominent part I was taking in favor of Tompkins was inconsistent with the friendly relations that had so long existed between Mr. Clinton, himself and myself, and that a proper respect for those relations demanded that my position, if not that of a Neutral, should at least be one of great reserve. I assured him that neither Mr. Clinton nor himself could feel more strongly than myself in regard to those relations but that I could not allow them to control my action in the way he proposed; that the support of Tompkins was the support of the War—in which cause I was engaged with all my heart and all my mind, and to which all my energies should be applied regardless of personal consequences. Seeing that he could not divert me from the course I had determined to pursue, he left me under great excitement and forthwith commenced a warfare embracing affairs of business as well as politics, that lasted for several years. Family connexion—my brother having married his daughter—and his advancing years ultimately brought him to a better state of feeling, which I eagerly reciprocated and our personal relations continued thence forward friendly during his life.

I was well aware of the inconsistency of my offer to support Mr. Clinton for re-election to the office of Lieut. Governor with the conclusive opinions I then entertained of his course in relation to the appointment of Senator, and with the bad treatment I believed myself to have received from him individually. But lingering attachments and the dread of being supposed capable of abandoning an old friend, and a great man in the then depressed state of his political fortunes had, I am free to confess, more influence upon my course than political justice or perhaps, to some extent at least, than a proper self respect. This disinclination to abandon a political friend in adversity has been with me a prevailing sentiment, and has been strengthened instead of weakened by the prevalence of a contrary disposition on the part of many from whom I had expected better things. I cannot bring my mind to the conclusion that Mr. Clinton himself entered into, or directly sanctioned such an understanding with the Federalists as that I have referred to, but I had at the time no doubt that, in the state of mind to which the loss of the Presidential election had brought him, aggravated by the apparent hopelessness of his ever regaining the confidence of the Republican Party, he suffered, by not attempting to prevent it, a sufficient number of his friends to deceive the party with which they professed to act, and to turn the election in favor of Mr. King. Judge Hammond [1] thinks that the Clintonian votes for Mr. King were promised to the Federalists by Thomas and Southwick, the agents of

---

[1] Political History of New York.

the Bank of America, to promote the passage of its charter. It is very possible that the Federalists, altho' they would have supported that bill in any event, imposed this tribute upon the agents. Thomas was a man of great address, and very unscrupulous. He may have managed the whole affair without letting Mr. Clinton know anything about it. The supposition is not in harmony with cotemporaneous and following events—but may notwithstanding be true. Instructed by a subsequent disclosure (applicable also to Mr. Clinton) how easy it is to be mistaken in similar matters, I pass from the subject without expressing or even entertaining a decided opinion in regard to it.[1]

The election of 1813 fortunately continued in his place the patriotic Tompkins but the federalists again succeeded in obtaining a majority in the House of Assembly. We were therefore doomed to struggle thro' another session without the ability to render any essential aid to the public cause. The indecorous violence of their answer to the Governor's speech (then the authentic exponent of party feelings) and of their speeches in support of it, exceeded those of the last session. They perseveringly refused to concur in any measure designed to support the war, and the session wore away in unavailing efforts on our part to strengthen the national arm, and in public conferences, in which the People took an increased interest, and which, tho' still fruitless in the Legislature, had a happy effect in preparing the public mind for the election of 1814. The spirit that actuated our opponents in the Assembly governed also the action of the same party in Congress, and in most if not all the State Legislatures, but most violently in the Eastern States. There matters were apparently in rapid progress which would tender to the Federal Government the alternative of a discreditable peace or a separation of the Union. It is believed that the subsequent peace alone, the news of which met the agents of the Hartford Convention on their way to Washington, saved that section 'from the full development of a treasonable design.

This humiliating state of things was discouraging to the supporters of the War, but they did not despair. To remove as far as possible the general gloom, a meeting was called of the members of the Legislature,° the Republicans of Albany, and those from the country who might then be at the seat of Government. It convened at the Capitol on the evening of April 14th 1814, and was well attended, altho' I can never forget the painful anxiety and apparent despond-

---

[1] Clinton, however, did conduct an intrigue with the Federalists in New York and in other States. The story is told in the memorandum printed in Life and Correspondence of Rufus King, V, 264 and subsequent pages. Some additional facts are given in Hammond, History of Political Parties in the State of New York, I, 315.—W. C. F.

° MS. I, p. 70.

ency visible on the countenances of those who composed it. I endeavoured to revive their spirits and rekindle their confidence in a speech of considerable length. Whilst speaking I was struck with the excited countenance of a stranger to me, wearing a fur cap and not distant from me in the crowd. When I closed, he took off his cap and without moving from his position, made a speech which by the remarkable sweetness of his voice, the grace and ease of his elocution, and the sanguine and inspiriting character of his remarks produced a thrilling effect upon the meeting. I soon ascertained that this was Peter R. Livingston, the son-in-law of Chancellor Livingston, who had that evening arrived in Albany as the Chancellor's agent to oppose Governor Ogden's petition to the Legislature. I thanked him heartily for his opportune and effective speech, and have not suffered the favorable impression he made upon me that night to be effaced by his subsequent unfriendly dispositions. As soon as he closed I offered a series of Resolutions, which were passed by acclamation, and the meeting broke up in excellent spirits.

I give a few brief extracts from the Resolutions to shew the temper of the time, and the plainness of speech by which it was characterized:

At this interesting period of our National Affairs, when our government is combating with a wily, vindictive, and sanguinary foe; when domestic disaffection and foreign partialities present their callous fronts at every corner and when the present hopes and future prospects of the people of New York are to be tested by the exercise of the elective franchise,—at a period of such anxiety and solicitude this meeting composed of citizens from almost every section of the State take the liberty of publicly expressing their sentiments on the subject.

That "every difference of opinion is not a difference of principle"—that on the various operations of government with which the public welfare are connected an honest difference of opinion may exist—that when those differences are discussed and the principles of contending parties [sought to be] are supported with candor, fairness and moderation, the very discord which is thus produced, may in a government like ours, be conducive to the public good—we cheerfully admit.

But that when on the other hand, the opposition clearly evince, that all their clamors are the result of predetermined and immutable hostility that, as between their own government and the open enemies of the land, they dare, as circumstances may require, unblushingly justify excuse or palliate the conduct of the latter and falsify, calumniate and condemn that of the former; when too in the means which are used to effect such unhallowed purposes, they are alike indifferent to the salutary provisions of the Constitution, to the requisitions of national interest, or the obvious dictates of national honor—that at such a time it is the duty of every sound patriot, to do his utmost to arrest their guilty career, and to rescue from their aspiring grasp his bleeding country—no good man will deny.

To prove that such has been the conduct, and that such are and have been the views of the party in this country which styles itself *Federal*—that their

" history is a history of repeated injuries and usurpations all having for their [direct] object," either the subjection of the rights and interests of their country to her ancient and unceasing foe, or a base prostitution of its fair fame for selfish and ambitious purposes " let facts be submitted to an intelligent and patriotic people."

Their opposition for the last thirteen years, has been universal, malignant and unceasing: their opposition was equally virulent when our country was basking in the sunshine of unparalleled prosperity, as it has been while her political horizon has been obscured by the clouds of adversity:

They opposed the abolition of [direct and] internal taxes when those taxes were rendered unnecessary by the general prosperity of the country: they opposed the imposition of the same taxes when their imposition became necessary to the maintenance of our National honor:

They opposed the reduction of the National debt, when the means of its reduction were in the power of the government: they opposed the increase of the national debt, when its increase, or an abandonment of every attribute of a free people, had become our only alternative: they clamored much on account of the aggressions on our commerce by the belligerents, and their Merchants presented petition after petition, and memorial after memorial, to Congress, that they should vindicate our commercial rights: they have uniformly calumniated and opposed every measure of the government adopted for their vindication or support: they opposed [and evaded] all commercial restrictions on the ground of their inefficacy, and that war, and war alone was the proper course for government to pursue, and on this subject they triumphantly declared " that the Administration could not be kicked into a war ": they opposed the war when it was declared on the ground that it was impolitic, unjust, and unnecessary:

They have always claimed to be the friends of order and the constitution, and as such friends of order and the constitution, their opposition to government, in the prosecution of the present just and necessary war, has been characterized by acts of violence, degeneracy and depravity without a parallel in the history of any civilized government on earth.

To enumerate the various acts with which the feelings of the American people have been wounded and insulted, the occasion will not admit of: Let their most prominent acts therefore, be alone considered. While the [undivided] combined power of the enemy and his savage allies has been directed against us, and our frontiers drenched with blood of unoffending women and children, the undivided powers of the opposition have been exerted

To destroy all confidence between the people and their government.

To misrepresent the latter, and to deceive, distract and cajole the former.

To deprive the government of the two great sinews of war—men and money :— preventing enlistments by discountenancing and calumniating both officers and soldiers—

Defeating the necessary loans, by attempting to shake the confidence of the people in the stability of the government:

To render the war odious and unpopular—

By the most flagrant perversions of the matters in controversy, and the pretensions of our government;

By the most criminal justification of the conduct of the enemy and the vilest extenuation of all their enormities;

To paralize the arm of the government and frighten the weak and timid from its support—

By exciting insurrection and rebellion in the east;

By openly threatening a dissolution of the union, and laboring incessantly to sow the seeds of Jealousy and disunion between the northern and southern states; and

By exercising in each state the same unworthy means as are practised by them throughout the union.

For while in this State they profess great solicitude for the sufferings of our citizens on the frontiers; they have inveterately opposed the raising a volunteer corps for their defence unless under the disgraceful stipulation,—that they shall not annoy the enemy—while also they seek to hide the deformity of their conduct in relation to our army, by professing attachment to the naval service; we find them opposing, with disgusting violence, a bill to encourage privateering, which passed the Senate of this State, but was negatived by the Assembly, because it had for its object to harass the enemy.

But we forbear the disgusting enumeration of acts so evincive of a deplorable degeneracy of a great portion of the American people, so well calculated to continue the war into which our country has been driven—to tarnish our national character and (unless successfully resisted) to drive our government to an injurious and disgraceful peace.

Therefore *Resolved*, That while we congratulate our fellow citizens on the happy revival of the feelings, sentiments, and spirit of the revolution which is every where manifesting itself; and our republican brethren in particular, on the heart cheering zeal and unanimity which pervades their ranks, which promises the total overthrow of that Anti American spirit which disguised under the specious garb of Federalism, has too long preyed upon the vitals of the nation— which excites a lively hope that the councils of this great and powerful state will speedily be wholly rescued from the hands of those who have disgraced them—

We warmly and earnestly conjure our Republican brethren, by the regard they have for their own rights; by the love they bear their country, and by the names of the departed worthies of the revolution, to be up and doing, and so to act that at the termination of the contest, each of them may triumphantly exclaim—" I have fought a good fight, I have finished my course—I have kept the faith." [1]

DANIEL WARNER Cha'n

P G CHILDS *Sec'ry.*

---

[1] A copy of the Notes and Resolutions of this meeting, together with Van Buren's autograph draft of the Resolutions, are in the Van Buren Papers, 1814, April 14.

CHAPTER IV.

The election of 1814 which followed in a few weeks was the most important of any ever held in the State, and resulted in the complete humiliation of our opponents by a triumph that gladdened the heart of every patriot in the land. We, for the first time since the declaration of War elected not only a large majority of our Members of Congress, but majorities also in both Houses of the Legislature, and thus secured our ascendancy in every branch of the Government. In the succeeding month of August the enemy captured the city of Washington, burned the Capitol and other public buildings, and drove the President and his Cabinet from the Seat of Government. The regret occasioned by this event—this desecration of our most consecrated spot by the ruthless tread of hostile steps—was in no small degree relieved by the knowledge that New York had been rescued from the hands of an unrelenting faction, and might now be relied on to furnish efficient aid to the general Cause.

The attention of the friends of the Country in all directions was therefore turned to Tompkins and the great State over which he presided. He did not disappoint their expectations but called an Extra-Session of the Legislature in the month of August,[1] and spread before it in an eloquent and patriotic Speech the actual condition of the Country—invoking its aid to support the National Arm. Never did a Legislative body assemble under circumstances of deeper interest, never one more solemnly impressed with a sense of the responsibilities resting upon it, never one more firmly and disinterestedly resolved to discharge all its duties. I was again appointed Chairman of the Committee on the Governor's Speech, and reported an answer which was adopted in the senate by acclamation and which I insert here.

The Answer of the Senate to the Speech of His Excellency the Governor.

Sir,

The Senate at the close of their last session indulged with your Excellency in the pleasing expectation, that before this period the blessings of peace would have been restored to their country on terms consistent with its honor & Interest. They are however by subsequent events reluctantly compelled to bear testimony to the insincerity of the professions on which those reasonable expectations were founded.

They have seen the enemy, while indulging in the vain hope that those professions would lead us into fancied but fatal impressions of security, applying

---

[1] The legislature met September 26, 1814.—W. C. F.

his energies to a vigorous prosecution of the war, and they have seen too with regret although not with dismay, that after having thus added duplicity to outrage, he has conducted the contest in a manner in the last degree disgraceful to a civilized nation & totally repugnant to the established rules of legitimate warfare.

That he is actuated by the most malignant hostility—that during the present season he contemplated the most extensive injury to the future welfare of our beloved country, if not the destruction of its constitution & the consequent prostration of our excellent political institutions—that intoxicated by the recent events in Europe which have given to the political complexion of the world a new character, and seduced by his unlimited confidence in the invincibility of his Legions, he fondly hoped to carry victory into the very heart of the country & by the wide spread desolation which should mark his course to compel the American people if not to acknowledge the legitimacy of his authority at least to recognize & admit the supremacy of his power—must be obvious to all.

The Senate therefore in common with your excellency and as they hope the whole American people " cannot but exult that thus far we have sustained the shock with firmness & gathered laurels from the strife "—that although he has succeeded in penetrating to the Capital & in the conflagrations of the monuments of art with which by the enterprise & public spirit of the nation it had been adorned, his success has before this time been embittered with the reflection that by their blaze he has kindled a flame of patriotism, which prevades every section of the union, by which he has been seriously scorched at *Baltimore*, & which threatens his compleat annihilation at every assailable point of the union to which his ambition or his resentment may lead him.

The Senate have witnessed with the same emotions, with the same enthusiastic admiration evinced by your excellency the brilliant exploits achieved by our army & navy during the present campaign—achievements, which in their consequences have been so immediately & extensively beneficial to our frontier citizens, achievements which will not lose in the comparison with the most gallant efforts of the veterans of the old world—exploits that have pierced the gloom which for a season obscured our political horizon & dispelled the fearful forebodings which past disasters had excited—exploits which have fully maintained if not enhanced the proud & enviable fame of our gallant tars—which have covered the actors in those bright scenes with never fading laurels and which will until public gratitude ceases to be a public virtue ensure the highest testimonials which a free people can yield to freemen—unceasing reverence for the memory of those who have died on the field of honor & acts of unceasing gratitude & esteem towards their noble survivors.

The Senate have seen with great satisfaction the prompt & efficacious measures adopted by your excellency to avert the dangers which impended [?] the State, and believing as they do that whatever excess of executive authority may have been indulged in, it has been not only exclusively intended for the promotion of the general good but was moreover rendered indispensible by the imperious nature of existing circumstances—they cannot doubt but that the acts to which your excellency has referred will be such as to command their approbation & support.

The Senate cannot forego the opportunity afforded them of uniting with your excellency, in an expression of the high satisfaction with which they have observed the increasing unanimity & noble ardour in our countries cause which pervades almost the whole community.

That on questions of local policy and the fitness of men for public stations we should ever be exempt from differences of opinion was not to be expected, divisions like those are inseparable from the blessings of our free constitution and although sometimes carryed to excess & made to produce a virulence & malignity which all good men must deplore, they are notwithstanding productive of much national good. But to have supposed that a people jealous of their rights & proud of their national character could, on the question of resisting the aggressions of the open enemies of the land—aggressions which have polluted the soil & which threaten the demolition of those fair fabrics which have been consecrated to freedom by the Blood & sufferings of their fathers—that on a question of such vital moment, so well calculated to excite all the patriotism, to arouse all the Spirit & to call into vigorous action all the latent energies of the nation—they would long continue to waste their strength in criminal and unprofitable collisions would have been a base libel on their character.

While therefore the Senate will at all times do all that in them lies to frustrate the efforts, to defeat the projects & to expose to public obloquy & reproach the conduct of all those who destitute of that noble love of country which should characterize Americans at this perilous crisis of our affairs, who preferring the Interests of party to those of their country, or actuated by motives more deeply criminal, shall attempt to aid the foe by heaping unfounded calumnies on the constituted authorities of the Country, or shall seek to excite distraction & alarm in the councils of the nation or in any other way attempt to paralize the arm of government, yet freely sensible that "every difference of opinion is not a difference in principle" they will on all occasions feel it to be their duty as it is their wish to afford to the meritorious soldier his due reward, without regard to sect or party.

The great Interest which the State of New York has in the prosecution & termination of the controversy in which our country is involved, the high destiny to which her local situation, the extent of her resources, the liberality of her legislature & the ardor of her sons may lead her, have been duly appreciated by your excellency. The Senate pledge their best exertion to realize those great & well founded expectations and relying on the Justice of our cause for the approvement of a Just God they cannot but flatter themselves, that in due season the American arms will be crowned with compleat success & the mild reign of peace be restored to our now oppressed & bleeding country.[1]

Among the first proceedings was my introduction of the "Classification Bill"—prepared by myself after full consultation with our friends in both Houses, and let me add, in justice to one who, with a capacity scarcely inferior to any, failed so sadly in the estimation of his Countrymen, after availing myself also of the military experience of Aaron Burr who was then at Albany. This Bill authorized the Governor to call into actual service Twelve Thousand of the State Militia, to be taken from or recruited by Classes to be formed out of the free white male inhabitants of the State, over the age of 18 years, according to their respective estates, abilities and circumstances. If any Class failed to produce an able bodied man, any member of the class might furnish him, and thereby entitle himself to the sum of Two Hundred Dollars, to be raised by assessment from the whole class, according to the appraisement or valuation ap-

---

[1] From the autograph draft by Van Buren in the Van Buren Papers, Library of Congress. The speech is printed in the Journal of the New York Senate under date of October 4, 1814, and was presented to the Governor October 5.

pended to the Enrolment, and if a man was not thus produced the Bill contained other stringent provisions to enable the proper officer to procure him, at the expense of the class in default, upon the same principle. The troops thus raised were to supply to that extent calls by the Federal Government upon the State Militia. The object was not only to improve the character of the aid rendered to the service, under calls for Militia, by the superior efficiency of troops thus raised over undisciplined recruits, but also to render the contributions of the People to Militia Service more proportionate to their interests and Means that was the case under the then existing law. The Bill proceeded upon the principle that all expenses incurred, or burdens imposed to preserve domestic order or to repel invasion should be borne as nearly as possible by each citizen proportionately to his interests, pecuniary as well as personal, in the benefits to be thus secured: in other words to apply to the Militia Service the principle that has always prevailed in regard to the support of the Army and Navy. The Bill excited the indignation of the wealthy classes generally, and particularly of those among them who were opposed to the War, and I was of course grossly abused by their mouth-pieces—so much so that in my own County the federal press advised its readers to withhold the courtesies of life from so bad a man. On one occasion I was accosted in the street by my great professional antagonist, Elisha Williams, (then a member of the House of Assembly) with this characteristic remark,—"Van Buren, my federal friends are such —— fools as to believe that you are in earnest with your Conscription Bill, and mean to carry it through, and I cannot convince them to the contrary." I told him that his friends were right, and that I was surprised to find that they understood me better than he, who ought to know me best. He raised both hands in amazement and replied that he had always regarded me as a man of too much sense to get into such a scrape.

We fought the Bill through against the violent opposition of the Federalists aided by General Root, who denounced it with great bitterness.[1] His opposition was, however, much more than counterbalanced by the manly and vigorous support of several of the [Federalist?] Senators. General Scott sent a copy of the Bill to Mr. Monroe, then Secretary of War, and it was believed to have entered into the composition of a somewhat similar plan that he recommended to Congress.[2] Governor Tompkins waited till the regular Winter session to obtain some amendments necessary to facilitate its execution,

---

[1] The bill became a law October 24, 1814.—W. C. F.

[2] Monroe's measure may be studied from his "Explanatory observations" and other papers in the State Papers, Military Affairs, I, 515, and in Henry Adams, History of the United States, VIII, 264.—W. C. F.

upon points which had been overlooked in our anxiety to establish
the principle; I applied at the opening of the session for a Committee, and we were engaged upon the subject when the Express arrived bringing the news of peace. The original draft of the Bill, in
my handwriting, is filed among the archives of the Senate, with the
following endorsement:—

The original classification Bill—to be preserved as a Memento of the Patriotism, Intelligence and Firmness of the Legislature of 1814-15.

M. V. BUREN.

Filed, Feby 21st 1815

The additional results of the active patriotism of the Republican
members were Bills to raise the pay of the Militia while in the
service of the United States,—to Encourage Privateering—to raise a
Corps of Sea fencibles,—and to raise two Regiments of colored men.
These laws were highly approved at Washington, and President
Madison, to testify the sense of the national administration of the
high stand taken by New York, offered to Governor Tompkins the
office of Secretary of State,[1] made vacant by [the transfer of James
Monroe to the War Department.]

Although surrounded by difficulties which were calculated to disturb the strongest nerves and constantly obliged to jeopard his
private fortune by personal responsibilities, indispensably assumed
for the public service, and thereby laying the foundation for the destruction of his future peace of mind, he [Tompkins] declined an
appointment which was then regarded as the stepping stone to the
Presidency. The reason assigned for his declension was his conviction that he could, during the continuance of the War, be of more
service to the country in the position of Governor of New York, than
in that of Secretary of State. There is no doubt that this was the
only consideration that determined his conduct, and it presented an
instance of pure and self sacrificing patriotism, rarely equalled and
certainly not surpassed by any single act during the War.

Chancellor Kent objected, in the Council of Revision, to the
Classification Bill, the Bill to raise a ° corps of sea-fencibles, and the
Bill to encourage Privateering, and delivered an Opinion, which
savoured more than was deemed suitable to the occasion of an appeal to popular prejudices. My friend Col. Samuel Young, who had
commenced his legislative career at the previous session, with much
promise, and was now Speaker of the Assembly, answered and successfully refuted the Chancellor's objections to the Classification
Act in one or two able numbers published in the Albany Argus, over
the signature of "*Juris consultus.*" The Chancellor replied over

---

[1] Offer made September 29, 1814.—W. C. F.   ° MS. I, p. 75.

that of "*Amicus Curiae.*" Col. Young, having confined himself principally to the Classification Bill, I took up the subject of the Chancellor's objections to the Bill to encourage Privateering, over the signature of "*Amicus Juris consultus.*" Finding that he had involved himself in a controversy uncongenial with his amiable and generally pacific disposition, the Chancellor retired with a Card, indicative of a sense of discomfiture. This was replied to by *Amicus Juris Consultus*, in the same form, and the discussion was closed.

The Chancellor's second and last number in reply to *Juris Consultus* appeared on the 28th of November 1814, and concluded with the following sentence;—"The public attention appears now to be properly awakened to the all important merits of our Conscription Policy. I am a great friend to the freedom and utility of public discussion, and I have no doubt it will be found now, as it has in all former times, that a free press is the great guardian of civil Liberty. So fully do I believe in its efficiency that if the Constituition was subverted and tyranny seated on the throne, surrounded by her sycophants, her parasites, her informers, her guards, her assassins and her executioners, a free press would restore the one and overturn the other."

The first number of *Amicus Juris Consultus* appeared on the next day, and the Chancellors card (which will be found with it), on the second day following.

I have deemed the portion of these papers in my possession worthy of preservation, and they accompany this Memoir,[1] not on account of their merits, but from higher considerations. The spirit with which the publick mind influenced and supported the legislation referred to, when regarded in connection with the actual position and pretensions of the enemy, afford, I cannot but think, a most gratifying exhibition of the character of our People under circumstances more trying than any to which our Country has been exposed since the War of the Revolution. The sacking of Washington—that wanton act of barbarity—and the temporary dispersion of the Government, have already been spoken of. These had been followed up by a formal announcement to the President by the British naval Commander on our coast upon pretences of the most unfounded character, that he intended to employ the forces under his direction "in destroying and laying waste such towns and districts on our coast as might be found assailable."[2] By despatches received from our Ministers at Ghent (during the brief Extra-session at which these laws were passed, and this objection interposed) it appears that the demands of the Enemy were as follows:

---

[1] In the Van Buren Papers under dates of Nov. and Dec. 1814.
[2] Cochrane to Monroe, August 18, 1814—before the sacking of Washington.—W. C. F.

1st. That their Indian Allies should be embraced in the treaty, and a boundary line between them and us permanently settled, beyond which we should not be permitted to purchase any land, or exercise jurisdiction; and a line was proposed by which the United States would have deprived themselves of the jurisdiction of at least one third of their original territory, including large portions of the population of Ohio, Michigan, and Illinois Territories, and which would also have annulled several Treaties we had made with the Indian Tribes by which the Indian Title to several millions of acres of land had been extinguished; and this article was declared to be a *sine qua non* to a Treaty of Peace:

2d. That the entire military command of the Lakes, from Ontario to Erie, inclusive, in the form of an exclusive right to maintain naval armaments upon them and military Posts on their shores should be secured to Great Britain; the British Commissioners declining to answer, for the present, the question whether this was also to be regarded as a *sine qua non* for the reason that they had already proposed one article of that character:

3d. That there should be a cession of as much of the territory of Maine as might be necessary for a direct communication between Halifax and Quebeck:

4th. That our Fishermen should no longer have the right to dry their fish on the coast of New Foundland; and

5th. That a new Boundary should be run between them and us from Lake Superior to the Mississippi.[1]

The indignation excited by these atrocious acts and insolent demands was intense, and soon satisfied the enemy that their crimes were also great blunders. It was at this crisis that Rufus King and other distinguished federalists withdrew their opposition to the War, and cast the weight of their influence on the side of their own Country,[2] and in our Legislature—hitherto, and still to a great extent, the hot-bed of faction—there were not wanting symptoms of relaxation.

Col. Benton, in his recent able work, places the subject of the conclusion of peace, without any stipulation of the subject of Impressment, upon its true grounds. That question was better disposed of than it would have been by any stipulation. We would now regard it as inconsistent with our national honor to ask or receive any promise on that point as the price of peace. The world knows that any action based upon such pretension in respect to our sailors would be tantamount to a declaration of War. During her recent war with Russia Great Britain has wisely taken a step in

---

[1] See Henry Adams, History of the United States, ix, 17.—W. C. F.

[2] See a memorandum, dated October, 1814, on the policy of the Federalists in the Life and Correspondence of Rufus King, V, 422.—W. C. F.

advance upon the general subject of maritime rights,[1] and there is no reason to apprehend that any similar questions will ever again be the cause of War between two Nations which have such strong inducements to be at peace.

Our exemption from further molestation in these respects is one of the results of the War of 1812 and one of the many reasons why that event should be regarded as having been of more advantage to us than any that has occurred since the adoption of the Federal Constitution.

I cannot allow myself to pass from the subject of the demands of the British Government without congratulating my countrymen on the dignity and immense power that the United States have acquired since that day. What nation in the world would now deem it either wise or safe to propose to us such terms as indispensable conditions to a treaty of peace? Not one.

The laws to which the Chancellor objected were passed in the Assembly by a vote of nearly three fourths, and, in the Senate, of about two thirds. In addition to this a Resolution passed the Assembly unanimously and was concurred in by the Senate, with equal cordiality, declaring "that the House of Assembly of the State of New York view with mingled emotions of surprise and indignation the extravagant and disgraceful terms proposed by the British Commissioners at Ghent; that however ardently they might desire the restoration of peace to their country, they would never consent to receive it at the sacrifice of National honor and dignity." But it was seen with pain and regret that a very slight portion, if any, of these feelings had reached the breast of the Chancellor, or it would perhaps be nearer the truth to say, of those by whose counsels his political course was greatly influenced. Objections founded on exclusively constitutional grounds, expressed with moderation, and accompanied by circumstances indicative of regret that official duty prevented a different conclusion, would doubtless have been received in a liberal and indulgent spirit, but the construction and temper of his Opinion closed the door against any such inferences, and the fact, charged at the time and never denied that he furnished a copy for the newspapers, shewed that it originated in a partizan spirit. It was under these circumstances that Col. Young and myself, both young men, then only in the second year of our public service, stepped forward and arraigned the conduct of the Chancellor at the bar of publick opinion in terms that we would, in a different state of things, have never thought of employing. If anything were wanting besides what appears in the

---

[1] This refers to the declaration adopted in April, 1856, by a congress of several maritime Powers assembled at Paris. The position of the United States is given in Wharton, Digest of the International Law of the United States, X, 342.—W. C. F.

articles written by me to shew the absence of any personal ill will on my part, it will be abundantly furnished by the following circumstances. The Chancellor, shortly afterwards, determined to abstain from all participation in party politics, and wrote a letter to that effect to his friend Josiah Ogden Hoffman, which was published. As soon as it appeared I wrote an article for the Argus, the original draft of which is still among my papers,[1] and the portion of which relating to this subject was as follows:—

Mr. BUEL.—I hope you will not fail to lay before your readers the very interesting letter from Chancellor Kent to Mr. Hoffman. It cannot fail to be gratifying to every real friend to the Judiciary. They have witnessed with regret the unceasing attempts which have been for some time making by his *Judicial friends* to draw him, with them, into all the petty intrigues of a Cabal which keeps the state in commotion, in the hope that if they could not derive a full excuse from his participation, they would at least divide the odium by his community. The determination to withdraw himself from the party dissensions of the day, and to devote his time and attention to the studies and duties of his office, expressed in this letter, is as it should be. His distinguished merits have been a subject of general admiration, and not unfrequently, it is feared, of sinister commendation. It is however but bare justice to him to say that among the list of worthies who have at periods filled our highest Judicial Offices, many of whom have descended to the tomb, accompanied by the benedictions of their fellow citizens, there has not been one who for spotless purity and exemplary industry in the discharge of his Judicial duties, has excelled the present Chancellor. There is no Equity Tribunal in this Country organized like our Court of Chancery; not one in which a single Judge ° possesses such extensive powers, and it is a source of just pride and satisfaction, that without subjecting ourselves to the charge of arrogance we can safely challenge a comparison in point of learning, industry and all the qualities requisite for a Judge, between the present incumbent and the brightest luminaries of the law throughout the Union. As such his character is the property of the State, and should be guarded against encroachments with the utmost jealousy, and as such too it is doubly important that by his total exclusion from the angry conflicts of party (with which this State is yet, for a season, doomed to be afflicted,) all obstacles to yielding him our united and cheerful applause should be removed; so that when Virginians, without regard to party, expatiate on the distinguished talents of their MARSHALL,— when our Eastern brethren dwell with enthusiasm on the memory of their justly celebrated PARSONS and boast of the erudition of

---

[1] Not found among the Van Buren Papers. ° MS. I, p. 80.

their STORY, we too may be able to point to a Judicial character, on which New York reposes her claims to a fair equality with the proudest of her sister States.

A steady adherence to the resolution contained in this letter is all that is necessary to secure this great End—every thing but that is already done. The Republicans of the State do not desire, nor would they approve the active co-operation of the Judges of our superior Courts in those party strifes which our free political institutions must and will produce. The utmost of their wish is to see them " *devote their time and attention to the studies and duties of their office.*" Let Chancellor Kent therefore persevere in his praise-worthy determination, and at the appointed day when, by the imperious provision of our Constitution, the high powers which have been delegated to him must be surrendered, he will find that that Party which can neither be intimidated by oppression, seduced by corruption, nor circumvented by artifice, is not wanting in liberality even to political opponents,—but there is no class of men who take more pleasure than they in bestowing the unbought and freewill offering of their approbation and support upon official merit.

While passing down the river on the morning after the appearance of my Card I met on the steamboat with a very clever lady and devoted friend of the Chancellor, who charged me with cruelty in exciting him to the extent she had herself witnessed that morning; and, which made it worse, she said, he was very far from being my enemy. I replied that she could not herself have seen the Card she referred to, or a person of her good sense would have perceived that the writer, whoever he might be, was none other than a true friend of the Chancellor. This profession in respect to my own feelings was entirely sincere. From my first acquaintance with him, until his death, I entertained for him sentiments of true esteem and great respect. If it is not a compliment too broad to be paid to any man, considering the frailty of human nature, and the bad influences to which the best are exposed at times, through their passions, I would say that I do not believe that he ever, in his long and honorable career, did an act, whatever may have been its error, that he at least did not conscientiously think to be right. I was first presented to him on my return home from the city of New York, where I had been studying law, at the Columbian Circuit which he was holding. He was sitting in the shade after the labours of the summer's day surrounded by a group composed of William P. Van Ness, Elisha Williams, Thomas P. Grosvenor, and others, who were greatly excited in consequence of some political occurrence, and were giving vent to their feelings in the severest terms. They retired one after another, and when he and myself were about the only persons present he rose from his seat and exclaimed, " Oh! these politicians! What trouble and vexation do they not cause! for myself I have been content to eat my cake in peace," and, tapping me on the shoulder, added—" don't you think that is the wisest course, young man!" Almost, if not quite the last time I had the pleasure of meeting him, was nearly forty years afterwards in New York and in the street, on my way home from Washington, after the expiration of my Presidential Term. He took both my hands, expressed his great satisfaction in having met me, and insisted on my accompanying him to his house which was near at hand; and on my consenting to do so, he said at once, " I have to ask your pardon, Sir, for the part I have taken in assisting to turn you out, and putting a man in your place, who is wholly unfit for it. I pledge you my honor, Sir, that I was then wholly ignorant of the fact, but now I know all about it! You made a very good President; I did not approve of all you did—but you did nothing of which either of us has reason to be ashamed; and we ought not to have turned you out, without placing a more competent man in your place, and in that matter I was sadly deceived, and I have, ever since I understood it, desired an opportunity to say to you what I now say!" I found it impossible to stop him until we had reached his house, when he introduced me to Mrs. Kent, and repeated to her what he had said to me. I spent an agreeable hour with him and parted with a promise on his part that he would pay me a visit in the country.

In my experience of men I have never known three men who received so nearly the same stamp from the hand of Nature as James Madison, Bushrod Washington and James Kent. In the simplicity, sincerity and inoffensiveness of their dispositions they were identical; each owned a delightful cheerfulness of temperament and an unvarying desire to develop that heaven-born quality in others. With a buoyancy of spirits and manners sometimes bordering on levity, they never for a moment hazarded the respect of their friends or of those about them. Mr. Madison's life having been devoted to politicks he was more reserved in regard to public affairs, but upon all other subjects they spoke their sentiments with the simplicity and directness of children. Kent possessed more genius and learning than his brother Judge, but Washington's mind was of a highly respectable order. Mr. Emmet, in speaking to me of Kent, said that he was a learned and able Judge—but a poor Jury-man. The justice of this distinction frequently occurred to me. Elevated to the Bench at an early age, and ardently devoted to domestic life, he had mixed but little with the world and was proportionally disqualified to sift and weigh testimony. This was strikingly exhibited at the commencement of his official duties as Chancellor. Being obliged in most cases to decide both law and fact, and too liable to be led into extremes, by his detestation of fraud, several of his first decrees failed to stand the test of review in the Court for the Correction of Errors. At the first or second Term of that Court, not fewer than six of his Decrees (speaking from memory) were reversed with the concurrence of his former brethren of the Supreme Court. Having occasion to call at his office the next morning on professional business, he displayed, in my presence, what, in almost any other man, would have been regarded as undignified violence of temper and manner, but would not, to one who knew him well, bear any such construction. The reversals of the preceding day having been referred to, he broke out into a mock tirade against the Judges, to the following effect;—" They are unfit for their places, Mr. Van Buren; You know that they are! SPENCER and VAN NESS are able enough, but instead of studying their cases they devote their time to politicks! You know that, as well as I do! As to Judge YATES "— raising his hands—" I need say nothing! *You should roll him back to Schenectady!*" (an allusion to Judge Y's personal appearance, borrowed from Mr. Clinton,)—"And as to my cousin PLATT! He is only fit to be Head Deacon to a Presbyterian Church, and for nothing else!"[1]

The memories of the older members of the Bar must abound in the recollection of similar ebullitions. On one occasion when I was present at his Chambers, a young attorney was applying for admission as Solicitor in Chancery. Finding (as was very evident) that he could not bring his case within the rules, he referred to the admission under similar circumstances of an attorney from a neighbouring city whose rough manners were notorious. Before he had finished his statement His Honor interrupted him in the following strain—" I deny it! Sir! It is not true! I did not *admit* him! HE BROKE IN! How would you keep such a fellow out?—But you are a gentleman, and must not try to imitate such a bad example. Wait till° the proper time and I will admit you with pleasure." At an earlier period he had been holding a tedious Circuit in Columbia, and, on the last day, tried an action for an assault and battery on a

---

[1] " To tell you the truth, I am discouraged and heartbroken. The judges have prevailed on the Court of Errors to reverse all my best decisions. They have reversed Frost *v.* Beekman, the Methodist Episcopal Church *v.* Jacques, Anderson *v.* Boyd, and others. After such devastation, what courage ought I to have to study and write elaborate opinions? There are but two sides to every case, and I am so unfortunate as always to take the wrong side. I never felt more disgusted with the judges in all my life, and I expressed myself to Judge Platt in a way to mortify and offend him. According to my present feelings and sentiments, I will never consent to publish another opinion, and I have taken and removed out of sight and out of my office into another room my three volumes of Chancery Reports. They were too fearful when standing before my eyes." *James Kent to William Johnson,* April, 1820. Kent, Memoirs and Letters of James Kent, p. 186.—W. C. F.

° MS. I, p. 85.

negro. It appeared that the negro's conduct had been improper, and the Jury gave him only six cents damages. He had brought another suit against another defendant for the same assault that was also on the Calendar, but had been passed. The Plaintiff wished to have it tried at the close of the circuit and the Judge refused, saying that he had had his chance, but on the representation of Plaintiff's counsel that his client was poor and would be liable to heavy costs, the Judge consented, with an admonition to the Counsel that if he did not recover more than six cents in the other cause he would not give him a certificate to entitle him to costs. The Clerk commenced calling the Jury, when the Judge looked at his watch and exclaimed, "Stop, Clerk! I'll be hanged if I will try the other Cause! *The Negro was saucy and deserved to be whipped!* Crier! adjourn the Court!"

CHAPTER V.

The return of peace naturally revived rival aspirations for political distinction which had been in some degree suspended, on the Republican side, by the engrossing cares and responsibilities of the War. The question in regard to Gen. [Obadiah] German's successor in the Senate of the United States took the lead in our State affairs. The personal and political relations between Judge Spencer and myself had been harmonious during the War; more so than ever before, and, I regret to be obliged to add, than they ever were afterwards. He was exceedingly anxious for the appointment of his old friend Gen. Armstrong, and pressed me with his accustomed earnestness to unite in his support. I could not consent to this proposal, but offered at once and with entire sincerity to support the Judge himself. He expressed his gratification at this offer, but declined becoming a Candidate, on the ground that his pursuits had not been of a character to qualify him for the place; and he did not discontinue his efforts to induce me to go for his friend. At our last interview that took place at his own house and by appointment, he submitted to me a great number of letters received by him from different parts of the state in favor of Gen. Armstrong to refute the opinion I had expressed that his efforts in favor of the General might prove a failure. I had, before this interview, come to the conclusion to support Nathan Sanford, of which fact I then apprised the Judge. He was somewhat excited, but received the communication in a much better spirit than was usual with him when his wishes were opposed, repeated his entire confidence in Gen. Armstrong's success, and expressed a hope that our difference would be an amiable one. Understanding his disposition and satisfied that when he found that he might fail in his design he would not be able to persevere in the liberal feelings he then professed, I deemed it an act of prudence to look out in season for the means of self defense. The Council of Appointment was in those days the only secure citadel of political strength to its possessors, and to that my attention was directed. In regular course Mr. Sanford would be selected for that Council from the Southern District; Ruggles Hubbard was the only Republican Senator from the Eastern District, and must therefore be chosen; with them and my friend Lucas Elmendorff from my own—the Middle District—we would have three out of the four members, and might feel ourselves safe from persecution for the act of rebellion we meditated against

Judge Spencer's long acknowledged supremacy. These we had the power, to elect, but at the Meeting of the Legislature Mr. Sanford declined a place in the Council, and recommended the selection of Judge [Jonathan] Dayton. By this act Col. Young, one of the most efficient of his supporters, was sacrificed to Spencer's resentment, as would have been the case with myself if I had had no other reliance than on Mr. Sanford's support. Dayton, Elmendorff, Hubbard and Col. [Farrand] Stranahan (a friend of the Judge) were chosen for the Council.[1] Judge Spencer continued for a season to support General Armstrong with great spirit but was finally compelled to abandon his case as hopeless. He then brought forward the name of his friend Elisha Jenkins but with no better success. Finally his own name was introduced into the Canvass, and the matter treated by his friends as if the only question was whether he would consent to take the office. When he was proposed in the Caucus, gentlemen who had dined in company with him but a few hours before made conflicting statements in regard to his willingness to take the place.[2] This produced a motion on the part of one of his friends that a committee should wait on him to ascertain whether he would serve if appointed. I opposed this motion, and cautioned his friends to reflect that the appointment of such a Committee would be tantamount to a declaration that a majority were in his favor—which I was very confident was not the case—and that if they should prove to be mistaken on this point they would practice a cruel deception upon their friend if they should obtain his consent. The motion was however persisted in and lost. I then moved for a recess of one hour, to give the Judge's friends an opportunity to consult him if they were so disposed. They availed themselves of it, reported his declension to stand as a Candidate,[3] and Mr. Sanford was nominated without an organized opposition.

Whilst we were proceeding in the election on the following day, Judge Woodworth came into the Senate Chamber, and directing Sanford's attention to him I said "There is the man who will be used by Judge Spencer to punish me for what we are now doing." When the Senate adjourned Woodworth stepped towards Sanford and myself, and invited us to drive to our lodgings in his sleigh, and on our way proposed a visit at his house. While there he was vociferous in his exultation at the triumph we had obtained over an "influence" (referring to Spencer) which had, he said, ruled the State too long. After we parted from him, Mr. Sanford asked me whether I did not regret the injustice I had done a friend. I an-

---

[1] The election occurred February 1, 1815.—W. C. F.

[2] Hammond says (I, 393, note) that it was Van Buren who stated that he did not believe Judge Spencer would consent to be a candidate.—W. C. F.

[3] "Because he would not put himself in competition with so young a man as Sanford."—(Hammond, I, 393 *note*).—W. C. F.

swered in the negative, and told him that Woodworth knew nothing of the matter yet, but that the Judge would send for him in the evening and obtain his consent to be a candidate against me for the office .of Attorney General. The desire of the party that I should be appointed to that office was so general that until that time no other name had been spoken of. The movement, as I told Sanford, would be founded on the assumption that Stranahan would certainly go with the Judge; that Hubbard who was a near relative of Woodworth, and had been to some extent brought up by him, could be easily induced to vote for him, and that Spencer's influence with the Governor, aided by the fact that considerable uneasiness had arisen between the latter and myself in respect to local appointments in my county, would be sufficient to induce him to give the casting vote against me.

A few days afterwards the Governor gave his first State dinner at which were present most of the parties to the political broil then in embryo, except myself—confined to my own quarters by a severe cold. In the evening Sanford and Ruggles [Hubbard] called at my room, in much excitement, and informed me that the Governor had shown them before they left him, Woodworth's application for the office of Attorney General, and had also told them that when the application was presented Woodworth had given him to understand that his friends contemplated the passage of a law for the appointment of two additional Judges of the Supreme Court, and that if my friends would sustain that measure and allow the appointment of Judges and Attorney General to proceed *pari passu* he would accept the office of Judge and withdraw his application for the Attorney Generalship. Mr. Hubbard knowing that he was to be in the Council and apprehending [*] that he might be embarrassed by an application from Woodworth had written me a letter expressing his preference for me for the office in question and pledging himself to vote in my favor. This he thought would furnish him with a satisfactory answer to all importunities. I took this letter from my desk, and after reminding Mr. Sanford of my anticipations, explained its contents and pointing out to Mr. Hubbard the impropriety of writing it offered to return it to him with a declaration that I should insist on his voting for Woodworth, and on his refusing to receive it, I threw it into the fire. I then told him that I was opposed to the proposed increase on the Bench upon principle, and that if I were not I could never consent to support the measure after so profligate a proposition had been attached to it, and requested Mr. Hubbard to inform Woodworth that if a movement in that direction was made in the Senate by any of his friends, I would repeat from my place his declarations to the Governor, and denounce the proposed arrangement as corrupt. Ruggles Hubbard was a noble hearted, enthusiastic and confiding young man and through these qualities he was liable sometimes to be misled by designing persons, whilst his motives were always honest and generous.[1] He was a zealous friend of mine, and as I have already said he was nearly connected with Woodworth (his sister having been Woodworth's first wife, I believe) and I was unwilling that he should gratify his feelings at the expense of a rupture with his relative. I therefore in the presence of Mr. Sanford, repeated my desire that he would take the course I had at first recommended. He answered that he was desirous to preserve the friendship of Mr. Woodworth, and could not at the moment say how far he might be induced to go to serve him, but that nothing on earth could induce him to give a vote that would defeat my appointment. After urging him farther on the point we parted. A few days later he called at my room in high spirits and told me that he had unbosomed himself to Governor Tompkins who had readily relieved him by the assurance that if there was a tie in the Council he would be glad of the opportunity to give the casting vote in my favor because he thought me entitled to the place and because he knew that the People desired that I should have it.

The practice of the Council had always been to meet at the Governor's Room, and to commence and finish their proceedings there. It was now proposed and agreed to that they should first meet at their own rooms in the city, and agree upon what they were to do, and then go to the Governor's office to record their decisions. The design doubtless was to lessen the influence of the Governor, but this was not suspected by Elmendorff and Dayton. A more active or a more indomitable spirit than Judge Spencer's never existed. Deeply offended by the choice of Senator, and seeing in the result, as he thought, a design on the part of the young men of the party to cast off his control over its action, he had determined not to content himself with my defeat, but had carefully prepared a blow with which to assail us in an unexpected quarter.

I was engaged to dine with my old friend Matthew Gregory on the day appointed for the first meeting of the Council, and on my way to his house I met Hubbard. Seeing in his speaking countenance indications of distress I enquired after the cause, and, in reply, he gave me a history of the proceedings of the Council at their informal meeting, which had just broken up. On my nomination there had been a tie; Elmendorff and Dayton voting for me, and Stranahan and himself for Woodworth, but Col. Young's nomination, as Secretary of State, in respect to which no question had been raised

---

[1] A different character is given by Hammond, I, 399, *note.*—W. C. F.

or was expected, had been defeated, and Elisha Jenkins had been
agreed upon. I begged him to go at once to Mr. Sanford and to
ask his interference. He answered that it would be useless, as Mr.
Dayton's pride had been assailed and his mind prejudiced by insinuations that he was Sanford's representative in the Council, and any
appeal from that quarter would therefore do more harm than good;
and any attempt to arrest the appointment in the afternoon, at the
regular meeting of the Council, he thought would be unavailing—
so that all he had to do was to apprise Col. Young of what had been
done. Judge Spencer had furthermore quietly operated upon Mr.
Elmendorff, who had acted with him so long that he could not refuse
to gratify him in regard to the appointment of his friend Jenkins,
as a sort of peace offering for the Judge's disappointment on the
question of Senator. Wounded by this result I was sufficiently rest-
less at the dinner table to attract the attention of the Company, who
very naturally attributed my anxiety to my own affair. While seeking relief, as men often do under such circumstances, by looking out
of the window, I saw Hubbard on his way to the Council. The
sight of him suggested an idea which I put into instant execution.
Calling Judge Atwater (a brother Senator) from the table to the
hall, I informed him of the condition of things, and begged him to
follow Hubbard, who was still in view, and to ask him from me to
nominate Peter B. Porter for Secretary of State,[1] the moment the
Council was organized, and to persist in his nomination until he
had a vote upon it. Atwater returned and reported that he had overtaken Hubbard at the Governor's door, and that he had promised to
do what was requested. I then asked the Judge to go to the Eagle
Tavern, where Porter had only arrived the evening before, to inform
him of what had been done, to ask him to accept, and, if he did not,
as we supposed, desire the place, to hold the office until we could recover our ground, and obtain the appointment of Young. He did
so, and Porter readily consented. The Council remained in session
until midnight, occupied almost every moment of the time with solicitations and remonstrances, addressed to Hubbard by his colleagues, to induce him to withdraw his nomination. When they
found every attempt of that character unavailing Porter was appointed by a unanimous vote. The General had fought gallantly
in the War, and on his arrival at Albany became the lion of the day.
Jenkins, on the other hand, had held a lucrative appointment in the
Commissary Department, without personal exposure to danger.

I was right in supposing that the Council would not venture
to reject Porter, under such circumstances, in favor of Jenkins.
The appointment was, of course, a surprise upon every body, and

---

[1] In place of Jacob Rutsen Van Rensselaer, removed.—W. C. F.

a source of deep mortification to Judge Spencer. The appointment of Jenkins under existing circumstances was an affair he had anticipated with delight and exultation, the expression of which would have speedily followed the action of the Council. Governor Tompkins was in favor of Young, and told me afterwards that he had heard from one of the members what had been agreed upon at the informal meeting and was much mortified by it. He said that at that moment he was called out to receive Gen. Strong, of Vermont, who had served with distinction in the War, and that he detained his visitor longer than he would otherwise have done to gain time for reflection, in the hope of being able to devise some scheme to save Young; but he returned to the Council without a plan, when Hubbard's motion presented him with a way to escape. Porter held the office for a year, and resigned it whilst I was detained at Hudson by sickness in my family, when Young was again disappointed thro' influences of which I need not speak.

The Governor deferred giving his casting vote upon the appointment of Attorney General until another day, when he promised to give it at his office in the Capitol. When that day arrived, Judge Woodworth and myself were invited to dine with his brother-in-law, the Patroon; and Woodworth came late to dinner, having waited to ascertain the result of the Governor's action. When he came in Gen. Van Rensselaer, who knew in advance, asked him provokingly who was Attorney General; a question that he was obviously not happy to answer.[1]

Peter B. Porter was a man of prepossessing personal appearance, good address and fine mind. He was fortunate and, in no inconsiderable degree, successful as well in the field as in our national Councils during the War, and yet he was at no time popular with the masses. The reason was a general conviction that the acquisition of wealth was his master passion, to which every other was made

---

[1] Mr. Van Vechten was, of course, removed from the office of attorney general, and Mr. Van Buren was appointed his successor. This appointment was made by the casting vote of the governor. Mr. Elmendorff and Mr. Dayton voted for Mr. Van Buren, and Messrs. Stranahan and Hubbard for Mr. John Woodworth. The circumstance is too trifling to deserve notice, except as an evidence of a jealous feeling which then began to exist between Judge Spencer and Mr. Van Buren. I do not impute the vote of Hubbard to the influence of Judge Spencer. Mr. H. was from Troy, and Judge Woodworth had many and powerful friends in that place, and in Mr. Hubbard's district. This accounts well enough for the vote of Mr. Hubbard. But Stranahan had no personal partialities nor any influential friends, in his district, in favor of Woodworth; on the contrary, they were for Van Buren. The truth is, Stranahan, at that period of his political life, was much if not entirely, devoted to the views of Judge Spencer. I apprehend that Judge Spencer perceived that Mr. Van Buren was acquiring a greater influence in the State than the judge desired he should possess, and, therefore, persuaded Mr. Stranahan to endeavor to defeat his appointment. From this period, down to 1817, when Mr. Clinton was nominated for governor, Mr. Van Buren and Judge Spencer, though both of them acting with the Republican party, and in good faith too, were very much inclined to thwart the individual views of each other." Hammond, History of Political Parties in the State of New York, I, 392.—W. C. F.

subsidiary. A partial illustration of this trait was exhibited in a transaction with which I was connected. Whilst we were holding the respective offices of Secretary of State and Attorney General, he proposed to me to unite with him in the purchase of an outstanding Class Right with a view to its location on Goat Island, at the head of the Niagara falls. I assented, and advanced him half the consideration money. The location was made, and no opposition or objection was raised to the completion of the title. But when it was found necessary to have the proceedings confirmed by the Commissioners of the Land Office, of which Board we were members, the objection to our being parties to any speculation that required such a step presented itself to my mind. I stated it to him and he laughed at ° what he called my fastidiousness, at the same time saying that if I persisted in it he would be too happy to return me my money— about a thousand dollars—and to take the whole purchase himself. I did persist, and he made a very considerable fortune out of the transaction.

Judge Spencer's feelings were somewhat soothed by his success in obtaining the removal of DeWitt Clinton from the office of Mayor of New York. Mr. Hammond [1] is right in assuming that I took no part in that matter. My friend Mr. Elmendorff could not have been induced to vote for it by any other consideration than his desire to save the Governor from the necessity of giving the casting vote—otherwise unavoidable, as Hubbard could not be brought to vote for the removal.

Mr. Clinton retired to his place at Flushing, to which he had often been sentenced in advance by Judge Spencer during their quarrel. Here he rusticated for two years, when strange to say he was recalled to public life mainly thro' the instrumentality of his imperious brother-in-law.

Mr. Elmendorff was always an anti-Federal politician without variableness or the shadow of turning, and an old school Dutchman, immovable, obstinate and imperturbably good natured. He was a member of Congress as far back as the days of William Cobbet in the United States, and received from that caustic censor the sobriquet of "The bird of wisdom."

The opening of the session of 1816 was marked by one of those occurrences that shew the facility with which men acting as a body, are led to confound power with right, and to do things that in their individual capacity they would regard as disgraceful. Experience has demonstrated that whenever distinterested justice is obtained from one Community—whether a great nation or a petty municipality—in behalf of another, it is due to the individuality and conse-

---

° MS. I, p. 95.   [1] Political History of New York, I, 397.—W. C. F.

quent responsibility of those who act for it; the substitution of motives of selfish advantage for those of fairness and right is the characteristic of souless corporations of all kinds, and political parties are very liable to become similarly demoralized.

At the election for members of the House of Assembly in Ontario County, Henry Fellows, the federal, was clearly chosen over Peter Allen, the republican candidate, if a few votes, in returning which the proper officer had abbreviated his name and written " Hen. Fellows ", were allowed to him. The Clerk of the County, being a mere ministerial officer, gave the certificate of election to Allen, who appeared and was qualified, as there was no proper tribunal for the decision of the question until the House was organized. The moment that was done, Fellows applied to be admitted. That his right would be ultimately established no one doubted, but the question was whether the investigation should take place before or after the choice of the Council of Appointment. With Allen's vote we could get the Council—if Fellows was first admitted, it would be against us. It is difficult to realize the idea that a great party would allow itself to take advantage of an accidental circumstance such as I have described, to secure to itself a patronage then supposed to amount to a million of dollars. But we did it, and there was not the slightest doubt that the other side would have done the same thing if the circumstances had been reversed. Fellows was admitted to his seat immediately after the choice of the Council, with only one dissenting voice. Although not a member of that house I was quite as much to blame in the matter as if I had aided the step directly, as I was pressed forward by my political associates to take a more active part in that body than was proper; so much so that Peter A. Jay, a federal leader in the Assembly, of fine talents and great personal worth, having occasion in debate to refer to a democratic member with whom I happened at the moment to be conversing, and affecting to forget his parliamentary designation, exclaimed, " I mean the gentleman who always speaks with the Attorney General at his elbow!" My then recent insurrection against him would prevent my attempting to screen my own delinquency, under the sanction and, of course, hearty co-operation of my quondam friend Judge Spencer, in the whole affair. The case was in truth one of those abuses of power to which parties are subject, but which I am sure I could never again be induced to countenance.[1]

I was at this time [1816] re-elected to the State Senate by a large majority, notwithstanding a factious opposition in our ranks by Judge Spencer's connections—acting however without his approbation. No one sooner perceived than himself that the political sceptre

---

[1] This political incident is fully described in Hammond, I, 412. See also Life and Correspondence of Rufus King, V, 501.—W. C. F.

that he had swayed so long in State affairs was dropping from his hand, and finding his power threatened by a body of spirited young men on whom his arts of seduction and intimidation had been equally tried in vain, he looked about for assistance. With this object he turned his attention, as no man but himself would have thought of doing, to Mr. Clinton. It was said, and I believe truly, that he consulted Gen. Armstrong on the point and that the latter remonstrated earnestly against the proposed step. I met him on the steamer on our way to attend the Term of the Supreme Court at New York, shortly after my re-election, when he took me aside immediately and assured me that so far from having countenanced the opposition of his friends to my election he had done all he could to prevent it. I begged him to give himself no uneasiness on the point as my friend Chief Justice Thompson had informed me to the same effect during the canvass, and I was very certain besides that he was wholly incapable of such conduct. He then proceeded to remark upon the happy results of the election throughout the State, and the uses we ought to make of our success; spoke of healing wounds and the importance and advantage of an harmonious party. Having had an inkling of what was in the wind I could, without difficulty, place the true construction on such unusual observations from him. I replied therefore that no one knew better than himself how well such sentiments corresponded with my own, and that he might safely count on my co-operation in all measures directed to that end, provided that they did not lead to such abrupt changes in our conduct and opinions, without a corresponding change in circumstances, as might impair the confidence of the People in our sincerity and cause them to believe that we were making a game of politicks, and playing it to serve our personal purposes. He said, certainly! that should be borne in mind, and the subject was dropped, but without the slightest idea on his part of abandoning his purpose; that he never did, when his mind was once set on a favorite object. We lodged at the same house in New York, and the matter alluded to on the steamboat furnished the occasion of many early walks together on the Battery. Finding that he could not prevail on me to become a party to the Movement he contemplated, he one morning halted suddenly in our promenade and facing me, exclaimed, with some feeling, "Why, You are a strange man! When I wanted to have Mr. Clinton removed, you were, in point of fact, opposed to it, and now that I want to bring him back you are opposed to that also!" I replied that I was not opposed to Mr. Clinton's restoration to the confidence of the party if it was brought about naturally, and facilitated by his own conduct, but that I could neither approve nor cooperate in the sudden and unwise way in which he proposed to bring it about, which could not fail, I thought, to have the effect I had alluded to in our first conversation. We were invited a few days after this to dine with Jacob Barker, then a great banker in New York, afterwards a lawyer in New Orleans, and everywhere and in every situation an extraordinary man, and always my personal friend altho' never my co-adjutor.

From his habitual devotion to Judge Spencer and his ambition to take part in such affairs, I was quite sure that this was a movement in furtherance of the Judge's project, and that we should meet Mr. Clinton at the dinner. On my way to the residence of Mr. Barker, in Beekman street, accompanied by Chief Justice Thompson and Judge Yates, I asked them whom they expected to meet. They mentioned several names, to which I added that of De Witt Clinton. "Why, Spencer is to be there!" exclaimed they, and "that is the very reason!" I responded. I then explained to them what was going on, which surprised them greatly. Mr. Clinton was the only guest present when we arrived. He had come in from the country, and I observed was plainly and rather carelessly dressed. We met him and were received by him very kindly. After a few moments Judge Spencer made his appearance, which caused some embarrassment on the part of all present. Although there was no direct recognition between him and Mr. Clinton, neither ° any conversation at the table between them, addressed to each other, they talked at each other through the rest of us in subdued and conciliatory terms. They had an interview in the evening of the same day, as I have always understood, at the residence of Dr. John A. Graham, and were formally reconciled. On the Friday following the Chief Justice called on me and informed me that, as the Court were to adjourn on Saturday, Judge Spencer had taken leave of his brethren and was going to Albany that afternoon. As the Legislature were to meet on the succeeding Monday for the choice of Presidential Electors we conceived his object and sending my papers to a friend by the hand of the Chief Justice, I packed my trunk and met the Judge and Mr. Clinton on the steamboat. Their familiar intercourse was matter of amazement to the uninitiated. Mr. Clinton left the boat at Newburgh, and I believe only made his appearance on it as an expedient demonstration preparatory to what was contemplated further. Very soon after he had left us Judge Spencer invited me to an interview in the small after cabin, when he opened his budget. He proposed that Chief Justice Thompson and Mr. Clinton should be placed on the Electoral Ticket as Electors for the state at large; that I might say which should stand first, and that he would pledge himself that Mr. Clinton should vote for Monroe for President and for Tompkins for Vice President. When I declined to come into

---

the arrangement he became much excited, and said that my unwillingness to confer a mere formal distinction of that character on Mr. Clinton betrayed a violence of party feeling that he could not have expected from me. I replied, without recriminations, that he misunderstood my motives; that if there were no ulterior purpose, I would not object to the choice of Mr. Clinton as he proposed, but that I believed it was his intention to bring Mr. Clinton forward as the candidate for Governor, to supply the vacancy that was expected to arise from the election of Gov. Tompkins to the Vice Presidency; and that as I would be opposed to that step he would think me weak indeed if I were to consent to a preliminary arrangement designed to promote it.[1]

Of course, if he had no such intention my course would be different. He was too truthful to deny this, and immediately turned the conversation upon the main question. He asked me, with his peculiarly emphatic manner, why I opposed the nomination of Mr. Clinton,

[1] " I understand that our Mr. Clinton has failed in the project, which he had formed of being one of the Electors of this State. He was at Albany, and with a view of reconciling himself to his old Friends and Party, as well as to advance a step in the accomplishment of his desire to succeed Tompkins as Governor, he made exertions to be put at the head of the Electoral Ticket ; but on a vote in caucus failed by a large majority against him." Rufus King to Christopher Gore, 22 November, 1816. Life and Correspondence of Rufus King, vi, 36.

The short session of the Legislature in the fall of 1816 had shown the Republicans to be divided between the Clintonians, of whom Judge Spencer was the recognized leader, and the followers of Tompkins and Van Buren, of whom James Emott said that they were " professing to be the true republican party, willing to support caucus nominations and to do all the things necessary to promote the views of the holy father [Monroe] at Washington, but in fact led by Van Buren and a few young men who mean to make the administration at Washington as well as the good people of this State, subservient to their particular views, which are in part ambitious but in main interested." It was with the idea of breaking the growing influence of Tompkins and Van Buren that Judge Spencer favored the advancement of Clinton and became reconciled to him. It was said that Clinton had given a pledge to vote for Monroe and Tompkins if his name were placed first on the electoral ticket. Seeing that such a concession would give the impression that Clinton had become firmly reconciled to the party and was pledged to support all its views and principles, Van Buren opposed it, and succeeded in defeating it. The Clintonians cried out that they had been " outmanaged," while their opponents boasted their superior strength and talent.

By removing Tompkins to the Vice Presidency the chair of the governor must be filled. Hammond describes the three distinct schemes entertained by Van Buren for defeating the project of making Clinton governor : 1. That Tompkins should hold both offices and be Governor of New York as well as Vice President ; 2, that the Lieutenant Governor should act until the regular gubernatorial election of 1819, a plan opposed by the Clintonians, who claimed that the Lieutenant Governor could act only until the next " annual " election ; and 3, to obtain a majority in the legislative caucus and nominate an opponent to Clinton. After the resignation of Tompkins, which occurred a few days before March 4, 1817, a measure passed the Legislature providing for the election of a successor, and Van Buren voted in its favor. It was thought to have been adopted "not so much to satisfy the terms and intent of the Constitution as the whims and expectations of the people." The question of succession was practically determined when the Clinton men obtained control of the Council, February 13, 1817. Walter Bowne, John Noyes, John I. Prendergast and Henry Bloom formed the new Council, and only Bowne was opposed to Clinton. Hammond says " This was a great point gained, and it seems to me Mr. Van Buren and Gov. Tompkins, if they possessed the power, should have prevented this. Whether they made any systematic effort to do so, I am not advised." Van Buren attributes the loss of the Council to the " inaction " of Governor Tompkins.—W. C. F.

and, after several earnest and impressive remarks, said he would be responsible for Mr. Clinton's good conduct towards me and my friends. I replied with a like proffer of responsibility in favor of Chief Justice Thompson, whom we then thought of nominating, on which Judge Spencer contracted his brow, rapped his snuff-box, as he was wont to do when highly excited, and exclaimed "There, Sir, you have touched a cord that vibrates to my heart! I was not ignorant that I expose my conduct to unfavorable criticism by my sudden reconciliation with Mr. Clinton, so soon after our violent quarrel and the many severe things I have said of him, and I am not sure that I could have brought my mind to that point had I not known that it was your intention to bring that man forward, against whom I have cause for resentment that neither time nor circumstances can appease!" I knew very well, without farther explanation, what he referred to.

The discussion between the Judge and myself terminated amicably but fruitlessly. On our approach to Albany he resumed the subject, spoke of his certain success with the Legislature, of the sure restoration of Mr. Clinton to power, ultimately, of his kind feelings towards me, of my age and prospects, and of the influence upon my future success of my course on this occasion. He continued these remarks until the moment of parting.

We met several times at the rooms of the Members, but had too much self respect to indulge in disputations on the subject in their presence. One or the other always retired, and left the field to his opponent, and we never had any difficulty in deciding whose turn it was to do so. A few hours before the Caucus he told me that they would certainly have a majority of twenty; and I asked him whether he would do us the honor to visit the Senate Chamber when we appointed the Electors, which was to be done on the next day. He replied "Certainly!" I had no doubt that he had received promises from several, who, tho' in their hearts for Mr. Clinton, were not yet prepared to support him openly.

As soon as the Caucus was organized I submitted two propositions: one, that the Members from each Congressional District should name the Elector for their district, and another that the two Electors for the State at large should be selected—one from the Southern and the other from the Western District. The first was the usual mode, and to the second there was no objection, as both Mr. Clinton and our candidate, Col. Rutgers, resided in the Southern District. They therefore both passed with perfect unanimity. As soon as the members had made and reported their district selections, I moved promptly that the two Electors from the State at large should be designated in the same way—the one by the members from the Southern District, and the other by the members from the West. As the members from the Southern district were nearly unanimous against Mr. Clinton, this proposition produced a perfect ferment in the meeting. The Clintonian leaders sprang to their feet, and contended with each other for precedence in denouncing the proposition, which they characterized by all sorts of hard names. They said that it was aimed at Mr. Clinton—as if it could have had any other aim—that it was unusual and unfair. A motion was made to amend it, so as to provide for a vote for the two Electors by ballot. Speech after speech followed on their side—our friends naturally waiting for me to defend my own proposition, and I to let the storm spend itself.

At the first pause I demanded the attention of the meeting as the mover of the resolution, which I ought, in common courtesy, to have been permitted to explain before it was so grossly assailed. The leaders of the opposition finding that they had been too hasty, more readily acquiesced in giving me a fair hearing. I then stated my object to be to bring the question of Mr. Clinton's appointment to a test by the *viva-voce* vote of the meeting; that everybody knew that if my resolution was adopted he would be excluded—those who were for his exclusion voting for the resolution and those who were in favor of his appointment voting against it; that in ordinary cases there might be no great objection to a vote by ballot, although it was always preferable that those who represented others should vote openly, and in this case there were circumstances that made the obligation to vote openly imperative. No one could doubt that when we were elected large majorities of our respective constituencies were decidedly against Mr. Clinton, and the proposition to give him the proposed proof of the restored confidence of the party was an affair of yesterday—brought forward without consulting the People or the possibility of consulting them. I was bound to presume, from the well known sentiments of our constituents, that the result of our vote would be the same whether we voted by ballot, or *viva voce* and in either case against Mr. Clinton, but if it should happen to turn out otherwise, there would, of necessity, be great excitements in the State—thousands would think that a March had been stolen on the party—there would of course be a desire to know who had done it—suspicion would be spread over the State, and the meeting owed it to itself to save each member from the consequences of the acts of others, which could only be done by an open vote on the resolution. If a majority of the Meeting were in favor of appointing Mr. Clinton, and should say so in an open and manly way, I would cheerfully submit to the decision, but no right-minded man could, upon reflection, desire such a result without being at the same time willing to bear the responsibility of it. After pressing these and similar considerations upon the meeting I resumed my seat, and after a few short speeches on the other side, the names of the members were called, and the resolution was adopted by a majority of nineteen, and our Electors were appointed.

Judge Spencer did not keep his promise to come to the Senate the next day, but appeared on the day after jaded and dispirited. He had not, however, the slightest idea of giving up the contest, but complained bitterly of the feeble manner in which their cause had been sustained in the Caucus, although he said that while they submitted to their present defeat, they would contest the nomination ° for Governor in the same way next winter and that he trusted that we would also acquiesce if they succeeded, to which I readily agreed.

Legislative caucuses were then, as has been shown, the regular mode of nomination, but, feeling doubtful of their success, the Clintonians commenced, at an early day, to elect delegates from the Counties represented in the Legislature by federalists, intending to claim seats for them in the nominating Convention.[1] We followed their example, but in those contests they had one advantage over us that we could neither prevent nor, in general, resist. The federalists, except a small section called "the high minded" (who brought but little aid from the masses) were favorable to Mr. Clinton. Having lost all confidence in their own success, and feeling assured that Mr. Clinton must ultimately come over to them, in addition to their indirect assistance of his Cause, which we felt everywhere, they sent to our Convention obscure men of their own who had no distinctive political character. In this way we were defeated in a large majority of the federal counties. They also obtained a preponderating influence, when the Legislature met, tho' not an absolute control, over the new Council of Appointment, in consequence of the inaction of Governor Tompkins, arising from his situation as a candidate for the Vice Presidency, and in a short time they obtained a complete ascendancy in respect to all new appointments.

Several meetings were held to establish regulations for the organization of the nominating convention, and notwithstanding the mass of influence that was brought to bear against us, the Clintonians had not yet obtained a majority of the Legislative Members. We resisted the admission of delegates not members of either House on the ground of precedent, and of the charge of federal interference, in

---

° MS. I, p. 105.
[1] See Hammond, History of Political Parties in the State of New York, I, 437.— W. C. F.

regard to which we fortified ourselves with well authenticated facts.[1] After a protracted debate at one of these preliminary meetings, with the reluctant assent of our friends, I proposed to abandon the elections that had been made, and to elect the delegates anew on the same day in each county, at a time to be fixed, and in case of such an arrangement being agreed to, to consent to their admission. This reasonable offer was violently opposed, and motion after motion made for an adjournment, which we were able to vote down. At midnight, Judge [Moak?] Swart, the Chairman, a family connection of mine, and a very upright man, but one of the Congressional protesters against the nomination of Mr. Monroe, and every inch a Clintonian, decided that the motion to adjourn was carried. Upon being asked to state the vote on the motion, he replied, with great simplicity, " Fifty odd to forty odd! " As this was rather too indefinite to be satisfactory, we demanded that the names of the members should be called and the vote taken more exactly. This was done and the result declared to be a tie. We finally consented to an adjournment. At the next meeting our proposition was accepted. The delegates were again elected, and as Mr. Clinton had undoubtedly made some favourable advance in public opinion, and the same influences were again applied, the election resulted as before. My own, the adjoining county and the small county of Broome were the only federal counties in the State that returned anti-Clintonian delegates.

Then ensued one of those *stampedes* that sometimes occur in all political associations; men running from a defeated party like rats from a falling house. A number of instances, some amusing and some distressing, were presented of individuals, once ranking among the firmest, now abandoning us under various but generally flimsy pretences. With both wind and tide in his favor and the Council of Appointment, that most formidable element of political strength in those days, to a very great extent under his control, Judge Spencer soon made a " practicable breach " in our Legislative defences. After much difficulty we had settled down upon Judge Yates, with his knowledge and virtual consent, as our Candidate, and his brother Spencer immediately set himself at work to induce or force Yates to decline, and succeeded. Only a few days before the Convention the latter invited me to his room, and told me that he must decline. He was apparently entering upon explanations more or less elaborate, when feeling indignant as well as grieved by his conduct but without asperity of manner, I said to him that it was unnecessary to give himself that trouble, as we had prepared ourselves for the

---

[1] The real point was whether the counties which were represented by Federalists in the Legislature should send delegates to the nominating convention. By resisting the admission of delegates "not members of either House" those Federalist counties would be without representation, and the Clinton support decreased.—W. C. F.

contingency, and would not be embarrassed by his declension. I then shewed him a letter from a friend of Gen. Peter B. Porter, giving his assent to be our candidate, if we desired it, and left him. I had before this communicated my apprehension on the point of Yates' firmness to Chief Justice Thompson, who scouted the idea. At our separate caucus a Senator from the Southern district, Mr. Crosby, with whom opposition to Mr. Clinton was an absorbing passion, presented his venerable and imposing figure to the meeting, and expressed a desire to ask a few questions of Mr. Van Buren, if he had no objections to answer them. On receiving a satisfactory assurance he asked for my opinion of the probable result of the approaching Convention. I gave him my impression in regard to our numbers, and my reasons for fearing that these would, under the circumstances, be diminished rather than increased, and that consequently we must be defeated. This, he said, was his own opinion, and he then desired to know whether in such an event I was willing to retire, with others similarly disposed, and to put Gen. Porter in nomination. I answered promptly and decidedly, " No! " and after stating the part that we had taken in getting up the convention, and our consequent obligation to acquiesce in the result, added that if we could be found capable of opposing its decision for no other reason than because we found ourselves in a minority, our bad faith would reduce us from our present elevated position as the main body, justly so regarded, of the Republican party of the State, to that of a faction, like the Burrites and Lewisites, which struggled for short seasons and then disappeared from the stage; but that if, on the other hand, we calmly pursued a steady and consistent course—upholding the time honored usages of the party and submitting to all that was done under them, until we could regain the ascendancy in the usual way—and if Mr. Clinton should, notwithstanding, subject his administration to federal influences, as we all supposed he would, and as I thought he would not be able to avoid doing even if he were so disposed, we would soon have the power to overthrow it, and to re-establish the Republican party upon its ancient foundations. These views, I added, were founded upon the assumption that the convention would be organized with tolerable firmness, but if the majority committed, in its organization, some act of violence, some palpable outrage that would be apparent to all, I would consider the binding character of their proceedings destroyed, and would in that case, and only in that case, unite with those who might be so disposed, retire from the Convention, and appeal to the People thro' the nomination of Gen. Porter. Mr. Crosby then asked me to specify what I would regard as a proceeding authorizing the step he had proposed. I answered that there were several cases of disputed seats in the Convention, all of which, except one, might, I thought, be decided against us without furnishing a ground of complaint of the character required. The exception was that of the Dutchess County delegation. There were serious objections to the regularity of the choice of our delegates, but for the admission of the Clintonian delegates there was no ground or pretence whatever. If the convention rejected our delegates and admitted the others I would be ready for opposition. Mr. Crosby, who religiously believed that there was nothing the Clintonian majority would not do to obtain power, declared himself entirely satisfied, and our caucus dissolved.[1]

In deciding on the representation from Dutchess the Convention took up first the case of our delegates and rejected them. It then proceeded to consider the claims of the Clintonian delegation, and the leading members from the Federal counties, such as Gideon Granger, John Woodworth, and Nathan Williams, made animated speeches in favor of their admission.

Our friends generally, and I among the rest, deeming the decision certain, took up our hats to repair to the Senate Chamber to nominate Porter, but the affair was destined to a different *dénouement*. Perley Keyes, a Senator on our side, and, tho' a plain farmer, a man of very rare sagacity, and Dr. Sargeant, long a distinguished Republican member, a sincere man, but drawn by special circumstances into the Clintonian ranks where he had become a leader, lodged at the same hotel. After the separate caucuses, which had both been held with closed doors, broke up, Senator Keyes invited the Doctor to a friendly consultation, and communicated to him confidentially what we had decided to do, and the latter agreed to exert all his power to prevent a rupture in the party by rejecting both sets of delegates from the county of Dutchess. I saw them together several times behind the Speaker's chair, during the debate, but had no idea of the subject of their conversation; Keys, it afterwards appeared, having sought these interviews to strengthen the Doctor's nerves under the violent[o] outpourings that came from his side. Dr. Sargent waited until the debate was drawing to a close, when he made, as he was very capable of doing, an able and effective speech against the admission of their delegates, dwelling mainly on the probability that their admission might break up the convention, and the folly of thus endangering the cause, when they had a sufficient majority of undisputed votes. Not one of the newly elected delegates voted with him, but he carried a sufficient number of those

---

[1] The convention was ehld at the Capitol 25 March, 1817.   [o] MS. I, p. 110.

who belonged to his party in the Legislature to carry the question. The next morning the principal part of the New York delegation, including a man of so much moderation as John T. Irving, called on me and insisted, without assigning any new reasons, that I should still unite with them in nominating an opposing candidate. The reception that I gave to this application offended them, and my political candle was thus lighted at both ends. Mr. Clinton was nominated and elected by an immense majority.

CHAPTER VI.

The Year 1817 was distinguished by the first and settled commitment of the State to the Canal policy that has since been prosecuted with such signal success. It is not to be denied that a large majority of the prominent men of the political party to which I belonged were very decidedly opposed to this policy. They regarded it, with few exceptions, as impracticable, and as brought forward principally thro' the influence of Mr. Clinton, at the most depressed period of his political career, with views rather to his own than to the interest of the State. As to the first objection there was room doubtless for an honest difference of opinion, but it must also be admitted that their prejudice against Mr. Clinton, personal and political, in some degree disqualified them from forming a safe opinion upon the subject. I did not in the least doubt that Mr. Clinton hoped to advance his political interests by the agitation of the question, but I could not concur with my friends in finding in that conviction sufficient ground for opposing the measure itself, if its prosecution should appear to me practicable and beneficial to the State. A Bill authorizing the commencement of the Erie Canal passed the House of Assembly at the previous session and came to the Senate near the close of it. The necessary information not having in my opinion been obtained to justify its passage I moved, successfully, that all the clauses of the Bill that authorized the commencement of the work should be stricken out, leaving only the section making an appropriation for further surveys and estimates. Mr. Loomis, a Western Senator, and friend of Mr. Clinton, but moderate in his politics, and an ardent advocate of the Canal, on its own merits, admitted that the views I had expressed in support of my motion were entirely correct. I believe that he voted with us, but am certain that he was content with the result, and I well remember the satisfaction he expressed that I had not fallen into the error so prevalent in both parties—that of looking upon the measure with eyes chiefly directed to its political bearings.

When the Bill was before us at the next session the necessary information had been obtained, and Judge Hammond (in his Political History) does me simple justice in the credit he concedes to me for the influence I exerted to secure its passage.[1] My brother-in-law,

---

[1] This measure, was adopted in the House by a vote of 64 to 36, the majority being composed mainly of the followers of Clinton and some Federalists. In the Senate the bill received 18 votes in its favor, and 9 in opposition. "There were five senators who were zealous anti-Clintonians who voted for the bill. Perhaps it is not too much to say, that this result was produced by the efficient and able efforts of Mr. Van Buren, who was an early friend of the measure." Hammond, History of Political Parties in the State of New York, I, 441.—W. C. F.

Senator Cantine, a very ardent politician, and a pure man in public and in private life, supported it earnestly. I believe our adverse votes would have caused its failure, but am quite certain that we could, if so inclined, have defeated it with the greatest ease. I made an elaborate speech in its favor, of which a report was attempted but acknowledged by its author Col. Stone,[1] (a life long political opponent) to be very imperfect—for which he assigned complimentary reasons, saying that he had found it difficult to report me generally from the rapidity and animation with which I spoke, and that on this occasion he was led to abandon the attempt by the great interest he felt in the speech, and his gratification at its character.

I perhaps pressed the subject with greater earnestness because a large majority of my political friends differed from me, and some blamed my course. Mr. Clinton was in the Senate Chamber, and listened very attentively throughout, and altho' it was only a few weeks after he had obtained the nomination for Governor, which I had so zealously opposed, and our personal intercourse was very reserved, he approached me, when I took my seat, shook hands with me, and expressed his gratification in the strongest terms. From that period to the end of my employment in the service of the State, I supported with fidelity and zeal every measure calculated to advance its Canal policy, and opposed as zealously, every attempt to prostitute that great interest to party purposes.

My shrewd friend, Senator Keyes, who was opposed to the Bill, informed me that he intended to offer an amendment providing for a branch canal from the main trunk to Oswego, in which place I was largely interested, and that the success of the amendment must depend upon my vote. I remonstrated with him on the unkindness of his course in seeking to connect my action upon so important a subject with my private interest, but told him that I should assuredly vote against the amendment on that ground, if there was no other. He notwithstanding offered it; I voted against it, and it was defeated. The construction of that branch many years afterwards proved of great advantage to the interests both of Oswego and of the State.

After the signal triumph of Judge Spencer in forcing the nomination of Mr. Clinton upon the party I did not much regret the necessity that presented itself to encounter him again at this session in one of those political skirmishes for which his passion was innate and insatiable, and in which, if I often succeeded, it was because I consulted my judgement more and my temper less, and because I took greater care to be right. In consequence of our respect-

---

[1] William L. Stone, conductor of the Albany Daily Advertiser, a leading federal newspaper, and later editor of the Commercial Advertiser of New York City.—W. C. F.

able force in numbers and the preponderance of talent in our Senatorial ranks, conceded by Judge Hammond in his Political History,[1] at the time of Mr. Clinton's election, we were not long in securing a majority in that body, which, tho' generally willing to support such of Mr. Clinton's measures as were not in themselves objectionable, could not be regarded as politically friendly to him. If matters were left to their natural course it was not likely that his friends could improve his condition in this respect, and it was not strange therefore that an administration that owed its existence to extraneous means, should find itself compelled to resort to similar appliances for its support. A case for this sort of interference was presented in this its first year.

The seats of Mr. [William] Ross, of Orange County, a Clintonian, and of my friend Mr. Cantine, of Greene, became vacant and were to be filled at the next election. The particular counties in each District from which candidates for Senatorial vacancies should be taken were then designated at the seat of Government by the representatives of the District in both branches of the Legislature. The counties already named were fairly entitled to be, and would, under ordinary circumstances, have been selected, but such a result would have left things precisely as they stood, the one being favorable and the other adverse to Mr. Clinton. A project was therefore started by Judge Spencer to give to the county of Otsego, already represented by Judge Hammond, a Clintonian, another Senator, to the exclusion of Greene, on the pretence that by a critical examination of the relative population of the counties composing the District, Otsego was better entitled to two Senators than Greene to one. On my way to the meeting of the representatives of the District at the Capitol, I was confidentially informed by a personal friend who generally acted with the Clintonians, that there had been private meetings of the members on that side, attended by Judge Spencer, in which it was agreed to give the vacancies to Orange and Otsego. I met Mr. Ross, at the door of the Senate, in the act of leaving the place of our meeting, called him aside, and denounced in strong terms the intrigue of which I had just been informed. He said he had nothing to do with the affair. I told him that could not well

---

[1] " Mr. Van Buren, of course, felt a deep interest in the choice of the council of appointment. His object would not be accomplished if men were placed in the council, a majority of whom were decidedly hostile to the governor. In that case the public would impute all the errors which might be committed, to the council, and judge of the executive by his speeches. Nor was he willing that Mr. Clinton should have a council which would accord with him in all his views, and be subservient to his wishes. It would, he thought, be more desirable to form a council which the governor could not control, but for whose acts the public would hold him responsible. In other words, Mr. Van Buren wished to create a council which should be nominally Clintonian, but which, at the same time, should be really hostile to the governor. Partly by management, and partly by accident, a council of the character last described, was actually chosen." Hammond, History of Political Parties in the State of New York, I, 457.—W. C. F.

be reconciled with the **fact** that some of the meetings had been held in his room; that if the perpetration of this outrage was persevered in we would not support him, and that he knew us well enough to judge whether we would keep our word. He showed confusion and alarm. Our meeting was soon after organized by placing Gen. Belknap of Orange in the Chair—a warm friend of Mr. Clinton and a very upright man. Judge Hammond, who was the leader on the Clintonian side, and whom, judging from the candour and integrity exhibited in his History of the times, it must have caused Judge Spencer some labour to bring into the support of the contemplated arrangement, moved that one of the Senatorial candidates should be taken from Orange, in regard to which there was no dispute. I moved to amend by adding Greene for the other, so that the question should be taken on both vacancies at the same time. Judge Hammond assigned plausible reasons against this course, without admitting that there was any opposition to Greene, and without knowing that I had been apprised of their plans. After skirmishing in this way long enough to be satisfied that he did not mean to be more explicit, I made a full statement of the information I had received, challenged a denial of its correctness,° and receiving none, denounced the projected scheme in decorous but severe terms, as a proof of a determination to break up the party. Mr. Hammond was not, as he says himself, an expert debater, and discomposed by a statement of facts, not complimentary to the fairness of those with whom he was acting, entered with evident embarrassment upon the exhibition of his statistics in regard to the population of the counties, and other pretences that had been constructed by the movers in the plot. We scouted all his calculations as indicating a chaffering disposition inconsistent with that confidence and fraternal feeling which had in time past characterized the action of the party. We affirmed that the treatment of the small counties, that constituted nearly half the district, had always been of the most liberal character, and that not an instance could be cited in which a double representation in the Senate had been given to a large county, as long as there was in the district a small county not represented, and finally we exclaimed against the propriety of a separate and private understanding by a portion of a political brotherhood about to assemble to promote the common cause, pledging itself to a particular course without hearing what the rest had to say against it.

Gen. Belknap, the Chairman, very unexpectedly to all, rose from his seat, and, tho' no speaker, said in impressive terms that he had attended the meeting alluded to, and had promised to vote for the exclusion of Greene, but that he was now satisfied that he had done

---

° MS. I, p. 115.

wrong, and that he would vote for my amendment. Mr. Throop from Chenango, who had been a clerk in my office, but was a zealous Clintonian, next made an elaborate explanation of his present views and his reasons for not voting as he had pledged himself to vote. Whilst he was speaking, Hammond turned to me and said, " Would you believe it, Sir! That young man has been one of the chief Agents in getting up this business! " When the vote was taken my motion to include Greene was carried by a large majority. I was detained in the Senate Chamber longer than the rest, and when I went out I found a solitary individual, walking to and fro on the Capitol Porch, whom in the uncertain light of the hour I did not at first recognize, but I soon made him out, by his habit of humming over the head of his cane, to be Dr. Davis, one of the Orange county representatives. I approached him, and asked him what kept him there at that time of night. He answered, with a hearty laugh, that he was positively afraid to go home; that Judge Spencer was waiting for him at his room, and he did not know how to explain their defeat, as they came to the meeting with a pledged vote of two thirds in their favor, and had been defeated by about the same number! I advised him to tell the Judge that their cause was not an honest one, and that was the reason of its failure.[1]

Gov. Clinton's inauguration was quite an imposing affair, as I understood, and conducted in excellent taste. Having, contrary to my usual course in such cases, agreed, on the suggestion of Judge Thompson, not to attend, I did not witness it, and was accordingly very much surprised to hear afterwards, that the latter was present, with his family, and that my absence had in consequence been more noticed than it might otherwise have been. This act, so inconsistent with his general conduct, was caused by an influence which in its usual and appropriate sphere is generally both benignant and auspicious, but when exerted in the uncongenial paths of politicks is rarely happy and always out of place. Knowing the Chief Justice to be.

---

[1] This incident of the senatorial election is more fully described by Hammond :
"Before the middle district convention adjourned, it was resolved to appoint a committee to draft an address to the electors of the district, on the subject of the approaching election. Mr. Van Buren was appointed chairman of that committee. Another person agreeing with him in political views, and myself, were of that committee. He drew an address, in which he reviewed the political contest between the two parties during the late war, and most soundly abused our old political opponents. The poor federalists, who were so far from being dangerous, that they had no idea of opposing our candidates, be they who they might, very justly might have complained of this treatment as illiberal, if not cruel. But on the part of Mr. Van Buren, the measure was politic and judicious. If the Clintonian republicans refused to sign the address, then it was evidence of what was charged against them,—a secret understanding with the federalists,—if they signed it, then the federalists might be told, that they had no more to expect from one class of the republicans than from another, for both had joined in the uncalled for denunciations against them. The address eventually was signed indiscriminately by all the republican members." Hammond, History of Political Parties in the State of New York, I, 471.—W. C. F.

when left to himself a perfectly straight-forward man, I did not, as I would have been justifiable in doing, break off my intercourse with him, but contented myself with making him sensible of the injustice he had done me, without asking or receiving explanations.

A few evenings afterwards I was visited by Gen. Solomon Van Rensselaer, the Adjutant-General, who brought me a message from Gov. Clinton to the effect that there was nothing in his feelings towards me that would prevent on his part the maintenance of friendly relations, and that he sincerely hoped that such would be the case; that he did not of course expect me to support any of his measures which I did not approve, but would be happy to find that I judged his administration fairly. I reciprocated these friendly assurances with much cordiality, and requested the General to say to the Governor that all I asked of him was such an administration of the Government as would satisfy our old political friends that he desired to sustain the Republican party of the State, in which event I could make myself useful to it, and would take great pleasure in doing so. I felt the awkwardness of sending such a response through a high-toned federalist, but thought it due as well to the Governor as to myself, to make him understand my position correctly. He and Judge Spencer might, at that time, by their joint influence, have prevailed upon two of the four members composing the Council of Appointment to consent to my removal from the office of Attorney General, and thus might have effected it by his casting vote. By omitting to make the attempt between July 1818, when he entered upon the duties of his office, and January 1819, when a new Council was chosen, he proved the sincerity of his professions made thro' Gen. Van Rensselaer. Of the new Council not a single member could have been induced to vote for my removal, and by the next—the only one in which his friends obtained a majority—I was removed.[1]

At the meeting of the Legislature in 1819 the Rubicon was passed by the Clintonians and a speedy separation of the party made certain. They decided to support for Speaker of the House of Assembly, Obadiah German, a Senator in Congress during the War, and its violent opponent. He was to our friends the most obnoxious man in the Clintonian ranks. It had for a series of years been the practice of the Republican members to meet in the Senate Chamber, and to select, by a majority, the individual to be voted for as Speaker, and the choice thus made was always regarded as binding

---

[1] The new council was composed of —— Yates, —— Barnum, F. William Ross and George Rosencrantz. It was elected with the aid of Federalist votes, only John A. King, Duer and Carman being opposed. These decided not to vote for the Clintonian council because of the treatment of the senatorial question by Governor Clinton. It was supposed that the Governor was hostile to the re-election of Rufus King, and this supposition was confirmed when Judge Spencer was put forward as the candidate of the governor's party.—W. C. F.

on the party. Owing, in some degree, to mismanagement, partly to
the unpopularity of German, and, to a small extent, to the absence
of members, we obtained a majority in the Caucus, and nominated
Mr. [William] Thompson, of Seneca, for Speaker. This result
astounded Mr. Clinton and his friends, who from having ridiculed
the idea of opposition to German were now filled with consternation.
Instead of uniting in the choice of Thompson, as they should have
done (the place not being one of primary importance) they decided
in the excitement and confusion of the time to elect, and did elect
German, by a union with the federalists.[1]

The effect was electrical, and from one end of the State to the
other there was a revulsion of feeling in the minds of Republicans
inclining them to join hands at the Governor's expence. This general sensation brought to Albany Jacob Barker, of whom I have already spoken, and who was always set in active motion by a crisis,
as had been shown on many occasions during the War. He possessed
the full confidence of Judge Spencer, and a large share of that of
the Governor and of his new friend Judge William W. Van Ness.
Barker confirmed the worst accounts they had received from the
counties and impressed them strongly with the necessity of taking
some step that might subdue the excitement, or at least divert the
public mind from the subject. A vacancy had been produced on the
Bench of the Supreme Court, and the *coup d'état* proposed by Barker
was that the Governor should nominate me to the Council for the
Judgeship without enquiring whether I would or would not accept
it. I have before described the relations that always existed between Barker and myself. He came to me, after a full consultation
with the three gentlemen I have named, and first requiring and obtaining my promise that I would say nothing in regard to my own
feelings upon the matter he was about to lay before me, proceeded
to inform me fully of his plan, to which, he said, all the gentlemen
referred to had assented. His argument was that whether I accepted
or not, it would be sufficient to repel the charge of Mr. Clinton's sub-
serviency to federal influence; and if I accepted it would remove me
from a place where I was very troublesome, to one where I could
exert less political influence. The only difficulty, he told me, arose
from a promise the Governor had made to appoint Mr. [John]
Woodworth, but that they thought could be overcome.

He subsequently described to me an interview between Judge
Spencer and Woodworth, the object of which was to induce the latter
to relieve the Governor from his promise, the particulars of which
were too characteristic of the parties to require, with me, any other
proof of their authenticity. But Mr. Woodworth stood fast on his

[1] A full account of this election is given in Hammond, History of Political Parties in
the State of New York, I, 477.—W. C. F.

bond. The interference of his brother-in-law, Gen. Stephen Van Rensselaer was next called into action, but with no better success. They were all greatly dissatisfied with this pertinacious selfishness, but the Governor, having received a personal favor from him, fulfilled his promise and nominated Woodworth. It is probable that when the result was found to be inevitable the proposition spoken of by Judge Hammond of appointing two additional Judges, and myself as one of them, was proposed by Mr. Barker, and abandoned on being opposed ° by Judge Spencer and the Governor.[1] I have no idea that either of these gentlemen knew that I had been apprised of these circumstances, or that they would have been much dissatisfied with the fact if they had known it.

The blunder of the administration in regard to the choice of Speaker, was, shortly after, followed by an event that served to strengthen us greatly. A vacancy occurred in the Board of Canal Commissioners, and I was told by a federal member of the House of Assembly, opposed to Mr. Clinton, and who subsequently became a member of the party known as " the high-minded," that if we would bring forward a candidate against Ephriam Hart the Clintonian candidate, who was not acceptable to him and his friends, there would be found votes enough on the joint-ballot to secure his election. I proposed my friend Henry Seymour, father of the present Governor [Horatio Seymour] to whom he at once agreed. On the joint-ballot, we, to the surprise and deep regret of the Governor and his friends, elected Mr. Seymour by a majority of one vote.[2] This gave us a majority in the Canal Board and I am quite confident that we derived more advantage from the patronage and influence attached to it than the Governor obtained from the Council of Appointment, which was embarrassed by the circumstance that it had to minister to the cravings of a party composed of discordant materials.

While things were going on in this way, I one day received, in court, a note from Judge Spencer, written on the Bench, saying that he desired a private interview that evening, and would meet me either at his house, or at mine, or at the residence of his son-in-law. I returned an answer before he left the bench that I would come to his house in the evening.

The state of party-feelings at the time may be inferred from the fact that we were both sensible that it was necessary to make our interview strictly private to prevent its being used by mischevious persons to foment jealousies among our friends. He received me very kindly at the door, introduced me into his library, and turned the key. He soon disclosed his object by expressing a strong desire

° Ms. I, p. 120.
[1] Hammond, History of Political Parties in the State of New York, I, 490.—W. C. F.
[2] Hammond, History of Political Parties in the State of New York, I, 495.—W. C. F.

to have the harrassing distraction in the party healed, and he had sought this interview to ascertain whether a candid talk with me might not lead, in some unexceptionable way, to the accomplishment of that result. He had not been able to digest any plan of his own, and was throughout, what was very unusual with him, embarrassed by his consciousness of the difficulties that surrounded the subject. I was pleased to find that the idea of any action on my part separated from my political friends, did not, at any time, appear to have entered his mind, and I observed to him that while my convictions of the impossibility of carrying his wishes into effect were very strong, I need give him no assurances in regard to my personal feelings and inclinations, as he had shown his sense of them by asking the interview. Among many other things, I urged the difficulty of bringing the Republicans on our side, and for whom we claimed that they constituted the main body of the party, to unite in the support of an Administration by which Judge William W. Van Ness, Elisha Williams, and many other prominent federalists were recognized as political and confidential friends and advisers. I could conceive of no way in which this objection could be obviated, that the Governor would feel himself at liberty to adopt; professions and assurances however honestly made, would, in the present state of political feeling, pass for very little, and nothing short of an open rupture with those gentlemen would inspire even the well-disposed on our side with confidence in any arrangement we might adopt. Mr. Clinton having received two Speakers and a Council of Appointment at the hands of those gentlemen could not now shake them off to conciliate old friends even if he could bring his own feelings to such a step. He admitted the difficulties that beset their path in that regard, and felt them the more sensibly as Judge Van Ness, whom he once heartily disliked, had by this time conciliated his esteem—and Judge Spencer was as sincere in his friendships as he was thorough in his aversions.

After conversing until a late hour we seemed both satisfied that nothing effectual could be done to further the object of our consultation, and were about to part, when he said that there was another subject on which he wished to speak, but was embarassed as to the manner of introducing it lest he might be misunderstood, and give offence where certainly none was intended. He proceeded to describe the pressure that had for a long time been made upon Mr. Clinton for my removal and the force that these applications derived from the circumstance that I was regarded as the leader of the opposition to his administration. I interfered at this stage of his remarks by begging him to permit me to anticipate what he desired to say which as I presumed was that if my opposition was continued the Governor would feel himself obliged to consent to my removal. I then observed that as this was not intended as a menace, of which I had not the slightest suspicion, and which he earnestly disclaimed, I could have no objection to its introduction; that I was not sorry it had been introduced, as I had for some time been anxious to be fully understood by the Governor and himself upon the point. I said that I had obtained my office from the same source from which the Governor had derived his place, and was earlier in possession. I sustained him in the leading measure of his Administration,—that of Internal Improvements—but it was complained that I was taking measures to prevent his re-election. This I had a right to do, and I denied that he had any authority to use his power, derived as it was, to coerce me into his support. But at the same time I admitted that these views, had, by the course of events, and conduct of parties, come to be regarded as mere abstractions;—that I was by no means certain that I would act upon them myself if our cases were reversed;—that I had for a long time regarded the loss of my office, when the Governor obtained the power to remove me, as the probable consequence of my persistence in the course I felt it my duty to pursue, and that he might rest assured that he would hear of no personal complaints from me or my friends on account of my removal.

Judge Spencer acknowledged emphatically the liberality of my feelings, and the regret he would experience if matters took the direction referred to, (in which I did not doubt his sincerity, for notwithstanding occasional exhibitions of great violence, he was capable of generous impulses)—and said, as I rose to leave him that he was happy we had met, because altho' we had accomplished nothing upon the main subject, our conversation could not fail to give a milder tone to our future differences.

The session terminated without any change in the posture of political affairs, but also without my removal taking place. In the heat of summer I received an order from the Governor to attend the Delaware Circuit, and to take part in a laborious and difficult trial for Murder in Delaware County, and meeting him the next day, at the Canal Board, he asked me whether I had received his order. I answered affirmatively but enquired whether he thought it quite fair as matters stood, (alluding to the called meeting of the Council of Appointment, and the expectation of my removal during my absence) to send me in such weather upon such a service, and proposed to him to consent that I should employ Counsel on the spot, at the expense of the State. He understood my allusion, and colouring, said, " No! Great interest is felt in the case, and the public will be disappointed if you do not go !"

Before the adjournment of the Legislature I said to Gen. German, in a jocose way, that his friend the Governor gave the State a great deal of trouble, that his adherents ought to apply to Mr. Monroe to send him on some distinguished foreign mission, and that he would be strongly tempted to unite in the measure, to which he made some reply, in a similar vein. On my return from the Delaware circuit I met the General on his way from New York, where the Council of Appointment was is session, to his residence in Chenango. He left his carriage, came to me and saluted me very cordially. I asked him the news—what was the Council about, and has it made a new Attorney General? He replied *"Not yet,"* and then referred to our former conversation, and said he had felt desirous to see me in the hope of being able in some way to arrest the divisions that were spreading in the party. I replied by giving to that conversation its true character, but adding seriously that if the Governor was willing to accept a foreign mission, I for one, would be happy to see him get it. He said "No, No."—on which I told him at once, but in kindness, that for anything else it was too late; that the Governor must either put us down, or be put out himself; that as matters stood the leading men of both parties would only discredit themselves with the People by attempting to patch up a truce. "Well," replied he, "it requires no prophet to tell us which of those results will happen"—and we separated. I have always supposed that the General had asked them to delay the removal until he could see me, and that he wrote to New York from the nearest post-office, after our interview, as I received my *supersedeas* almost immediately thereafter.[1]

Chief Justice Thompson, having received the ° appointment of Secretary of the Navy, and there being besides strong objections to his nomination for Governor on the part of some of our best men, we determined, before the Legislature separated, informally, to bring forward Vice President Tompkins. All admitted the Chief Justice to be honest and sincere but it was thought that he did not understand the feeling of the party sufficiently, and might quarrel with it before his term of office expired. Although I had been very instrumental in giving him the political prominence he possessed, I

---

[1] "In July [1819] the Council met again. Although the removal of minor office holding Bucktails and the appointment of Clintonians had been very general; yet Mr. Van Buren, who stood at the head of the opposition to the Governor, and led on the attack, had been allowed to hold one of the most important, influential and at that time lucrative offices in the State, the office of Attorney General, undisturbed. It was urged that this inconsistency in the conduct of the administration ought to be obviated; and after much and long hesitation the Council removed him, and appointed Thomas J. Oakley in his place . . . Mr. Van Buren, according to the maxim which before had, and since has governed his political conduct, had no right to complain, and in fact, I believe, he did not; but an outcry was of course raised in the newspapers, on account of the removal of a republican from an important office, and the appointment of a federalist in his place." Hammond, History of Political Parties in the State of New York, I, 507. Oakley was the Dick Shift of the Bucktail Bards.—W. C. F.

° MS. I, p. 125.

came to pretty much the same conclusion—for many reasons, one of which I will mention by way of illustration. We went together to the Delaware Circuit—in which county Gen. Root lived and then exercised undisputed and indisputable political sway—and on our way I expressed a hope to the Chief Justice that he would shut his eyes to the General's foibles, and treat him kindly. For a few days their intercourse was mutually satisfactory—so much so that the latter confessed to me that there were good points about Thompson of which he had not before been sensible; but before the Circuit closed his prejudices were more than ever aroused and I could not even prevail on him to take a respectable leave of the Chief Justice.

The knowledge of our intention in regard to the Vice President was the signal for opposition to the settlement of that portion of his accounts for War expenditures that had to be audited by the States officers before it could be allowed at Washington. Until then all went on smoothly and his accounts would have been without a doubt, but for that circumstance, satisfactorily settled. He soon came to an open rupture with the Comptroller McIntyre (a zealous friend of the Governor) who made an appeal to the public in the form of an official letter, signed as Comptroller, and addressed to the Vice President.[1] I went to the residence of the latter at Staten Island, as well to obtain his consent to be our candidate, as to tender all the aid in my power in preparing an answer to the Comptroller's letter, with copies of which the State had been inundated. I soon found that he was strongly impressed with the idea that I wanted the nomination myself, and persisted in declining, until I alluded in terms to his motive, and gave him assurances of his error which he could not but believe, when he consented to our wishes. But when we came to the examination of his papers I found him, in comparison with what he had been, exceedingly helpless. Conscious of his integrity in all things—sensible of the great services he had rendered to the country at periods of its utmost need, and of the disinterestedness of his motives, (which had been strikingly displayed by his refusal to be drawn from his Post, by the temptation of the office of Secretary of State) his feelings had not been callous or his resolution strong enough to enable him to bear up against the injustice, the ingratitude and the calumny of which he was now made the victim. He could not speak on the subject of his accounts with composure, or look at McIntyre's letter without loathing. When told of the indispensable necessity of giving to those matters prompt and thorough attention, he said, he could not help it, and throwing down a bunch of Keys, exclaimed, " There are the keys of my private papers, without reserve—here is

---

[1] A letter to his Excellency Daniel D. Tompkins, late governor of the State of New York. The answer was entitled: A Letter to Archibald McIntyre, comptroller of the State of New York. It ran through two editions.—W. C. F.

my friend Mr. Leake—he knows a good deal about the papers and will cheerfully give you all the aid in his power, and, when you want explanations come to me."

On examining his private letter-book I found a correspondence between him and Thomas Addis Emmett containing an offer of the office of Attorney General, and its acceptance. I immediately went to the garden where he was, with the book in my hand, and said to him "Vice President, I find here that you were the author of an appointment that I have always attributed to Mr. Clinton," and showed him the correspondence. He replied "Certainly, Gov. Clinton knew nothing of the matter. I wanted to have Thomas and Southwick convicted of the bribery they practiced on the passage of the Bill to incorporate the Bank of America, and thought you too young for that service; and I knew besides that you would come to the office early enough."

The knowledge of the injustice that I had for so many years done to Mr. Clinton in this regard distressed me and made me afterwards more cautious how I trusted to mere inferences in important matters. There was then an impassable political gulf between us, and no suitable opportunity was presented for explanation, but I am sure this discovery had its influence on my dispositions towards him at another and very critical period of his life.

In the course of my early interviews with the Vice President I imbibed a suspicion that the habit of intemperance, to which he, in the end, fell a melancholy victim, had commenced its fatal ravages upon him. The Secretary of the Navy, (Thompson) whose son had married the Vice President's daughter had taken a cottage for the summer on the island, but was absent from home when I arrived. On his first visit I proposed a walk, and in reply to his question as to the condition in which I found the Vice President's papers, I answered "So far, very well, but there is another matter that has afflicted me more." I then asked him whether it had ever occurred to him that our friend was becoming intemperate. He paused a moment, and replied, with more feeling than was common to his nature, but with his habitual truthfulness, that he could not say that the idea had not at times passed thro' his mind, but that he had watched him as closely as he could, with propriety, and satisfied himself that his indulgence was temporary, occasioned by his troubles, and would soon wear off. I hinted at the fearful responsibility I was assuming in pressing his nomination if it should turn out differently. He concurred very fully in this and said that he trusted I knew him too well not to be satisfied that he would be the last person to advise me to persevere if he thought there was any real danger, and that he would not fail, if my apprehensions were realized. to step forward, and share the responsibility with me.

This relieved my mind, but I prepared, notwithstanding, an anonymous letter to the Vice President which I intended to put in the post-office, when I reached the city, but my courage, which was never yet equal to such a performance failed, and when I got to New York I destroyed it.

I soon found not only satisfactory but highly creditable explanations of transactions that figured largely in the Comptroller's letter, in the federal presses, and in the pamphlets which the enemies of the Vice President had written on the subject of his accounts. When my examination was finished and he was delighted with the case he was about to present, I was pleased to witness the revival of his spirits and, with them, of his adroitness, tact and power. He proposed to read his Reply first at a private meeting of the most distinguished of his personal and political friends—a step of the utility of which I became very sensible when I found that these numerous gentlemen, after having been thus consulted, identified themselves, in some degree, with the document, and were as much interested in its success, as they could have been if they had themselves written it. My experience on this occasion had its influence in inducing me ever afterwards to submit my own papers destined for publication to the widest inspection of my friends, with liberal permission to suggest improvements, and unaffected dissatisfaction if they failed to avail themselves of it. There was one, and only one point on which the Vice President and myself differed, and that will show the effect that injustice had produced on a mind naturally the most disinterested and self-denying, by tempting him contrary to the usage of his life, to become the trumpeter of his own glory. I desired to give the largest share of credit for results that had in fact been produced by his individual efforts and sacrifices, to the patriotism of the People, but he thought he had acted on that principle long enough, and that the time had arrived when he ought to claim what belonged to him. His version of the matter was inserted in the letter, with an engagement on his part, to state to the meeting our difference of opinion on the point, when he reached it, and to abide by their decision. When I looked at the list of persons he had prepared to compose the meeting I was amused with the complexion of some of its parts, and yet nothing could have been more judicious than such a selection. At the door of the place of meeting I met Martin S. Wilkins, the Vice President's class-mate and early friend, who, altho' an honest man in all respects, was substantially a monarchist in his politics. Recognizing him, in the obscure light of evening, and notwithstanding my previous knowledge that he was to be one of the company, I said, " Mr. Wilkins you have made some strange mistake in coming here!"

"Not at all," he answered, "is not this the house of Jonathan Thompson?"

"Yes!" said I—"but there is to be a *democratic* meeting here tonight" (that term having come into use instead of Republican) "and I am very sure that you do not go to such gatherings."

"That is true enough" replied Wilkins, "I don't care a d—n for your democracy, but I take an interest in the success of honest men, and believe my old schoolmate Daniel D. Tompkins to be one, and I come here to-night to be confirmed in that opinion!"

The Vice President made some very impressive remarks illustrating the truth of the statement upon the expediency of publishing, on which he and I had differed—justifying the inferences he had drawn, and strengthening the propriety of his position and concluding with the declaration that the time had arrived when he ought to do himself justice. Forming their° opinion upon these grounds only, there appeared to be a general sentiment in the meeting that I was wrong, followed by a remonstrance with me for my opposition. In reply I dwelt for a short time on the danger of a man who had always been so modest in speaking of his own merits changing his character in that regard, particularly under his present circumstances, which as they stood were well calculated to excite public sympathy; but when I came to describe the uses that Mr. Clinton's caustic and busy pen would make of such seeming self adulation, in a degree at the expense of the People, and at a moment when we were seeking their favor, there was a change of sentiment, except on the part of Mr. Wilkins, who contended that this flattering the People was all —— stuff, and that the better way was to tell the truth and abide the consequences. The rest advised the Vice President to yield for the sake of policy—notwithstanding the truth of what he proposed to say—which he did with a good grace. The letter was received with the greatest favor, and embarrassed Governor Clinton and his friends exceedingly.

The country was filled with the most exaggerated reports in regard to the claims preferred against the State by the Vice President. I offered a resolution, early in the next session, calling on the Comptroller to report the claims made, whether the accounts had been settled according to the provisions of an act passed at the last session,[1] (before it was suspected that he would be a candidate) and if not, the reason for the omission. That officer sent in an elaborate reply which was referred to our committee. We made a report, simple and unvarnished, stating the whole case in a way to be easily understood by the People, and accompanied it by a Bill directing the Comptroller to pay to the Vice President Eleven Thousand Dollars,

---

° MS. I, p. 130.

[1] Session Laws of 1819, p. 286.   See Hammond, History of Political Parties in the State of New York, I, 508.—W. C. F.

as the balance fully due to him from the State. When this Bill was before the Senate I made a Speech that was very extensively published and was entirely satisfactory to the friends of the Vice President.[1] Gideon Granger, the Post Master General under Mr. Madison, who had been elected to the Senate from the Western District, was expected to reply, but did not do so, nor was any answer made, and the Bill passed the Senate by a vote of two to one. To prevent the influence of his silence, it was said and published that Mr. Granger had temporarily lost his voice by a severe cold; which was partially true, but from the sympathy of which he gave unmistakable signs, whilst listening with respectful and undivided attention to the recital of Tompkins' services, persecutions and sufferings, I inferred a better reason for his disinclination to speak against him, and gave him credit for his forbearance. Mr. Lot, a Member from Long Island, and an ardent friend, was so far moved by the same cause that he wept like a child and was obliged to leave the chamber.

The Vice President arrived at Albany from Washington about this time, and was received by our friends with wild enthusiasm. A meeting[2] composed of the Democratic members of the Legislature, and citizens in great numbers and from all parts of the State, and over which I presided, was, a short time afterwards, held at the Capitol, by which Tompkins was nominated as a Candidate for Governor with great unanimity and enthusiasm.[3] After an unusually animated contest in which each party exerted itself to the utmost, Mr. Clinton was re-elected by a small majority, but neither of the results I proposed to Gen. German occurred: we did not turn the Governor out, nor did he put us down. Although we lost our Governor we chose a Legislature by which I was appointed a Senator in Congress, and which turned McIntyre out of the office of Comptroller, in which he had worked so hard against us.

Several other stirring events transpired at the session of 1820. Mr. Clinton called the attention of the Legislature, in his speech, to the Missouri Question, and recommended action upon that subject. I was not favourable to his recommendation, but unwilling to give him the advantage of wielding so powerful an influence against us as it would have proved to be, if we had opposed it. Incessant attempts were made by his friends to place me in that attitude. Permission was asked, and given, to use my name in a notice signed by

---

[1] Speech in the Senate of New Pork, on the Act to carry into effect the Act of 13th April, 1819, for the settlement of the late Governor's accounts. Albany, 1820.—W. C. F.

[2] Feb. 22, 1820. In an account of the meeting, written by John A. King to Rufus King, he said: " A well written address and Resolutions were then submitted by Mr. Van Buren, the chairman to the meeting, and were adopted with long and repeated cheering."—W. C. F.

[3] The question of Tompkins' accounts remained open until after the election, and undoubtedly played some part in defeating him. In November. 1820, a measure was introduced, and passed without opposition, ending the controversy by enabling the accounts to be balanced.—W. C. F.

the most respectable citizens of Albany, of all parties, calling a meeting to take the sense of the People on the subject. I was necessarily absent, on a foreign circuit, when the meeting was held, and refused my assent to their proceedings when they were presented to me, because they bore on their face the stamp of political and partisan designs. A letter was written to me by the gentleman who obtained permission to use my name, evidently intended for publication but it was deemed inexpedient to publish my answer when they received it.[1] When the Resolution was acted upon in the Senate there was neither debate nor a call of the Ayes and Noes; and it was silently passed. I was in my seat and would have voted for it if a formal vote had been taken and I always afterwards therefore admitted my share of responsibility for its passage. It may be said that in overlooking the bearings of the question upon the happiness of the People for whom Congress were acting, and allowing myself to be influenced by a desire to prevent the Governor from making political capital out of his recommendation, I placed myself on the same footing with him. As to motives I can only say that I state mine truly; that I acted on the defensive, and that I had no hand in bringing the matter forward.

The re-election of Mr. Rufus King to the United States Senate was another feature of this session that excited much feeling and not a little surprise from the circumstance that it was unanimously made by men, most of whom opposed him at the preceding session. An appointment had been attempted then and failed because of the three candidates brought forward respectively by the Clintonians, Republicans and Federalists neither could obtain a majority of the whole vote, necessary to obtain a majority in either House; the strength of the Democrats and Clintonians being nearly equal, and divided between Col. Young and John C. Spencer.[2]

In the recess I became, I believe for the first time, acquainted personally with Mr. King, and from my connection with the defense of Vice President Tompkins, in which the subject was noticed, became also better informed of his patriotic course in support of the War after the capture of Washington, and his urgent appeal to the Vice President, then Governor, to assume every responsibility and to trust for indemnity to the justice of his Country. Influenced by

---

[1] Henry F. Jones, Jan. 19, 1820, to Van Buren and draft of Van Buren's answer, Jan. 21, are in the Van Buren Papers.

[2] The three candidates proposed were John C. Spencer by the Clintonians, Samuel Young, by the republicans or "Bucktails" and Rufus King, by the federalitsts. "In the assembly Mr. Spencer received fifty four votes, Mr. Young forty four, and Mr. King thirty four. Some of the members, who, on the resolution, voted for Col. Young, when the resolution was lost, voted for Mr. King. The whole number of republican votes, in both houses, for Col. Young, were fifty seven, while those given to Mr. Spencer were sixty four; showing evidently, at that time, a republican majority in the legislature in favor of Mr. Clinton; but the preponderance of talent was decidedly with the Bucktails." Hammond, History of Political Parties in the State of New York, I, 486. The details of the proceedings are told in John A. King to Rufus King, February 2, 1819. Life and Correspondence of Rufus King, VI, 202.—W. C. F.

these considerations, and doubtless stimulated by a desire to obtain for Tompkins the votes and support of that section of the federalists called "the high-minded"—then supposed to be quite influential— I resolved, before the meeting of the Legislature, to support his re-election. To this end, I prepared, under the pressure of my numerous other avocations, a Pamphlet in his favor, which I submitted to the examination of Mr. William L. Marcy, by whom it was much improved, 'from which circumstance Judge Hammond, in some degree correctly describes it as our joint production. The pamphlet was sent to the Members before they left home, and had, it was believed, considerable effect upon their opinions. It was signed "A Member of the Legislature" but generally understood, and not denied, to come from me. With the exception of a few members of the delegation from the city of New York, who never forgave my refusal to unite in an adverse nomination to Mr. Clinton, the vote of the Legislature was unanimous in favor of Mr. King's re-election.

No one supposed for a moment that Mr. Clinton and his friends were otherwise than hostile to the measure, but it was well understood that they voted for it for the same reason which they charged influenced us; that of gathering strength for the Gubernatorial election. The part I took in the affair was a stereotyped charge against me for the remainder of my political career, brought forward by different parties and factions in turn as the shifting phases of party politics made it their cue to lay hold of the subject. That good natured but most unscrupulous politician, Major Noah, then the Editor of the National Advocate, applied for and obtained a confidential communication of my views on the subject as necessary to the proper discharge of his editorial duties. When he became, in the progress of time, opposed to me, he furnished to my enemies for publication extracts from my letter, shamefully garbled, but even in that state harmless. In 1840, when he felt rather friendly again, he, to my amusement, offered the letter to a political friend to save himself from the importunities of the Whig Committee of Richmond, who he said were anxious to obtain it, having evidently forgotten the roguish use he had himself, years before, made of its contents.[1]

---

[1] This letter is printed on p. 138 of the Autobiography. The autograph draft is in the Van Buren Papers. Rufus King gracefully noted his indebtedness to Van Buren, in the following extract of a letter to John A. King, January 14, 1820: "The part taken by Mr. Van Buren has indeed been most liberal, and as I conceive at the risk of impairing his high standing and influence among his political friends; do not fail therefore to inform him that I can never be insensible of his generosity and that no occasion can arrive, that I shall not be ready to prove to him the personal respect & esteem with which he has inspired me." Two months later (March 18) he wrote: "To the Vice President I am not a little indebted for the support without which Mr. Clinton and his' federal friends would have succeeded in degrading me. To Van Buren more especially am I most particularly obliged; whose views and principles, as far as I have understood them, deserve my hearty approbation."—W. C. F.

102 AMERICAN HISTORICAL ASSOCIATION.

The election of 1820 resulted in the choice of a Democratic majority in the House of Assembly, and we availed ourselves of our full possession of both branches of the Legislature, at the Extra session called for the choice of Presidential Electors in the fall of that year, to pass a Bill providing for a Convention to amend the ° Constitution of the State, which was rejected in the Council of Revision by the casting vote of Gov. Clinton.[1] Two friendly Judges, Platt and Van Ness, were absent on their circuits; Chancellor Kent and Judge Spencer were known to be against the Bill, and the vote of Judge Woodworth, who had been recently nominated by Governor Clinton was confidently counted on to save the latter from the necessity of giving the casting vote. To the surprise of every one, and the indignation of the Clintonians, he voted with Judge Yates, and thus produced the tie.[2] A law was passed early in the winter session to submit the question of Convention or No Convention to the People in the spring, who decided in favor of holding it by a majority of seventy thousand.

° MS. I, p. 135.

[1] In the session of 1817–18 Ogden Edwards, of New York, brought a bill into the assembly for calling a State convention to consider such parts of the constitution as related to the appointment of offices. The object was to substitute for the council of appointment some other method of appointing officers. Hammond advised Clinton to adopt the suggestion and couple with it an alteration and extension of the right of suffrage. "All men had become disgusted with the appointing power, under the old constitution, and so universal was the opinion that a change ought to be made, that I was satisfied that the council of appointment could not much longer form a part of our governmental machinery. The right of suffrage, too, was more restricted in this State than in any other of the northern or middle States; and I was satisfied that public opinion, in a State so highly democratic, would not much longer endure the restriction" (Hammond, I, 469). Although Clinton controlled one branch of the legislature and could have directed the course of the question he refused to support it, presumably on the ground that the project had originated in the opposition. Edward's bill was rejected.

The idea of a convention was not abandoned by those opposed to Clinton, and his re-election in 1820 produced the necessary unanimity. Local meetings were held advocating a convention, and the democrats, "perceiving that the only sure means" of getting rid of Clinton was by changing some of the methods of government, "availed themselves, with great skill and adroitness, of the propensity of the people for an alteration of the constitution to effect that object." It was to be a convention with unrestricted powers, not confined only to the machinery of appointments. Clinton was now in favor of the plan, and wished the question of calling a convention to be submitted to the people; but the democrats were in a majority in both houses of the Legislature, and passed a measure providing for a convention, the results of which were to be submitted to the people for confirmation or rejection. The Clintonians feared that it was the purpose of those favoring a convention of unlimited powers to abolish the existing judiciary system, and introduce a new one not containing the present judges and chancellor, who had created a prejudice by their political activities. Gaining confidence in their ability to manage the convention after their own wishes, they yielded and joined in favoring the movement. The bill was thrown out by the Council of Revision, as related by Van Buren. To overcome the opposition of the Council some leading Federalists proposed to have the Council of Appointment appoint three additional judges, and if experience should show there were then too many judges, a convention might be called to modify the judiciary department so as to "insure an unpolitical tribunal." Rufus King refused to give his support to this suggestion, and it was never seriously discussed.—W. C. F.

[2] The same story, with other details, is told by Hammond, History of Political Parties in the State of New York, I, 545.—W. C. F.

These circumstances seemed to overthrow the popularity of the Governor, already greatly shaken, and induced his friends to advise him to retire to private life at the end of his term, as he decided to do. The Assembly also chose at the Extra-session a new Council of Appointment of which Skinner, Bowne, and Evans were members.[1] Evans came to Albany, an honest and intelligent young man from the Western District as a Clintonian, but being disgusted with his Associates in the Legislature, he sought me out, in one of our Caucuses, before they separated from us and when their leaders were trying, against our opposition, to obtain an adjournment, and told me that he had lost all confidence in the men with whom he was acting, and asked me to consent to an adjournment, which I cheerfully did, from which time to the end of his life he was my fast and active friend politically and personally.

[1] This election was held on November 8, 1820. The full council was Walter Bowne of the southern district, John T. Moore, of the middle, Roger Skinner of the eastern, and David E. Evans, of the western. The Clinton candidates were Townsend, Ross, Frothingham and Barstow. Skinner was at this time United States Judge of the northern district of New York, as well as a member of the State Senate.—W. C. F.

CHAPTER VII.

The first question that presented itself at the ensuing winter session was that of filling the vacancy in the office of United States Senator, occasioned by the expiration of Mr. Sanford's term. Our friends came to Albany in the opinion that the time had arrived when my services ought to be transferred to the Federal government. Mr. Sanford received a few votes in Caucus, but on the appointment every democratic member voted for me, while he received the votes of the Clintonians. I had neither solicited the place nor taken a single step to promote my election, but was gratified by the distinction. My old professional opponent, Elisha Williams, then in the Legislature, offered to support me in return for my having once sustained him against one of my political friends, in a matter by which the fortune of his family was made; I told him that he was mistaken in supposing that he was under any obligation to me, as I had only done in that case what I thought was right—but that I was pleased with his sense of the act, and had certainly no objections to his easing his mind by returning the supposed favor, which would be better done by voting with his federal friends for Mr. Sanford. This amused him very much and induced him to say in the House, in his own way, that he thought I was the fittest man for Senator, but as he was the very incarnation of old Federalism, I would not let him vote for me, and he therefore voted for Sanford.[1]

In April 1820, some forty gentlemen, of the federal party, most of them young men of talent and all occupying respectable positions in society, came out with an Address in which they insisted that no " high-minded federalist " would support Clinton. The use of this expression obtained for them the designation of " the high-minded " in the political nomenclature of the times, while their demonstration against the Governor secured for them from his friends the less flattering *sobriquet* of " the forty thieves." [2] John Duer was their ablest man, but his Federalism was so deeply dyed as to neutralize

---

[1] The caucus for the purpose of naming a candidate for the United States Senate was held on February 1, 1821. Sanford was nominated by Mr. Romaine, of New York, and Mr. Eldred, of Otsego, brought forward the name of Van Buren. No charges of neglect of duty or want of loyalty to the party were made against Sanford, and, it was urged, that to set him aside without cause, would be equivalent to a vote of censure, seal his political usefulness, and destroy his political character in the public estimation. His great knowledge and experience in commercial affairs peculiarly fitted him to represent the State in the Senate. Col. Young acted as Van Buren's advocate, saying that with Rufus King in the Senate the commercial matters would have proper attention, and on a ballot Van Buren received 58 votes against 24 for his opponent. A resolution was adopted expressive of the confidence of the meeting in Sanford, as balm to his wounded feelings.—W. C. F.

[2] A list of the forty who signed the address of April 14, 1820, will be found in Hammond, History of Political Parties in the State of New York, I, 529.—W. C. F.

all his efforts to become a democrat. The sons of Rufus King were prominent members. The whole number were indeed Mr. King's devoted friends, and his advancement was the object nearest their hearts. Their opposition to Mr. Clinton, to whom they allowed no credit for the support his friends had given to Mr. King, was cordially reciprocated. Tompkins was not to their taste as a candidate for Governor, but when his nomination was decided on they supported him with zeal and fidelity.

Pleased with their society and with the spirited manner in which they sustained their position, I became more intimate with them than was the case with any other prominent democrat, and formed sincere attachments to several of their number. Our friendly relations were strengthened by the early stand I took in favor of Mr. King, and their conviction that he was principally indebted for his election to that circumstance, as they well knew that the friends of Mr. Clinton would not otherwise have supported him. My partiality for them produced heart-burnings on the part of many democratic young men, which, in regard to some, were never entirely removed. Federalists from their birth, and of the oldest and strictest sect, they could not make much impression by their efforts upon the democratic ranks, and failing to draw after them those from whom they had separated, their success was not equal to their expectations, neither were they treated by our party with the consideration which they thought they deserved. Resentments engendered on the first moments of separation between political associates are always accessible to the mollifying influences of former sympathies not entirely extinguished, and the recollection of common struggles and triumphs in the old cause paves the way for re-union. These are more efficient when the cause is one in which they or their ancestors have acquired distinction. Most of these gentlemen had from early manhood enjoyed high and influential position in what was called good society, and the supposition that they expected to occupy, on that account, greater consideration in the democratic organization was not acceptable in that quarter. There was a warm concurrence in feeling and opinion between us upon the point that brought us together—opposition to Mr. Clinton—but in regard to other matters we were far from entertaining similar views. Upon some of the latter we were called to act together at a period when the ardour of our first embraces had in some degree subsided. The first occasion of that description was presented by the Convention for the Revision of the State Constitution, which met at Albany in August 1821.[1]

The County of Albany, where I resided, being then hopelessly federal, the democrats of the large agricultural county of Otsego

---

[1] The convention assembled at Albany August 28, 1821, and did not close its sessions till November 10.—W. C. F.

elected me to the Convention without even apprising me of their intention.

The federalists insisted, and generally believed that we maintained our ascendency in power mainly thro' the influence of the Council of Appointment, and were therefore feverishly anxious for its abolition. Convinced by full experience that the possession and distribution of patronage did us more harm than good, as a party, I early determined to advocate its diffusion to the widest extent that should be found practical and consistent with the public interest. When asked by the President of the Convention (Tompkins) on what Committee he should place me, I replied, on that " on the appointing power ". Not understanding, or rather misunderstanding my object, he smiled, but complied with my wish. The fact that I was placed at the head of that Committee[1] strengthened the opinions of the federal members and made them quite confident that an effort was to be made to preserve the Council of Appointment in a form perhaps changed but of unabated efficiency. The President gave me an excellent Committee, embracing however, but under proper control, some of the most violent denouncers of the Convention. Among these was Judge Ogden Edwards, of the New York delegation, an honest, capable and well-meaning man, but always overflowing with political prejudices. His disposition in this respect was vouched for by his own father, as related to me by my friend, Roger Skinner, who, on his return from a visit to Connecticut, his native state, told me that he had met the celebrated Pierpoint Edwards, the father of Ogden, and that he had added to the usual enquiries about his son the question whether " he had got through damning De Witt Clinton yet ? "

I rather mischievously delayed calling my Committee together until the suspicions I have referred to had time to mature. When we were assembled I proposed to call on each member for his general opinions upon the subject committed to us. Mr. Edwards immediately suggested that the Chairman should give his views first. This I declined to do, on the ground that such a course would be contrary to parliamentary usage, according to which the Chairman is regarded as a mediator, and, to some extent, an umpire between the conflicting opinions of the Committee.

The process I proposed was then entered upon, and when finished I deferred giving my own views until the next meeting. At that meeting I submitted my propositions which were in substance.

1st To abolish the existing Council of Appointment without substituting any similar institution in its place;

---

[1] The full committee contained Martin Van Buren, ——— Birdseye, ——— Collins, Jesse Buel, ——— Child, Ogden Edwards, and ——— Rhinelander.—W. C. F.

2nd To provide for the election of all military officers by the choice of Companies, Regiments and Brigades;

° 3d To give the appointment of high Judicial Officers to the Governor and Senate, and

4th To provide for the choice of all other Officers, save only Justices of the Peace, by the People, either through appointment by the Legislature, or by direct election. The Justices of the Peace, as Judicial Officers, ought not, I said, to be elected, but to bring them as near to the People as possible and avoid the objections to their election, I proposed that two lists should be made in each county, one by the Board of Supervisors (who were themselves elected by the People in each town) and the other by the county court Judges; whenever these two lists agreed the choice should be complete, and whenever they differed the Governor should select the Justices from them.

The jealous members of the Committee were not only disappointed, but some of them confounded by my propositions. They went so far beyond their expectations, in distributing the patronage of the Government, and in removing the grounds upon which they expected the battle in regard to the appointing power to be fought, as to draw from some the charge of radicalism. The question in regard to Justices of the Peace was the only remaining point on which speeches that had been prepared, in expectation of a different report, could be directed. My recommendations were substantially adopted by the Committee, but the portion of them relating to the choice of Justices was violently assailed in the Convention by the federal members and also by the "high-minded" gentlemen. I stated frankly the principle upon which that part of my report was founded, and that I considered it a fair subject for differences of opinion. The questions were whether the spirit of the rule, to which every body then assented, that the higher Judicial Officers ought not to be elected should be respected in providing for the choice of Justices of the Peace; and, if so, whether the mode proposed by the Committee for their selection was the best.

Mr. Rufus King attacked the proposition with great earnestness, and scarcely concealed acrimony. After enumerating a few objections to its practical operation, he took up the subject of the old Council of Appointment, and denounced it as a machine that had in times past been used and abused to monopolize central power. Although his remarks were not directly aimed at me or at my friends, they were, I thought, sufficiently susceptible of that construction to require notice from me.

I replied at considerable length and with some warmth and in the course of my remarks alluded delicately but intelligibly to *one*

° MS. I, p. 140.

of the uses that had been made of what he denounced as the Central
Power of which he had not complained. This affair caused a reserve in our personal intercourse which continued for some time, and
until the period arrived when our franking privilege as United States
Senators commenced. He then came to my seat and announced the
fact to me as a matter that might have escaped my notice, and at the
same time pressed me to dine with him.

After dinner he proposed a walk, and in the course of it spoke
feelingly of the collisions which political life almost unavoidably
produced between the best of friends, and the inquietude growing
out of them, and said that the best remedy he had discovered was to
forget and forgive—to sleep upon the matter, and rising in the morning to wash, shave, put on fresh linen, and think no more of it. Understanding the object of these suggestions, I also came to the conclusion to dismiss the subject from my thoughts, and our personal relations resumed their previous footing.

Some time afterwards, and during the session of the Convention,
an editorial article appeared in the Argus remarking upon this and
other differences of opinion between this section and the great body
of our party—admitting that to some extent they had been anticipated as likely to occur in the course of time, but saying that it was
not expected that they would present themselves so soon. When I
came into the Convention, John Duer, in a courteous and not unfriendly manner, repeated to me the closing words—" not so soon "—
with significant emphasis. This led to a farther conversation in
which I admitted that the article spoke my sentiments. We dined
together at his brother's lodgings with a few mutual friends, and
had an animated conversation upon points in regard to which we
entertained diverse views, in the course of which, becoming convinced that there were radical differences in our feelings and opinions which must prevent us from long acting together, I involuntarily
struck my hand upon the table with unusual earnestness, when he
instantly turned to me, and said " that is the indication of a grave
conclusion! May I know what it is, Sir?" I laughed at his interpretation and turned the conversation into a different channel.

These occurrences produced distrust, but no personal hostility, or
even determination to separate. That was brought to pass by the
ensuing Presidential election, and the influences it called into action.
A large majority of the Democrats supported Crawford, the rest
dividing upon Adams and Clay. The " high-minded " espoused the
cause of Mr. Adams zealously, and the feelings produced, or rather
revived by that contest carried them back into the federal ranks,—
then called National Republicans—where the survivors are still
serving as Whigs.

CHAPTER VIII.

All personal intercourse between Charles King, Editor of the New York American, and myself was for many years broken off. After he had retired from the Editorial profession, and had, I believe, received the appointment of President of Columbia College, we happened to meet at an entertainment given at the opening of a new Club House in New York. He approached me and entered into a familiar conversation upon the topicks of the day. So long a time had elapsed since I had seen him that I took him for his brother James[1] and reciprocated his address very cordially, but the idea of my mistake soon occurring to me the conversation gradually stiffened on my part, and he, perceiving and understanding it, rather abruptly but gradually withdrew. My son, Col. Van Buren, standing at some distance, and witnessing and comprehending the whole scene, advanced towards me as Mr. King walked away, and said " I saw that you did not at first recognize your old friend Charles." I confessed that I had not, but as it had ever been my practice to continue the war as long as my adversary desired it, but always to be prepared for peace, I sought him out, and renewed a friendly intercourse that has since been uninterrupted.

Thus disappeared from the political stage a party which, though small in numbers produced nearly or quite as great an impression as its predecessor and counterpart, in respect to size, the *Burrites*—in their day distinguished by the name of the " Little Band." The latter were heard and felt through the pamphlet of "Aristides " written by William P. Van Ness.[2]—a production of great celebrity in its time,—the Morning Chronicle, edited by Peter Irving, elder brother of Washington Irving, and the " Corrector," a stinging little sheet, edited by a number of young men and to which, I believe Washington Irving was a contributor. The New York American, edited with great ability, and a series of clever publications, of which " Dick Shift "[3] (supposed to have been written by John Duer) was the most piquant, were the oracles of the " high-minded." The Burrites were headed by Aaron Burr, and the sons of Alexander Hamilton were prominent members of the " high minded " party.

To the latter belonged indisputably the paternity of one public measure, namely the attempt to impeach William W. Van Ness, one of the Justices of the Supreme Court, for receiving a bribe from

---

[1] James Gore King.
[2] An examination of the various charges exhibited against Aaron Burr, Vice-President of the United States, and a Development of the Characters and Views of his Political Opponents. By Aristides. 1803.—W. C. F.
[3] See the letter from Johnston Verplanck to Van Buren, December 25, 1819, in the Van Buren Papers.—W. C. F.

109

the Bank of America, to secure the assent of the Council of Revision, of which the Judges were then members, to the act of incorporation. The fact that the Bank obtained its charter thro' the most daring and unscrupulous bribery practiced upon various persons, occupying[o] different positions in the public service, is undeniable. The matter was investigated with great solemnity by a Committee of the House of Assembly, appointed on the motion of Erastus Root, upon the exhibition of the charge made by the Editors of the New York American, Charles King, Johnston Verplanck and James A. Hamilton, over their own signatures. The Judge appeared before the Committee, supported by an imposing array of Counsel, and the principal part of the session was occupied with the examination.[1] The Committee finally reported that there was no ground for the interference of the House, but the public mind did not respond favorably to the conclusions of the report. The consciousness of this fact preyed upon the Judge's spirits, and hurried him to a premature grave.

Judge Van Ness was by nature the ablest man among his associates in public life. His facilities for early improvement had been but limited, and he had no taste for deep study; the brilliant reputation he established as a lawyer and Judge was therefore mainly founded on the raw materials with which nature had liberally endowed him. His personal figure was imposing and his manners peculiarly fascinating—so much so that even his enemies courted his society. He was a member of the Constitutional Convention of 1821, which was the last public station he held. In that body a proposition was introduced by Gov. Tompkins, and supported by Erastus Root and a host of other democrats, to vacate the offices of the Chancellor and Justices of the Supreme Court by the new Constitution. Although the Convention had the power to do this, it had certainly not been expected by the Legislature or the People that such a step would be taken. Sincerely desirous to secure the respect and sanction of the public for our proceedings and opposed upon principle to a course so proscriptive, I threw myself in the breach against the weight of my party and opposed the proposition. To neutralize the prejudices of friends, and to conciliate moderate men, whilst resisting a measure, the success of which threatened all that remained of the former greatness of Judge Van Ness, I deemed it a fit if not a necessary occasion to allude to our past relations. This was done in a speech delivered in his presence, from which the following in an extract:

The judicial officer who could not be reached in either of those ways, ought not to be touched. There were, therefore, no public reasons for the measure,

[o] MS. I, p. 145.
[1] See Proceedings of the Committee appointed to inquire into the official Conduct of William W. Van Ness, New York, 1820.—W. C. F.

and if not, then why are we to adopt it? Certainly not from personal feelings. If personal feelings could or ought to influence us against the individual who would probably be most affected by the adoption of this amendment, Mr. Van Buren supposed that he above all others would be excused for indulging them. He could with truth say, that he had through his whole life been assailed from that quarter, with hostility, political, professional and personal—hostility which had been the most keen, active and unyielding. But, sir, said he, am I on that account, to avail myself of my situation as a representative of the people, sent here to make a constitution for them and their posterity, and to indulge my individual resentments in the prostration of my private and political adversary. He hoped it was unnecessary for him to say, that he should forever despise himself if he could be capable of such conduct. He also hoped that that sentiment was not confined to himself alone, and that the Convention would not ruin its character and credit, by proceeding to such extremities.[1]

A sufficient number of my political friends voted with me to defeat the proposition. The Chancellor and three of the Judges were members of the Convention. The latter left soon after to hold the Term at Utica, and the democratic portion of the Convention, no longer irritated by the active intermeddling of Judges Spencer and Van Ness in matters supposed to have partisan tendencies, was losing the memory of my rebellion against party discipline and of the whole subject; but the return of those gentlemen with renewed ardour to their work of political intrigue caused a new proposition, sufficiently varied in form to evade the parliamentary rule, to be promptly introduced by a lay member, and procured for it a vigorous support. I felt that I could now do no more than give a silent vote against the measure. The proposition was adopted, the offices of the Judges were vacated, a new Governor was elected before the time arrived to fill the vacancies, and neither Spencer nor Van Ness were renominated. They both resumed the practice of their profession, but his misfortunes preying upon Van Ness' proud spirit his health failed, and he went to South Carolina in the hope of re-establishing it, but there, soon after, died at the house of his connexion, Mr. Bay, a highly respectable resident of Charleston. I was informed by Mr. Bay, many years afterwards, that, in the closing scenes of his life, the Judge spoke often and feelingly of his political and personal controversies, and that whilst he referred with much severity to the conduct of some of those with whom he had been in collision, he took pains to say that he should die without complaint or bitterness against me, who, altho' among the most uniform of his opponents, had always treated him frankly and fairly. His unfriendliness throughout his public life did not prevent my sincere sympathy with him when he fell, and with his friends in their prayers over his ashes.

---

[1] Reports of the New York State Convention, 1821 (Carter and Stone), p. 535.

A new Constitution was adopted by the Convention providing for increased action on the part of the People themselves in the management of public affairs, and liberalizing and elevating the political institutions of the State to the standard required by the advances made by public opinion in that direction.

I have noticed the part that I took in regard to two questions that were acted upon by the Convention because they were more or less complicated with other matters. To do as much in reference to all, would require more space than I think it would be proper to devote to the subjects here. There was scarcely any question raised in the discussion of which I did not participate to a greater or less extent, and those discussions as well as the votes that followed them are to be found reported in the official proceedings and published accounts of the doings of the Convention, which publications, altho' not accurate throughout, are sufficiently so for all important purposes.

On one point only will I add a few words of explanation, because it has been the subject of much remark, and of much partizan misrepresentation.

At one stage of our proceedings I was alarmed at the ground taken by a number of my political friends upon the question of suffrage. They seemed willing to go at once from a greatly restricted suffrage to one having but the appearance of restriction, which I considered very hazardous as well to our institutions as to the success of the work of the Convention. I preferred to move upon this truly important point step by step, and to advance as we should find ourselves justified by experience. The partizan policy of advocating extreme measures of seeming popularity, trusting that somebody else would prevent their adoption, or that perchance they might not work as badly, if adopted, as my reason anticipated, has never, I can conscientiously say, been mine. I therefore exerted myself to moderate the extreme views of my friends, and, when necessary, to oppose them until the suffrage was established on what I deemed safe and reasonable grounds. For this, and upon the ground of expressions loosely and inaccurately reported I was for many years much censured, but, I believe, not injured, because the People saw the soundness of my motive even thro' the distorted and false views in which, for sinister purposes, the subject was presented to them.

The new Constitution was approved and adopted by an immense majority of the People.[1] Judge Joseph C. Yates was elected Governor, under its provisions, without opposition, Governor Clinton retiring to private life, and I soon after took my seat in the Senate of the United States.

---

[1] The result showed 75,422 votes in favor of the Constitution and 41,497 votes against or a majority of 33,925 on the side of adoption.—W. C. F.

CHAPTER IX.

The transfer from the State to the Federal Service has generally been considered as a discharge from responsibility for the management of the affairs of the former, but neither friends nor foes would permit such a result in my case. The first had claims upon my gratitude and good offices that I was not inclined to disregard, and the latter found or fancied a party benefit in charging me with influencing the action of the State Government from Washington thro' the agency of representatives at home to whom they gave the name of the " Albany Regency."

The inconvenience, to say the least of it, of this ubiquitous responsibility was strikingly and very disagreeably illustrated by bringing me very early into disfavour with the new Governor whose nomination I had preferred and aided in effecting. Judge Yates was an honest man, possessed of a good understanding, who always designed to do what he thought was right. He warded off too strict a scrutiny into his mental capacities by a dignified and prudent reserve—a policy that long practice had made a second nature. He had been strongly tempted, by his marriage connections, to depart from the simplicity of life and manners characteristic of his race. His first wife was a Kane, a family which almost without exception was distinguished for the personal beauty of its members, and their natural dignity of carriage, and which had made considerable advances towards the establishment of a sort of family aristocracy before it gave way under the pressure of adverse circumstances. His second wife, with whom he acquired a good estate, was a De Lancey, a powerful family at the commencement of the revolution, jealousy of whose superior position at Court was said to have had great influence in inducing the Livingstons, and other families who figured in that contest, to espouse the popular side. My acquaintance with Mrs. Yates has led me to regard her as a good woman of superior mind and sedulous in the performance of duty. I paid the Judge a visit at Schenectady at the time when we were preparing to bring him forward as a candidate for Governor, in company with several of the " high-minded " gentlemen to whom he was very partial. While we were at dinner the conversation was mischievously turned by one of the guests for his own amusement to a matter in regard to which our host ° and myself had, in past times, stood in opposition

---

° MS. I, p. 150.

x

to each other. The Judge promptly and courteously said in reference to it, "Ah! that was at a time when I did not understand Mr. Van Buren as well as I do now!" On which Mrs. Yates turned to her husband, and asked with unaffected simplicity whether he was sure that he understood me now! The question of course was received with a general burst of laughter, and not having the slightest idea of incivility or unfriendliness, she began to apprehend that she had shown both—an apprehension that it cost me no small effort to efface from her mind. The circumstance slight as it was, strengthened my impression that she was not in all respects well adapted to the office of guarding her husband against the effects of a suspicious temperament, which had been always an obstacle to his advancement, and was the principal cause of his failure in public life.

On my way to Washington, in the fall preceding the Judge's assumption of his official duties, I remained some time in New York winding up professional concerns at the November Term of the Supreme Court. Many of my friends were there in the prosecution of their professional engagements, and some were doubtless brought there by their fondness for political gossip, and by a desire to take leave of me. I had not been long in Washington before I learned, thro' a source entitled to my confidence, that the Governor-elect had been told that I had assembled my friends in a private meeting at New York, at which we had marked out a course for the Governor to pursue as the indispensable condition of our support. There was of course not a word of truth in this story, and under ordinary circumstances I would have taken no notice of it. But I knew the Governor's disposition, and that he was surrounded by men in whom I had little confidence, who owed me no good will and who had personal objects which they might hope to promote by availing themselves in this form of an infirmity to which they knew him to be subject. I therefore determined to address myself to him directly, and to make a serious effort not only to disabuse his mind upon the particular point, but to prevent the recurrence of similar misunderstandings. In the propriety of this course, Mr. King, to whom I mentioned the subject, fully concurred, and I wrote a letter to the Governor in which I referred to the story I have mentioned as a vile falsehood, expressed my apprehension that other misrepresentations of the same character would be made by bad men for selfish purposes, avowed my disinclination to the slightest personal interference in affairs which had, with my hearty approbation, been committed to his hands, and closed with what appeared to me a clear and conclusive argument to show that I could have no possible interests that would be benefitted by his overthrow and an assurance that the first wish of my heart was that he might sustain himself successfully and honorably in his responsible position. With most men this would have been sufficient, but as to him the soil was too favorable to the rank growth of the seed I, endeavoured to eradicate and the sowers were too numerous and industrious to admit of any success to my efforts. He had weakened his position by his jealousy to an extent that enabled the friends of Col. Young to nominate the latter in his place during the succeeding winter. Irritated by this result and distrusting almost every body he was induced to take an official step which I will have occasion to refer to hereafter, and which finally prostrated him as a public man.

I entered the Senate of the United States in December 1821, at the commencement of Mr. Monroe's second Presidential Term. John Gaillard, of South Carolina, was then, as he had been for many years, President *pro tem.* of that body. I need add nothing to the eloquent description given of his character by Col. Benton, in his Thirty Years' View, except the expression of my full concurrence in what has been so well said. I was first placed on both the Judiciary and Finance Committees, and soon succeeded to the Chairmanship of the former, a compliment to so young a man, on his first appearance in the Senate, which I could not fail to appreciate.

There was at this period a perfect calm in the public mind upon political subjects, and the Administration continued the course it had pursued during the previous term, unlike any since that of Washington, without an organized opposition. The important questions that occupied the attention of Congress during the Presidency of Mr. Monroe were those of Internal Improvements by the Federal Government and a Protective Tariff. Stronger proof could not be required of the capacity of our system of Government to deal with difficult public questions, and the strength it derives from that source, than the fact that those disturbing questions, which (particularly the latter) semed, in the hottest day of their agiation, to threaten the continuance of the Union, in so brief a period not only ceased to inflame the People, but, in the sense in which they were then advocated and opposed, have become virtually obsolete. It is also worthy of remark that neither of these great questions originated with the Administration, or were regarded as Administration Measures. They found their origin in other sources and were called into existence by other considerations than those of Executive recommendation.

Mr. Monroe was universally regarded as the last of that class of Statesmen to which the country had invariably theretofore looked for Presidential candidates. This fact was sufficient to bring forward for the succession the names of those of the succeeding generation who deemed themselves, or were deemed by their friends, as possessing sufficient claims to the distinction.

The most prominent of these were Clay, Calhoun, Crawford and Adams. I name Messrs. Clay and Calhoun first because, from very nearly the beginning of Mr. Monroe's Administration, their respective courses were most definitely shaped to that end.

Mr. Clay was Speaker of the House of Representatives, had returned with *éclat* from his Mission of Peace, and enjoyed an extensive popularity with uncommon facilities for its enlargement.

Mr. Calhoun was Secretary of War, the undoubted favorite of the President, and in point of talent, industry and the art of winning popular regard scarcely inferior to Mr. Clay.

A better field for the display of political ability and tact than that presented to these distinguished gentlemen could not have been imagined. The old Federal Party, yet strong in numbers and rich in its traditions, had been reduced to a low condition by the course it had taken in regard to the War. Its former leaders, either from policy or conviction, acquiesced in the condemnation that had been pronounced upon it, and the future allegiance of its members seemed to be offered as spoils of conquest to democratic aspirants to the Presidency.

Relaxation of the rigors of party discipline and acts of amnesty in favor of vanquished federalists—splendid schemes of Internal Improvement at the expense of the Federal Treasury with munificent bounties in the form of encouragements to Domestic Industry to the North, the East, and the West, were the popular appeals and blandishments with which Mr. Clay and Mr. Calhoun, each secure in his position at home, entered into the Presidential Canvass. Hence the continued Agitation of all of these questions from near the beginning to the end of Mr. Monroe's Administration—leaving them at its close as unsettled as they were at any stage of their discussion and as it was expedient to Presidential aspirants that they should be. These topicks for a political campaign were wisely selected, and produced apparently extensive effects upon the public mind. The great States of Pennsylvania, New Jersey and New York, with the entire West, swallowed the baits that were held out to them under such alluring disguises, in which they were joined by the Eastern States as soon as our Yankee brethren saw that the protective policy had acquired a sufficient hold upon the country to make it safe for them to divert their superior skill and industry from Commerce to Manufactures. So irresistible did the current seem to have become that even Gen. Jackson, with all his repugnance to equivocation, and all his fearlessness of responsibility, was fain, when he was brought into the Presidential Canvass, to take refuge under the idea of a "judicious tariff."

These, as I have said, altho' the prominent Measures acted upon, could not be regarded as among those of Mr. Monroe's Administration. Although he knew that the protective policy was supported by several members of his Cabinet, he never recommended it in his Messages and he interposed his Veto against a Bill for the repair of the Cumberland Road in a message in which the whole subject, so far as it related to the exercise of Federal jurisdiction over the territory embraced, was elaborately discussed.

The Cumberland Road was established under the Presidency of Mr. Jefferson, and whilst Mr. Gallatin° was Secretary of the Treasury. It was originally contemplated to be made out of the avails arising from the sales of the public lands, and was established to promote such sales. But Congress soon fell into the habit of anticipating the receipts from that source by appropriations from the Treasury and this [practice] had been almost annually repeated for more than twenty years and had received the Executive approval from Jefferson and Madison.

The jurisdiction by the Federal Government, which constituted the foundation of Mr. Monroe's objection had never been exercised; but he was, I think, quite right in assuming that the establishment and support of the Road involved the claim of a right to its exercise and therefore fairly presented the constitutional question upon which he took, as to that point, the true ground. The Bill came up soon after I had taken my seat in the Senate and I voted for it rather on the ground of its paternity and the subsequent acquiesence in it, than from an examination of the subject. The whole matter was afterwards very thoroughly investigated by me when I found reason to regret that vote and to take not only an early opportunity to avow my error but also a decided stand against the claim in both aspects of Jurisdiction and Appropriation.

The unavoidable and improper conflict of jurisdiction between the Federal and State authorities that must arise from the establishment of the Internal Improvement System advocated by its friends, was apparent, and the objections arising from that source was insuperable. Pressed by the force of this argument the friends of the Road almost always shunned the discussion of that branch of the subject and insisted that the Federal Government could exercise a salutary agency in the matter by appropriations of money without cessions of jurisdiction. This power was fully conceded by Mr. Monroe, and the exercise of it was sure in the end to impoverish the National Treasury by improvident grants to private companies and State works, and to corrupt Federal legislation by the opportunities it would present for favoritism. I shall hereafter have occasion to speak as well of the part I took in this matter subsequently, as of the total and, I hope, final overthrow of the principle.

°MS. I, p. 155.

The subject of Piracy became prominent in the discussions of the Senate, and I made a speech upon it.

Several Amendments of the Constitution, in regard to the election of President and Vice President were also offered and discussed. Upon one introduced by Gov. Dickerson of New Jersey, and hence called the New Jersey Plan, proposing to district the States, I delivered a Speech of which I have only the preparatory notes; these may be found to contain suggestions of some interest and are given in [1]

The wise disposition of our People to deal prudently with matters touching the safe action of their political system in times past is strikingly illustrated, in view of the inadequacy of the provisions of the Constitution and laws for the government of Congress in canvassing the votes for President and Vice President, by the success with which they have avoided difficulties for so long a period upon a point in which their feelings are always so deeply excited. Apprehensive of danger from this source at the election of 1824–5, when, from the number of Candidates, it was generally assumed that the election would come to the House, the Senate instructed its Judiciary Committee to consider the subject and to report thereon. After consulting with the older and more experienced Senators, I reported a Bill supplying omissions in the old law, which passed the Senate but failed in the House. As the law is still in the same imperfect State, and the matter may some day become one of considerable interest, the notes of my Speech upon the Bill, which were furnished to me by the Reporter, but have never been published, are given in [1]

---

[1] In the Van Buren Papers, under date of December 29, 1823.

CHAPTER X.

The period covered by Mr. Monroe's Administration was made memorable by the canvass for the succession to which I have alluded, and by his efforts to bring about a fusion of Parties.

Mr. Monroe's character was that of an honest man, with fair, but not very marked capacities, who, through life, performed every duty that devolved upon him with scrupulous fidelity. He had been honorably connected with our Revolutionary Contest, and from the beginning of our party divisions was found in the same ranks with Jefferson and his friends, although, like Mr. Madison, he was, while perfectly sincere, yet from a difference in temperament, neither so earnest nor so eager in his devotion to their common cause. But two circumstances occurred, at early periods in his political career, well calculated to stir his feelings and to whet his political zeal.

Having been appointed Minister to France by Washington he was recalled under circumstances implying dissatisfaction. He appealed to the People for his vindication in a publication of some length, characterized, as it has appeared to me, by great fairness.

The second matter alluded to was as follows:—a man by the name of Reynolds having, on several occasions, thrown out intimations that he was possessed of information that would inculpate criminally the administration of the Treasury Department by Alexander Hamilton, Congress appointed a Committee of Investigation consisting of Monroe, Venable and Leiper.[1]

Knowing that the relations between himself and Reynolds would require explanations which it would not be agreeable to offer on a public investigation, Hamilton invited the Committee to an informal meeting at his own office, and there made to them a confidential communication shewing that his connection with Reynolds grew out of a criminal intercourse between himself and Mrs. Reynolds, in all probability begun with the connivance of her husband, and ended, after the lapse of a certain time, in the pretended discovery by him, and the pecuniary extortions, under menaces of exposure, common to such cases. This statement was accompanied by the exhibition of a series of letters, receipts for money and other papers, placing its truth beyond all doubt. The Committee reported that the imputation was groundless, and the subject soon passed from the public mind; but a history of the United States subsequently appeared written by the well known James Thomas Cal-

---

[1] Congress did not appoint a committee. An informal investigation was made by Speaker Fredk. A. Muhlenberg, James Monroe and Abraham Venable. Leiper was not in Congress until 1829.

lender, in which the charge of peculation against Gen. Hamilton was repeated with much solemnity. The latter sent the publication to Mr. Monroe, and made a respectful and friendly application to him to be relieved, thro' his agency, from the odium of the charge by a statement that would have that effect. Party spirit ran high, and Mr. Monroe omitted to comply with this request. This omission drew from Gen. Hamilton a letter that was not a challenge absolute or conditional in its terms, and contained no expression from which an intention to make it the prelude to a challenge could be positively assumed, but no one doubted on reading it that such was the General's ultimate expectation. This was answered by Mr. Monroe with a few but slight words of explanation in regard to the course he had adopted, and with a declaration in conclusion—from all that appeared in the correspondence, quite abrupt,—that if the General's letter was intended to convey a demand for personal satisfaction his friend Col. Burr was authorized to make the necessary arrangements. Gen. Hamilton denied that such was the intention of his letter, but said, in reply, that if an invitation to the field was intended to be conveyed by Col. Monroe's letter he should not decline it, and his friend Major Jackson was authorized to make the arrangements that would in that event become necessary. Mr. Monroe disclaimed such an intention, and the affair was terminated by a letter from Gen. Hamilton which concluded with a declaration that he did not regard the case as one calling for the resort that had been referred to.

Gen. Hamilton, thinking that the only way to wipe off the reproach that it was attempted to fasten upon his official character, published to the World, a complete history of the transactions, including all the documents submitted to the Committee, and the correspondence with Monroe, in a Pamphlet written with much feeling and signal ability.[1] This having been done without consultation with his friends, they took unwearied pains to suppress the publication, deeming it neither necessary nor expedient. But few copies escaped their efforts, and one of these was sent to me, many years ago, as a curiosity by an old gentleman whose antiquarian tastes led him to collect and preserve such things, but I have °not seen it for a long time, and what I have stated is from a recollection of its contents.

I read it at an early period of my life with great interest, and could not but be strongly and favorably impressed by the readiness with which Gen. Hamilton exposed his moral character to just censure and the feelings of his family to the greatest annoyance, while

---

[1] Observations on Certain Documents contained in Nos. V and VI of *The History of the United States for the Year 1796*, in which the charge of speculation against Alexander Hamilton, late Secretary of the Treasury, is fully refuted. Written by himself. Phila. Printed for John Fenno, by John Bioren, 1797.

° MS. I, p. 160.

vindicating his official conduct from unmerited reproach. But notwithstanding my partiality for his personal character, and my confidence in his courage, I could not resist the conclusion, on reading the correspondence, that Colonel Monroe's disorderly inversion of the regular steps of such affairs, by his bull-dog avowal of a readiness to fight before he was challenged, having divested the contest of its formal chivalry and dignity, induced the General to bring it to a different result from that which he had at first contemplated.

It is not unlikely that these collisions with gentlemen at the head of the Federal Government, whilst they afforded a useful stimulus to Mr. Monroe's partizan zeal, attracted towards him, under the political excitements of the periods when they occurred, a larger share of popular attention and led to more numerous public employments, than, not being either a good speaker or a good writer, or remarkable for any striking accomplishment, he might otherwise have enjoyed. Having, besides, been born and reared on the red clay grounds of the Old Dominion, so celebrated for the production of Presidents, it is quite natural that he should, at an early period, have come to the conclusion that to be among the successors of Washington would not exceed his deserts. That he did not think his own pretentions unreasonably postponed by the preference given to Jefferson, his senior in years and whose claims upon the confidence and favor of his country were incomparably superior to his own, I can well imagine. But it became a very different affair when the day arrived for the choice of Mr. Jefferson's successor, and when the dwellers on the red soil could hardly believe it possible that the other portions of the Union would be sufficiently self-denying to acquiesce in any further selections from that already highly favored spot. It is well known that Mr. Monroe's feelings were deeply soured by the choice of Mr. Madison for the succession through the influence of Mr. Jefferson—not seen or heard or exerted by improper means but not the less effectual. The celebrated Protest of John Randolph and his associates,—for a long time distinguished by the cognomen of "the Protesters,"—was made in the interest of Mr. Monroe, and long and bitter were their denunciations of the latter for accepting office under Mr. Madison. Jefferson and Madison, placable, just and sincere, were doubtless desirous that their neighbour and friend with whom they had long been associated in the public service, and whom they respected and esteemed, should enjoy the same high distinction which had been conferred on themselves, if that could be effected without doing violence to the feelings of the rest of the country. But, with the exception of a single act, they trusted the result to the well known and oft experienced partiality of the Republican Party for the distinguished men of the Ancient Dominion. The office of Secretary of State had become a stepping stone to the Presidency, so much so that Mr. Clay, at a subsequent period and in an unhappy moment, spoke of the selection of Presidential Candidates from that station as following " *safe precedents.*" Mr. Madison had, as has already been said, with that single heartedness and high sense of justice that formed a part of his character, offered the place to Governor Tompkins as a proof of the estimation in which he held his patriotic and useful services.

Gov. Tompkins' declension and the consequent selection of Mr. Monroe, in all probability, controuled the question of the succession to Mr. Madison.

I visited Washington during the session and enjoyed good opportunities to observe the movements that were on foot. The friends of Clay, Lowndes, Calhoun, Cheves and others of less note evidently looked to their respective favorites as not yet ready for the course, but expected them to become so by the end of Mr. Monroe's term, and were unwilling that the place should be pre-occupied by one of their contemporaries. Crawford, also, but not so clearly, fell within the scope of these considerations.

Mr. Crawford was by far the strongest of these aspirants, and might perhaps have been nominated, if his friends had taken open and unqualified ground in his favor. But they were seriously divided in regard to the policy of such a course. Many of them, influenced by an apprehension that decided opposition to Mr. Monroe might be unsuccessful and injurious to Crawford's future prospects, were disposed to leave the question to be decided by time and chance.

The nomination of Gov. Tompkins for the Vice Presidency was generally favored, and I never understood that he expected or desired that his friends should attempt to bring him forward for the Presidency, nor could any efforts in that direction have been successful.

Notwithstanding this inaction on the part of rivals, Mr. Monroe obtained only a very small majority in the Congressional Caucus; a result not soothing to his feelings. The Republican Party was greatly in the ascendant, and Monroe and Tompkins were elected by a large majority.

The Party which had raised Jefferson and Madison to the Presidency elected Mr. Monroe under the expectation that his Administration would be similar in its political aspects to those of his predecessors. The People of the United States had, during both of those Administrations, been divided into two and only two great political parties. It is not necessary and would only serve to render complex the views intended to be expressed to make any reference here to the particular character and tendency of their conflicting principles. For the present it needs only to be stated that in the ranks of one or the other of these parties were arrayed almost all the People who took an interest in the management of public affairs. These differences were first developed in Congress and in Society during the last term of Gen. Washington's administration, had a partial and comparatively silent influence in the election of his successor, but were openly proclaimed and maintained with much earnestness during that successor's entire administration. The result of this conflict of opinions was the expulsion of John Adams from the office of President and the election of Thomas Jefferson in his place. Not intolerant by nature Mr. Jefferson made an ineffectual effort to allay the warmth of these party differences and to prevent them from invading and poisoning the personal relations of individuals. But, true to his trust, he not only administered the government upon the principles for which a majority of the People had shown their preference, but he carried the spirit of that preference into his appointments to office to an extent sufficient to establish the predominance of those principles in every branch of the public service. This he did, not by way of punishing obnoxious opinions, or to gratify personal antipathies, but to give full effect to the will of the majority, submission to which he regarded as the vital principle of our Government. Mr. Madison, elected by the same Party, tho' proverbial for his amiable temper and for the absence of any thing like a proscriptive disposition, pursued the same course, and upon the same principle—the performance of a public trust in regard to the terms of which there was no room for doubt.

The Administrations of Jefferson and Madison, embracing a period of sixteen years, were, from first to last, opposed by the federal party with a degree of violence unsurpassed in modern times. From this statement one of two conclusions must result. Either the conduct of these two parties which had been kept on foot so long, been sustained with such determined zeal and under such patriotic professions and had created distinctions that became the badges of families—transmitted ° from father to son—was a series of shameless impostures, covering mere struggles for power and patronage; or there were differences of opinion and principle between them of the greatest character, to which their respective devotion and active service could not be relaxed with safety or abandoned without dishonor. We should, I think, be doing great injustice to our predecessors if we doubted for a moment the sincerity of those differences, or the honesty with which they were entertained at least by the masses on both sides. The majority of the People, the sovereign power in our Government, had again and again, and on every occasion

---

° MS. I, p. 165.

since those differences of opinion had been distinctly disclosed, decided them in favor of the Republican creed. That creed required only that unity among its friends should be preserved to make it the ark of their political safety. The Country had been prosperous and happy under its sway, and has been so through our whole history excepting only the period when it was convulsed and confounded by the criminal intrigues and commercial disturbances of the Bank of the United States. To maintain that unity became the obligation of him whom its supporters had elevated to the highest place among its guardians. Jefferson and Madison so interpreted their duty. On the other hand, Mr. Monroe, at the commencement of his second term, took the ground openly, and maintained it against all remonstrances, that no difference should be made by the Government in the distribution of its patronage and confidence on account of the political opinions and course of applicants. The question was distinctly brought before him for decision by the Republican representatives from the states of Pennsylvania and New York, in cases that had deeply excited the feelings of their constituents and in which those constituents had very formally and decidedly expressed their opinions.

If the movement grew out of a belief that an actual dissolution of the federal party was likely to take place or could be produced by the course that was adopted, it showed little acquaintance with the nature of Parties to suppose that a political association that had existed so long, that had so many traditions to appeal to its pride, and so many grievances, real and fancied, to cry out for redress, could be disbanded by means of personal favors from the Executive or by the connivance of any of its leaders. Such has not been the fate of long established political parties in any country. Their course may be qualified and their pretentions abated for a season by ill success, but the cohesive influences and innate qualities which originally united them remain with the mass and spring up in their former vigour with the return of propitious skies. Of this truth we need no more striking illustrations than are furnished by our own experience. Without going into the details of events familiar to all, I need only say that during the very " Era of good feelings," the federal party, under the names of federal republicans and whigs, elected their President over those old republicans William H. Crawford, Andrew Jackson and John C. Calhoun—have, since his time, twice elected old school federalists—have possessed the most effective portions of the power of the Federal Government during their respective terms, with the exception, (if it was one) of the politically episodical administration of Vice President Tyler—

and are at this time in power in the government of almost every free state. We shall find as a general rule that among the native inhabitants of each State, the politics of families who were federalists during the War of 1812, are the same now—holding, for the most part, under the name of Whigs, to the political opinions and governed by the feelings of their ancestors.

I have been led to take a more extended notice of this subject by my repugnance to a species of cant against Parties in which too many are apt to indulge when their own side is out of power and to forget when they come in. I have not, I think, been considered even by opponents as particularly rancorous in my party prejudices, and might not perhaps have anything to apprehend from a comparison, in this respect, with my cotemporaries. But knowing, as all men of sense know, that political parties are inseparable from free governments, and that in many and material respects they are highly useful to the country, I never could bring myself for party purposes to deprecate their existence. Doubtless excesses frequently attend them and produce many evils, but not so many as are prevented by the maintenance of their organization and vigilance. The disposition to abuse power, so deeply planted in the human heart, can by no other means be more effectually checked; and it has always therefore struck me as more honorable and manly and more in harmony with the character of our People and of our Institutions to deal with the subject of Political Parties in a sincerer and wiser spirit—to recognize their necessity, to give them the credit they deserve, and to devote ourselves to improve and to elevate the principles and objects of our own and to support it ingenuously and faithfully.

Two affairs grew out of the agitation of Mr. Monroe's fusion policy which from their relation to prominent individuals and the developments of character they produced, may be considered of sufficient interest to be described here.

In no state in the Union was party discipline in so palmy a condition at this period as in New York, and a vacancy about to occur in the office of Post Master at Albany, the Capitol of the State, presented to the Administration a fitting, if it was not also a desirable opportunity for the inauguration of the policy in regard to appointments by which it had determined to be governed.[1] Van Rensselaer was, notwithstanding, appointed. Among the papers published at the time of and in connection with this affair was a letter addressed

---

[1] It had evidently been the intention of Mr. Van Buren to give an account of the controversy over the appointment of Solomon Van Rensselaer to be postmaster at Albany in place of Solomon Southwick, removed for defalcation. The Federal side is well given in Mrs. Catharina Van Rensselaer Bonney's " Legacy of Historical Gleanings," I, 366.— W. C. F.

by Vice President Tompkins and myself to the Republicans at Albany, which contained the following:

That you will be disappointed and mortified we can readily believe, but we trust that you will not be disheartened. While there are no men in this country more inured to political sufferings than the Republicans of New York, there are none who have stronger reason to be satisfied of the irrepressible energy of the Democratic party, and that no abuse of its confidence can long remain beyond its reach and plenary correction.

It would have been impossible at any moment during the administrations of Jefferson and Madison, or at any period since that of John Quincy Adams, to have comprehended the degree of odium brought upon me by this language within the precincts of the White House and in most of the circles, political and social, of Washington. The noisy revels of bacchanalians in the Inner Sanctuary could not be more unwelcome sounds to devout worshippers than was this peal of the party tocsin in the ears of those who glorified the "Era of Good Feeling."

Whilst this excitement was at its highest point I took a trip to Richmond, Virginia, and visited Spencer Roane whom I had never seen but long known, by reputation, as a hearty and bold Republican of the old ° School. I found him to my great regret on a bed of sickness, from which, although he lived some time, he never rose. But in all other respects he was the man I expected to meet—a root and branch Democrat, clear headed, honest hearted, and always able and ready to defend the right regardless of personal consequences. He caused his large form to be raised in his bed, and disregarding the remonstrances of his family he insisted in talking with me for several hours. He at once referred to the Albany Post Office Question, told me that he had read all the papers in the case and thought that we were perfectly right in the grounds we had assumed. He condemned in unqualified terms the course pursued by Mr. Monroe, spoke freely of past events in his career, and of his apprehensions that he would, if elected, be governed by the views he had avowed.

Mr. Roane referred, with much earnestness, to the course of the Supreme Court, under the lead of Chief Justice Marshall, in undermining some of the most valuable clauses of the Constitution to support the pretensions of the Bank of the United States, and placed in my hands a series of papers upon the subject from the Richmond Enquirer, written by himself over the signature of Algernon Sidney.

On taking my leave of him I referred to the manner in which he had arranged the busts of Jefferson, Madison and Monroe in his room, and said that if there had been anything of the courtier in his character he would have placed Mr. Monroe, he being the actual President, at the head instead of the foot. He replied with empha-

---

° MS. I, p. 170.

sis, "No! No! No man ranks before Tom Jefferson in my house! They stand Sir, in the order of my confidence and of my affection!" The other matter to which I allude as an incident of the history of the fusion scheme, was a Pennsylvania affair. Mr. Monroe and his cabinet appeared to have determined to take the bull by the horns—a plan worthy of the strength and standing of the members who abetted his favorite policy. New York and Pennsylvania were not only the largest and most influential states in the Union, but also, perhaps, the most devoted to the maintenance of existing political organizations, and especially did this sentiment prevail in the Western Judicial District of Pennsylvania.

If the republicans of those States could be seduced or forced into an acquiesence in the fusion policy, there would have been the best reason to anticipate its success everywhere. A vacancy occurring in the office of Marshal for the Judicial District referred to presented a fair opportunity for a display of the Administration scheme in regard to appointments, parallel to that of the Albany Post Office. A man by the name of Irish—an out and out federalist—was one of the Candidates. His application was of course earnestly opposed by the republicans, and proofs of their opposition in the shape of protests from the members of the state Legislature and from State officers, from their Representatives in Congress and from private persons innumerable, were laid before the President, but without avail. Irish was nominated to the Senate and the nomination was confirmed. Although I happened not to have opened my lips on the question of the passage of this nomination in secret session, yet, as it was generally my lot to be held on such occasions justly or unjustly to some measure of responsibility, my quasi friend David B. Ogden circulated a report that I had made a most violent and jacobinical speech against it, and thus disturbed the sensibilities of my personal friends among the federalists, of whom I always numbered many. Mr. Ogden was a sound lawyer and possessed a vigorous intellect, but although an amiable man naturally, he was a violent politician and liable to " welcome fancies for facts " in matters having partizan relations.

CHAPTER XI.

Before I enter upon the engrossing subject at Washington, during Mr. Monroe's last term, to wit, the election of his successor, I will give a brief account of my senatorial *début.*

A Bill for the confirmation of the title of Mr. Cox of Philadelphia to an extensive territory in Louisiana called the Maison Rouge Tract was referred to our Committee. Having from unaffected timidity and ° respect for the body of which I was so new a member, withheld myself from debate until an advanced period of the session, I determined to make my first appearance on the floor upon this Bill. To this end I gave to its merits a thorough examination, and became satisfied that it ought not to pass. James Brown, an old and prominent Senator and lawyer from Louisiana, being an early and warm friend of Mr. Cox, and very decidedly in favor of his claim, Mrs. Brown brought to the Senate Chamber several distinguished ladies, among whom were Mrs. Cox and Mrs. Johnston, the wife of his colleague, (now Mrs. Gilpin, of Philadelphia) to hear her husband's speech.

It being my business as Chairman of the Committee to open the matter to the Senate, and to state the objections to the Bill, I rose for that purpose, and very soon met with a regular " break down"— as such catastrophes to young speakers are called. However strange it may appear in view of my previous public and professional career, it is nevertheless true that timidity in entering upon debate in every new situation in which I have been placed, and consequent embarrassment in its first stages, have been infirmities to which I have been subject in every period of my life. Finding that I could not proceed I made my retreat with as good a grace as possible and resumed my seat.

Mr. Brown was a respectable, tho' not, in my estimation, a very strong man. He had been long at the bar in Louisiana, where the lands in question were situated, was familiar with the Civil Law— which was in force there—with the laws and ordinances of the Colonies and the Statute laws of the State, all of which had a bearing upon the validity of this title, and was withal an easy speaker, plausible in his manner and much inclined to sarcasm. I can never forget either the triumphant air with which he threw himself into the debate, or the irritating condescension with which he explained the causes of my failure. This he did by enlarging upon the difference in the legal systems of Louisiana and New York, particularly in respect to the prevalence of the Civil law, and by obligingly expressing his confidence that if the question had arisen in my own section of the country I would doubtless have done it fuller justice— only regretting that I should have allowed myself to make up so confident an opinion against so valid a claim without a better understanding of its merits. He then proceeded in a long discussion of the points involved in the claim; but he had done more to prejudice the passage of the Bill in his opening remarks than his subsequent argument, able as it undoubtedly was, could remedy. He had totally extinguished the timidity by which my capacities had been for the moment paralyzed, and had excited in its place a glow of feeling and an anxiety for the reply which public speakers will appreciate. He soon perceived the mischief he had done, and which the vote confirmed in the rejection of the Bill by a large majority, altho' it had passed the Senate at a previous session with only six votes against it.

When I resumed my seat Father Macon,[1] as he was called in the Senate, came to my place and shaking me cordially by the hand, thanked me for the service that I had rendered to the public, and said he had always believed the matter to be a dishonest concern. The Bill to confirm the title having thus failed, another was introduced, or the old one modified to make it a Bill granting leave to implead the United States and to try the question at law. So bad had the character of the claim become in consequence of this discussion that it failed even in that form. It was with the Judiciary Committee an annual visitor, acted upon at almost every session and invariably rejected. The Committee were at one time nearly or quite unanimous against it; changes in its members, personal influence and solicitations of the worthy claimant and his numerous friends, and those various considerations which are often successfully brought to bear on the decision of Congress in regard to private claims, after a time brought me into a minority in the Committee, but not in the Senate. In the session of 1827–8, when I had reason to expect that my friends would take me from the body, I told my friend, Mr. Seymour, of Vermont,[2] a member of the Committee, who was in favor of the Bill and had charge of it, and who had made a report in its behalf, that I had a presentiment that I should die before the next session, and submitted to him the expediency of deferring the action of the Senate upon it until that period. Understanding my meaning he adopted my suggestion.

---

[1] Nathaniel Macon of North Carolina.   [2] Horatio Seymour.

Twenty-six years have since elapsed, and the claim has been through that period and I learn now still is the subject of legal investigation.

The late Mr. Cox, the claimant, a worthy citizen of Philadelphia with some peculiarities in his disposition, retained to a very late period his dislike towards me on account of my persevering and obstinate opposition. I remember on one occasion meeting him on board of a steamboat when he was not a little amazed at my civil salutation, and while I was President he called at the White House and, in a manner somewhat confused, told me that he called to discharge what he regarded as the duty of every citizen—to pay his respects to the Chief Magistrate of the country. I thanked him as President, and added in the kindest spirit that I had allowed myself to hope that other feelings might have formed a part of his inducements, but that it was not for me to quarrel with his motives, so long as they were of so justifiable a character. This interview entirely removed the asperity of his feelings, and when I visited Philadelphia after my retirement and a short time before his death, he evinced towards me the most cordial friendship.

The reappointment of Mr. King did not, in its consequences, I am inclined to think, realize the anticipations of either of us. It is not possible that any such proceeding could have been freer from preconcerted arrangement or intrigue of any description. I am quite sure that I never exchanged a previous word with Mr. King upon the subject of his appointment, or that I required or received any assurance or intimations from his friends or from anybody else in regard to his political action if appointed. He was therefore at perfect liberty to pursue any course his conscience dictated, so far as we were concerned. Yet I must admit that I expected in view of the general condition of the country in regard to party politics, and the changes that had taken place in his own relations with his party, in consequence of the patriotic course he had pursued in respect to the War after the destruction of the Capitol, to find in him a disposition to look with more complacency on the success of democratic measures and democratic men than proved to be the case.

But I did not allow this to excite in my breast any unkind feelings towards him. He was, altho' yet in the full possession of his faculties, between twenty five and thirty years my senior—had occupied with ° distinguished credit a succession of high public stations, and might be disposed, with good motives and friendly views, to turn to my advantage the stores of knowledge and experience he had acquired. So long as the means he employed were unexceptionable and his efforts to turn my mind to conformity with his own

---

° MS. I, p. 180.

were conducted with becoming delicacy, I could not be annoyed by them—and he shewed himself incapable of acting otherwise.

I arrived at Washington almost without a preference between the Candidates for the succession, save that I was strongly inclined to regard Mr. Adams as excluded by the political bias and opinions by which I thought he would be governed. Both Mr. Clay and Mr. Calhoun were personally more agreeable and prepossessing in their manners, and I regarded Mr. Crawford, from our first acquaintance, as an honest and true man—an opinion which I never found reason to change. His friends seemed more anxious to preserve the unity of the Republican party, and on that account I imbibed an early inclination to give him the preference. But feeling that I was not acting for myself alone, but for many confiding friends at home, I deferred coming to a conclusion upon the subject until I could have an opportunity to advise with them during the recess.

Mr. King and myself made our approaches to Washington, in the succeeding fall, very leisurely—remaining some days at Philadelphia and also at Baltimore. We were treated with much kindness at both places and spent our time very agreeably. The Presidential Question was introduced by him in the course of our journey, and discussed on his part in our daily walks, and on most occasions not otherwise pre-occupied, with much earnestness. He spoke handsomely of Mr. Crawford and without special disparagement of either of the candidates, and placed his preference solely on the ground of the influence which the subject of slavery had exerted and was likely to exert in future on the administration of the Federal Government. In the course of several conversations he spoke of the long periods during which the office of President had been held by citizens of the slave States and the power they had thus possessed to elevate the public men of their own section and to depress others, and he discussed their claims to this preponderance—comparing the talents, native and acquired, of the People of the different sections, the services, they had respectively rendered toward the establishment of our independence, and the extent of their respective interests most affected by the action of the Federal Government. He did not regard Mr. Adams as particularly well adapted to be the leader in such an issue, but he was placed in a condition to make him the best we had; he was by no means sanguine in regard to his success—a question he thought of inferior importance to the opening of the proposed issue, which he firmly believed when once fairly started must speedily succeed.

In the course of these protracted reasonings I acted the part of listener rather than that of a contestant. Respect for their source and the eloquence and earnestness with which they were made secured from me a close and interested attention, but they did not make the desired impression. My opinion was very decided that the Southern States had dealt with the subject of slavery, down to that period, in a wise and liberal spirit, and that they owed the disproportionate influence which they had possessed in the Federal Government to other causes than to the concentration of feeling and effort produced by that interest. I was therefore unwilling to give so controlling an influence in the Presidential election to the considerations advanced by Mr. King, and I communicated this conclusion to him with delicacy and unfeigned respect for his character, and we proceeded on our journey without change in our feelings, much less in our social relations.

As I acted at the time on the opinion I have mentioned, and as there has subsequently been, in my judgment, a wide departure from the policy which then commanded my approval, which has also in its turn governed my action, I will here give my views of the matter as it then stood, leaving the consideration of the change and its consequences to its proper period and place.

At the time when the oppression of the Mother-Country compelled our ancestors to resort to arms for the defence of their liberties, the condition of the old Thirteen States was not materially different, in respect to the institution of Slavery, from that which existed at the period of which we are speaking. In those where it still exists, it had been so deeply planted as to forbid the hope of seeing it eradicated except thro' Providential means not then discoverable by human intelligence; whilst in those which are now free from it, it had obtained but a slight hold upon the interests or upon the habits and feelings of the inhabitants—none that would not be sure to yield to wise and prudent legislation. But no obstacle was found to arise from the difference in their condition in respect to the existence of slavery, to their cordial and devoted union in the struggle which, by the blessing of God, resulted in the establishment of our national independence.

No sooner had that great end and aim of all their secrifices and sufferings been accomplished than the leading men—those who swayed the councils of the States in which slavery existed and still continues to exist, on all sides a race of great and good men—proceeded to the consideration of this difference in regard to slavery in the condition of the states, and the possible consequences which it might in time produce. They took up the subject with earnestness and sincerity and with a determination to deal with it justly and thoroughly. They foresaw that the day was not distant when slavery would have ceased to exist in a majority of the states; that its abolition would in all probability produce a more rapid increase in the population of the non-slaveholding States; that this would continue in a constantly augmenting ratio; that questions would arise as to the relative value of free and slave labor and as to the degree of encouragement to which each was entitled, and they apprehended that these might lead to invectives against the institution of slavery, which the changed condition of States would naturally increase, and that in this way the subject itself would come to be regarded as one of political power, creating sectional parties and in the end overthrowing the glorious fabric which had been raised by the joint labors of all, if these sad results were not prevented by timely and comprehensive measures.

They did not apprehend a disposition on the part of their Northern and Eastern brethren to disturb the domestic peace of the States in which slavery had long and fixedly existed, by interference with the subject within their borders. This would have been a desecration of the fraternal spirit of the Revolution so gross that their pure breasts could not harbor a suspicion of it. They never doubted that ample Constitutional protection for the possession and use of this portion of their property would be secured to them, and that was all that they required.

The spread of slavery and the increase of slave States was the source and the only source from which trouble was apprehended.

The advance of liberty—the sign under which they had fought and by which they conquered—and the growth and maintenance of free institutions were the objects of that Revolution from which they had just emerged. The existence and continuance of slavery in so many of the States was a sad qualification of these noble aims and glorious results—but it was impossible, positively and absolutely impossible to avoid it, and its existence was without fault on the part of those who had inherited it from ancestors many of whom were as little responsible for its creation.

Shall the exceptional feature in the free system about to be organized be enlarged? Shall the influence and action of the Federal Government be employed for the multiplication of slave States, or to discourage their increase?

These were the questions that presented themselves to all patriotic and thinking minds before and at the period of the adoption of the Constitution; and it is an historical truth, worthy of all honor, that the great preponderance of opinion on the part of all that was imposing in character and venerable in authority in what are still the Slave States was in favor of a course most in harmony with the principles of the Revolution—that of discountenancing the increase of Slave States. Such men as George Washington, Thomas Jefferson, Patrick° Henry, George Mason, James Madison

---

° MS. I, p. 185.

and other patriotic citizens did not hesitate to express their repugnance to slavery, their regrets at its existence, their desire to see it lessened and abolished, if possible, by proper means, and not only their unwillingness to contribute to its extension, but their readiness to co-operate in proper measures to limit its farther spread by the increase of free states.

They were wise and experienced men and knew that such a subject could not be trusted to professions or acts which would be open to different constructions, and could only be safely dealt with by such measures as must carry conviction to the most prejudiced minds because they went directly to the accomplishment of their object.

From such considerations and from such sources issued the Act of July 1787 for the government of the North Western Territory. By this Memorable Act its author and supporters intended not only to provide effectually for the peace and safety of their beloved country, but to repel, as far as was in their power, the suspicion of their fidelity to the cause of freedom which their enemies had attempted to fix upon them. Whether we regard the source from which it originated, the support it received on 'its passage, or its efficiency in promoting the great object of its enactment, this Law deserves a place in our National Archives side by side with the Declaration of Independence and the Federal Constitution. Attempts have been made to deprive Mr. Jefferson of the credit of this great measure, as there have been cavillers against every truth of history however firmly established. Nothing can be more certain than that it was to his master mind that the country is indebted for its conception, and to his perseverance in its support seconded by the Legislature of Virginia and the old Congress for its completion.

By its provisions the North Western Territory which was, in the hands of Virginia, slave territory, was set apart for the creation of six new states—the precise number of the slave states then, to all appearance, destined to remain such—and it was made an irrevocable condition of the cession that slavery should never be tolerated within their boundaries. The Executive and Legislative Departments of the State of Virginia, and the prominent men of the State, of all parties, lent their aid to promote the measure and it passed the old Congress by the unanimous vote of the Representatives from the slave-holding states. Its adaptation to exigencies of the occasion to the promotion of the policy of which I have spoken are too obvious to require a single remark. It embraced all the vacant territory of the United States which was at all likely to be converted into Slave States and promised to balance the influence of the irredeemable slave holding states in the Federal Councils—leaving the progress of Emancipation in the Middle and Northern States to work out a preponderance of free states qualified, to a limited extent, by the new states that might be made out of vacant territories still belonging to the States of North Carolina and Georgia by divisions of those states.

The Act was passed but a short time previous to the meeting of the Convention [1] which framed the Federal Constitution and its patriotic promoters were not disappointed in the character and extent of the influence which a measure so wise and liberal was destined to exert upon the other members of the Confederacy. They found them ready to secure the citizens of the Southern States in the full enjoyment of the rights they claimed as slave holders by adequate constitutional guarantees and the Southern members of the Convention reciprocated that disposition by their significant consent that the word slavery should not be used in the Constitution, and with the exception of the members from South Carolina and Georgia they insisted that the Slave trade should be forthwith abolished. The prolongation of the period for its suppression was, it is well known, the consideration given, in pursuance of an arrangement between the members last mentioned and some of our Eastern brethren, for the right in Congress to pass Navigation Acts.

The six new States provided for by the ordinance of 1787 have all been admitted into the Union as free States, according to its provisions, and have now a representation in the U. S. Senate exactly equal to that of the six Slave States of the old Confederacy and a representation in the House of Representatives of —— members to —— members, the present representation of the latter. As late as the year 1809, the territory of Indiana, under a momentary delusion in regard to her best interests, applied to Congress for temporary relief from the prohibition of the Ordinance against slavery. The petition was referred to a Committee of which John Randolph, distinguished for his devotion to Southern rights, interests and feelings, was Chairman, reported against promptly and firmly and the report acquiesced in with perfect unanimity by his Southern associates. Add to all this the Declaratory Act of Congress by which the Slave trade was declared Piracy, in the passage of which Southern men took the most prominent part, and we have a series of Acts all showing the absence of anything like a desire to advance their political power by the spread of Slavery or the increase of Slave States.

What subsequent steps have been taken bearing upon the relative powers of the slave and free states, before the agitation of the Missouri Question, and how far do they afford evidence of a different design !

---

[1] Van Buren confused the adoption of the Constitution by the Convention, September 17, 1787, with the date of convening which was May 14.

Tennessee had been cut off from North Carolina—made a State and admitted into the Union as had been the case with Vermont and Maine taken from the states of New York and Massachusetts. Georgia had ceded her vacant lands to the Federal Government for a stipulation to be relieved from the occupation of certain Indian tribes, out of which lands the states of Alabama and Mississippi had been carved. The Floridas and Louisiana had been purchased, and the state of Louisiana had been admitted into the Union. These were all proceedings, except the purchase, anticipated by the acts of the Government, and neither they nor the purchase last men- tioned afforded indications of a design to increase, or exclusively aggrandize the slave interest or power, nor were they at the periods when they occurred, to my knowledge, objected to on that ground. It may have been otherwise in respect to Louisiana, on the part of some of our Eastern people, but their objections were not very ear- nestly insisted on. These purchases were not in contemplation when the Ordinance of 1787 was passed. The settlement of the Valley of the Mississippi made the acquisition of the Mouths of that River a state necessity which could not be disregarded or much longer delayed without hazarding the peace of the Country or the sta- bility of the Union. The admission of Louisiana as a slave state necessarily resulted from the stipulations in favor of the inhabi- tants which the treaty unavoidably contained. I firmly believe that if Mr. Jefferson had thought it practicable to acquire the territory and to obtain its admission as a State without such stipulations, he would have made the attempt. His whole course upon the subject of slavery warrants this opinion. If the existence of slavery in the state was an insuperable objection with the Northern states they had only to withhold their assent from the treaty and the whole proceeding would have fallen to the ground: But the paramount necessity for the purchase banished that consideration from their minds, if it existed there to any considerable extent—which in the then state of public feeling upon the subject is not very probable.

The territory was too large for a single state, and a portion of it comparatively thinly settled, but by a congenial population, was set off as a separate Territory by the name of Missouri. Eight years afterwards the latter applied to be admitted as a state, having in the mean time acquired a sufficient number of inhabitants. Having grown up as a slave territory under the territorial laws, and her people being then, for the most part, slaveholders, Missouri claimed to be admitted as a Slave State and had framed her Constitution ac- cordingly. On that ground—that is because her constitution recog- nized and sanctioned the existence of slavery within her borders— her admission into the Union as a state was opposed by large portions of the Northern people. This opposition they had the right to make. Thinking that it would be for the interest of the new State that she should be free, and thinking also that from the smallness of her population, and the limited number of slaves within the territory—even now not large—the State would find not more difficulty in relieving itself from the existence of slavery than many of the Northern states had experienced, they had a right to press those considerations upon° the applicant by all fair and proper means. If the unbiased opinion of Missouri could now be obtained I should not be surprised to find it one of regret that she had not yielded to that opposition and made herself a non-slave holding state.

The opposition that was made to the admission of Missouri takes its character from the motives by which it was actuated and the manner in which it was conducted. That opposition was unexceptionable where it arose from an honest conviction that the previous abolition of slavery within her territory would be advantageous to her, and that the admission of more slave states into the Union would be adverse to its welfare, and where no improper means were employed to carry out these views; but where it was, on the contrary, the fruit of an outside policy—where the principal design was to produce political and partisan effect by seizing on the question as an opportunity to bring the politics of the slave states and the standing of their supporters in the free states into disrepute through inflammatory assaults upon the institution of slavery, which we are under constitutional obligations to respect in the states where it exists,—the opposition was culpably factious. Disguise the matter as we may such agitation must, in the light of reason and justice, be regarded as alike offensive to the spirit and derogatory to the memories of the Revolution. If our participation in the protection which the Federal Constitution extends to the institution of slavery had become intolerable to us, and we had satisfied ourselves that the interests of humanity would gain more by our release from that obligation than they would lose by a dissolution of the Union, there was one way in which we could obtain an honorable discharge and that was by tendering to our brethren of the slave holding states a peaceable and voluntary dissolution of that Union which our Ancestors had formed with them under a different state of feeling. To hold on to its advantages and at the same time to lessen if not destroy through the agency of such agitations, that security to their slave property which was one of the principal benefits promised to them by its adoption, was the reverse of such a course.

° MS. I, p. 190.

From all that I saw of it I could not divest my mind that such was the intention of the movement against the admission of Missouri on the part of its leaders. I thought so then—I think so still. I feel less embarrassed in speaking of it thus freely because I have always admitted my share of the responsibility so far as the New York Resolutions went—but no farther. Although I did not actually vote for them I allowed myself to be prevented by political and partisan considerations, which have been heretofore alluded to, from meeting them by open opposition.

While it affords me no satisfaction to say this I would the more regret the necessity of this sacrifice to the truth of history if I did not also know that at a later period and at a critical period, too, for the South the Northern States stepped forward and screened her from the assaults of the abolitionists in a manner and to an extent that called forth the strongest expressions of approbation and thankfulness from the Slave States, with acknowledgment that more could not have been done or desired. What return has been made for this conduct on our part will be seen in the sequel. All I wish is that the simple truth of these matters should be told.

In confirmation of the statement of my own feelings at the time of the Missouri agitation, I now for the first time publish two letters written at that period; one addressed to William A. Duer, recently President of Columbia College,—(The letter to Mr. Duer has been mislaid.) a zealous and active friend of Mr. King and of his appointment as Senator—and the other to Major M. M. Noah, at the time Editor of the National Advocate in the city of New York. The occasion of the latter epistle and certain circumstances in its history have been heretofore related.[1]

LETTER TO M. M. NOAH, ESQR.

"HUDSON *Dec. 17, 1819.*"

D^r SIR

Your letter has reached me here in the midst of a Circuit and I have but time to say a word to you on the interesting points you speak of. Advise Thompson by no means to have such a meeting—it would as you say set an example for Mr. Clinton for which he would give the world. The dire necessity to which he will be subjected of resorting to such nominations galls him to the quick. Such a measure would therefore be intolerable in us, and I am astonished that any discreet man should dream of it. *Make yourself perfectly easy on the subject of the nomination.* If such designs as you speak of exist they are perfectly harmless. There is the most unprecedented unanimity on the subject among Republicans. Tompkins will be the man unless he himself declines. Let the few individuals who entertain different views talk on, but don't notice them in your paper. They will soon be lost in the general mass. I should sorely regret to find any flagging the subject of Mr. King in New York. We

---

[1] Page 101 of the Autobiography.

are committed to his support. It is both wise and honest, and we must have no fluttering in our course. The Republicans of the State expect it and are ready for it. I know that such is the case. There was not in the Senate a dissenting voice that I could find. Mr. King's views towards us are honorable and correct. The Missouri Question conceals *so far as he is concerned* no plot, and we shall give it a true direction. You know what the feelings and views of our friends were when I left New York, and you know what we then concluded to do. My *Considerations*[1] &c and the aspect of the Argus will shew you that we have entered on the work in earnest. We cannot therefore look back. Our fair, consistent and manly course has raised our party in the estimation of all, and its contrast with that of our opponents has cast much contempt on theirs. Let us not therefore have any halting, but come out I beseech you manfully on the subject and I will put my head on its propriety." * * *

At the time of my conversation with Mr. King, the Missouri Question had been settled—most of the Candidates were slave-holders, and there was scarcely a ripple on the political waters produced by slavery agitation.

It was not surprising that Mr. King and myself should differ upon this point as we viewed it from opposite positions. Although not in the Country during the administration of the elder Adams and perhaps not approving of all its measures, he nevertheless sympathized with its conductors and had through life been the political friend and associate of its principal supporters. He had regarded its overthrow and the election of Mr. Jefferson as national misfortunes. He had been in opposition—respectful indeed but not the less decided—to the administrations of Jefferson and Madison during the sixteen years of their continuance, with the exception of the support he gave to the War after the sacking of Washington. With his political feelings moderated by time and circumstances, he was still, as I found upon a nearer approach, on all essential points, the same old fashioned federalist that he had been from the start. Under a bias so potent he was wholly unwilling to allow, indeed incapable of believing that the lodgment which Jefferson's political principles had acquired and was likely to maintain in the minds of the People, in preference to those of his own school, was well deserved on public grounds, and he was ready to attribute it to the unanimity of the slave states caused by the slave interest or by the " black strap " as he called it. His feelings against the institution as a philanthropist were thus stimulated by the prejudices of the politician, and he was by their combined influence induced to embark with so much earnestness in the Missouri agitation.

° My feelings were of a very different character. My earliest political recollections were those of the day when I exulted at the

---

[1] Considerations in favor of the appointment of Rufus King—a pamphlet of 32 pp. (Dec., 1819). A copy is in the Toner Collection, Library of Congress. See the long extracts published in Holland's Life of Van Buren (Hartford, 1836), p. 129.
° MS. I, p. 195.

election of Mr. Jefferson, as the triumph of a good cause over an Administration and Party, who were as I thought subverting the principles upon which the Revolution was founded and fastening upon the Country a system which tho' different in form was nevertheless animated by a policy in the acquisition and use of political power akin to that which our ancestors had overthrown. I had ever since regarded the continued success of Mr. Jefferson's policy as the result of the superiority of the principles he introduced into the administration of the Government over those of his predecessor, and was sincerely desirous that they should continue to prevail in the Federal Councils. I had not, as I have before stated, sympathized in the Missouri Agitation because I could not conceal from myself the fact, to which all we saw and heard bore testimony, that its moving springs were rather political than philanthropical, and because I thought nothing had arisen that would justify us in making the subject of slavery a matter of political controversy.

These conflicting views, coloring all our conversations, soon convinced us of the parts we were to take in the Presidential election. I announced by intention to support Mr. Crawford soon after my arrival at Washington, and Mr. King was, from the beginning, the known friend of Mr. Adams. But this difference did not then produce the slightest effect upon our social or friendly relations. We messed together during the session, and notwithstanding the disparity in our years, which was still greater between some others of our associates and himself, our social intercourse was not only unembarrassed, but so genial and entertaining as to have kept a pleasant and lasting place in my memory.

A circumstance occurred in the succeeding recess affecting me personally that served to draw forth his friendly regard. Chief Justice Thompson, having been transferred to the Navy Department,[1] disposed to testify his sense of the intimate relations that so long existed between us, inquired of me by letter whether I would accept the office of Judge on the bench of the Supreme Court of the United States, to supply the vacancy caused by the death of Brockholst Livingston. My impression, upon receiving the letter, was decidedly against the acceptance of the offer, but on mentioning the subject to Mr. King he took very earnest ground in favor of my accepting it, and begged me not to decline, as it was my intention to do immediately, until we could give the subject a fuller consideration. At subsequent interviews he prevailed upon me to consent to the appointment. Having felt myself called upon to oppose an Act of Mr. Monroe's administration in regard to an appointment in which a large portion of my constituents was interested, I informed the

---

[1] Smith Thompson transferred in April, 1823.

Secretary that if the President was disposed to confer the office upon me I would accept it, but I was desirous that it should be understood as having been done exclusively on public grounds, as I had no desire for the position and could not consent to be regarded as an applicant for it. Mr. King wrote of his own accord to Mr. Adams, who took a friendly part in the matter.

From some source[a] which I never perfectly understood obstacles were thrown in the way of the appointment and considerable delay intervened. An expression in one of the Secretary's letters induced me to repeat my request that in whatever he said or did in the matter, I relied upon his friendship to prevent me from appearing before the President as an applicant for the office. After a while I received a letter from him asking me whether, after what had happened between us, I thought he could with propriety take the office himself. Mr. King had taken much interest in the subject and was much displeased with the conduct of Secretary Thompson. He thought I ought to leave him to his own course; but feeling best satisfied with an avoidance of the appointment, I wrote to him at once absolving him from any obligation to myself and advising him to take the place, for which, by the way, he was as eminently qualified as he was unfit for political life.

Now, altho' I was very sensible that one inducement with Mr. King, on this occasion, was a willingness to withdraw me from the Presidential canvass, I was yet perfectly satisfied that he sincerely thought the appointment a desirable one, and that it could not be otherwise than beneficial to me to accept it. I was not therefore disposed to undervalue the zealous and friendly part that he took in the matter, because his success would favor other objects in which he felt an interest and which he was quite justifiable in seeking to advance by such means.

---

[a] On referring to my correspondence with Secretary Thompson, to which I could not have access when the above was written, I find that, previously to the offer of his influence in obtaining the Judgeship for me, he had solicited in his straight forward way my support of himself for the Presidency, and had become not a little impatient of my silence. This circumstance, which, from the slight impression that it made on me, had altogether escaped from my memory, may throw some light upon the course and disposition of the judicial appointment after it was ascertained that my inclinations in regard to the Presidential Question were not in that direction. I cannot say that I have at this moment any decided opinion as to the source from whence the obstacles arose which prevented my appointment. The correspondence which accompanies this Memoir will be found to possess interest from the light it throws upon the ways of men and of several distinguished individuals in particular. I have myself fancied on reading it now that I could discover traces of views and feelings on the part of others which from the unsuspicious character of my mind did not occur to me at the time.

CHAPTER XII.

° My notice of the Presidential election of 1824–5 will be confined mainly to the State of New York. An unforeseen occurrence gave the principal part of her electoral vote to Mr. Adams, and an accidental circumstance, bearing upon that vote, turned the question finally in his favor in the House of Representatives.

By the law of the State, passed at a very early period, the Electors of President and Vice President were directed to be appointed by the Legislature. The election of members of the latter body in 1823 was held with direct reference to the Presidential question and resulted in the choice of a very decided majority supposed to be and which was, at the time, favorable to the election of William H. Crawford. The friends of the other Candidates, recognizing their defeat, demanded a second trial. A transaction something like this occurred in 1800—the object being to defeat Mr. Jefferson. After a Legislature had been chosen known to be favorable to him an application was made to Gov. Jay (as appears from his Life, by his son,) by a prominent federalist, to call the old legislature, whose time had not expired, to choose the Presidential electors, which Mr. Jay very properly refused to entertain.

The movement now made was of a far more plausible character. It was demanded that the Electors should be chosen by the People, instead of being appointed by the Legislature, as had been the previous usage and as the existing law directed. The unreasonableness of this demand under the circumstances was apparent, but its rejection was nevertheless a matter of great delicacy. It was an awkward affair for a party which prided itself on being most in favor of employing the direct agency of the People in the conduct of public affairs, to refuse such an application when there was yet time enough to accede to it and to carry it into effect. It seemed, at least, in thus refusing, to place itself in a false position. Our opponents pressed this view of the subject with much earnestness and considerable influence. But I have never doubted that we would have been able to sustain ourselves before the country if it had not been for a very unexpected and badly advised step taken by our friends at the moment when the Legislature adjourned to the Extra-session for the choice of electors.

Gov. Clinton had listened to the advice of his friends and had avowed his determination not to be a candidate for re-election—his chance of success being regarded by them as hopeless. He did not lack troops of devoted personal adherents, but his failure to maintain his position in the favor of the People, under the auspicious circumstances which had attended his public service, even when strengthened by the complete success of the Erie Canal—a measure to which his name was so closely and meritoriously linked—induced them to think that he did not possess the faculty of making himself generally and permanently acceptable to the People under any state of affairs. They had therefore employed themselves in looking for an office or employment for him which would be adequate for his support, of sufficient dignity and independent of the popular vote. He had confessedly done more than any other man to secure the success of the great Public Work to which I have referred. The office of President of the Canal Board which had been conferred on him at an early day had no salary attached to it nor did he receive any compensation for his services. Having the best right to be regarded as the founder of the Work, that post as a mark of distinction only, without reference to his usefulness in the performance of its duties, was justly due to him.

Such being the state of things Mr. Clinton was removed by a vote of the Legislature, on the last day of the session,[1] without notice or specific complaint.

It has been truly said that this removal " operated like an electric shock upon the whole community." It secured to Mr. Clinton a full measure of what he had never before possessed—the sympathies of the People. The friends of Mr. Adams, generally, in the Legislature and their leaders Wheaton and Tallmadge[2] voted for the removal, but we had the majority—the motion came from our side— and ours was the responsibility.

A public meeting was forthwith held at the Capitol, at which the measure was severely denounced. Similar meetings followed in every part of the State, and an excitement in the public mind was produced which disinclined it to receive dispassionately the explanations of our conduct in refusing to pass the electoral law. Our excuses for declining to fight a battle over again that we had once fairly won, which, but for this disturbing question would have been favorably heard by the majority, would not be listened to by an irritated community.

---

[1] April 12, 1824.—W. C. F.   [2] Henry Wheaton and James Tallmadge.

Mr. Clinton's re-election to the office of Governor was the redress that instantaneously presented itself to the minds of the masses. The people's party "—a temporary faction generated by the refusal of our friends to pass the Electoral law and most of whose members in the Legislature had voted for his removal—could not prevent his nomination at a State Convention in the call of which they had united. The current of public feeling, overwhelmingly in his favor, carried him in by the largest majority ever given in the state. So violent was the excitement that when I, to whom the removal had occasioned much regret and who had no knowledge, being in Washington, of the intention to make it, made my appearance at the polls the shout of " Regency! Regency! " was raised by the crowd and my vote was challenged by some dozen persons. The efforts sincerely made by the Board of Inspectors and by some of Mr. Clinton's most attached friends to get the challenge withdrawn were ineffectual, and I was obliged to take the prescribed oath. The first returns from the Western Counties were astounding, but at a meeting of a few friends, held at my lodgings, we canvassed the State and still claimed success. On the following morning, however, my excellent friend Judge Roger Skinner came into my room and furnished me with returns shewing that we had been, as I have stated, completely routed.

A feeling of bitter personal hostility towards Gov. Clinton— foreign to his generous nature, but for which he thought he had adequate grounds—had made Judge Skinner more instrumental in accomplishing the removal of Mr. Clinton than any other of our friends. Knowing that if informed of the design I would have done what I could to prevent it, he took especial pains to keep it from me and laughed at the apprehensions I expressed on being informed of the act. He was standing at the window, tapping the glass with his fingers, whilst I was taking my breakfast with what ° appetite his news had left me. I could not resist saying to him— " I hope, Judge, you are now satisfied that there is such a thing in politics as *killing a man too dead!* " an observation sufficiently absurd to the general ear, but full of significance and matter for painful reflection to him. He left the room immediately without saying a word. Conscious that I had wounded him deeply I followed him to his lodgings, begged his forgiveness with perfect sincerity and succeeded in obtaining it. But nothing could soothe the pang inflicted on his heart by Mr. Clinton's success and by the conviction that he had contributed to it. His health, always delicate, gave way, and he died not long after in my arms. He was among the worthiest and most valued of my friends, and I long

---

° MS. II, p. 5.

and deeply mourned his loss. He was the second person whose death was obviously hastened by grief and mortification at Mr. Clinton's success. The other was Judge[1] Crosby, Senator from Westchester County, of whom I have already spoken in connection with Mr. Clinton's nomination three years before.

To those familiar with the action of public bodies under the influence of panic it cannot be necessary to enlarge upon the injurious effects produced by these election results, received at the time that the Legislature was in session for the sole purpose of appointing Presidential Electors. Gen. Peter B. Porter, a sagacious man, well versed in political management and, tho' never popular himself, very capable of influencing others, was at the head of Mr. Clay's friends. His ablest associate and co-worker was John Cramer, a veteran politician, who had been one of the Electors at Mr. Jefferson's second election, had almost ever since been in public life, lived on political intrigue, and having been familiar with legislative corruptions was consequently well acquainted with the worst portion of the members and the ways by which they might be operated upon. Following the example of their Principal their first step was to prevent a *Caucus*, in which, if its decision was adhered to, we would have been entirely safe. In this step they would not have succeeded but for the fact that the election had deprived us of the prestige which the long possession of power had given us. They coalesced with the friends of Mr. Adams, and this union enabled them to hold out reasonable expectations of a share in the favors of the new Government to members friendly to Mr. Crawford. The two sections made a regular bargain for the division of the Electoral ticket and succeeded, but so close was the vote that only thirty-two electors out of thirty-six were chosen on the first ballot. On the second ballot four of our ticket were elected, by which result Mr. Clay was excluded from the House of Representatives and Mr. Crawford's name was returned to it as one of the three highest.

We had formed our ticket upon a principle that brought on it several of Mr. Clay's supporters, equal in number to the share they were to have under their arrangement with the friends of Mr. Adams, and four of these were lost. Although I did not suspect it at the time, I had reason subsequently to believe that these were intentionally lost from a desire on the part of the Adams men to exclude Mr. Clay from the House.

Our Governor in office, Judge Yates, and our new candidate for that station at the election, Col. Young,—two very honest men but impracticable politicians,—did each their part in breaking down the

---

[1] Darius Crosby.

party by which the one had been and the other hoped to be elected. I have already alluded to the unfounded prejudices in regard to myself which had unhappily been created in the breast of the former. These were not removed in the Recess, and I left home for Washington in December, 1823, in the full belief that we were destined to encounter his opposition upon the Presidential question in the shape of the recommendation, in his second Message (January 1824) to alter the mode of appointing electors,[1] and I remained under that impression until I heard that document read under the following circumstances.

My colleague, Mr. King, resting confidently upon the almost universal impression that such must be its character, manifested more curiosity for its arrival than I either shewed or felt. It was brought to us at the close of our mess dinner at which were present our mutual friends Gen. Stephen Van Rensselaer, Messrs. Andrew Stevenson, Louis McLane & others. Mr. King·immediately proposed that it should be read aloud, and Mr. Stevenson was, I think, designated as the reader. Mr. King folded his handkerchief on the table before him and resting his arms upon it, as was his habit, his complacent countenance indicated the confidence and satisfaction with which he prepared himself to hear the welcome tidings. The ordinary topics of the Message were run over hurriedly until the reader came to the interesting subject of the choice of electors, when, to the amazement. of all, we were favored with a string of generalities studiedly ambiguous, but susceptible of only one interpretation which was that in his Excellency's opinion it would be better to leave the law as it

---

[1] The paragraph in the Governor's message read as follows :

" The choice of electors of president and vice-president, has excited much animadversion throughout the nation ; and it is to be regretted, that a uniform rule on this subject is not prescribed by the constitution of the United States. It is manifest, that the manner of electing may have an essential effect on the power and influence of a state, with regard to the presidential question, by either dividing the votes, or enabling the state with greater certainty to give an united vote ; and until a uniform rule is ingrafted in the constitution of the United States, the manner of electing will continue to fluctuate, and no alteration made by any one state will produce a material change in the various modes now existing throughout the union. In some states the people will vote by a general ticket ; in some by districts, and in others by the legislature ; and no practical remedy probably does exist, competent to remove the evil effectually, except by an amendment to the national constitution.

"Although this state has heretofore sanctioned an attempt to accomplish that important object, which proved unsuccessful, the measure on that account should not be abandoned ; and as the subject has recently been brought before congress, it is to be expected that another opportunity will shortly be presented for the legislature of this state to sanction an amendment, not only establishing a uniform rule in the choice of electors, but also securing the desirable object of directing such choice to be made by the people. A more propitious period of evincing its propriety and consequently affording a more favorable prospect of obtaining a constitutional number of the states to assent to it I am inclined to think has not presented itself since the organization of the government. Persuaded that you as the representatives of a free people, will only be influenced by reason and true patriotism, it is submitted to your wisdom and discretion, whether, under existing circumstances, the present manner of choosing electors ought, at this time, to be changed."—W. C. F.

stood. A lowering frown chased the smiles from Mr. King's face, and being observed by all produced an unpleasant pause, interrupted by himself when, turning to me, he said " I think, Mr. Van Buren, that Mr. Crawford's friends ought to send the Governor a drawing of the Vice President's Chair." I asked for his reason. " Because " said he, " I presume they have promised its possession to him." I replied with some feeling, but respectfully, that I could not of course say what had been promised him by the friends of the other candidates, but that I was quite sure that Mr. Crawford's friends had held out to him no allurements. " I hope so! " on his part, and " I *know* so! " on mine followed in rapid succession, when he picked up his handkerchief and walked out of the room. Mr. King was entitled to credit for his government of a naturally warm temper. We saw no more of him that evening nor did he come to the breakfast table in the morning, but at night following he pressed me to accompany him to a party given by the French Minister, which I did. On our way he said what was proper in regard to the unpleasant occurrence of the day before, and at the party he shamed my unprompt gallantry by dropping on his knee, in my presence, to retie her loosened shoe-string for a very interesting young lady—the grand daughter of Mr. Jefferson and my warm friend—a duty that his greater age should have devolved upon me.

How Gov. Yates' mind had reached a conclusion so unexpected by all of us I never ascertained. He lost a renomination and before I left Washington I had the mortification to see his proclamation calling an extra session of the Legislature in August to reconsider the subject of the Electoral law.[1] This served to increase the agitation in the public mind caused by Mr. Clinton's removal but gave us little farther trouble, our majority not having then been disturbed as it was afterwards by the tornado of Mr. Clinton's election. I wrote a communication for the *Argus* to shew the impropriety of the call, and our friends in the Legislature, on the motion of Mr.[2] Flagg, resolved that nothing had arisen in the Recess to justify the call under the Constitution and adjourned.

---

[1] In April, 1824, in caucus Yates received only 45 votes and Young 60. The unpopularity of Yates was said to have been due to his opposition to an electoral law. Hammond writes (II. 166) : " He pursuaded himself that the party in favor of that measure, which he knew was composed as well of the Clintonians as the people's men, were so much divided in opinion about the selection of a gubernatorial candidate, that if he were to place himself in an attitude which would enable them with any decent regard to consistency to support him as their candidate, in all probability they would do so ; or if in this view of the case he was mistaken—if he was to come out publicly in favor of the measure which had recently excited so much attention—it would create such confusion in the ranks of the supporters of Col. Young, as would, in all probability, defeat a rival for whom it cannot be supposed he entertained much affection. It must have been under some such impressions, that, contrary to the expectations, and to the surprise of all parties, on the 2nd day of June he issued a proclamation requiring an extra session of the legislature on the 2nd day of August."—W. C. F.

[2] Azariah C. Flagg.

Gov. Yates' future political prospects were by this act totally destroyed. Col. Young, who obtained the nomination for Governor on our side, not aware of Mr. Clay's want of strength with the rank and file of the party in the state, allowed himself, in an evil hour, to be persuaded to come out with a Card substantially avowing his preference for that gentleman's elevation to the Presidency. This disgusted the Republicans by thousands and I had great difficulty to prevent a meeting at the Capitol to renounce his nomination.

These antecedent weaknesses and disastrous results were relieved by a single amusing feature, and that was the very characteristic tho' somewhat irreverent reply of Gov. Yates to his relative, John Van Ness Yates, then Secretary of State, who, designing to console him in his adversity, said to him, " Well, after all, Governor, one thing is true of you that cannot be said of any of your Predecessors. You are the only Governor who came in unanimously!" "Yes, John, by G—," was the reply, " and, it may be added, *who went out unanimously!*"

CHAPTER XIII.

I left Albany for Washington as completely broken down a politician as my bitterest enemies could desire. On board of the small steamer that took us to the larger one that waited for her passengers below the *overslaugh* it was my luck to meet Mrs. Clinton (the Governor's wife) and her brother James Jones. The latter said to me whilst we were ° seated at the breakfast table, " Now is the time admirably fitted for a settlement of all difficulties between Mr. Clinton and yourself." I thanked him for his friendly suggestion—the sincerity of which I did not in the least doubt—but replied that my fortunes were at too low an ebb to be made the subject of a compromise, and that when they improved a little I would remember his generous offer.

I stopped at New York only long enough to pay the bets I had lost on the State election and then went on for the first time without Mr. King. I was dissatisfied with his course in the election, with which I had no right to meddle; but, as I was not in a mood to form a very correct estimate of my rights in that regard, I indulged my feelings. I found at New York the good old Patroon Van Rensselaer, who with the Dutch pertinacity and fidelity saw in my distressed political fortunes a reason for sticking to me and insisted on our journeying together. At Philadelphia we were overtaken by Mr. King who said, in his peculiar way, that he had been enquired of by his servant William " why it was that Mr. Van Buren had for the first time passed on without calling," and that the only answer he could make to William's natural question was that he knew of no reason and did not believe that a good one existed. I muttered some civil explanation that explained nothing and when we reached Washington Messrs. Van Rensselaer, McLane, Cuthbert [1] and myself took a furnished house and Mr. King joined a mess at the Hotel; our accustomed social relations were, however, in most other respects, maintained.

The Presidential canvass in the House of Representatives soon commenced and was carried on to its close with intense feeling and interest. I obtained a meeting of the friends of Crawford in the New York delegation and proposed to them in a few remarks that we should abstain to the end from taking a part in favor of either of the three gentlemen returned to the House—Jackson, Adams or

---

° MS. II, p. 10.
[1] Stephen Van Rensselaer of New York, Louis McLane of Maryland, and Alfred Cuthbert of Georgia.

Clay [Crawford]. I assured them that there was no danger that an election would not be made by others and that if the friends of Mr. Crawford stood aloof from the intrigues which such a contest would produce unavoidably they would form a nucleus around which the old Republicans of the Union might rally if the new Administration did not act upon their principles as we apprehended would be the case. They resolved with perfect unanimity to pursue that course, and I do not believe that a single individual of our number ever thought of departing from it: certainly not one did so depart. Judge Hammond was therefore misinformed in regard to their intention to vote in any event for Mr. Adams.[1]

On one occasion Francis Johnson, of Kentucky, a prominent supporter of Mr. Clay, called, by appointment, upon Mr. McLane and myself, and in a long conversation endeavoured to prevail upon us to unite with the friends of Mr. Clay in making Mr. Adams President. Finding us unyielding, and standing with his hand on the door he said that with our aid that result could be easily realized and that he was not absolutely certain but thought that they could accomplish it without our assistance. I stepped to the door and said " I think that very possible, but, Mr. Johnson, I beg you to remember what I now say to you—if you do so you sign Mr. Clay's political death warrant. He will never become President be your motives as pure as you claim them to be." He was a light hearted man and not apt to take anything gravely, but replied with a sensibility unusual to him that I might be right, but yet that he believed they would do it and trust to the purity of their intentions for their justification. The friends of Crawford lacked but one of being half of the New York delegation, so that the diversion of a single vote from Mr. Adams would produce a tie. Gen. Van Rensselaer was, through his first wife, a brother-in-law to Gen. Hamilton, and had, at an early age, imbibed his dislike to the Adamses. He at no time entertained the idea of voting for Mr. Adams and communicated his views to me at an early period and without reserve. On the morning of the Election he came to my room and told me he had some thought of voting for Gen. Jackson, and asked me whether it would make any difference in the general result, adding that as he had uniformly told me that he intended to vote for Crawford he did not think it proper to change his determination without letting me know it. I told him that as his vote could not benefit Mr. Crawford it was of no importance to us whether it was given to him or to Gen. Jackson, but submitted whether, as his intention was known to others as well as myself, there was an adequate motive for subjecting himself to the imputation of fickleness of purpose by a change which would pro-

---

duce no beneficial result to any one. He reflected a moment and then said I was right and that he would adhere to Crawford. When he arrived at the Capitol Messrs. Clay and Webster had an animated conversation with him in the Speaker's room. The first intimation I had of the hesitation they produced in his mind was a message from Mr. McLane, through Mr. Archer,[1] that Mr. Van Rensselaer had been staggered by the representations of those gentlemen, accompanied by a request that I would come to the House and talk to him. I refused to do so on the ground that I had no right to interfere with his action in that way; the communications that had passed between him and myself having all been voluntary on his part and the great disparity in our ages rendering any attempt to influence him at such a moment indelicate and inadmissible. Mr. Archer fully concurred in these views, but in a few minutes returned with a request of the same character, and from the same source, of increased urgency. I consented to go into the House, and if Mr. Van Rensselaer, of his own accord, addressed me upon the subject to do what I could to dissuade him from the course it was feared he would take.

As I entered the Chamber Mr. Cuthbert met me and said that it was not necessary that I should do anything in the matter, as Mr. Van Rensselaer had that moment assured him that he certainly would not vote for Mr. Adams on the first ballot. I remained to see the voting which took place presently afterwards, and was pained to witness Mr. Van Rensselaer's obvious agitation and distress. When the votes of the New York delegation were counted it was found that Mr. Adams had a majority of *one*. The vote of the state was of course given to him and he was elected. Mr. Van Rensselaer at once admitted that he had voted for Mr. Adams and thus changed the anticipated result. The excitement was of course very great, and I hurried to our lodgings to prevent a breach between him and Mr. McLane. I found the General and Cuthbert sitting at opposite ends of the sofa, both much excited tho' not a word had passed between them. As I entered the former said "Well, Mr. Van Buren, you saw that I could not hold out!" I replied that I had no doubt he had done what he conscientiously believed to be right, that was enough and I hoped the subject would now be dismissed from our minds. I then went to Mr. McLane's room and found him still more stirred up and it required the greatest effort on my part and a plenary exercise of Gen. Van Rensselaer's amiability to prevent a breaking up of our Mess.

Gen. James Hamilton, of South Carolina, had enquired of me in the morning what would be the result of the vote of our state and I assured him as I was fully authorized to do, that it would be a

---

[1] William S. Archer, of Virginia.

tie. It had been ascertained that one of the Maryland delegation would, on the second ballot, vote for Gen. Jackson, and would continue to do so. This would cause Mr. Adams' vote to fall short *two* of the number required by the Constitution, and it was confidently calculated that rather than submit to a failure to make an election, a sufficient number of his supporters would feel themselves constrained to go for Gen. Jackson, who had received a large plurality of the popular vote. This calculation was broken and every hope dissipated by Gen. Van Rensselaer's sudden and unforeseen change. The excitement caused by it was therefore not surprising.

I had asked no explanations of the General nor did I intend to do so, as I was satisfied he could not give any that it would be agreeable to him to make. But an evening or two after the election, whilst on our way to visit Mrs. Decatur,[1] he volunteered an explanation which he did not make confidential but of which I did not speak until a long time afterwards, and, to the best of my recollection, for the first time to Mr. Clay. He said that after what had passed between us he felt it to be due to me that he should explain the change in his vote which I had so little reason to expect. He then proceeded to inform me that when he arrived at the Capitol Mr. Clay invited him to the Speaker's room where he found Mr. Webster; that they took the ground that the question of election or no election would depend upon his vote: that they portrayed to him the consequences that would in all probability result from a disorganization of the Government, and referred in very impressive terms to the great stake he had in the preservation of order from his[o] large estate, and kindred considerations. He said that his mind was much disturbed by these views which he had not before regarded in so serious a light, but that he returned to the Chamber determined not to vote for Mr. Adams on the first ballot whatever he might be induced to do ultimately if their anticipations of a failure to make an election should prove to be well founded. He took his seat fully resolved to vote for Mr. Crawford, but, before the box reached him, he dropped his head upon the edge of his desk and made a brief appeal to his Maker for his guidance in the matter—a practice he frequently observed on great emergencies—and when he removed his hand from his eyes he saw on the floor directly below him a ticket bearing the name of John Quincy Adams. This occurrence, at a moment of great excitement and anxiety, he was led to regard as an answer to his appeal, and taking up the ticket he put it in the box. In this way it was that Mr. Adams was made President.

---

[1] Mrs. Stephen Decatur.   [o] MS. II, p. 15.

When I spent some days with Mr. Clay at Ashland, upon his invitation in 1842, he rallied me considerably upon the General's vote, and spoke of the labor it had cost him to correct the heresies I had sown in his mind. Altho' there was, as I have said, no injunction of secrecy upon the General's communication and it was not impossible that he omitted it to enable me to satisfy my friends in regard to his conduct, I yet felt a delicacy in speaking of it on account of its peculiar character, and therefore submitted in silence to Mr. Clay's pleasantry. Upon his visit to me in 1849, he happened one evening to recur to the subject, when I told him that I had on a former occasion omitted to place that matter before him in its true light from a feeling of doubt in regard to the effect that a true relation of the subject might have upon the reputation of a man whom we both esteemed so highly, but that upon farther reflection I had come to the conclusion that as it would be only strengthened in the point upon which his merit was most conspicuous and real, that of sincere piety and honesty, I felt that there could be no objection to my giving him the General's explanation of his vote in his own words, to which he listened with great interest.

I joined the immense throng at Mr. Adams' house on the day of the Inauguration and after paying my respects to him passed on to the White House to take leave of the retiring President. I found Mr. Monroe literally alone, and was as usual kindly received. I remained an hour without being joined by a single individual, when I parted from him for the last time. Owing to an early and somewhat excited difference in opinion upon what I could not but regard as an unfortunate point in his administration, our relations had never been confidential. I nevertheless always respected and esteemed him. Although not possessed of remarkable talents, he passed through an almost unequalled number of responsible public employments without leaving a stain upon his character.

Near the close of this session I was pained to witness once more the extent to which advancing years had impaired the power of self-control for which my worthy colleague had been much distinguished. This exhibition was the more distressing on account of the place where it occurred. The Society of Shakers, residents of my native county, sent to me their petition to Congress praying to be allowed exemption from military services and from other duties which conflicted with their religious faith. I presented the Petition with a brief reference to the characters of the petitioners and moved that it should be referred to the Committee on the Militia. Mr. King immediately rose, made for him, a very violent attack on the applicants, as a band of fanatics, and ended by a motion to lay the Petition on the table, adding that it would be but justly treated were it thrown *under* the table.

There was something so extraordinary, so unexpected and to all present so amazing in his concluding remarks, as they related to myself, that they failed to disturb my own temper. I was thus enabled to describe very calmly, in reply, the true character and condition of the petitioners,—concurring in the condemnation by my colleague of their religious views, but giving them credit for their charities, their sobriety and their industry,—claiming for them the common right to petition Congress for a redress of grievances even tho' they were not real,—stating what I considered due to myself in the matter, and concluding with a declaration of my intention, for reasons which the Senate would not fail to appreciate, to postpone all comments upon the treatment which the petitioners had received from my colleague until it should appear that he persisted in his opposition to my motion in the spirit which had been exhibited. The Senate was evidently relieved by the direction thus given to the subject, and after a moment's pause, without farther remarks from any quarter, met the motion to commit by an emphatic aye without a single negative vote.

The occurrence produced a suspension of personal intercourse between us, but Mr. King's good sense and correct feeling soon put an end to it. Within a day of two thereafter he approached me at the adjournment of the Senate and proposed to take a seat in my carriage. On our way from the Capitol he expressed his great regret on account of the occurrence which I have described,—his strong feelings against the Shakers having caused him to overlook what was due to myself. He apprised me of his intention to leave Washington in a day or two, never again to resume his seat in the Senate, and said that he would embrace that opportunity to make his acknowledgments for the respect and kindness with which I had treated him. He regarded it as a remarkable circumstance that we should have passed as opponents thro' so exciting a Presidential canvass as that which had just closed without more incidents to disturb our feelings and to threaten our friendship than the few which had unhappily arisen, and that he owed it to me to say, before we parted, how sensible he was that we were in a very great degree indebted for that exemption to my amiable disposition and self command; and he concluded by pressing me earnestly to pay him a visit on my return home after the adjournment.

I need not speak of the extent to which my feelings were allayed by this seasonable and kind explanation. I visited him on my return and was received with his usual cordiality. He said that some of his friends had told him that I would not keep my promise to come to him, but that he understood me better than they did, to which I might have added that there were not a few of mine who censured me for doing so. Some time afterwards I received a letter from Mr. King informing me of his acceptance of the Mission to England, tendered to him by Mr. Adams. I assured him in reply of my gratification that he had found himself in a situation to accept a place so honorable and for the duties of which he was so well qualified, and wished him very sincerely a successful mission and safe return. His health, however, soon failed and in about a year he came home an invalid. I called at his home in the city, and he directed that I should be admitted, but his old servant William informed me that he was very ill and suggested the propriety of deferring my visit for a day or two, in which I acquiesced. He grew rapidly worse and shortly after died, and I was thus prevented from seeing him again.

Mr. King's career as a public man, tho' it failed to fulfill the expectations which were justified by its early promise, was highly distinguished. He was appointed a Senator in Congress by the state of Massachusetts as early as 178–, and also a delegate to represent that State in the Convention which framed the present Constitution of the United States, was made Minister to England by Gen. Washington in 1796, and represented the country at that court until the accession of Mr. Jefferson to the Presidency, when he requested his recall, was twice elected to the U. S. Senate by the state of New York, to which he had removed, and was actually one of its representatives in that body when he was nominated by Mr. Adams and appointed to the English Mission. In politics he was from first to last a federalist of the Hamilton school. The only material difference between him and his old associates arose from a diversity of sentiment not upon any general principle but in regard to the extent to which upon a particular occasion and a special question ° their country required an intermission of party. He understood too well the working of the public mind not to know that, after the sacking of the Capitol by the enemy, the War, whatever might have been its previous character, must become national, and that those who failed to support it would fall under the ban of popular opinion. Viewing the matter in this light and moved also by a genuine partriotic impulse he dissented from the course pursued by his party in that crisis, arrayed himself on the side of his country and zealously sustained the Government. This gave him a position in the public estimation which was denied to the mass of his former associates and contributed largely to his re-election to the Senate. A man of sound sense and good taste, having through the greater part of his life associated with eminent men, as well in Europe as in his own Country, he had acquired a thorough knowledge of what belonged to the proprieties of every

---

° MS. II, p. 20.

situation in which he was placed, and possessing withal a natural dignity of manner was well fitted to adorn high public stations. Mr. Jefferson, comparing him intellectually with others, spoke of Mr. King as a "plausible man." Although I did not consider his mind remarkable either for vigor or comprehensiveness, it yet struck me that this remark did not do justice to it. Plausible he certainly was, but he was also always impressive, at times eloquent and forcible. He generally selected one or two of the principal points presented by any subject under discussion, and applying to their elucidation all the power of his mind, seldom failed to do them ample justice. He never attempted what Hamilton scarcely ever omitted to do—to follow the subject into all its legitimate bearings and bringing into view the collateral issues which sprung out of it and were logically entitled to influence its solution, to bend the whole matter to a great point most favorable to his argument,—a practice that caused Callender to say of him that "he beat his guinea into an acre of gold leaf." If Mr. King had attempted this I think he would have failed.

CHAPTER XIV.

Although far advanced in Federal politics I must not lose sight of those of my own state. I will therefore, before I touch upon the course of the Adams Administration, notice the most interesting portions of her political history anterior to the very sudden and lamented death of Gov. Clinton. His prospects were never more promising than in the early part of the year 1825. His triumphant election as Governor of the largest state in the Union by the greatest majority she had ever given to any candidate, produced by a wide spread conviction in the public mind that he had suffered great injustice, required only ordinary tact and discretion on his part to ensure a continuing prosperity. The Erie Canal—the success of which was his richest source of strength in the state—was completed this season, and in the month of November a few days previous to the state election, the mingling of the waters of the Atlantic and of the Lakes was celebrated through the country lying between them. The re-election of Mr. Adams was considered, from his well understood want of popularity, highly improbable; Mr. Clay, by accepting the office of Secretary of State, had for the time put himself out of the line of competitors for the Presidency; Mr. Crawford had been withdrawn from public life by indisposition; the sanguine efforts in behalf of Mr. Calhoun had proved signally abortive, and the leading politicians inclined to the opinion that Gen. Jackson's strength could not stand the test of a four years exposure to the public scrutiny. Under such favoring circumstances it was not surprising that Mr. Clinton and his friends should have regarded his chances for the Presidency as better than those of any other aspirant, yet strange as it may seem, it is nevertheless true that the popular impulse in his favor recently so strong was at the time of his great Canal celebration already subsiding, and the elaborate demonstrations of joy at the completion of that work coldly received by the mass of the People. Having, as they considered, justly rebuked the violence of his opponents, they seemed disposed to leave his future fortunes to his own management and to the course of events.

I did not accompany the *Cortége* from Buffalo to New York, but joined in the procession at Albany and attended the public dinner given on the occasion. My companion, in the former ceremonial, was J. W. Taylor, who was a few weeks afterwards chosen Speaker of the House of Representatives. Satisfied by my own observation and by the accounts I had received from different parts of the state that the injurious effects upon the harmony and efficiency of our own party by the combined agitation of Mr. Clinton's removal and the Electoral question had substantially spent themselves, I replied to Taylor's observations in regard to the imposing character of Mr. Clinton's position by pronouncing a very confident opinion that we should defeat him in the elections for the legislature to be held within a few days. He expressed his surprise at my delusion and repeated the conversation to Gen. Van Rensselaer. The latter informed me that he had told the Governor what I had said to Taylor, who had assured him that there was but one senatorial district in the state in which we stood the slightest chance, and that the majority against us in the House of Assembly would be overwhelming. Gen. Van Rensselaer was evidently distressed by my confidence in a different result for tho' perhaps liking me personally quite as well as he liked the Governor, he was on political grounds desirous that the latter should be sustained.

We elected three of the eight Senators, and a decided majority in the House of Assembly. Although in this election the Democratic party acted in undisguised opposition to Gov. Clinton it is an undoubted fact that their prejudices against him had then already considerably abated. Their distaste for Mr. Adams—a strong and I believe well founded belief that the Governor sympathized in that feeling—and the fact that many of the leading friends of Mr. Adams in the state and a large proportion of the members elected to the Legislature on the same ticket with Mr. Clinton at the election of 1824, were as hostile to him as they were to us, contributed to that change. Informal conferences took place at Albany, during the session of the Legislature of 1825–6, between prominent democrats and some of the friends of the Governor with a view to bring this feeling to practical results. The Governor nominated his connexion by marriage, Samuel Jones, always before a zealous Federalist, to the office of Chancellor, and the Senate, in which our friends were largely in the majority confirmed the nomination promptly and unanimously. It was expected that he would give an indication that he reciprocated the feelings of returning good will which had been, in various ways, manifested, and the nomination of Mr. Redfield[1] for the office of Circuit Judge was looked to as the proof of such disposition. He was believed to be personally favorable to this measure, but there was a lion in his path. Although he had obtained his election by temporary secessions from the democratic ranks the great body of his supporters was composed of the remains of the old federal party and they never could be taught the wisdom or expediency

---

[1] Heman J. Redfield.

of foregoing the full enjoyment of present power with a view to future advantages. He disappointed the wishes of our side, but selected a democratic adherent the least obnoxious to us.

The sayings and doings of this winter, altho' they ameliorated the prejudices against Mr. Clinton in the Democratic ranks, and excited friendly feelings in the breasts of many which did not altogether subside during the brief remainder of his life, yet carried conviction to the democratic mind, on the whole, that he had become so connected with the federalists by the support he had received from them, by social intercourse and latterly by family ties—all cemented by a common antipathy against the ascendency of Southern principles in our National Councils, as to render his support by us impossible without our° consent to an amalgamation of parties in the state—which was deemed neither possible nor desirable. I had a long and friendly conversation, neither private nor confidential, with Gov. Clinton, on my way to Washington, at the house of a mutual friend, to which we were both invited, and returned in the Spring with a sincere desire that he should be re-elected without opposition. My views were confined to that single object. I had long been thoroughly convinced that his entanglements with the federalists would always present an insuperable obstacle to anything like the re-establishment of old political relations between him and the democratic party. As an individual I was influenced by feelings of personal kindness and not a little by a consciousness of the unintentional injustice I had done him in the matter of the appointment of Attorney General; as a member of the democratic party I felt that his re-election without a contest would be a compliment that would go far to efface the severity of their treatment of him in his removal from the Canal Board, and I saw no adequate motive and some embarrassment in a contest for Governor in the then state of National politics. I have heretofore mentioned Dr. Cooper,[1] then President of Columbia College in South Carolina. He was son-in-law of the celebrated Dr. Priestly,[2] and himself in many respects a remarkable man. Mr. Jefferson expressed his regrets to me that they could not avail themselves of his services as President of the University of Virginia, on account of objections that were raised by many of the Trustees to his religious views, as he thought him by far the fittest man he knew of for the place. The active, probably violent part he took in politics during the administration of John Adams subjected him to indictment and trial under the sedition act, and he was on conviction sentenced to suffer imprisonment and to pay a fine of, I believe,

---

° MS. II, p. 25.   [1] Thomas Cooper.   [2] Joseph Priestly.

four hundred dollars. The imprisonment he endured, and I introduced and supported a Bill to refund to him the amount of the fine—which has, I believe, been since refunded. This induced him to write me several friendly letters, continued to a period when, as he expressed it, he had not, in Quaker phrase, " freedom " to vote for me for President however much he esteemed me personally. One of these letters was written during the administration of John Quincy Adams, on the subject of the candidate to be brought forward against him. He expressed great respect and much good will towards Mr. Clinton and could see but one objection to him, and that was an apprehension, expressed in his usual strong style, that Mr. C. would be too much under the influence of the clergy—an apprehension founded upon an address then recently delivered by him before the Bible Society. Coming up the river in the same boat with Mr. Clinton shortly after its receipt, I informed him that I had a letter from the Doctor in which he was particularly mentioned in connection with the Presidency, but that as he might not be pleased with its contents I would not offer to shew it to him—but would do so if he desired it. He was well acquainted with the Doctor's character and I handed him the letter at his request. He coloured as he read it, but smiled and said that there was no ground for the apprehension.

Doctor Cooper came north the same summer and brought me a letter of introduction from Thomas Addis Emmett. I invited Mr. Clinton to meet him at dinner, and the latter was much pleased with the originality and invariable force of the Doctor's observations.

Mr. Clinton was, in a little more than a year afterwards, forever removed from the political stage by the hand of death, and the Democrats of South Carolina took early ground in favor of Gen. Jackson. To this Dr. Cooper was earnestly opposed insisting that it would be far better in them to go for the re-election of Mr. Adams and giving reasons for his opinion which were characteristic of the man. These were that if they intended to carry their opposition to a protective tariff to the extent contemplated by them, as to which as a nullifier he trusted that there would be no flinching, Gen. Jackson was the last man they should think of for the Presidency because he would be very apt to *hang* them, whilst they might hope to intimidate Mr. Adams.

Having reason to apprehend that the impression that there might be no opposition to the re-election of Gov. Clinton was causing considerable uneasiness among our political friends I made diligent enquiries in regard to their dispositions and to that end visited several parts of the state. The result was an entire conviction that any attempt to prevent a counter-nomination would produce serious discord in our own ranks and ought not therefore to be made. A considerable number of our delegates on their way to the Herkimer convention met together at my house. Among them were Silas Wright and Perley Keyes, two of the most influential leaders of the party. Finding after the lapse of some time, that no one introduced the subject of their Convention about to be held, and understanding the cause of their reserve, I introduced it myself by observing that it was an extraordinary circumstance that we should have been so long together without a word being said in regard to the business they had been appointed to perform. The ice being thus broken Mr. Keyes expressed a desire to hear my views upon the subject. These were given without reserve. Commencing with an admission that I would myself have preferred acquiescence in the re-election of Gov. Clinton and the reasons for that preference, I proceeded to inform them of the enquiries I had made and the result of them, which was that I was satisfied that a nomination could not be omitted without seriously distracting our party and that I could not urge that course in view of such a consequence. They were relieved and gratified by this explanation, assuring me that there was great unanimity among our friends in favor of a nomination, that they had heard with regret that I was averse to it, and one of the delegation told me that the meeting at which he was appointed had gone so far as to advise him and his colleagues to nominate one of themselves, if they could get no other candidate.

On being asked whom they had thought of as a candidate they without a dissenting voice named Gen. William Paulding of Westchester. I expressed the greatest respect for Gen. Paulding saying that I would with pleasure make him Governor if it was in my power to do so, but that there were, in my judgment, strong objections to his nomination. The place of his residence and his well known participation in the feelings of his neighbors, adverse to the construction of the Erie Canal, would alone make his selection inexpedient. But there was another and strange as it might seem to them a still more formidable objection. I alluded to the report already extensively circulated that the General was the subject of a singular monomania in regard to his physical condition—one well adapted to be made the subject of ridicule. Knowing Mr. Clinton's proclivity to that species of assault, and having on several occasions witnessed his ability to make it effectual, I feared that he would turn this report into a weapon for that purpose and whether true or false that it would be in his hands very damaging against one who was from other causes a weak candidate. These remarks naturally led to a call upon me to name a candidate more likely to be successfull. I replied that since I had changed my views in regard to a nomination I had reflected much upon that question as one likely to involve our future success as a party and that I had come to a conclusion to which I was quite sure they would not upon first impressions agree, but I desired that they would hear me patiently and then do as they thought best. I confessed that in making my selection I had looked beyond the election of a Governor, and had been materially influenced by a deep sense of the disastrous consequences that would follow anything like a signal defeat in the present condition of National politics and so near a Presidential election in which I hoped to see the democracy of New York act an important part. °I said that I had never known an occasion on which I was so willing as at present to make sacrifices to *availability*, or one on which that point was entitled to so much consideration;—that it should be remembered that we had been overwhelmed at the previous election of Governor by a union between the friends of Clinton, Adams and Clay, for although our candidate Col. Young, had on the eve of the election declared for Mr. Clay and had received the votes of a few of his supporters, most of them had acted upon the principle which on such occasions usually controls the action of minor factions, that of striking at the strongest, and had voted for Clinton to put down Crawford;—that a similar union between the friends of Adams, Clay, Jackson and Calhoun had broken us down in the Presidential election;—that Mr. Adams had offered Mr. Clinton the first seat in his Cabinet, which upon his declension was given to Mr. Clay, and that there was, at the moment when I spoke, apparently, a more cordial union between the friends of Clinton, Adams and Clay than existed in 1824, and, if we so acted as to compel them to go together, that something like the same result might be produced. It was well understood that we intended to support Gen. Jackson, and I urged that if we nominated a candidate who was avowedly in his favor we would present to those three political interests the same inducements they had in 1824 to coalesce, but that having good reasons to believe that the apparent union between the friends of Clinton on the one hand, and those of Adams and Clay, now identified, on the other, was a hollow one, if we nominated a candidate whom the latter would regard as their friend, and would therefore favour or be only suspected of favoring by his election, we would drive a wedge into that union that would sever it forever. I then named William B. Rochester as the man whose nomination would produce that result. His father had been a partner in business with the father [-in-law] of Mr. Clay, and he was at that moment on his return from a Mission which had been conferred on him through Mr. Clay's influence. He was also, as I remarked, eligibly situated-

---

in regard to the Canal, had so conducted himself as to avoid creating strong prejudices on the part of our friends, and altho' we might have some trouble with him if elected we should probably succeed in electing reliable men to all the other Departments of the Government and in that event would be able to prevent him from doing much injury to our cause. I believed him honest and had obtained a small appointment for him from the General Government, and was personally very partial to him although I did not suppose that I could influence him against the wishes of Mr. Clay.

My exposition made a favorable impression upon the majority of my auditors, but Wright and Keyes remained immovable.[1] They would consent to take Rochester for Lieutenant Governor, but his nomination for Governor, all other considerations apart, would be such a surprise upon the public that it would for that reason fail. They held to the old rule of a regular progression, and could not believe in the policy of starting a new man for so important a place. The objection had no weight with me but they persisted in it. I called those gentlemen back after the others left, and begged them to think the matter over again on their way to Herkimer and to sacrifice their prejudices against Mr. Clay, which I knew lay at the bottom of their opposition, to the demands of the crisis.

William L. Marcy, then Adjutant General of the State, having official business with Gov. Clinton on the following day was asked what his friends would do at Herkimer, and on his replying that they would probably make a nomination, the Governor exclaimed, in a lively tone, "Gen. Paulding, I suppose!" On being informed that it might be Rochester, Marcy told me that he sobered down and became thoughtful to a degree that embarrassed the latter and induced him to propose to postpone their business, to which the Governor readily assented. Although not apt to place a very high estimate upon the influence of his opponents, Gov. Clinton saw at a glance the direction in which such a nomination would point and the danger that would flow from it. Keyes and Wright acknowledged to me afterwards that they saw the matter in the same light before they got to Herkimer and used their influence upon their arrival to secure the nomination of Rochester which was made. The matter worked as we anticipated. The nomination was reputed to have been made through the influence of the National Administration, and that report received no contradiction from Washington. The frail cord that united the latter with the Clintonians was snapped, and could never have been reunited if Mr. Clinton had lived. For many days after the election, Rochester was supposed to have succeeded, and Gov. Clinton was finally found to

---

[1] Silas Wright, jr., and Perley Keyes,

have been saved by the votes of our friends on the Southern borders of the state, given to him and to our Candidate for Lieut. Governor because they were the open friends of a State Road from the River to the Lakes along that border, the construction of which Mr. Clinton had recommended to the Legislature whilst there was reason to believe that Rochester would entertain different views of that project.

We gave to Rochester a faithful support but had not much reason as a party to grieve at the result. We carried the Legislature, and every thing except the Governor, and cleared the way for our success in the Presidential election. I had been doubtless in some degree induced to recommend the course that was pursued by the circumstance that my re-appointment to the Senate of the United States would depend upon the Legislature then chosen. But I am very sure that the influence arising from that source was subordinate to my desire for the promotion of the cause I had heartily embraced and actively supported. The readiness with which I had before sacrificed high official station for its success must go far with candid minds to sustain this assertion.

I received daily accounts of the feelings of Governor Clinton during the time when the election was supposed to have gone against him from one of his most devoted/friends and I can say with perfect truth that I listened to his account with no other feeling than regret that circumstances beyond my control had compelled me to contribute to the result he so painfully deprecated. Of this his friend was well convinced or he would not have made his communication to me. In explanation of the supposed loss of this election and of other adverse results in his political career the Governor said to this friend, who was an old democrat, that he had by the force of circumstances been connected with a party which was under the ban of public opinion and whose unpopularity would render their support disastrous to any public man. The suspense as to the result continued, as I have already mentioned, for several days as we were not then favored with the facilities to convey information we now possess. On the last night of its duration, the Governor's friend to whom I have referred, called upon me in high glee with a report that Steuben County, from which we confidently expected more than one thousand majority, had, in consequence of the State Road question, given more than that majority to Mr. Clinton, and wished to know before he communicated it to the Governor what I thought of its truth, and effect if true. I told him that I considered it an improbable rumour, but that we had all along been apprehensive about that part of the State—that it might be true and if so that

Mr. Clinton was undoubtedly reelected. He literally ran ° from me for fear that some other person might anticipate him at the Governor's house with the good news. The next morning being Sunday a few moments before I started for church I heard the sound of the steam being blown off, signaling the arrival of the Southern boat, and immediately after I saw a busy friend of Mr. Clinton pass my window in hot haste in the direction of the Governor's residence. I directed Gen. Marcy's attention to him, saying that the steamboat had, I did not doubt, brought the news from the Southern tier of counties which reelected the Governor, but this he did not credit. As we walked to the church I told him the mystery would be solved by the late arrival at church of the Governor and Mrs. Clinton. After considerable progress had been made in the services they arrived and Mrs. Clinton had no sooner settled herself in her seat than she turned towards us and favored us with a look which induced Marcy to whisper to me that the election was indeed lost.

This election ardently as it was contested and intense as was the excitement caused by its closeness, did not in the least aggravate the political hostility that had long existed between Mr. Clinton and the democratic party. He did not the less respect them for having supported with good faith and zeal a nominee who was not at heart the object of their preference, and the great addition to his previous prejudices against Adams and Clay made by the conduct of their friends in the recent elections went far to neutralize his antipathy towards his fair and open opponents. I had every reason to believe that such was the case in regard to myself personally. Altho' not a word had ever passed between us, either directly or through friends, he was made to understand,—in what way I never knew but have guessed that it was thro' Mr. Knower, the father-in-law of Gen. Marcy,—the nature of my feelings towards him [Clinton] and the extent to which I had been willing to go to place him on an equal footing with his compeers in the Presidential canvass, and he appreciated correctly the necessity which overruled that disposition.

The election placed a sufficient majority of my friends in both branches of the Legislature to secure my re-appointment to the Senate against all opposition, yet I had the best reason to believe that great efforts were made by the friends of the National Administration to prevail upon Gov. Clinton to unite in an attempt to prevent my return, and that he promptly and definitively refused to do so. Some of his friends over whom he had the most influence voted for me and I was informed by his aid, Col. Bloodgood,[1] that a day or two before he died he had spoken of me in kind and complimentary terms.

° MS. II, p. 35.   [1] De Witt Bloodgood.

The public mind at Washington was deeply agitated by the news of the Governor's sudden death. Political rivalry, so rife at the moment, was hushed for a season and rooted prejudices displaced by feelings of sincere regret. The silencing of animosity and the awakening of charity and sympathy in the human heart in the presence of death is always a grateful subject of contemplation to the benevolent mind, and when these effects are produced by the sudden close of a prominent and influential public life, while yet in mid career, it is no less matter of satisfaction to the patriot. At a meeting of the representatives in Congress from the State of New York, convened for the purpose of expressing their feelings on this occasion, the following remarks were made by me,[1] which I here insert from a report published at the time.

The honorable Martin Van Buren of the Senate addressed the meeting nearly in the following words:

Mr. Chairman: We have met to pay a tribute of respect to the memory of our late Governor and distinguished fellow-citizen, De Witt Clinton. Some of our brethren have been so kind as to ask me to prepare a suitable expression of our feelings: and I have, in pursuance of their wishes, drawn up what has occurred to me, as proper to be said on the occasion. Before I submit it to the consideration of the meeting, I beg leave to be indulged in a few brief remarks. I can say nothing of the deceased that is not familiar to you all. To all he was personally known, and to many of us intimately and familiarly, from our earliest infancy. The high order of his talents, the untiring zeal and great success with which those talents have, through a series of years, been devoted to the prosecution of plans of great public utility, are also known to you all; and by all I am satisfied duly appreciated. The subject can derive no additional interest or importance from any eulogy of mine. All other considerations out of view, the single fact that the greatest public improvement of the age in which we live was commenced under the guidance of his counsels, and splendidly accomplished under his immediate auspices, is of itself sufficient to fill the ambition of any man, and to give glory to any name. But, as has been justly said, his life and character and conduct have become the property of the historian, and there is no reason to doubt that history will do him justice. The triumph of his talent and patriotism cannot fail to become monuments of high and enduring fame. We cannot indeed but remember that in our own public career, collisions of opinion and action, at once extensive, earnest and enduring, have arisen between the deceased and many of us. For myself, sir, it gives me a deep-felt, though melancholy, satisfaction, to know, and more so to be conscious that the deceased also felt and acknowledged, that our political differences have been wholly free from that most venomous and corroding of all poisons—personal hatred. But in other respects it is now immaterial what was the character of those collisions. They have been turned to nothing, and less than nothing, by the event we deplore, and I doubt not that we will, with one voice and one heart, yield to his memory the well deserved tribute of our respect of his

---

[1] Oakley's note to Van Buren Feb. 18, 1828, suggesting that the latter take the lead in the matter is in the Van Buren Papers in the Library of Congress. The remarks are from The National Journal, Washington, D. C., Feb. 22, 1828. The meeting was held in the Capitol, Feb. 19.

name and our warmest gratitude for his great and signal service. For myself, sir, so strong, so sincere and so engrossing is that feeling, that I, who whilst living never no never envied him anything; now that he has fallen, am greatly tempted to envy him his grave with its honours.

Of this the most afflicting of all bereavements that has fallen upon his wretched and despondent family, what shall I say? Nothing—their grief is too sacred for description—justice can alone be done to it by those deep and silent, but agonizing feelings which on their account pervade every bosom.

Mr. Van Buren then submitted the following resolution:

The Delegation from the State of New York to the Senate and House of Representatives of the Congress of the United States, having been informed of the sudden death of De Witt Clinton, late Governor of that State, feel it due to the occasion, as well as to their own feelings, to unite with the people they represent, in expressing their deep and sincere sorrow for a dispensation of Providence which has, in the midst of active usefulness, cut off from the service of that State, whose proudest ornament he was, a great man, who has won and richly deserved the reputation of a distinguished public benefactor.

Sensibly impressed with respect for the memory of the illustrious dead, they will wear the usual badge of mourning for thirty days; and they request that a copy of these, their proceedings, be communicated to the family of the deceased, with an assurance of their condolence at the greatest bereavement that could have befallen them on this side the grave.

After a lapse of more than a quarter of a century and after having enjoyed the highest political distinctions known to our system, I can truly say that I feel upon the subject now as I expressed myself then.

Mr. Clinton's political advancement did not realize either the anticipations of his early friends or perhaps his own expectations. But he left traces upon the times in which he lived which were made indelible by his connection with the great Public Work of his period—the Erie Canal. In all the relations of private life his conduct and character were, if not faultless, certainly without just reproach. His social habits for a season excited the apprehensions of his friends and were made the subject of unfavorable censure by his opponents, but the former were dispelled and the latter refuted before he died. His talents are admitted to have been of a high order and were favorably exhibited in his writings; his speeches also were carefully and well constructed but delivered in an awkward and unimpressive manner. He never enjoyed extensive popularity with the masses, altho' there can be no doubt of his desire to acquire it, and the failure of his efforts in that direction has been variously accounted for. His official communications were filled, sometimes overloaded, with expositions and recommendations of measures which he thought calculated to subserve public and advance private interests. His friends generally attributed his want of popularity to the stateliness and seeming *hauteur* of his manners, but when the limited extent of his personal intercourse with the People is considered the correctness of this interpretation of results so diffused may well be doubted.

In this matter of personal popularity the working of the public mind is often inscrutable. In one respect only does it appear to be subject to rule, namely in the application of a closer scrutiny by the People to the motives of public men than to their actions. When one is presented to them possessed of an ardent temperament who adopts their cause, as they think, from sympathy and sincerely regards their interests as his own, they return sympathy for sympathy with equal sincerity and are always ready to place the most favorable constructions upon his actions and slow to withdraw their confidence however exceptionable his conduct in many respects may be. But when a politician fails to make this impression—when they on the contrary are led to regard him as one who only takes the popular side of public questions from motives of policy their hearts seem closed against him, they look upon his wisest measures with distrust, and are apt to give him up at the first adverse turn in his affairs. The process by which they arrive at one or the other of these conclusions is not easily described. Feeling has of course more to do with it than reason, yet, tho' sometimes wrong, it must be admitted that they are much oftener right in their discriminations. Jefferson and Jackson were favorites of the character I have described, and justly so. Clinton was not. For his conduct in regard to the Erie Canal he received from the public all the credit to which he was entitled notwithstanding the unfavorable criticisms that were made as to his motives—criticisms of which we would not have heard if that great public service had been rendered by either of the statesmen I have referred to. A striking illustration of the truth of this view was furnished by the fact that when he was for the last time a candidate for popular suffrages he was not as well supported by the people on the line of the Erie Canal (making allowances for their political preferences) as his competitor, a young man who had rendered no aid to that great enterprise deserving to be mentioned in comparison with his own.

CHAPTER XV.

Circumstances occurred in the summer of this year which from their bearing upon a great public question are deserving of notice. The annual petition of the manufacturers to Congress for increased protection, presented at the previous session, resulted in the report of what was called the ° Woollens' Bill. Having promised to accompany a friend on a visit to the Congressional Cemetery, I was absent from the Senate when the Bill was reached and rejected by the casting vote of Vice President Calhoun. My absence was assumed to have been intentional and was made the ground for the usual newspaper vituperation, according to which my delinquency was greatly aggravated by my accompanying Gen. Hamilton and Col. Drayton to South Carolina at the close of the session. Whilst at Charleston I received a letter from Comptroller Marcy urging my immediate return to arrest the use that our opponents were making of the materials with which I had thus supplied them. Having had some experience of his propensity to *croak*, and being withal not ready to comply with his unreasonable request, I replied that if my standing at home was not sufficient to protect me against such assaults it was not worth preserving and that I should not hasten my return for such a purpose. On my way homewards I learned at West Point from a reliable authority that the Tariff champion Mallary had informed his friends that it was the intention of the Protectionists to denounce my course at a State Tariff Convention which was to meet at Albany within a week or two, and that my old friend the Patroon[1] had agreed to preside at the meeting. I immediately determined to face the assemblage and to speak for myself, but without communicating my intention to a single friend.

To the very able exposition of the system and the persistent assaults upon its injustice and impolicy by the New York Evening Post, the country is more indebted for its final overthrow, in this state at least, than to any other single influence.

On the morning of the Tariff meeting at the Capitol I sent for my friends Benjamin Knower and Charles E. Dudley, and for the first time informed them of my intentions and asked them to accompany me. They vehemently remonstrated against the proposed step and told me that they had been reliably informed of the intention to pass a vote of censure upon my course in regard to the

---

° MS. II, p. 40.   [1] Stephen Van Rensselaer.

Woollens Bill,[1] and that altho' there would be many of my political friends at the meeting, a very large majority would be enemies who would avail themselves of my presence to make the proceeding more humiliating. I agreed with their opinion as to the meditated assault, but observed that it would not be contained in the Report of the Committee, as well to save the feelings of my friends at the Commencement as because the managers would know that Gen. Van Rensselaer would not make himself a party to such a Report by a Committee of his appointing, and that as the censure, for these reasons, would doubtless be reserved for a motion to amend, at the close of the proceedings, if I could unexpectedly appear before them after the organization of the meeting I would take my chance for what was done afterwards. They still objected, but were of course willing to go with me, and after ascertaining, by a messenger dispatched for that purpose, that the assemblage was organized for its work we repaired to the Capitol.

My appearance occasioned evident surprise. The good Patroon who presided asked me to take a seat by his side, which I respectfully declined, and chose an eligible position in the crowd. At the end of every speech the eyes of the assemblage were directed towards me, but I waited until every one had spoken who desired to do so, and I then addressed the meeting for nearly two hours. Some of the speeches previously made contained or insinuated enough to justify me in regarding myself as accused of delinquency in the matter of the Woollens Bill and thus to open the whole subject. I was listened to throughout with silent but respectful attention. During the whole time my friend Knower sat directly before and with his eyes fixed upon me, and when I spoke of the injustice that had been done to me he was so much moved as to attract the attention of the meeting. He was then extensively engaged in the purchase of wool, but being a Republican of the old school and withal a singularly upright man and sincere friend, those fine qualities had not yet been affected by the ardent pursuit of money. At a later period he separated from many of his early friends, myself among the rest, in consequence of their anti-tariff opinions, but a short time before his death he addressed me a letter replete with the sentiments and the spirit of his best days.

At the close of my speech Mr. J. Townsend a son-in-law of Judge Spencer and a rich manufacturer, expressed a desire to pass a vote of thanks to me for it, but some of his more sagacious associates, who did not think as favorably of its probable effect, interfered and overruled him. The meeting dissolved without anything being further

---

[1]A bill for the "Alteration of the acts imposing duties on imports" introduced Jan 27, 1827, by Rollin C. Mallary, of Vermont, and designed to amend the tariff of 1824.

said or done, and we moved down State Street from the Capitol with every indication of exultation on the part of my friends at its *dénouement*, and of dejection on the other side.

Mr. Knower came to me in the evening and told me that, on his way home from the Capitol, Mr. Wood, one of his wool buyers and a sensible man, said to him—"Mr. Knower! that was a very able speech!" "Yes, very able!" he answered. "Mr. Knower!" again said Mr. Wood, after a considerable pause,—"on which side of the Tariff question was it?" ° "That is the very point I was thinking about when you first spoke to me, Mr. Wood!" replied Knower.

I have frequently been told and have always believed that I rendered much service to the cause of truth by that speech, but this conversation between two intelligent and interested men would seem to indicate that directness on all points had not been its most prominent feature.

In the course of my remarks I had referred to the fact, by way of putting myself in good company, that the Chairman of the Meeting, my very good friend the Patroon, had been also absent from his seat in the House of Representatives when the Woolen's Bill passed that body. The recollection of this fact, and especially my reference to it, had made him quite uneasy in a position which, as I understood, he had promised, even before he left Washington, to occupy altho' he had not been apprised of the intention to assail me. In the evening, being desirous to see how he had relished the proceedings, I proposed to Gen. Thomas Pinckney, of South Carolina, who had called upon me, a visit to the Manor House. We found Gen. Van Rensselaer in the act of giving Mrs. Van Rensselaer an account of the meeting and our arrival created an embarrassment, unpleasantly obvious to both of us, that made me regret that we had interrupted him.

I had sustained the protective policy by my votes and speeches under instructions of the Legislature, but the more I became acquainted with its true character and with the views of its advocates the more my repugnance to it became strengthened. Compelled to regard it is a system equally unwise and illiberal, kept on foot by politicians to secure the support of a class of men whose selfish appetite increased by indulgence, I became sincerely solicitous for its overthrow; but experience having shewn that it had acquired, by the plausible pretences upon which it was sustained, a hold upon the public mind which could only be loosened by degrees and by means which would not rouse the prejudices of its supporters, I determined to assail it in that form. Whatever may be thought of the morality

° MS. II, p. 45.

of such a conclusion it was to my mind quite clear that an obstinate error like this, fostered by positive private gains to a busy few and promises of individual advantages to large and influential classes could in no other way be successfully combatted, and I considered it a case in which the end would justify means so little exceptionable. President Jackson pursued a similar course, and, as I know, for similar reasons, in his Maysville Veto.[1] The great influence which that Message exerted in overthrowing the entire system of Internal Improvement by the Federal Government, altho' it was only directed against a part, is universally conceded. How much was done towards correcting public sentiment on the subject of high tariffs in our state by the course I pursued, it is not for me to say. Governor Marcy, who will not, by those who knew him, be remembered as a flatterer even of his best friends notwithstanding this instance of exaggerated praise, in a letter to me some months after this period, referring to his solicitude as to the political effect that must be produced by the tariff feeling and his apprehension that it had disturbed his relations with Mr. Wright, wrote as follows:

There was last spring a more than half formed opinion that you was hostile to the Tariff; this opinion was settling down into a conviction accompanied with some excitement and was doing (or rather was about to) infinite mischief to the cause of Genl Jackson in this State, when, at the most auspicious moment that political sagacity ever selected, and by the most successful effort that talent ever made, you destroyed in the speech you made at the Capitol all the works which long premeditated mischief had contrived, and the industry of political enemies had been many months employed, to raise up for the prostration of yourself and the cause you had espoused.[2]

In every subsequent National canvass until my final retirement from public life my Woollen's Speech (as it was called) was made a prominent subject of a partizan agitation. It was denounced by my opponents at the South as proof of my being a Protectionist and by those at the North as proof of my hostility to the system. So frequent and continued were the applications for explanations that I was obliged to have an edition of the speech published for the benefit of my friends at the South. At the north its drift and design were soon understood and in the end favorably appreciated.

In the fall of this year Thomas Addis Emmett was seized with paralysis whilst engaged in the trial of a cause, and died almost immediately. I was one of the opposing counsel in the cause, and as the court adjourned on the preceding day he [Emmett] expressed to me his surprise that we had kept our suit—the claim of Bishop Inglis, of Nova Scotia, to the immense estate called the Sailor's Snug Harbor—on foot so long, but added that we could not prolong its life

---

[1] Message of May 27, 1830, with veto of bill authorizing a subscription of stock in the Maysville, Washington, Paris and Lexington Turnpike Company.

[2] This letter, Marcy to Van Buren, 1828, Jan. 29, is the Van Buren Papers in the Library of Congress.

beyond twelve o'clock of the next day. When that time arrived I followed him from the bar to the stove, whither he had been called by an acquaintance, and said " Well, Mr. Emmett, the hour has come and we are alive yet!" " Yes," he answered—" but you cannot live much longer!" Immediately after my return to my seat David B.'Ogden said to me " Look at Emmett! He is going to have a fit!" I looked and replied that it was a mistake. In a few moments he repeated the alarm more emphatically. I went to Chief Justice Thompson, before whom the cause was tried, and informed him of Mr. Ogden's suspicions. The Judge observed Mr. Emmett closely, and replied pleasantly " No! No! Ogden is mistaken—his under lip hangs a little lower than usual, but that is natural to him when he is writing!" At that instant and as I turned towards my seat I saw Mr. Emmett reel in his chair and extend his hand towards a neighbouring pillar. I endeavoured to intercept his fall but without success; he was carried to his house and died in a few hours.[1]

I had considerable professional intercourse with Mr. Emmett, admired his talents, and always found him liberal, honorable and just. His conduct and character as a public man are known to the country. He soon lived down the censures and hatred which pursued him in his emigration and were for a season troublesome, and died universally lamented as an honest man and faithful citizen.

There were circumstances in the life of my ill fated friend Samuel A. Talcott, connected with the same trial in the course of which Mr. Emmett died, which lead me to take here a brief notice of his brilliant yet melancholy career. About the year 1819 I chanced to see a number of articles in a western newspaper criticising and censuring my course in regard to a public question, the marked ability of which caused me to make enquiries in respect to their paternity. I soon ascertained that they were written by Mr. Talcott, a young federal lawyer of Oneida County whom I had never seen. Happening afterwards to be on the same boat with him, on our way to attend the Supreme Court at New York, I sought and made his acquaintance, and finding him undetermined, on our arrival, where to lodge, I invited him to accompany me to the Parke Place Hotel where I usually staid, to which he consented. The house being very full I ordered a bed in my room for his temporary accommodation. This arrangement led to frequent conversations which impressed me with the highest opinion of his character and intellectual endowments. I told him, one day, between jest and earnest, that he was misplaced in the political field, and that he ought to be on our side. At the moment I had not the least idea that any consequence would flow from the remark, but I soon dis-

---

[1] Nov. 27, 1827.

covered that he had thought seriously upon the subject, and was desirous to talk farther with me about it. I gave him a very unreserved account of my own political opinions and, as far as I understood them, of those of the mass of my party, and pointed out to him the reasons why his chances for fame and public usefulness would be increased by joining us; but advised him at the same time to come to no hasty conclusion—to think the matter over deliberately at home, and, if he found his way so clear as to afford a reasonable confidence that the change when made would be satisfactory and permanent, to make it—if not, to stay where he was, for I had too much respect for him to wish him to adopt a time serving policy.

Some weeks after this I received a letter from him informing me of his intention to attend a democratic meeting and to avow his adhesion to our party and that I might rest assured that he had not come to the conclusion without a solemn resolution that in politics as it was his first so it would be his last change.

His great talents soon made him conspicuous in our ranks and as early as the year 1821 he was appointed Attorney General of the State in the place of my successor in that office Thomas J. Oakley. The selection of so young a man and so recent a convert from the federal side drew down considerable censure upon the Council of Appointment from disappointed candidates and their friends and not a small portion of it was diverted against myself on the suspicion, better founded than usual, that I had exerted myself in his favor. I felt no uneasiness about this, as I was certain that it would soon satisfy all disinterested friends that it was the best selection that could have been made. This he accomplished in a short time and very thoroughly, and whilst the man, who had busied himself in an unavailing effort to get up a Legislative meeting to denounce us for making a federal appointment, himself joined the other side, young Talcott attained a solid popularity in our party and an eminent professional standing.

But these bright prospects were destined to be early blasted by habits of intemperance, which grew upon him with fearful rapidity, and filled the hearts of his friends with sorrow. The wane of his professional fortunes, before his fall, was protracted by the respect which he inspired as a man and by the admiration which he compelled by his remarkable professional talents and acquirements. After the fell disease had made great progress his clients, unwilling to dispense with his services, often resorted to the expedient of enlisting the good offices of some mutual friend to remain with him and to keep him for a time from the intoxicating bowl. Many instances of this were known to me of which I will notice a few. Under such training (which he perfectly understood and aided as far as his infirm nature would allow) he made an argument in the Supreme ° Court of the United States which called forth the strongest applause of Chief Justice Marshall and all his brethren, greatly excited a numerous and intelligent audience and attracted the attention of the country to an almost unprecedented extent.

In a very important trial between the State of New York and John Jacob Astor, in which Chancellor Kent, Mr. Webster and myself were employed as Counsel on behalf of the State, and Mr. Talcott represented it as Attorney General, it became necessary to have a consultation in regard to several difficult questions of law which arose in the case. We agreed to meet at the Chancellor's office in Greenwich street, and Mr. Talcott was to call for me on his way down to the appointed *rendezvous*. When he arrived at my room I was shocked to find that he was very much intoxicated and taking his arm I led him past Rector street, down which lay our direct route, as far as the Battery, and there walked with him to and fro for a long time and beyond the hour fixed for our meeting. When in one of our turns we came to the gate which was nearest the Chancellor's residence, he looked me in the face and, expressing by a smile his consciousness of my object, said—"I think it will do now!" "Well," I replied, "if you think so we will go!"

The other gentlemen had been waiting for us and he at once proceeded, as his official station required, to state the several questions in their order, the difficulties of each, and the manner in which he thought it best to deal with them. He did this in so full, able and vivid a manner, as to leave us nothing to do but to adopt his recommendations. After he left us to fulfill an appointment, the Chancellor and Mr. Webster expressed very earnestly their admiration of the general accuracy of his views, the simple power of his language, and his extraordinary familiarity with questions as abstruse and difficult as any in legal science. They referred also with delicacy and obvious sincerity to their regret at hearing of the unfavorable impressions which existed in regard to his habits, but not one of them dreamed of the narrow escape they had just had from an exhibition of them.

In the suit on the trial of which Emmett fell, which was, as I have mentioned, an action brought by Bishop Inglis of Nova Scotia for the recovery of real estate in the city of New York, even then of great value and now worth several millions of dollars, Talcott was one of his associate counsel. The Bishop claimed as heir at law of the last owner, Mr. Randall, and the defendant claimed under his will, by which the whole property was devised as a charity for the support and comfort of aged and infirm seamen. We contested this

---

° MS. II, p. 50.

devise as illegal and had, for reasons not necessary to be stated here, satisfied ourselves that if we could obtain possession of the property we would have no difficulty in maintaining it. During the early stages of the trial, Talcott was in an unfit state to come into court, and his associates under the lead of Emmett, desirous to avoid the issue on the validity of the devise, had for several days managed the defence in a way which shewed a determination to rely on their possession as a sufficient bar to our claim. On the day before the sad occurrence that filled us all with sorrow, Talcott walked into court, looking fresh and well, and took his seat among his associates. After some conversation between them Mr. Emmett asked the indulgence of the Court while they retired for consultation, and gave as a reason that they had until that moment been deprived of the assistance of Mr. Talcott by his indisposition. As they walked out I said to Mr. Ogden, my associate, that I was quite sure that Talcott would induce them to produce the will, but he thought that the opposite policy had been too firmly settled. The first thing after their return was Mr. Emmett's offering the will in evidence.

We were defeated and I had the curiosity immediately after the trial was ended to ask the Chief Justice what he would have thought of the cause if they had not introduced the will. He replied that, assuming from the course pursued by the defendant's counsel that they did not mean to rely upon it, he had considered the cause in that light, and had come to a very decided conclusion that they could not prevent our recovery on the strength of their possession. I have therefore ever thought that the chances were at least equal that if Talcott had not come into court that large estate would have gone in a different direction.

Within an hour after the fall of Mr. Emmett I took a long walk with Talcott and pressed upon his attention the vacancy in the profession now certain to be created in New York by Mr. Emmett's death, and the fact that he was the most able man in the state to fill it. After talking some time I paused and added that there was but one obstacle to his success, and that he must understand what I alluded to. He said he did *well* understand! I exclaimed with vehemence—" is it not possible to remove that?"—to which he answered characteristically, " I can try!" He moved to the city and endeavoured to break the hold of his insidious enemy, but in vain. In the course of a few years he became an inmate of the Hospital for the Insane where he died. Thus perished, alas! how ingloriously, a mind of the highest order; a counsellor of well earned and brilliant distinction—the best black-letter lawyer I ever knew—; a man of the purest personal character and friend the most sincere.

CHAPTER XVI.

Of the action of the Federal Government during the administration of Mr. Monroe I have nothing farther to say, but I cannot
pass without noticing two visits I made to Virginia during his
last term, the incidents of which were interesting to me and the
relation of them may be somewhat so to others. It seems unavoidable in writings of this kind to make oneself to a great extent
the hero of the narrative, although the offensive intrusion of "the
eternal I" is as disagreeable to me as it can be to the reader. I
doubt not that when Mr. Jefferson feelingly exclaims in his autobiography, that he is tired of speaking of himself, he disclosed
the true reason why that work was not continued to its proper
termination: and I am continually tempted by the same inducement to bring my story to an abrupt close.

I paid my first visit to Mount Vernon on the invitation of Judge
Bushrod Washington to spend Christmas with him, accompanied
by Gen. C. F. Mercer who had been the bearer of the invitation.
A closer acquaintance confirmed my impressions of the purity of
the Judge's character, and I was agreeably surprised by the vivacity of his disposition. His mental qualifications were of a highly
respectable order, and united to the simplicity and frankness of
his manners made his society peculiarly agreeable, and his cordial
hospitality assisted by the Herberts,[1] Mrs. Washington's nephews
who besides their other accomplishments sang remarkably well,
made ours a merry Christmas. Mrs. Washington had been a long
time bed-ridden, but the singing drew her to the head of the stair
case and it was delightful to see how much this circumstance excited the Judge's sensibilities and added to the general hilarity.
In the course of the evening we availed ourselves of the fine weather
to take a stroll on the lawn, and leaving the young people to their
amusements he led the way to a covered walk in the adjoining
grove. I spoke of the extent to which my interest in the beautiful
scene about us was enhanced by the associations, to which he assented and added that my observation reminded him of an occasion
when he paced that walk as we were now doing, but with a more
troubled heart.

"I received" said he, "a letter from the General" (his invariable synonym for his uncle) "in the spring before his death re-

---

[1] Judge Washington's nephews, Bushrod W. and Noblet Herbert.

questing Mr. Marshall, as he always called the future Chief Justice, and myself to come to Mount Vernon. The court was sitting and a compliance with his request of course inconveninent, but it never occurred ° to either of us to postpone his business to our own. Our brethren of the bar readily acquiesced in a postponement of our causes, and we started, as was the fashion of the time, on horseback and with no other wardrobe that what we carried on our persons. I mention the latter circumstance because of an accident to which equestrians are peculiarly liable, having occurred to Mr. Marshall, which frequently exposed to view the nether extremity of his shirt, causing infinite amusement on the journey and much embarrassment at Mount Vernon. On our arrival in the evening, the General took me into the library and informed me that he wished Mr. Marshall and myself to offer for Congress at the approaching election—Mr. Marshall for Henrico district and myself for Westmoreland. As I resided in Richmond, altho' my property lay in Westmoreland, it might be safest, he said, to make a partial removal there to satisfy the law, which could not give me much trouble.

"Having explained his wishes and briefly assigned his reasons he desired me to break the matter to Mr. Marshall so that he could have our answer at supper. I called Mr. Marshall out, and on this walk we had our consultation. We had of course the strongest possible desire to conform to the General's wishes, but could not bring our minds to any other conclusion than that to do so in this instance would be destructive of our prospects in the pursuit we preferred, and injurious to our families. Altho' it was not so with Marshall, I was myself deeply conscious of an unfitness for political life. It was made my duty to state our objections to the General which I did very earnestly. He heard me through without interruption, and then answered in his usual grave and emphatic way—"Bushrod, it must be done!" With this I returned to my friend, still lingering in this grove in painful suspense. We resumed our walk and finally agreed that me must comply with the General's wishes at all hazards. We returned to him and informed him of our assent to his proposition. He expressed his satisfaction in very kind terms and said that he was sensible of the inconvenience to which a compliance with his views might subject us, but was certain that he had asked nothing from us which he would not have done himself if our situations had been reversed. We left Mount Vernon early in the morning and returned to Richmond with feelings of great anxiety.

"I had entered upon the steps deemed advisable to qualify myself to represent Westmoreland when I received a letter from the Secre-

---

° MS. II, p. 55.

tary of State informing me that President Adams had appointed me one of the Justices of the Supreme Court of the United States, and I was advised by the same letter that a circuit court was to be held in Georgia in so short a time that it would be necessary to start immediately for that state if I accepted the office. I took the official oath immediately, threw myself into the stage coach, proceeded to Georgia and informed the General from that place of what I had done and my reasons for doing it."

General Washington died in the month of December in the same year.[1] Marshall offered for the Henrico district, was elected and made his justly admired speech in defence of the administration for its course in the case of Jonathan Robbins, which raised him at once to the first rank in that body. He was appointed Secretary of State by Mr. Adams, on the removal of Timothy Pickering, and, just before the end of his term, Chief Justice of the United States.

I listened to the Judge's narrative with interest but with a painful sense of the danger to which it showed that Gen. Washington had been exposed of becoming involved in the conflicts of party, at that moment as violent as they have ever been,—a danger from which, in the inscrutable providence of God, he had been withdrawn by an early and otherwise premature death. No man entertained a sounder sense of what belonged to his position, possessed more self command or could be more ready to sacrifice personal feelings to the public good than Gen. Washington. These high traits had all been strikingly exhibited in the course of the trying years of his administration, as well as in his subsequent retirement. Nor was it possible that any extent of personal irritation could ever bring his mind to sanction public measures that he did not conscientiously believe would be beneficial to the country. He was yet a man, and as such subject to some extent to the passions and infirmities of his nature, and the state of his feelings described by Judge Washington at a period and under circumstances so inauspicious to their continued restraint, gives us reason to apprehend that had he lived longer his wise and self imposed reserve would have been farther and farther relaxed until he would have become more deeply involved in the angry conflicts of party than was to be desired in one who at that moment possessed, with rare if any exception, the warm affections and the respect of the whole country.

Who can think without pain upon the consequences of his withdrawal from that enviable position which made the sacred appellation of Father of his Country so acceptable to all his countrymen and the loss of which would have robbed not only our History but Human Nature itself of one of the brightest glories of both. Who

---

[1] December 14, 1799.

that has been enabled to comprehend the violence of party spirit—
to know that the influences neither of religion nor of kindred nor of
any other earthly relation or situation have sufficient strength to
avert animosities or denunciations between partizan belligerents, can
regret that Washington's fair fame was snatched from farther exposure to that fiery ordeal, or can hesitate to acknowledge that the
goodness of Providence which had, for his own and his Country's
welfare, directed all his actions through his most useful and brilliant
life, was scarcely less signally displayed in his death.

CHAPTER XVII.

In the course of the winter of 1824, preceding the Presidential election, Ninian Edwards, one of the Senators in Congress from the state of Illinois, set in motion the famous A. B. plot, by causing to be published in the "Washington Republican," *newspaper*, several articles signed with those initials, in which Mr. Crawford was charged with culpable mismanagement of the public funds at different and remote points in the Western Country. Having thus sown his seed, he obtained from Mr. Monroe the appointment of Minister to Mexico, and after the nomination had been confirmed and his commission delivered him, he sent to the Speaker of the House of Representatives copies of those articles, with a letter avowing himself the author of them and affirming that the charges they contained could be supported by legal proofs if the House directed their investigation. At this stage in the proceedings and a short time before the close of the session he started on his Mission, assuming from the nature of his charges and the remoteness of the places from which the testimony was to be obtained that the matter could only be acted on in the recess, and intending that Mr. Crawford's friends instead of giving their attention to the election should find their time engrossed for the few months which yet remained before it was to take place in defending him before a committee of investigation.

Governor Floyd of Virginia, a political friend of Mr. Crawford, moved instantly for such a committee, and one was selected by Mr. Speaker Clay (himself a rival candidate) with equal delicacy and discretion. It was composed of seven of the most respectable members of the House, viz: Gov. Floyd, and Mr. Randolph, of Virginia, and Mr. Owen, of Alabama, friends of Crawford, Daniel Webster and John W. Tayler, supporters of Adams, Edward Livingston, who was in favor of Gen. Jackson, and ° Gen. McArthur, of Ohio, a friend of Clay.

The public mind was greatly shocked by the ruthlessness of the attack and was prepared to find it unfounded as well because of the conduct and reputation of its author as of Mr. Crawford's exemplary character. The Committee seemed similarly impressed and entered upon the immediate investigation and conducted it throughout in a spirit and with a degree of impartiality that reflected the highest

---

° MS. II, p. 60.

honor upon themselves and upon the Speaker by whom they had been selected. Mr. Crawford was at the time confined by a disease which had brought him to death's door and deprived him almost entirely of the use of his eyes during the whole investigation. His friends were of course ready to render any assistance not inconsistent with the proprieties of their positions, but the laboring oar was in the hands of his Chief Clerk, Asbury Dickins, who discharged his duties with fidelity and consummate ability. The Defence, which was almost altogether prepared by Dickins, drew forth loud and earnest applause from friends and foes. Whilst it left no matter of fact or argument unattended to, it did not contain a single harsh comment upon the conduct of Mr. Crawford's accuser, a feature which I was very desirous it should possess and to which I took some pains to reconcile our friends who were naturally excited and justly indignant.

The Committee immediately despatched the Sergeant at Arms after Edwards, who pursued him fifteen hundred miles on his way to Mexico. Edwards had left the prosecution of the case in the hands of his son-in-law, Mr. Cook, then a member of Congress, and holding in his hands the vote of Illinois upon the Presidential question in the House—where it was almost certain it would have to be decided, and with the cunning and unscrupulousness which characterised all his actions in the matter he evidently placed great reliance on that circumstance; but in this too he was disappointed. The Committee satisfied themselves of the utter falsity of the charges before Edward's return and, to prevent him from injuring Mr. Crawford in the public estimation at so critical a period, made and published a report,[1] in part, exonerating his conduct from the slightest impeachment. They however thought it proper to give Edwards an opportunity to be heard and to that end adjourned to meet again after the close of the session, when he was examined, but proved nothing to change the character of the report which was reaffirmed. He resigned his appointment and sank into an inglorious retirement.

Our friends being desirous that I should remain at Washington until the Committee reassembled, I spent the intervening time after the adjournment of Congress in making a visit I had long contemplated to Mr. Jefferson, accompanied by Gov. Mahlon Dickerson. Altho' suffering at the time from the pressure of pecuniary embarrassments, brought upon him by responsibilities incurred for an old friend, Mr. Jefferson received us with unaffected cordiality, and exerted himself cheerfully and heartily to make our visit agreeable. He had known and highly esteemed Gov. Dickerson when

---

[1] Report of select committee of the House, 18th Cong., 1st sess., vol. 6, No. 128.

he resided at Philadelphia during the most stormy period of the administration of John Adams, and he referred in a lively but tolerant spirit to many scenes of those stirring times, in not a few of which the Governor had himself been an actor,—such as his accompanying Dr. Cooper (of whom I have spoken) arm in arm to prison upon his conviction under the sedition law, altho' at the time Recorder of the City,—and to various exciting articles which had appeared in the *Aurora*, newspaper, supposed to have been written by Gov. Dickerson. The gratification of the latter in finding the most interesting events of his early political life thus brought step by step under a sort of commendatory review was unconcealed and pleasant to witness. On the next and subsequent days, leaving the Governor to be entertained by our host's grand-daughter, an accomplished and very agreeable young lady, now Mrs. Coolidge,[1] of Boston, (whose future husband paid his first visit to her while we were at Monticello) we employed our mornings in drives about the neighbourhood, during which it may well be imagined with how much satisfaction I listened to Mr. Jefferson's conversation. His imposing appearance as he sat uncovered—never wearing his hat except when he left the carriage and often not then—and the earnest and impressive manner in which he spoke of men and things, are yet as fresh in my recollection as if they were experiences of yesterday. I have often reproached myself for having omitted to make memoranda of his original and always forcible observations and never more than at the present moment. Uppermost in my mind is the recollection of his exemption from the slightest remains of party or personal prejudice against those from whom he had differed during the stormy period of his public life. Those who like myself had an opportunity to witness his remarkable freedom from the common reproach of political differences would find it difficult to doubt the sincerity of the liberal views he expressed in his Inaugural Address in regard to parties and partisan contests.

The bank of the United States was at this time in the plenitude of its power, and Mr. Jefferson was much disturbed by the sanctions which its pretentions received from the decisions of the Supreme Court, under the lead of Chief Justice Marshall, which he regarded as tending to the subversion of the republican principles of the Government. He expressed his belief that the life tenure of their offices was calculated to turn the minds of the Judges in that direction, and that the attention of our young men could not be more usefully employed than in considering the most effectual protection against the evils which threatened the Country from

---

[1] Miss Ellen Wayles Randolph, late Mrs. Joseph Coolidge.

that source. He spoke of the power of Impeachment with great
severity not only as a mockery in itself, but as having exercised an
influence in preventing a resort to a more thorough remedy, which
he thought was only to be found in a change in the tenure of the
judicial office. Annual appointments, as in the New England states,
were, he thought, the best, but he would be content with four or
even six years, and trust to experience for future reductions. Fresh
from the Bar, and to some extent at least under the influence of
professional prejudices, I remember to have thought his views extremely radical, but I have lived to subscribe to their general correctness.

In a speech in the Senate delivered years ago[1] I referred to the
Bank of the United States as having been the great pioneer of constitutional encroachments, and our subsequent experience has confirmed the justice of the remark. It is worthy of notice that since
that Institution has happily ceased to exist we have not only been
exempted from any such overwhelming pecuniary convulsion as
those caused by it, but the Supreme Court has occupied itself with
its legitimate duties—the administration of justice between man and
man—without being, as formerly, constantly assailed by applications for latitudinarian constructions of the constitution in support
of enormous corporate pretensions. We might, perhaps, have expected that in such a calm even Mr. Jefferson's alarm, if he had lived
to see it, would at least in some degree have subsided; but this
state of things can only be expected to last until a similar or equally
strong interest is brought under discussion of a character to excite
the whole country and to enlist the sympathies of a majority of the
Court and requiring the intervention of that high tribunal to sustain its unconstitutional assumptions by unauthorized and unre-
strained construction. Whether the institution of domestic slavery is
destined to be such an interest remains to be seen. The experience of ages proves that with exceptions too few to impair the rule,
men can not be held to the performance° of delegated political trust
without a continued and practical responsibility to those for whose
benefit it is conferred. The theory of the independence of the Sovereign in the case of the Judges in England, which we have copied,
entirely fails when applied to us. There they are rendered independent of the Crown to secure their fidelity to the public against
the influence of the power to which they owe their appointment
here their life-tenure renders them independent of the People for
whose service they are appointed. Irresponsible power of itself ex-

---

[1] " Substance of Mr. Van Buren's observations in the Senate " [Feb. 12–13, 1828] a
pamphlet of 16 pp. in which two speeches are welded into one, is in the Van Buren
Papers. Cf. Congressional Debates. iv. 1 : 313, 338.
° Ms. II, p. 65.

cites distrust, and sooner or later causes, on the part of its possessor, an impatience of popular control and, in the sequel, a desire to counteract popular will. The only effectual and safe remedy will be to amend the constitution so as to make the office elective, and thus compel the Judges, like the incumbents of the Executive and Legislative departments, to come before the people at stated and reasonable periods for a renewal of their commissions.

The subject of Internal Improvements by the General Government was another matter which occupied Mr. Jefferson's attention and caused him much concern. He spoke of it, with some feeling, as a mode of wasting the public revenues, without the probability of adequate returns, and involving violations of the constitution injurious to the interests it professed to advance, and expressed his approbation of the course I was pursuing in regard to the system in flattering terms.

I derived the highest gratification from observing that his devotion to the public interest, tho' an octogenarian and oppressed by private griefs, was as ardent as it had been in his palmiest days. Standing upon the very brink of the grave, and forever excluded from any interest in the management of public concerns that was not common to all his fellow citizens, he seemed never to tire in his review of the past and in explanations of the grounds of his apprehensions for the future, both obviously for my benefit. In relation to himself he was very reserved—taking only the slightest allowable notice of his agency in the transactions of which he spoke. Happening to notice a volume in his library labelled curtly and emphatically—" LIBELS "—I opened it and found its contents to consist entirely of articles abusive of himself, cut out of the Newspapers; and shewing it to him he laughed heartily over the *brochure*, and said that it had been his good fortune thro' life to be, in an unusual degree, indifferent to the groundless attacks to which public men were exposed. My inquiries in regard to individuals who had been prominent actors on the political stage in his day, were naturally as frequent as was consistent with propriety, and his replies were prompt and made with apparent sincerity and absolute fairness. Of Gen. Washington and of his memory he invariable spoke with undisguised regard and reverence. The views he took of his political character and career are fully stated in his letter to me of the ——, to which I shall have occasion presently to refer. The residence so near to each other of two such men, and the change which had taken place in their political relations presented an irresistible opportunity to mischievous busy-bodies, and no effort of theirs or of political rivalry or private enmity was omitted to impress Gen. Washington with a belief of Mr. Jefferson's ill will towards him. In speaking to me, in the letter I have mentioned, of the feelings of the old republicans, himself included, towards Gen. Washington, he uses this eloquent and, on its face, truthful language:

He lived too short a time after and too much withdrawn from information to correct the views into which he had been deluded, and the continued assiduities of the party drew him into the vortex of their intemperate career, separated him still further from his real friends, and excited him to actions and expressions of dissatisfaction which grieved them but could not loosen their affection from him. They would not suffer the temporary aberration to weigh against the immeasureable merits of his life, and altho' they tumbled his seducers from their places they preserved his memory embalmed in their hearts with undiminished love and devotion, and there it forever will remain embalmed, in entire oblivion of every temporary thing which might cloud the glories of his splendid life.[1]

If anything could be required to establish the truth of this statement in regard to Mr. Jefferson himself it would be sufficient to refer to the fact that all the great statesmen, his contemporaries, have gone hence, and that their papers have been ransacked and published without reserve, as well as his own, by friends and foes, and that not a fragment has been found to cast a doubt upon it.

Observing that in describing party movements he almost always said " The republicans " pursued this course, and "Hamilton " that— not naming the federalists as a party, except by the designation of a sole representative, I brought this peculiarity to his attention. He said it was a habit that he had fallen into at an early period from regarding almost every party demonstration during the administrations preceding his own, as coming directly or indirectly from Hamilton. He spoke of him frequently and always without prejudice or ill will, regarding him as a man of generous feelings and sincere in his political opinions. In answer to my question whether Hamilton participated in some step that he condemned, he replied— " No ! He was above such things ! " His political principles Mr. Jefferson condemned without reserve, save only their sincerity, regarding them in their tendency and effects as more anti-republican than those of any of his contemporaries.

Mr. Jefferson's account of the humble position from which Patrick Henry raised himself to eminence and the limited means of education and study with which he had been able to make a never to be forgotten impression upon the age in which he lived, interested me exceedingly. He described his agency in facilitating Mr. Henry's admission to the Bar, which was, in substance, that happening to be in the vicinity of the residence of Mr. Henry who was then a clerk in a small country store, the latter called upon him and asked him to use his influence with Mr. Wythe and Mr.

---

[1] A signed draft of this letter, dated June 29, 1824, by Jefferson, is in the Jefferson Papers, Library of Congress. Ser. 1, v. 14, 298.

Pendleton to induce them to unite with him in giving a certificate of qualification which was necessary to enable Mr. Henry to procure a license to practice law. In reply to Mr. Jefferson's enquiry in regard to the extent of his legal studies, Henry acknowledged that it was but very recently that he had resolved to ask admission to the Bar, and that he had not as yet opened a law book, but offered to pledge his honor that he would not practice until he had pursued the proper course of study. It was upon that assurance that they consented to give him a certificate, and Mr. Jefferson added that such was Henry's aversion to reading that he did not believe that he had ever read the whole of any book! Taking up a volume of Blair's lectures, one day at Monticello, and glancing over a page or two, Henry exclaimed "this is a very sensible book and if you will lend it to me I think I will read it." On his returning it months afterwards Mr. Jefferson, as a matter of curiosity, asked him whether he had read it through, and he acknowledged that he had not. In Mr. Jefferson's Autobiography, published by Congress, will be found a statement of similar import. Yet such was the strength and acuteness of his intellectual powers and so impressive and efficient his native eloquence, that of all the able men of whom Virginia then boasted there was not one whose speeches produced as great effect as did those of Patrick Henry. Mr. Jefferson did full justice to his services in the Legislature during the Revolutionary War, and in the State Convention for the adoption of the Federal Constitution, and ° described to me the singular effects produced by some of his addresses to juries. When the eminent position he attained as an orator as well at the Bar as in the public councils is considered in connection with the circumstances under which he was admitted to practice (as to the main facts in regard to which I am certain of having stated them correctly) it presents a most remarkable illustration of the power of genius unaided by education.

Our host pressed us with much earnestness to remain a few days longer, when we proposed to leave, and in reply to my excuse for returning to Washington, the desire to be in season for the meeting of the A. B. Committee, he said that his experience justified him in assuring me that a few days would make no difference in that respect, as I found to be true enough. When parting from him he said he would take the liberty of an old man to give us some advice upon the subject of being in a hurry. The first fifty years of his life had been harassed by the habit of thinking it indispensable that things should be done at a certain time and engagements kept to the moment; but upon summing up results he had found

---

* MS. II, p. 70.

that his punctuality had proved a losing business and that in a thousand instances things would have gone on rather better if he had given himself more latitude, and that subsequently he had adopted a different, and as the result had satisfied him, a wiser rule. Hoping that we would do likewise he bid us an affectionate farewell. In Gov. Dickerson he had met an old friend whom he had proved in the times which were then and long afterwards not inaptly called the "Reign of Terror," and whom he had not expected to see again, and for me he manifested a regard which I might safely construe into an approbation of my public course, and I could not fail to be highly gratified by such an assurance from one whose character, conduct and principles formed my *beau ideal* of thorough patriotism and accomplished statesmanship.

I had spoken of a political pamphlet by Timothy Pickering[1] which, as appeared by the newspapers, had just made its appearance and Mr. Jefferson requested me to send him a copy—which I did. A few weeks afterwards I received the letter from him to which reference had already been made, and which accompanies these memoirs. I am sure that no intelligent mind can peruse it without being deeply interested by its graphic views of circumstances and events not generally understood and in which no American citizen can fail to take the deepest interest.

I visited the elder Adams, at Quincy, the next summer after I was at Monticello, and I do not recollect ever to have seen a more striking and venerable figure than he appeared at that day. The traces of advanced age were more perceptible in him than in Mr. Jefferson, but did not appear to affect him either in mind or body, beyond the unavoidable infirmities of the decline of life. He received me kindly, and during the short period that I felt myself justified in occupying his attention conversed with uniform good sense, and a degree of animation and decision seldom witnessed in so old a man.

The Adamses, including that public spirited patriot Samuel Adams, were an extraordinary race and made indelible impressions on the times in which they lived. John Adams was, in the estimation of his successful rival, the most effective orator of the Revolution—a post of danger as well as of honor, as was shewn by the exception of his name, among others, from the offers of pardon which the Crown, from time to time, tendered to her rebellious subjects.

I need hardly say that his greatness was not without alloy, but happily for his country the defects of his character did not affect his usefullness until after her independence had been established.

---

[1] A Review of the Correspondence between the Hon. John Adams, late president of the United States and the late Wm. Cunningham, esquire * * * by Timothy Pickering. (Salem, 1824.) A copy is in the Library of Congress.

Whatever these defects may have been, one thing was at all times clear, as Dr. Franklin, in a brief sketch of his character (quoted below and not designed, as a whole, to be particularly complimentary) said, "he was always honest," and so were Samuel and John Quincy Adams. Indeed such, to their honor be it said, has, with very rare exceptions, been the character of our high public functionaries at all periods. In the times of John Adams the political atmosphere had been so thoroughly purified by the Revolutionary fires that no man, whatever his talent or his services, who was wanting in that the first qualification for public trusts could have been sustained for a day. Arnold was corrupted by the enemy, and scorn will never cease to designate, with her unmoving finger, his infamy. Edmund Randolph who possessed the confidence of Washington and Jefferson, and was appointed by the former Secretary of State when the latter resigned, ranking among the highest in personal position and in talent, was unhappily exposed to suspicion as to his official integrity, and he fell at once to rise no more. An attempt was made to attach suspicion to the acts of Alexander Hamilton as Secretary of the Treasury—as I have heretofore described. We have seen at what a sacrifice he vindicated the purity of his official conduct, and manifested his sense of the indispensable necessity of such a vindication whenever it should be questioned.

It is always hazardous for one whose judgments are deductions from what he reads to pass upon the personal characters of public men, yet it is the motive and sincerity with which this is done which makes it excusable or otherwise. My own impression has always been that Mr. Adams's subsequent failure in public life was, in no considerable degree, owing to an overweening self esteem and consequent impatience under honors conferred on his cotemporaries. Frequent exhibitions of this feeling, with—not too high, certainly—but perhaps too exclusive an appreciation of his own services, were, I cannot but think, among the causes of his unpopularity. It was this, doubtless, which gave a feverish character to his relations with Dr. Franklin, during their residence in Europe. The same causes produced wider and still more injurious effects on his return to the United States. The attention of public men, engrossed during the War by the enemy, was diverted by the peace and more closely directed towards each other, and anticipated rivalries doubtless added keenness to those examinations. The previous friendly relations between himself and Mr. Jefferson were, not improbably, then weakened and suspended: with Hamilton, who was himself not deficient in the same quality, he was soon in open hostility: he looked down upon Hancock, and an impression was made upon the minds of many that he yielded, with less complacency

than the other leading men of his day, to the universal preference
accorded to Washington. These well known circumstances, in connection with his after expressed admiration of the English system,
always excepting its corruptions, gave rise to the imputation, undoubtedly unjust, that his resistance to the Crown did not arise
so much from opposition to Monarchy in the abstract as to a natural
preference for the House of Braintree over that of Hanover.

The election at which he was chosen President passed off without
anything like a partizan canvass. The seeds of future party divisions had begun to sprout at the seat of Government, but in the
country at large these divisions were yet unseen and unfelt. The
election was suffered to drift to its conclusion without serious efforts to control its direction. In Mr. Madison's correspondence
may be found a letter from Mr. Jefferson, authorizing ° Mr. Madison to announce to the House of Representatives if the vote proved
to be equal, as it nearly turned out to be, as the earnest desire of
the writer that Mr. Adams might be preferred.[1] Mr. Adams was
a man of strong feelings and those to which I have particularly
alluded had lost none of their force by his long previous occupation
of an office without patronage or power. Mr. Jefferson tells us that
consultations between them on public affairs, tho' at first invited,
were in the end studiously avoided, and we know that his relations
with Washington were not free from embarrassment. The latter
had, as Commander in Chief of the Provisional Army, recommended
for Major Generals Hamilton, Pinckney and Knox; Mr. Adams
made the appointments, but was induced, it was supposed by his
prejudices against Hamilton, to reverse the order by placing Knox
first and Hamilton, last. Washington, as might have been anticipated, took exception to this arrangement of the names and insisted upon the order he had proposed, which was finally adopted.
I need not say that such a transaction could not pass to its consummation without offending the feelings of both.

Of Mr. Adams' support of the Alien and Sedition laws I have
elsewhere spoken. These laws were the legitimate fruits of principles which Hamilton had instilled into the federal party yet the
largest share of public odium they excited fell upon the head of
Adams. Divisions arose in that party and Hamilton took ground,
covert at first but finally avowed against his reelection. Fearless
in spirit and bold in movement the President removed from the
office of Secretary of State that remarkable man Timothy Pickering
who had been appointed by Washington, but whom he suspected of

---

° MS. II, p. 75.
[1] Dec. 17, 1796. In the Madison Papers, Library of Congress. It is printed in Ford's
Works of Jefferson. (N. Y. 1904), v. 8, 254.

being too much influenced by Hamilton, and threw himself upon the country for support.

Public services have their stipulated rewards, and all beyond, the People proudly regard as reserved for free-will offerings. Nothing is so likely to offend and repel their confidence as appeals for their support which wear the appearance of claims of right on the part of the applicant. Mr. Adams found it difficult, constituted as he was, to make any to which his enemies could not cause that objection to be plausibly set up. He was consequently never popular save during the war of the Revolution, when his appeals to the People were for their own interests and defence, and under the weight of this personal and administrational unpopularity, which his Revolutionary services could not surmount, he not only fell himself but drew down upon his party imperishable odium.

In a letter from Dr. Franklin to Robert R. Livingston, the Secretary of Foreign Affairs to the Congress, dated "Passy 22d. July, 1783," he alludes to Mr. Adams as follows:

* * * It is therefore I write this, to put you on your guard (believing it my duty, though I know that I hazard by it a mortal enmity) and to caution you respecting the insinuations of this gentleman against this Court, and the instances he supposes of their ill will to us, which I take to be as imaginary as I know his fancies to be that Count de Vergennes and myself are continually plotting against him, and employing the news writers of Europe to depreciate his character &c. But as Shakespeare says, "Trifles light as air" &c. I am persuaded however that he means well for his country, is always an honest man, often a wise one, but some times, and in some things, absolutely out of his senses.[1]

In the recently published Life and Works of John Adams, his grandson, the author and compiler, has incorporated in the Diary of Mr. Adams a paper left by him entitled "Travels and Negotiations", which appears to have been commenced in December 1806, and from which the following is extracted:

Dr. Franklin, one of my colleagues, is so generally known that I shall 'not attempt a sketch of his character at present. That he was a great genius, a great wit, a great humorist, a great satirist, and a great politician is certain. That he was a great philosopher, a great moralist, and a great statesman is more questionable. (Vol. III, p. 139.)

Whether the venerable diarist, when the above was written, had been apprised of the notice which had been taken of him by his renowned and equally venerable co-negotiator we can never know. Its resemblance to an excusable *retort courteous* is certainly not a little striking.

To return to the commencement of the administration of John Quincy Adams, efforts were made by its friends to excite public

---

[1] In the Department of State, Continental Congress Mss. It is printed in Wharton, Diplo. Corres. (Washington, 1889), v. 6, 580.

odium against its opponents by charging that their opposition was personal, predetermined, and made without reference to public measures. In this they were aided by an unwise and somewhat inflammatory declaration attributed to one of the South Carolina members. In point of fact our opposition commenced at the threshhold of the new administration but our course was nevertheless not justly deserving of the imputations that were cast upon it. The fact that the election of Mr. Adams had been made against the known wishes of a majority of the People was at least sufficient to justify us in standing aloof until we were officially informed of the views and principles in the administration of the Government by which the President-elect would be guided. The vote of non-concurrence in the nomination of Mr. Clay as Secretary of State, was confined to a portion only of our friends and avowedly given on personal grounds. Beyond that nothing was done until the delivery of the Inaugural Address in which the new President disclosed the principles of his administration—principles of which neither he nor his Cabinet expected our support.

Mr. Adams was an honest man, not only incorruptible himself, but, as I have before said (and in these days it cannot be too often said or too favorably remembered) an enemy to venality in every department of the public ser-ice. He loved his country, desired to serve it usefully and was properly ambitious of the honor of doing so. At a time and under circumstances highly creditable to his patriotism he left his party and came to the support of Mr. Jefferson's administration. Knowing that in voting for the embargo he opposed the opinion of his State he resigned the place of Senator in Congress which he held by her appointment and was, in the following year, sent as Minister to Russia by Mr. Madison. He occupied several prominent public stations abroad during Mr. Madison's administration and was recalled at the commencement of Mr. Monroe's term to take the leading position in his cabinet. The appropriate duties of these high offices, commencing very soon after his rupture with the federalists and continuing through the entire administrations of Madison and Monroe, he discharged not only with great ability but with equal fidelity and honor. He doubtless embraced fully and sympathized cordially in the feelings and opinions of Jefferson, Madison and the republican party, by which they had been elected and by which alone the administrations were sustained, on the subject of the War with England. The same may be said in regard to most if not all the public questions that arose out of our foreign relations between the imposition of the embargo and the close of Mr. Monroe's Government.

But such we are bound to believe was not the case in respect to the political creed of the old republican party on the subjects of the proper and only legitimate objects for the institution of governments among men, and the purposes for which they should be employed,—of the true theory of our complex Federal and State system in its operation upon domestic affairs, and the uses for which they were respectively framed and could only be rightly applied, and of the binding effects of written constitutions; a creed which having caused the Revolution subsequently, in the same spirit and significancy, triumphed in 1800, °and was throughout faithfully sustained by Jefferson, and, with a solitary exception, by Madison. The influence which that party had exerted in the overthrow of the Founder of his House was not calculated to conciliate the feelings of a man of Mr. Adams' temperament. He had too much self respect to profess that, on these points his original views of opinions which had met with his warmest opposition in the early part of his political career had undergone any change. He therefore embraced with avidity and supported with zeal the project of Mr. Monroe to obliterate the inauspicious party distinctions of the past and to bury the recollection of their causes and effects in a sepulchre proposed by himself—to wit in "the receptacle of things lost on earth."

With such feelings and amidst the distractions and consequent temporary overthrow of the republicans he was elevated to the Presidency. The condition of parties at that moment, the feelings that pervaded them and the effects produced by the preliminary steps and subsequent measures of the new Administration are matters of interesting review, at least to one who had opportunities to judge of them correctly and thinks himself able to speak of them with reasonable impartiality.

The election of the son of the statesman whom the ancestors of some among them had deemed it such a triumph to overthrow in the great civil struggle of 1800—a son believed to be imbued with many of the strong prejudices and obnoxious opinions of his father—as the first fruit of their own distractions, was a source of keen regret to the old republicans, save the comparatively few who had decided to follow the fortunes of Mr. Clay. The power which the old federal party had exerted in the recent contest and the alacrity and exulting spirit with which its votaries rallied to the standard of Mr. Adams as to a complete restoration of their influence in the Government, soon satisfied those who had yielded to the idea of the extinction of that party of their delusion—a conviction mingled with self reproach. These latter, attached as strongly as ever to the principles of their own party, and convinced by their

---

° MS. II, p. 80.

unexpected defeat of the continued necessity of organization to make them ascendant, became early desirous for its restoration. Always under similar circumstances, the rank and file of a political party, taught by adversity the folly of their divisions, look to a discontinuance of them to soothe its mortification, and long delays in accomplishing a cordial reconciliation are invariably attributed to the policy and ambition of leaders. In the present case the difficulties of this kind were not formidable, as the friends of Mr. Clay were readily made scape-goats for all delinquencies. A short interval to soften the minor irritations produced by the asperities of the canvass, and an outside pressure from the successful candidate were alone necessary to the formation of a hearty and effective union between the friends and supporters of Jackson, Crawford and Calhoun. That pressure was quickly applied by Mr. Adams in his Inaugural Address. Believing that the steps that had been taken to break up old party organizations had been successful, a large portion of that paper was employed in demonstrating and applauding the result. The merits and demerits of the two great political parties which had divided the opinions of our country were, in felicitous terms, placed upon a footing of equality; the policy of our Government towards foreign nations was assumed to have been their principal source; the catastrophe of the French Revolution and our subsequent peace with Great Britain were alluded to as having uprooted the baneful weed of party strife; no differences of principle, it was declared, either in relation to the theory of government or to our foreign intercourse, had since existed sufficient to sustain a continued combination of parties; animosities growing out of political contention had consequently, he said, been assuaged and the most discordant elements of public opinion blended into harmony.

The scattered members of one of those great parties, of that, too, which when united had for a series of years possessed the confidence of the country and been intrusted with the administration of the government, but which had now been defeated mainly by the concerted action of its old opponents—could not be expected to listen with complacency to this description, by their successful rival, of a state of things which they had discovered to be "a delusion and a snare." But this was not all: the new President announced among the subjects of Federal legislation which he favored that of Internal Improvement by means of Roads and Canals. He admitted that some diversity of opinion had prevailed in regard to the power of Congress over the subject, but it was alleged that a great advance had taken place in public sentiment in favor of the power and confident hope was expressed that its extent and limitation would soon be established to the satisfaction of all, and "every speculative scruple solved by practical public blessings." In his first annual Message he dwelt with much earnestness and at great length on the same subject—pressed the transcendant importance of the policy recommended and the obligation to promote it, and recommended to the persevering consideration of Congress "the general principle in a more enlarged extent;" embraced among several other specified objects a University and Astronomical Observatories, describing the latter as "light houses of the skies!"—a name sufficiently felicitous in regard to the subject, but indiscreetly used as conceded by his friends in reference to the circumstances under which he spoke,—and closed with an admonition as to the consequences of attempting to excuse our failure in duty by proclaiming to the world that we had allowed ourselves "to be paralized by the will of our Constituents."

These papers were written with the ability for which Mr. Adams's pen was justly distinguished. They were filled with well-wrought encomiums on the Federal Constitution, plausible definitions of the grants and limits of powers between the General and State Governments, and eloquent injunctions in favor of their faithful observance; and yet not one of the followers of the old Republican faith—no intelligent friend of the reserved rights of the states could fail to see in them the most ultra latitudinarian doctrines. The expressions which I have quoted, and especially that in which he spoke of the Representatives allowing themselves to be palsied by the will of their constituents, tho' couched in terms of professional ambiguity, were well calculated to strengthen that conclusion. Even Hamilton, who had always been placed at the head of the latitudinarians, whilst avowing, in the ingenuousness of his nature, his admiration of the British Constitution, admitted that the establishment of a monarchy here ought not to be attempted because it would be against the known wishes of the people, while it was the duty of their representatives to conduct the government on the principles elected by the constituency.

Mr. Adams's description of the then state of public opinion in respect to the constitutional power of Congress over the subject of Internal Improvements was, in the main and particularly in respect of those who had constituted the great body of the Republican party, very incorrect. It was true that several prominent Republicans had, after the peace, entered warmly into the support of that system, evidently under the impression that° it was the path to the confidence and support of the people, and there were of course not a few, in every section of the country, who, stimulated by self interest, were willing to have their "speculative scruples solved" by so-called, "practical public blessings." But the thinking and disinterested minds of the party, as well as the mass who were influenced by their counsels, continued to regard the claim of this power as dangerous heresy and to oppose it by every effort—an opposition of which the Journals of the National Legislature through several administrations furnish abundant evidence.

I never entertained a moment's doubt, after the delivery of the Inaugural Address, of the speedy reunion of the Republican party— excepting the personal adherents of Mr. Clay, but including a majority of its former supporters in the eastern states who had been drawn off to Mr. Adams by the consideration of his being an eastern man.

It suited the policy of the friends of the Administration, taking advantage of an article in the *Albany Argus*, newspaper, which was published without my knowledge and in well understood opposition to my opinions, and of the near expiration of my Senatorial term, to charge me, through their presses, with a concealment of my views in regard to the new government until I might secure my reelection: hence the imputation of *non-committalism* which became thence forward the parrot-note of my adversaries throughout my public career always applied to my sayings and writings except when it was supposed that more injury could be done by attributing to me the sentiments which I meant to express. My son, Col. Van Buren, on his return from the campaign in Mexico, described to me an incident amusingly illustrative of the tenacity with which this party catch-word of more than twenty years maintained its place in the vocabulary of those who had been accustomed to use it. At the hottest moment of the battle of Monterey, when it required all the circumspection of Gen. Taylor and his staff to avoid the cannonade of the enemy, directed against the position they occupied, Col. Baylie Peyton rode up to the General with a message from Gen. Worth who was stationed on the opposite side of the city. Having made his communication, he added that a letter had been found in the pocket of a dead cavalry officer from Santa Anna in regard to whose movements and plans there was great uncertainty and of course great interest. "Well," said the General, "which way is he moving?" "Upon that point" replied the Colonel, "his letter is quite *Van Buren-ish* and leaves us altogether in the dark!" Gen. Taylor, who knew enough of party politics to recognise a portion of its vocabulary so notorious, and to his credit as a soldier very little more, turned to my son at his side and said, somewhat sharply, "Col. Peyton, allow me to introduce you to my aid Major Van Buren." Peyton, altho' a violent political partisan, was a generous hearted man and had, in the excitement of the moment, been unmindful of my son's presence. Regardless of the constant salutations to the company of the enemy's artillery he insisted on acquitting himself on the spot of intentional want of courtesy, either towards him or myself—for whom he protested, notwithstanding political difference, he had always entertained the kindest and most respectful feelings; which was doubtless true, and he was of course readily excused upon the single condition that he would allow my son to give me the benefit of a hearty laugh by describing the scene to me.

There was never perhaps a more unfounded imputation, and no two men in the country were less in doubt in respect to my course than Mr. Adams and Mr. Clay. They understood too well my feelings on the subject of Mr. Monroe's fusion policy which they both promoted, and they had seen too much of my opposition to the principles and measures which they knew would become leading features of their administration to expect me to sustain it. I feel that I can say with truth that throughout my political career it was my invariable desire to have my opinions upon public questions distinctly known. I publicly answered, without hesitation or unwillingness, more questions put to me by opponents whom I knew to have sinister purposes in putting them and whose predetermined votes were not to be affected by any assurances or explanations, than have been answered by all the Candidates for the Presidency together from the commencement of the Government to this day. Notwithstanding that these are by-gone affairs, in their time of very limited importance and now of none, yet in view of the extraordinary success of this partisan accusation and of its striking illustration of the power of the Press, I will record the proof of its original falsity which has at this late date accidentally fallen under my notice. In looking over some old papers for another object, I accidentally laid my hand on a letter from Mr. Croswell, at the time Editor of *the Albany Argus*, in which the article in that newspaper which was so confidently attributed to my dictation and which gave rise to the charge of my pursuing a non-committal policy in regard to the administration of Mr. Adams, is directly referred to. The letter is dated April 3d, 1826, and the following extract is all that it contains upon the subject:

* * * I must ask you not to be surprised at the tenor of the leading editorial article of this morning. It has not been written without deliberation. The truth is, whilst there is an increasing aversion towards Mr. Adams amongst the Republicans of the State, there is a great aversion on their part to any collision with the administration which shall drive them to the support of Mr. Clinton, or that shall force them to encounter the hostility of both. They prefer, *for the present, at least*, to stand in the capacity of lookers on, believing that the natural hostility between A and C will be certain of shewing itself, and the sooner if we afford them no other aliment than themselves. It is for this reason and because it is believed that little advantage and very great evil may arise from a contrary course that we propose to let the National politics alone.[1]

The *italicising* in the above extract is my own. It thus appears that the position assumed by my friends at Albany was taken without my previous knowledge, and to shew how inconsistent it was with my known opinions and acts it is only necessary to say that I spent the month of March immediately preceding the date of the letter in earnest and active participation with the opposition in the Senate in their efforts to defeat the Panama Mission, and the month of April, in which it was written, in resisting the project of the Administration in respect to the Judiciary Bill. The former was its favorite measure, whilst it acquiesced in the loss of the latter rather than agree to the Jeffersonian restriction of the act of 1802, confining the residence of the Judges to their circuits, (upon which we insisted) notwithstanding our assent to the number of Judges which they proposed, and of which they had the appointment, or rather nomination.

My views in regard to the then next Presidential election were formally asked by that estimable man and inflexible old Republican, Judge William Smith, of South Carolina in an interview which I had with him at Boston, within three months after the commencement of Mr. Adams's Administration. I informed him that as Mr.° Crawford was removed from further competition by the state of his health my next candidate would be Andrew Jackson. To his questions in regard to the probability of success and to the safety with which we might rely on the General's present political opinions—his confidence on the latter point having been shaken by the famous letter to Mr. Monroe[2] and by the incidents of the last election,—I answered that by adding the General's personal popularity to the strength of the old Republican party which still acted together and for the maintenance of which the Judge and myself had been strenuous colaborers, we might, I thought, be able to compete successfully with the power and patronage of the Administration, then in the zenith of its prosperity; that we had abundant evidence that the General was at an earlier period well grounded in the principles of our party, and that we must trust to good fortune and to the effects of favorable associations for the removal of the rust they had contracted, in his case, by a protracted non-user and the prejudicial effects in that regard of his military life.

---

[1] Edwin Croswell to Van Buren, Apr. 3, 1826, in the Van Buren Papers. It is indorsed: "Origin of the non-committal charge, M. V. B. 1842."

° MS. II, p. 90.

[2] Jackson's letter of Oct. 23, 1816, and a certified copy of Monroe's reply, Dec. 14, to this and the Jackson letter of Nov. 12 are in the Jackson Papers, Library of Congress.

Pleased with these views the Judge asked my consent to speak of them freely as coming from me, which was readily given, and he entered upon their support with characteristic spirit. It was at my suggestion that Gen. Jackson afterwards offered to Judge Smith a seat on the Bench of the Supreme Court of the United States, which he declined.

From that period to the election there never was a moment in which my intention to oppose the reelection of Mr. Adams was not universally known, notwithstanding which fact the Administration presses succeeded extensively in imposing the non-committal fiction upon the credulity of their readers. I spent a few hours, not long since, with Mr. Walsh, formerly Editor and Proprietor of the *National Register*,[1] (a journal politically opposed to me, published in Philadelphia) and with his amiable family, at their residence, in Paris, and we all laughed heartily together at his allusions to some of the absurd anecdotes which the party spirit of that day had put in circulation on this point. Among many others of equal pretensions to truth he related this:—a bet was offered by one partisan to another that the latter could not put to me a question on any subject to which he would receive a definitive answer, which was accepted and the question asked was whether I concurred in the general opinion that the sun rose in the East; my answer having been that I presumed the fact was according to the common impression, but, as I invariable slept until after sun-rise, I could not speak from my own knowledge. Mr. Walsh heard this reported by persons who *believed it to be true:*—a strong illustration of the influence of a party press and of the fatuity of a blind party spirit.

The acceptance by the President, in behalf of the United States, of an invitation received from the American States of Spanish origin to send a Minister to represent us at their proposed Congress at Panama, was the first great measure of Mr. Adams's administration. This extra-territorial action of the Executive branch of the Government, being without precedent in its history, contrary to the scope and spirit of the Constitution and at variance with one of the most prominent recommendations of the Father of his Country in regard to our foreign policy, presented the first tangible point for the opposition which had been anticipated and could not have been avoided without an abandonment of cherished principles and which there was in truth no disposition to avoid.

Mr. Calhoun had, to use his own words, "taken a perfectly neutral position between Gen. Jackson and Mr. Adams," and there was not a little curiosity to learn what his course .would be towards the

---

[1] The National Gazette and Literary Register, edited by Robert Walsh.

Administration after these developments of its views. I called upon him, at his residence in Georgetown, at the commencement of the session and found him as decidedly hostile to the Panama Mission as I was myself. Although nothing to that effect was then said there was also an obvious concurrence in opinion between us that opposition to so prominent a measure of the Administration could not fail to lead to an ultimate union of efforts for its overthrow. This followed and from that period to the election of Gen. Jackson there was a general agreement in action between us, except in regard to the Tariff policy of which I have already spoken.

The Panama Mission was a very imposing measure and well calculated, on first impressions, to be very popular. An assemblage of the free states of a Hemisphere by their representatives in one Congress, to deliberate upon the most effectual means to protect their own sovereignties, to advance the great cause of free governments and, thro' their instrumentality, the dignity and the happiness of their people, in contrast with, and, in some degree, at least, in antagonism to the so-called "Holy Alliance" of the absolute Governments of another Hemisphere, assembled in another Congress to maintain and promote their despotic sway over the minds of men, was a scheme apparently well planned to captivate republican citizens. It seemed also well devised to soothe the public mind, to lessen the irritation unexpectedly produced by angry discussions during the recess growing out of the appointment of Mr. Clay and the doctrines broached in the Inaugural Address, and to bury the recollection of former discrepancies in the views of the leaders of the Administration by presenting them to the Country as the cordially united and enthusiastic advocates of a noble National undertaking. Indeed, no project could have been better adapted to produce the latter result, for attempts to dazzle the public mind by gala-day measures of that description formed the ruling passion of Mr. Clay's political life to which he sacrificed bright prospects that could doubtless have been easily realized by simpler means.

Yet it was not difficult to show that the scheme was ill-advised and could not fail if carried out to cause incalculable evils to the Country. The first question was in regard to the point at which the assault should be commenced—whether in the Senate, on the nomination of the Ministers, or in the House on the appropriation for their salaries. Our greatest strength, in regard to talent as well as comparative numbers being in the Senate, that body was selected as the principal field of contest. The nomination of Ministers was referred to the Committee on Foreign Affairs of which Nathaniel Macon was Chairman, who made an able report against the mission.[1] Our objection

---

[1] Executive Proceedings * * * on * * * the mission to the Congress at Panama, 1826, Jan. 16. S. Docs., 19th Cong., 1st sess., No. 68 p. 57.

being to the measure and not to the men nominated as Ministers, and therefore wholly unprecedented, I thought it a case in which the discussion should be public and introduced a resolution, which was adopted, to that effect " unless in the opinion of the President, the publication of documents, necessary to be referred to in debate, would be prejudicial to existing negotiations."

Mr. Adams, on receiving a copy of the resolution, refused to give the opinion respectfully asked by the Senate, not content with that, he, in his return message, said he would leave it to the Senate itself, (who were of course to a great extent ignorant of existing negotiations) to decide " the question of an unexampled departure from its own usages, and upon motives, of which, not being himself informed, he ° did not feel himself competent to decide." This refusal, and the unauthorized allusion to and virtual condemnation of our motives gave great offense to the Senate, and was the first act of discourtesy in a series of proceedings which produced unprecedented excitement and ill-blood as well in the Senate as in the Country. A retaliatory movement was proposed, but as the original resolution had been introduced by me, our friends conceded to me, in a great degree, the suggestion of any action to be adopted on our part. I was sensible of the importance of the proposed opportunity to repel the censure that was cast upon us for obstructing the passage of a measure represented by the Administration press to be eminently patriotic, but my anxiety to avoid anything that might be construed as a factious opposition was so strong as to induce me to prefer to waive it, which was accordingly done.

The discussions occupied several weeks and became earnest and sometimes violent. After unmistakable indications of effects produced by Governmental influence, the nominations were confirmed by a vote of 24 to 20,[1] and the measure received the sanction of both Houses of Congress, but it was undeniably thoroughly discredited with the Country by the opposition it had received. The Ministers went out but they found no Congress. Several of the Treaties among the South American States authorizing it were not ratified by them, nor were any other steps taken to carry the plan into effect.

This general abandonment of the grand enterprise by its *putative* fathers, together with suspicious signs in the correspondence, satisfied me that altho' it had been apparently organized in South Amer-

---

° MS. II, p. 95.

[1] With Van Buren voted Findlay of Pennsylvania, Chandler and Holmes of Maine, Woodbury of New Hampshire, Dickerson of New Jersey, and Kane of Illinois, making seven Northern and twelve Southern senators. Against Van Buren were eight senators from Slave States, Barton of Missouri, Bouligny and Johnston of Louisiana, Chambers of Alabama, Clayton and Van Dyke of Delaware, Richard M. Johnson of Kentucky and Smith of Maryland. It was an incipient but a true party division.—Shepard, Martin Van Buren, American Statesmen Series (Boston and New York, 1899), p. 131.

ica, the inspiration which suggested it was of Washington origin. Mr. Adams, in his next annual Message, sang a graceful requiem over the lost project, accompanied by exculpatory observations to which, as no danger of resurrection was apprehended, there was no reply.

A copy of a speech delivered by me on the subject will be found in——.[1]

---

[1] The pamphlet edition of Van Buren's speech, Washington City, Gales & Seaton, 1826, 41 pp. 8° is in the Van Buren Papers under date of March 14.

CHAPTER XVIII.

The proposition for the Mission to Panama was accompanied by a measure not less obnoxious to public feeling and alike indicative of great ignorance of the current of public sentiment on the part of the President and his Secretary of State, or a recklessness in encountering it in the prosecution of favorite schemes inconsistent with the character of prudent statesmen. That which we have just described was pressed upon the Country in open disregard of a familiar principle in our foreign policy, the observance of which had been coeval with our Government and which had acquired a permanent and favorable lodgment in the public mind. The measure now referred to was the concession to Great Britain by treaty stipulation of the Right of Search to prevent the prosecution of the slave trade under our flag, a pretension against which, when attempted to be put in practice for the purpose of recovering British seamen from our service, we had waged a war—the cause of which was yet fresh in the recollection of the People, as well as the irritations produced by it.

We opposed the treaty and defeated it by a decided·vote.[1] The condition of the Country in its foreign and domestic relations was so favorable at this time that with discreet men at the head of the Government, and ordinary prudence in the conduct of its affairs, there could not have been the slightest doubt of the success of the Administration, but unfortunately, as well for the Country as for themselves, neither Mr. Adams nor Mr. Clay were either discreet by nature or instilled by experience with a proper appreciation of the humble virtue of prudence in the direction of public business. Munificently endowed with genius and talents, their passion for brilliant effects, of which I have spoken as peculiar to Mr. Clay but which was common to both, was not crowned with a degree of success proportionate to the hazard of its indulgence. In the career of the military leader this is often otherwise, but in the administration of civil affairs statesmen of sober judgment and

---

[1] The Convention with Great Britain was finally disposed of by the Senate May 22, 1824. The votes on the various amendments are given in the Executive Journal of the Senate (Washington, 1828) V. 3, pp. 380–387. As ratified, by a vote of 29 to 13, the convention was well nigh worthless as a means of suppressing the American slave trade. For the final end of this negotiation see Clay's letter to Addington, Apr. 6, 1825, in American State Papers, Foreign 5, No. 414, p. 783.

prudence though possessed of less shining talents are generally the most prosperous.

Among other occurrences at the seat of Government during this stirring period the duel between Mr. Clay and Mr. John Randolph produced by a denunciation of the Administration on the floor of the Senate, by the latter, as a "coalition between the puritan and the blackleg" was one of the most exciting. In his "Thirty Years' View," Colonel Benton has given an account—clever and impartial—of this affair. The subject was frequently adverted to by Mr. Randolph during our rides together and the details recited in his peculiar way. He invariably admitted that laying out of view the place where the offensive words were spoken and its immunities, which he said he had waived as far as he could, Mr. Clay had incurred no blame in calling him to the field. On one occasion he told me that the latter had been six years in bringing his mind to that point, during which he had, on several occasions, furnished him ground for such a step, but as he had always given the offense in a way that left it optional with Mr. Clay to give the matter that direction or to let it pass, he had taken the latter course. Perhaps no man ever lived more qualified to do such a thing successfully than Randolph. He insisted that he at no time intended to take Mr. Clay's life and assigned as a reason his respect for Mrs. Clay and his unwillingness to make her unhappy, but he admitted that, after certain occurrences, he had determined to wound him in the leg—his failure to accomplish which design he attributed to an anxiety to avoid the *kneepan*, to hit which he regarded *as murder!*

Mr. Randolph's intemperate speeches during the whole of the Panama discussion attracted a large share of the public attention, and the Vice President was much censured by portions of the public press for omitting to call him to order. Randolph justified himself on the ground that a corrupt and tyranical administration could not be overthrown without violence, and quoted in his defence the text of scripture which says "the Kingdom of Heaven suffereth violence and the violent take it by force." Mr. Calhoun held that he did not possess the power to call a senator to order, as the rules conferred that power on the members of the body only—that he could not claim it by implication, and that as he was not placed over the body by their own choice or responsible to them, he ought not in so delicate a matter to act upon doubtful authority. He therefore, very properly called upon the Senate to express its opinion upon the subject, and to confer the power upon him by their rules if they wished him to exercise it and if they concurred with him in supposing that he did not already possess it. This led to an elaborate discussion of the question and of the true construction of the Constitution in regard to implied powers, in which I took part and delivered a speech which will be found in——.[1]

Mr. Randolph was in every way a most extraordinary man, and occupied wherever he went a large share of public attention. There was not a session of Congress during his —— years service as a member in which his sayings and doings did not contribute the principal staple of the political gossip at Washington. This was particularly the case at the commencement of Mr. Adams's administration, when he appeared for the first time in the Senate where his whole course was one of annoyance to his opponents and of not a little uneasiness to his friends. He spoke day in and day out, and sometimes for several successive days, upon matters and things in general having political and personal bearings but not always even directed to the business before the Senate—an abuse in which others have since been largely participant, but in which perhaps there has never been so great an offender. His speeches attracted great attention from the severity of his invectives, the piquancy of his sarcasms, the ° piercing intonation of his voice and his peculiarly expressive gesticulation. He could launch imputations by a look, a shake of his long figure, or a shrug of his shoulders, accompanied by a few otherwise commonplace words, which it would require in others a long harangue to express. These rare oratorical accomplishments were never suffered to grow rusty for want of use, and he kept us in constant apprehension that he would still further thin our ranks in the Senate, already somewhat weeded by Executive favours, by the character of the stimulus with which he was in the habit of urging the sluggish zeal of some of our brethren. He had for some time been desirous to take in hand the case of John Holmes, of Maine, whose party fidelity was doubted by his associates long before he quitted them, and Randolph at length found a more justifiable ground for his assault than he could have anticipated. Holmes had made a speech which Randolph thought bore upon its face satisfactory evidence of being designed to propitiate the Administration, and either in it, or in some collateral remarks, had spoken of the Vice President and himself as personal friends. Randolph, finding these remarks in the papers, called the attention of the Senate to the subject, denied the right of Mr. Holmes or any other person to define his personal relations in delicate and guarded terms but in a way entirely respectful to that Senator, and, as an excuse for not saying what he now said when the remark was made, explained that he had not heard it and presumed it must have been made whilst he was

---

[1] See Holland's Life of Van Buren (Hartford, 1836) p. 279 for a long extract of this speech and note to p. 184 " Substance of Mr. Van Buren's observations in the Senate."
° MS. II, p. 100.

out of the Senate. Holmes, thrown off his guard by the courteous manner in which Randolph had excused his omission to notice the circumstance on the spot, not only insisted that Randolph was in his seat, but that he heard the remarks to which he now took exception, and evinced a degree of pertinacity in doing so which amounted to rudeness. From the moment that Randolph understood such to be the drift of Holmes' remarks, his face assumed its sternest expression, and he sat stiffly in his chair with folded arms, manifestly tortured with suppressed rage. On Holmes' resuming his seat, he rose and recapitulated, with a self possession that surprised us, what had occurred—shewed the length he had gone to satisfy the Senator from Maine that he had no cause of complaint in the matter referred to and the persistence of that Senator in an attempt to impeach his veracity. Having done this in a cold and unimpassioned manner, his appearance and style suddenly changed, and he charged Holmes with a premeditated design to make a personal attack upon him as a peace offering to the Administration, and a prelude to his political apostacy, and proceeded in an assault the most severely personal that had perhaps ever been heard within that chamber and seeming at the moment to annihilate his antagonist.

Altho' of course there were repeated cries of " Order ! Order !" there was no specific and responsible call, and, if there had been, his words were so skillfully chosen and his peculiar gestures contributed so largely to the conveyance of the most offensive imputations, that a Senator calling him to order would have found the greatest difficulty in writing down, as the rule required, the disorderly words on which the motion could be founded. The Senate immediately adjourned under great excitement. Randolph came to me and insisted that I should go home and dine with him, and on our way to his lodgings I remonstrated with him on his course in breaking down our party strength, admitted that Holmes had given him a fair excuse for a reply of great severity, but not for an attack like that he had made which would unavoidably drive him from our ranks. " I deny that," he vehemently replied, " I have not driven him away. He was already a deserter in his heart; if you examine the body you will find that *the wound is in the back !*"

I could not at the time account for the respectful and mild character of his preliminary explanations to Holmes, as I knew the state of his feelings towards him, but was in the end satisfied that it was a part of his design to make sure of his victim by first putting him as far as possible in the wrong. This affair was the cause of an extraordinary scene in the Senate a few days afterwards.

Mr. Randolph's speeches became more and more annoying to the Administration and its friends, in and out of the Senate, and yet no one seemed willing to incur the responsibility of calling him to order. I inferred from circumstances a design on the part of the administration Senators to administer a corrective to Mr. Randolph by severally quitting their seats when he was speaking to an extent sufficient to leave the Senate without a quorum. This was practicable as the call of the House, usual in the other branch of Congress, was unknown in our body. Having engaged one day to dine with my friend Gen. Van Rensselaer at an hour earlier than the ordinary adjournment of the Senate, I gave Randolph notice in the morning of the necessity I should be under of leaving whilst he was speaking and of my desire to avoid setting such an example on account of my suspicion as to the game of our opponents. He promised to close his speech in season, but did not. Whey my hour arrived I held up my watch, and he pointed to the door. I left and the example was quickly followed by the members of the opposition; in a very short time the flag of the Senate was lowered and the body adjourned for want of a quorum. This unusual proceeding having been once adopted—was soon to a considerable extent, converted into a practice, to the great annoyance of Randolph whose vanity was wounded by an apparent indifference to his speeches which he had seldom experienced and was little able to brook. The circumstance sensibly increased the bitterness of his denunciations and finally led to that which caused the duel between himself and Mr. Clay whose impatient spirit could no longer endure the invectives which were incessantly hurled at him by Randolph.

He [Randolph] visited Virginia soon after and whilst there became satisfied that his chance for a reelection was far from favorable. This increased the acerbity of his temper, and he returned to Washington with a determination to leave it for England almost immediately. He sent a message to me, on his arrival, asking me to call upon him at his old quarters. Being engaged in the Senate, it was not in my power to do so before the adjournment, of which I informed him by a note, adding also that I should expect him to dine with me. When I reached his lodgings I entered what I supposed to be his bedroom, but which proved to be that of Mark Alexander, a member of the House from Virginia. I found Randolph booted and spurred, stretched at full length on his colleague's bed, and fast asleep, with his letters and papers scattered about him. I was so much interested in the appearance of his tall and gaunt figure, extending beyond the foot of the bed, and in observing the striking resemblance of his features to the Indian race, from which it was his pride to claim descent, that some moments elapsed before I could make up my mind to awaken him. When we reached my lodgings and found that the members of the Diplomatic Corps were expected guests, some of whom indeed had already arrived, he for a few moments insisted on returning, but, as I had foreseen, he was easily induced to abandon that idea, and I could not have afforded my company a greater treat than was furnished by his presence. He took the *parole* at once, and kept it till a late hour, talking upon a great variety of subjects with more than his usual ability and with the most entertaining raciness and originality. He began the meal with calling for toast-water, pleading that wine was too strong for him, but yielding to the excitement of conversation and the grateful consciousness of appreciative listeners he gradually advanced through wine and water to wine, brandy and water and, before he left, to clear brandy. After the company retired he sat with me 'till long after midnight describing the condition of things in Virginia, and his reasons for apprehending his defeat at the Senatorial election. Mr. Tyler, who had 'till that time always been in the Republican ranks, would, he said, be brought forward as a Candidate or supported° by his enemies and his explanation of the causes which would induce a sufficient number of Republican members to vote with them, brought into view the hostility which had at different periods of his life existed between himself and Jefferson, Madison, Monroe and others and of which he gave me graphic and very interesting accounts. Having engaged no lodgings, in consequence of a determination, as he declared, never again to "have any in that corrupt hole" (as he called Washington), I sent my servant out to find a bed for him and afterwards to conduct him to it.

On the following morning he appeared in the Senate, dressed with unusual care and apparently in excellent spirits, having ordered his carriage to be sent to the Capitol, with his luggage, at noon, to convey him to Baltimore. Mr. Calhoun had, at his instance, appointed him a member of the Committee on Rules and his object, in coming to the Senate, was to report one or two very proper amendments to the standing rules of the body.

Mr. Holmes had manifested more sensibility in regard to Randolph's attack upon him that was supposed to belong to his nature, and his inflamed appearance after it, in the Senate excited the apprehensions of his friends in regard to his habits. His excitement on the morning referred to was greater than usual and he carried a huge cane which indicated that he meditated or expected a personal attack. He took the floor immediately after Randolph resumed his seat and read from a paper a series of amendments of the Rules which he proposed. These with scarcely an exception referred to acts with which Randolph had been charged and which it was proposed thereafter to prohibit. Among them was one declaring it a

violation of order in a Senator to make personal references to gentlemen who had been introduced on the floor of the Senate by other
Senators. Mr. Russell,[1] of Boston, Editor of the *Columbian Centi-
nel*, a newspaper which had made a reckless opposition to the War
of 1812, had been so introduced during the session, and Randolph
had attracted the attention of the body to him by a general and
seemingly not personal reference to a notorious feature in his political career; it was at that occurrence that the proposed amendment
was aimed.

Immediately after Holmes finished the reading of his propositions,
Randolph asked Mr. Tazewell, his colleague, to take the clerk's seat,
and to write, as he dictated, a series of amendments to them "in the
form of instructions to the Committee,"—designed as answers to
them by successive recriminations. Mr. Tazewell, one of the best
tempered men I ever knew, complied, and when the proposition
which I have particularized was reached, under the impression that
Russell had been introduced by Holmes, Randolph dictated the declaration, as an amendment, that the "personal reference" which it
was now designed to stigmatize as disorderly was no more than a
suitable reproof of the Senator who was so wanting in a sense of
what was due to the dignity of the Senate and to his own character
as to introduce such a man within the Bar!

At this point the affair received an unexpected complication.
Senator Lloyd of Massachusetts, a man of undoubted courage, who
felt no insurmountable scruples upon the subject of private combat, and between whom and Randolph there had already occurred
some *newspaper* sparring, sprang to his feet the moment the offensive words were uttered, announced himself as the Senator who
had introduced Russell, repelled with great vehemence every assault upon that gentleman, whom he pronounced to be quite equal
in respectability to Randolph himself, and indignantly shaking his
closed hand at the latter, declared his readiness to give him satisfaction there or elsewhere! Randolph, entirely taken by surprise,
sought an opportunity to explain, and disclaimed all hostile feelings
towards Lloyd; but the latter could neither be appeased or silenced
and continued his minatory gestures and denunciations with undiminished vehemence. In this condition of things Mr. King, of
Alabama, called both the Senators to order, and Mr. Calhoun requested him to reduce the objectionable words to writing, as required by the Rules. Sensible of the difficulty of committing to
paper expressions used in such a squabble, which was yet going
on, Mr. King declined to do so, and in the excitement of the moment
said abruptly, that he would not! Mr. Calhoun, anxious from

---

[1] Benjamin Russell.

what had passed, to do his whole duty when a case occurred within the Rules, rose from his seat and, pale with agitation, said "The Chair *orders* the Senator from Alabama to reduce the words to writing." The Senate at this moment presented a striking *tableau*—Calhoun, King, Lloyd and Randolph on their feet, intensely excited, and every Senator present inclining from political and personal sympathy to take sides in the fray—when the last moved deliberately from his place, which was on the extreme outer range of seats, and passed in front of the Chair to the door, exclaiming as he walked along, "I will have no more of this! I am off for England! Good bye, Tazewell! Good bye, Van Buren! They are all against me! They are all against me Tazewell, in Virginia too!"—and still uttering these words the doors of the Senate closed behind him.

The Vice President and Messrs. Lloyd and King resumed their seats: Mr. Tazewell returned to his place leaving his unfinished papers on the Clerk's desk and for a little while nothing was said or done. A sense of relief from the excitement in which Randolph lived and moved and had his being, as his native element, prevailed, and the Senate after a pause took up the order of the day without, either then or at any future time, giving further attention to the proposed amendments.[a]

---

[a] This account of these proceedings is according to my best recollection of them, which is unusually fresh, as the subject is one to which my attention has been frequently directed, and of which I have often spoken. Mr. Tazewell's officiating as Secretary is entirely left out in the published proceedings, a point in which I know I cannot be mistaken, and a form given to the whole proceedings in some respects more consistent with the dignity of the body, about which the gentlemen charged with the publication of the details were always, much to their credit, very solicitous. Some allowance is certainly due to that consideration, in judging of the partial, and not very important, differences between their account and mine, which I cannot but think conveys with substantial accuracy their true character.

CHAPTER XIX.

An act for the relief of the officers of the Army of the Revolution in relation to their half-pay became a law about this time, and upon its passage I delivered the speech which will be found in——[1] Its merits will doubtless be found to fall below the reputation it acquired, yet I derived as much satisfaction from the effect it was believed to have produced as from anything in my legislative experience. The Bill had been long under discussion, and the Senate had adjourned on the previous day on my motion, which constituted a notice according to usage that it was my intention to address the Senate upon the subject. Before the hour arrived for taking up the order of the day my friends pressed me not to speak as the Senate had been sufficiently canvassed to make the defeat of the Bill certain. Louis McLane of Delaware, a member of the Senate, and a son of one of the officers for whose relief it was the object of the measure to provide, backed this advice so earnestly that I was induced to yield to it. When the Bill was announced the Vice President turned his eyes towards my seat and seeing no intention on my part, or on that of any other Senator to speak, rose and stated that the question would be on final passage and was in the act of taking the sense of the Senate upon it when two ladies, friends of mine, who had come to the Senate to hear me, shook their fans at me in token of their disappointment and I rose from my seat intending to go to them with an apology. The Vice President assuming that I rose to speak announced "the Senator for New York" and, suddenly changing my mind, I proceeded to address the Senate, at length, in favor of the Bill.

When I had concluded, Gov. Branch,[2] of North Carolina, an impulsive but always honest man, who had been violently opposed to the proposed° measure, moved to adjourn the question saying that views of the subject had been presented which were new and upon which he desired an apportunity to reflect. His colleague, the venerable Macon, scouted the idea of an adjournment, said that a good speech had undoubtedly been made, but that lawyers knew how to make good speeches on either side of any question, and hoped that the Senate would without further debate proceed to the vote and reject the Bill.

---

[1] Gales and Seaton's Register of Debates, under date of Jan. 28, 1828, vol. 4, pt. 1, 167–182.
[2] John Branch.
° MS. II, p. 110.

Gov. Branch replied with feeling that his course in regard to it was well known, that he had several times spoken against it, but that he had no other feeling in the matter than a desire to do right and that unless the views which had now been taken of the subject were satisfactorily refuted, he would, if driven to the vote, support the Bill. This declaration produced an adjournment. It was soon discovered that others had also given way and a proposition was submitted to us the next morning that if we would accept certain amendments, of a character not very objectionable, a sufficient number would change their votes to secure a majority. We consented and the Bill became a law [1]—gladdening the hearts of many yet surviving soldiers of the Revolution and of the descendants of their departed brothers-in-arms, by the appropriation of large sums of money in satisfaction of their just claims.

Imprisonment for debt, the rigour of which had been greatly relaxed by state laws, being still in force against debtors to the United States, attracted a considerable portion of the attention of the Congress. My own efforts for its abolition commenced in the State Legislature at an early period of my connection with that body and were continued in the Senate of the United States in conjunction with Col. Richard M. Johnson, whose truly philanthropic feelings made him an enthusiast in the cause.

My plan from the beginning was:

1st To provide for the most searching inquiries into the property of the debtor, however invested, and to arm the creditor with all necessary facilities to secure the application of it to the payment of his debts; and

2d To punish fraudulent concealments as crimes, by confinement, upon executions, to the walls of the prison.

Those facilities being secured to the creditor, I regarded every other *lien* on the body of his debtor as alike inhuman and immoral, and advocated a repeal of the law by which it was authorized. The subsequent adoption of these views of the subject and the extent to which a practice, that had become, by inflicting punishment upon misfortune, the opprobrium of the age, has accordingly been abrogated, is highly honorable to the country. Although a professional man, not wanting in *esprit du corps*, I yet must admit that this great reform is perhaps indebted for its success less to our lawyers and merchants than to almost any other class. I generally found them the most obdurate and inflexible in their adherence to the old system arising rather from the force of habit than from less humane or less liberal dispositions. The merchant had been educated to look upon the security founded on the fear of imprison-

---

[1] Approved Feb. 12, 1828.

ment as a vital element in a well regulated credit system, and the lawyer had been blinded to the immorality of such *liens* by the long and frequent enforcement of them under the sanction and with the cooperation of the Courts. But all such ideas and arguments have been exploded by the steady progress of liberal opinions, and there are none now who would more cordially resist the restoration of imprisonment for debt, in the absence of fraud, than those classes. So certain and so generous indeed is now the indulgence of the American Merchant to his unfortunate debtor as to place him in that respect in a more creditable position than is occupied by his mercantile cotemporaries in any part of the world.

The subject of a Bankrupt Law was also seriously agitated in the Senate whilst I was a member of that body. The abuses practised under the law of 1800 not only led to its speedy repeal but attracted a degree of odium to the system itself which prevented its reenactment until 184–; a spasmodic effort was then made to close up the appalling chasm which had been made in the business relations of the Country through the instrumentality of a Bankrupt law, which, so soon as it had effected a sort of general jail delivery, was, like its predecessor, sent to an early and ignominious grave.

During that long interval there had been several unsuccessful attempts to revive the system. Mr. Hayne,[1] of South Carolina, who had moved in the matter previously, introduced, upon leave, at the commencement of the session of 1827 "A Bill, to establish a uniform system of Bankruptcy throughout the United States." It contained the usual provisions applicable to merchants and traders, and also a section (the 93d) extending to all classes, whether traders or not, upon the principle of an Insolvent law, and was referred to a select committee composed of Messrs. Hayne, Berrien, Silsbee, Smith of Maryland, Johnson of Kentucky, Sandford[2] and myself.

The proceedings of this Committee and the action of the Senate upon them have been kept fresh in my recollection by the striking exhibitions they afforded of the working of that spirit of rivalry so common to political life and so influential in the business of legislation. The leading and most active friends of the proposed Bill were Col. Hayne, the Chairman of the Committee, and Judge Berrien,[3] of Georgia. They were co-adjutors in politics and among the foremost in organising and forwarding the Party then in course of development which had for its objects the overthrow of the existing Administration and the election of Gen. Jackson. Col. Hayne possessed a lively imagination and an intelligent and dis-

---

[1] Robert Y. Hayne.

[2] Nathaniel Silsbee of Massachusetts; Samuel Smith, Richard M. Johnson, and Nathan Sandford, of New York.

[3] John Macpherson Berrien.

criminating mind. Judge Berrien was not less highly favored in both respects, and had besides, acquired a greater wariness in debate by a long and more busy professional life. They were both ambitious and looked forward, as they had a right to do, to high rank in the party of which they were members.

When called upon in the Commitee for my opinion of the Bill, I declared myself ready to vote for a Bankrupt law proper, applicable to merchants and traders, but opposed to the ninety-third section as unauthorized by the Constitution and in every respect inexpedient. I was prepared to assign the reasons which had brought my mind to those conclusions but was prevented from doing so by finding no disposition such as I had anticipated, on the part of the leading supporters of the measure in its original shape, to make me a convert to their opinions. The sense of the Committee was at once taken and a majority declared in favor of the whole Bill. Differences of opinion in regard to the disputed section were regarded with indulgence as results which had been expected, and dissentients were referred to the Senate Chamber for the explanation and vindication of their views.

I was certainly somewhat piqued at this course but having witnessed similar proceedings among political friends when acting upon subjects supposed to be of great interest in the public mind I determined to be no further influenced by it than to give the Bill a more thorough examination after stating more distinctly to the committee my intention to ° oppose it if the objectionable clause was retained. I went to the Senate intending to confine myself to a simple and brief statement of the ground I occupied, notwithstanding that I had, as I believed, made myself master of the subject and notwithstanding the feelings produced by my construction of the course pursued in the committee. I came to this conclusion because my support even of the constitutional parts of the Bill was little more than an acquiescence in the opinions and wishes of my friends—my own impressions being then as they have been since that the frauds inseparable from the execution of a national bankrupt system are likely to outweigh its advantages and I could therefore feel no great solicitude for its passage. Besides I feared that I could not present the encroachment of the ninety-third section upon a state sovereignty in its details and in the proportions which the subject allowed without mortifying the pride of my southern friends by holding them up to their constituents as unfaithful to a principle which was the corner stone of our Party and particularly so regarded in the states they represented.

° MS. II, p. 115.

A motion was made by Gov. Branch to strike out the 93d section, and upon this and other motions a debate ensued which occupied the Senate for more than a week. When the question was about to be taken I made the brief statement I contemplated, and which appears in the Congressional Debates. The motion failed, and the section was retained by a vote which indicated the passage of the whole Bill, but a motion to reconsider was made the next morning by Senator Barton of Missouri, who had upon more reflection changed his opinion and was now against the section. On this motion the debate was renewed embracing the whole subject and in the course of it the principles I had briefly advanced were reviewed to an extent that made it my duty to sustain them. I thereupon delivered a speech of considerable length which was not published for the reasons assigned by Gales & Seaton in their volume of the debates of that session, but which I have always regarded as the most successful of my senatorial efforts.[1] Whatever may have been its merits, or its lack of them, there was no difference of opinion as to its effects upon the disposition of the question. It placed the provisions of the ninety-third section in lights that had not before occurred to many of those who sustained it and made them anxious to get rid of it without an immediate change of votes. They became in consequence disaffected to the Bill, and, although the vote on the section was substantially the same as before, the whole Bill was rejected by a vote of 25 to 15. On motion of Col. Hayne it was recommitted to the select Committee with instructions to strike out the obnoxious section, and in that form reported to the Senate where protracted efforts were made for its passage, but without success.

Upon the conclusion of my speech the Senate adjourned and before I had left my seat Messrs. Hayne and Berrien approached me with vehement complaints of the course things had taken and of my agency in producing it. I proposed to them to join me in the carriage and to talk the matter over on our way to our lodgings. Our conversation was of that eager and earnest character usual to Southern men when highly excited. Judge Berrien being asked to specify the ground of his complaint said that I had taken them by surprise—not having given them reason to expect that I would oppose the ninety-third section in debate altho' I had disapproved of it. Col. Hayne, however, without waiting for my reply, ex-

---

[1] Van Buren spoke on the bill on Jan. 23, 25, 26, and 27 and again on Feb. 1, 1827. The surviving portions of these speeches are in Gales and Seaton's Register of Debates, vol. 3, 82, 104, 119, 121, 160 and 226. The principal speech was delivered on Jan. 27 and under that date Gales and Seaton (3, 160) explain that this and Van Buren's preceding speeches are not reported because their reports, forwarded to Van Buren for revision, were mislaid by him. Van Buren's auto-notes for his speech are in the Van Buren Papers under date of Jan. 23, 1827.

claimed that he felt bound to admit on the contrary that I had given them distinct notice that I would make active opposition to the Bill if that section was retained:—" But what I complained of " said he, " is that Mr. Van Buren did not state his objections, which now appear to have been of so grave a character, that he did not make an effort to convince us of their importance and give us such information upon the subject that we might have been prepared either to admit their weight or to rebut them."

I at once admitted that this complaint would have been well founded had not circumstances occurred which excused me from doing what he suggested, and informed them that I attended the Committee intending to give them a candid account of the [my] reasons but their attitude -compelled me to think that they did not desire me to do it. We could not agree entirely as to all the facts on which my opinion was founded, but my statement evidently modified their complaints. In the subsequent discussions Col. Hayne made no further attempt to sustain the ninety-third section nor did Judge Berrien make material reference to it otherwise than to repel as unfounded the charge he attributed to me of a want of proper respect on his part for state rights.

Although the Judge and myself were afterwards members of Gen. Jackson's Cabinet and our personal relations were always respectful they were never confidential nor particularly cordial. From my first acquaintance with him I felt that the cultivation and maintenance of such an intercourse with him would be impracticable, a sentiment which surprised me because it was inconsistent with the general current of my disposition and indeed then for the first time entertained. I refer to the fact only on account of its singularity and not in a spirit of complaint, as the fault, if any existed, may as likely have been with myself as with him.

Col. Hayne I always regarded as a fair and generous hearted man. His course towards me on the question of my nomination as Minister to England, unjust as it was, did not change this opinion. I found no difficulty in attributing it to other influences than the unbiased dictates of his own heart. He was an improving man and if his life had been spared would doubtless have risen to still higher distinction, at least in his own state. He possessed a tolerably good opinion of his own capacity, but whatever may have been the degree of this estimate of himself it was not sufficient to blind his eyes to what was passing about him. The Senate was at that time composed of much older men that at present, who were at least not less able. One consequence of their long experience in public life was that they spoke less for effect and sometimes discussed questions of considerable importance with seeming carelessness and comparative feebleness. Newly appointed Senators often spent portions of the session previous to the 4th of March on which they were entitled to take their seats at Washington and much of the time in the Senate Chamber preparatory to becoming actors themselves, and I seldom failed to discover in the faces of the younger men of this class a disappointment in the character and proceedings of the body to which they had been chosen; a feeling which frequently inspired them with a degree of confidence and self-sufficiency on their first appearance which the Senate always understood and seldom omitted to correct in a way alike efficacious and decorous. Col. Hayne was a marked subject of this feeling as he was also of the appliances designed to remove it. He entered at once into the debates and without the slightest embarrassment spoke fluently, intelligibly, sometimes forcibly but often without the slightest effect. Whilst he was himself treated with proper respect, motions, arguments and opinions which he deemed very conclusive, were sometimes disposed of in a summary and unceremonious way not [at] all consistent with the weight to ° which he deemed them entitled. In short, altho' no one appeared to be specially disposed to thwart him there was an invisible but continual filling of his pockets with lead by which his career was seriously obstructed. His disappointment was always seen in his expressive countenance and once to my knowledge spoken out. No one informed him of the cause, but he did not fail to discover it himself, or to take promptly the steps to remedy the evil. From originating propositions himself he became obviously desirous to follow the lead of others—instead of the usual confident and *ex-cathedra* way of advancing his opinions they were now expressed with diffidence in moderate terms with well conceived expressions of deference to those of the elder and more experienced members of the Senate. The change was observed and appreciated. He had not only thereafter no more reason than any other member of the Senate to complain of its want of consideration for what he said or did, but he contracted a habit of acting and speaking in the body which was of great value to him there and would have been equally useful to him in any after stage of public life.

The revulsion in trade and business of every description in 1837 produced a clamor for a revival of the Bankrupt system from large portions of the people who had ruined themselves by their own improvidence. Among the many questions put to me by my opponents in the canvass of 1840—numerous enough to fill a volume— and answered notwithstanding the silence in which by their advice their own candidate was shrouded, there were several calling for my opinion upon that subject. I took in my replies the same

---

° MS. II, p. 120.

ground that I occupied on the occasion of which I have been speaking and in so doing was not unaware of the costly sacrifice I made of votes which I would otherwise have received.

The subject of the Judicial system of the United States and its improvement was also elaborately discussed at this session. The increase of the number of states and the inability of the Judges to do equal justice to all made some alteration in the existing organization of the courts a matter of high necessity. Several plans were considered one of which I will notice here because I think it involves a principle of great importance and because after repeated ineffectual efforts for its establishment it seems yet to have supporters in and out of Congress and will in all probability be again proposed. This arrangement separates the Justices of the Supreme Court from the performance of circuit duties and devolves them upon circuit Judges, to be appointed for that purpose, or upon the district Judges.

Although the attempt to require by law that the Judges of the Supreme Court in the event of the establishment of such a system, should reside at the seat of Government has not to my knowledge been actually made yet its propriety has been sustained in Congressional discussions and it is moreover generally conceded that that consequence would naturally follow without legal requirement. The struggle for the accomplishment of this object, seldom avowed but always meant, may be traced through our legislative history for more than half a century. The Act of 1789, first organizing the Judicial system of the United States, authorized the Judges to make temporary allotments of the Circuits among themselves, but made no provision in respect to their places of residence. So the law remained until the celebrated Act of 1801, passed at the close of the administration of the elder Adams, which provided for an entire reorganization of the system. It converted the Supreme Court into a Court of Appeals, relieved its Judges from Circuit duties and directed the appointment of nineteen Circuit Judges for their performance.

The appointment of so large a number of officers for life by an administration from which the People had already withdrawn their confidence, and the extension of the Judiciary so far beyond the wants of the public service, aided by the extraordinary excitement of the period, drew down upon that Act and its authors the greatest public odium. The incoming administration of Mr. Jefferson procured the repeal of the law, the abolition of the offices of the new Judges, and the substantial reestablishment of the old system. The talents of the federal party then most conspicuous, were employed in brilliant but vain efforts to resist these measures. Their enactment was denounced as a violation of the Constitution and was held up to the People, in the forum and in the press, as the first fruits of victorious jacobinism. But these exertions were unavailing. The system then in substance restored has ever since prevailed and still exists because it is the best of which the subject is susceptible.

But one material alteration of the former system was made, and that was upon the point to which I have referred.

Mr. Jefferson and his associates in the Government saw, as they believed, in the bold measure of their retiring opponents the extent to which the latter counted upon the Judicial power as a political engine, and they saw in the Judiciary the only portion of our political system that was virtually irresponsible to the People. They knew that the possessors of such a power must in the sequel by the workings of the human heart and the irresistible law of human nature be hostile to the principles upon which the Government should be conducted and by which its Republican spirit could be alone upheld. Although the law they were about to repeal did not require the Judges to reside at the seat of Government, they could not doubt that such would be the effect and was probably the design of its provisions, of which they foresaw the evil political consequences, and they applied the only remedy within their reach in providing by law that the Judges should reside within their respective circuits. The only exception of this rule was in relation to the state of Virginia. That state had two judges on the Bench, Chief Justice Marshall and Justice Washington. In deference to the Father of his Country the case of Judge Washington was excepted from the otherwise general provision, and he was not withdrawn from Mount Vernon. Seven years afterwards when the appointment of an additional Judge became necessary for Ohio the same provision was adopted and has been preserved in every subsequent law by which the system had been extended to meet the growing exigencies of the service.

But it has not been preserved without a struggle. On the occasion of the proposed appointment of three new Judges, during the administration of the younger Adams, the adoption of a clause compelling them to reside in their respective circuits was one of two questions upon which the Houses of Congress differed and through their non-concurrence in which the Bill was lost. The proposition of the House of Representatives was reported and sustained by Mr. Webster, and that of the Senate by myself. Portions of my observations at the time upon the subject will be found in ――――.[1]

It will be perceived by the remarks here referred to that I have subsequently changed my opinion in regard to the proper tenure of

---

[1] Van Buren's entire speech, which was delivered Apr. 7, 1826, is in Gales and Seaton's Register of Debates, vol. 2, pt. 1, 410–423.

Judicial officers. Some of the reasons for this change are elsewhere stated. It was founded on observation and reflection and without prejudice. The tide of public opinion on the subjects of the jurisdiction of the Federal courts and the term for which their Judges should hold their offices ° has had its ebbs and floods, and it is my firm belief that the time is not far distant when these questions will be more seriously agitated.

The future fortunes of Mr. Clay became dependent in a very great degree upon the success of Mr. Adams. This consideration added to his views of the public interest, enlisted all his faculties in the struggle. The contest between Mr. Adams and Gen. Jackson, who was with great unanimity selected as the republican candidate, was an arduous one, but was not, after the lapse of a year, considered of doubtful result on our side. The common rally of the old Republicans in favor of the General caused many Federalists, who had supported him in the last trial, to leave him now, and with the exception of a few prominent men in different states the masses of that party went cordially for Mr. Adams. But a zealous union between that portion of the republican party who, adhering to its usages, had shown themselves willing to sacrifice personal preferences to its harmony, the numerous supporters of Gen. Jackson in the preceding election who constituted the majority in several of the states, and the friends of Mr. Calhoun, who controlled South Carolina and were formidable in many other states, encouraged by the tried popularity of their candidate, and strengthened by the mismanagement of the administration was too powerful to be resisted, and Jackson and Calhoun were elected to the offices of President and Vice President by large majorities.

The same fall my friends called on me to stand as their candidate for Governor of New York with a degree of unanimity and earnestness that did not admit of a refusal, and I was elected by a plurality of more than 30,000 over my quondam friend Smith Thompson, who was run for the office without resigning his seat on the bench of the Supreme Court. The anti-masonic excitement, which is too well understood to require explanation, made its first political demonstration at this election. The criminal transactions [1] which produced it were perpetrated in the midst of a district of country in the Western part of the state which since the War of 1812 had been strongly on the republican side in party politics, and owing to this circumstance and to the fact that dislike of secret societies had always formed a more marked feature of our creed, the sincere converts to the new party were principally drawn from our ranks. The votes given for Mr. Southwick, the anti-

---

° MS. II, p. 125.
[1] The abduction and probable murder of William Morgan in the fall of 1826.

masonic candidate for Governor, exceeding in number the majority by which I was elected over Judge Thompson, were almost exclusively given in this region and at least two-thirds of them taken from our side.

I entered upon the duties of the office of Governor early in January, and sent a Message to the Legislature which convened at the same time. I received soon after a letter from John Randolph communicating his own and Nathaniel Macon's congratulations upon the character of that paper. Few men were better instructed in the principles of the republican party than Mr. Randolph and there was not one on whose good opinion I placed a higher value than on that of the venerable Macon.

I held the office of Governor only ——[1] days and during that short period succeeded in obtaining the action of the Legislature on three subjects in which I felt great interest. These consisted of adequate measures, *first*, to protect the public and more particularly the laboring classes, who were most concerned in a sound currency because they were the most dependent upon it and the least able to detect what was otherwise, from losses through bank failure; *second*, to prevent as far as possible the use of money at the elections, and *third* to abolish a particular monopoly[2] and thereby to relieve a valuable portion of the business of the community from unnecessary and therefore injurious interference on the part of Government.

Of my consistent opposition to the multiplication of banks and my readiness to suppress and punish the frauds they have committed on the public I have before spoken. I think in these respects the record will not produce the evidence of any man having gone beyond me, be the merit great or small. Thoroughly satisfied of the hopelessness of the task of putting a stop to the improper increase of banks I turned my attention to the consideration of the most effective measures to protect the most helpless against losses by their failures. Joshua Forman, of Onondaga county, a plain but practical and far-seeing man, apprised of my general views in the matter, submitted for my consideration a plan for the accomplishment of my object of which I thought favorably and which contained in a rough state many of the features of the Safety Fund System which was finally adopted.[3] I opened communications with those whom I regarded as the most competent and trustworthy bankers of New York and Albany and submitted to them the project of Mr. Forman with my own views of the subject, and after full discussion we

---

[1] From Jan. 1, 1829, to Mar. 12, 43 days.
[2] The bank monopoly, created by the practice of the State accepting a money bonus for a bank charter.
[3] Forman's letter dated Jan. 24, 1829, is in the Van Buren Papers.

settled upon the plan ultimately submitted to and adopted by the Legislature. Having an abiding faith in the wisdom and efficacy of the system, if honestly administered, I have requested my friend, Major Flagg,[1] who as Comptroller of the State had much to do with its administration, and in whose statements all who knew him will confide, to give me a brief statement of its workings throughout. His reply will be found——

The law which I assisted in framing to restrain the use of money in elections is still, I believe, on the statute books, and no one can doubt its sufficiency if the provisions were fairly executed. I exerted myself to the uttermost before I left Albany and afterwards from Washington, by letters to induce my political friends to take a strong stand in its support at the first election after its passage urging upon them considerations founded on the unprincipled character of the practices it was intended to suppress, the special obligation upon them to abstain from and resist such practices as claiming a purer political faith than their opponents and finally the inferior motive of expediency. I assured them that experience had satisfactorily established the fact that as to the two great parties which divided the country the spontaneous feelings of a large majority of the People were on our side; that whenever we were defeated the result could generally be traced to specific and extraneous causes; that with this truth before our eyes nothing could be more unwise in us than to tolerate practices which exerted an influence upon the elections in utter disregard of the conduct or principles of the respective parties or of the unbiased inclinations of the People; that in the use of money the struggle was altogether unequal—the banks, incorporated companies of all descriptions and the monied interest being generally against them and able to raise more dollars than they could cents and that whilst they paid out their driblets their adversaries, emboldened by their participation, would carry all before them by the lavish expenditure of thousands.

I urged them in view of these and other similar considerations to forbear the use of money themselves, to appoint at their town meetings a committee whose duty it should be to attend the polls and to institute prosecution in every case where they had reason to believe that the law had been violated. But my efforts were unavailing. Not a single committee was appointed or any efforts to my knowledge made to carry the law into effect. It has stood[o] as a dead letter on the statute book ever since. Excuses were given by some of my friends that its provisions were too stringent and that they could not carry an election without violating some of

[1] Azariah Cutting Flagg. His statement is missing from the Van Buren Papers.
[o] MS. II, p. 130.

them. Partisans have since waded through seas of corruption in the profligate use of money in elections—neither side has been free of offense although nine tenths of the effects produced have without doubt enured to the benefit of our opponents.

I have ever advocated the abolition of patronage that was not acquired for the despatch of public business and limiting the interference of the Government in the business concerns of the People to cases of actual necessity, and [have been] an enemy to monopoly in any form. Our state being eminently commercial a large and very valuable portion of its trade was carried on through the medium of sales by auction. The exclusive right of making such sales had, from the commencement of the Government, been conferred on officers called auctioneers, appointed and commissioned like the other officers of the Government. Appointments of this nature were like others usually given by both parties to their political supporters, but as meritorious politicians are neither necessarily or even usually good men of business or possessed of the means required to carry on business to advantage, they fell into the habit of transferring their official rights to those who were more fortunate in those respects for a share of the profits. A species of official brokerage was thus kept on foot and sanctioned from the necessity of the case discreditable to the administration of public affairs.

Looking upon the creation of these offices as an extension of patronage by Government to be a case where it was neither necessary nor advantageous, and upon the exclusive privileges attached to them as an injurious monopoly, and satisfied that the business would be better attended to when left to those who had no other claims to be employed than those which arose from established character and proved capacity I recommended to the Legislature to abolish the offices and to throw the business open to public competition. This was promptly done, and the results have satisfactorily vindicated the wisdom of the policy.

CHAPTER XX.

° I received a letter from Gen. Jackson, soon after his arrival at Washington, offering me the place of Secretary of State of the United States [1]—a wholly unsolicited step. I had expressed no desire to receive that or any other appointment at his hands, either to him or to any other person and I have every reason to believe that no advances to that end were ever made on the part of my personal friends. He said in a published letter: " I called him [Mr. V. B.] to the Department of State influenced by the general wish and expectation of the republican party throughout the Union." This position, like every other office or nomination save one, bestowed upon me in the course of my long public life, came to me without interference on my part, direct or indirect, and in the execution of the well understood wish of the great majority of the political party of which I was a member. My election to the New York State Senate, the first elective office I ever held, was the exception referred to. The circumstances under which I then felt myself constrained to interfere personally in support of a nomination, which I not only did not wish but stood ready to decline, have been unreservedly stated in an earlier part of this work. With that single exception my observance of that abstinence from personal efforts to acquire political advancement, which was once inexorably demanded by the habits and feelings of Northern people, has been uniform. On the most interesting occasion of all—when my acts and motives were most unsparingly assailed—that of my acceptance of the Presidential nomination, I flung before my opponents, including a large number whom I had been constrained, by views of public duty, to make such, altho' previously close and confidential friends, a challenge upon this theme, to which it will be admitted no one would have ventured to resort, at such a time, who was not well assured of his invulnerable position.

My second nomination for the State Senate was made with perfect unanimity. The opposition made to my appointment as Attorney General, under the State Government, in 1815, was an individual effort by Judge Spencer, whose influence in such matters had before been irresistible, to punish me for refusing to sustain his views in relation to the choice of U. S. Senator, by defeating an appointment against which there was not, until that attempt, a known dissentient in the party to which we both belonged; an appointment by the way, of which he was, at an earlier period,

---

° MS. III, p. 1.
[1] This letter, Feb. 15, 1829, is in the Van Buren Papers.

the first to suggest the fitness and of which he was an advocate until his favor was changed into hostility in the way I have stated. The principal features of that affair have been described already and I will only add here the Gov. Tompkins delayed his casting vote, at the Council, between Judge Woodworth and myself—giving to it a quasi-public character by announcing it at the Capitol—and declared in giving it that he decided the question in my favor because he believed me to be competent to discharge the duties of the office and because he knew that my appointment was confidently expected by the party by which he had himself been elected. To this it may with truth be added that there was at the moment some coolness between the Governor and myself growing out of his appointments in my county, and 'that altho' the question upon the tie vote of the Council was pending before him some days, he was not approached upon the subject either by myself or by any of my friends, to my knowledge or belief. Having been removed from the office of Attorney General under circumstances already noticed I was, upon the return of my political friends to power, appointed U. S. Senator, without disagreement among them. After the expiration of six years, my re-nomination in caucas was made with great unanimity and received no opposition in the Legislature save from my political opponents. My nomination for the office of Governor was also made without opposition, and against my wishes, by a State Convention. Of my appointment as Secretary of State I have just spoken, and to that of Minister to England there was no dissent, save by the antagonists of my party. I was made a candidate for the office of Vice-President of the United States in pursuance of the spontaneous and united demand of the democracy of the Nation; a complimentary vote was given in Convention to two other gentlemen by the delegates of their respective States, who were, in point of fact, as friendly to my selection as were those who advocated it from the first, but the nomination was forthwith made unanimous in form as it was in the wishes of the mass of the democratic party.

I received my nomination as the democratic candidate for the office of President of the United States from the National Democratic Convention of 1835* and again, after a four years incumbency,

---

* At the *election,* following this nomination, I was deprived of the votes of the States of Tennessee, Georgia and even of that of the thoroghly democratic State of Alabama, by a combination between the friends of Judge White, of Tennessee, and of Mr. Calhoun with the undivided opposition to President Jackson's administration in those States. The Judge had not been a candidate before the convention. He was naturally honest, alhto' open to prejudices, and more self-willed by far than General Jackson himself. When Major Eaton quitted the War Department I advised the President to offer the place to Judge White, and, as his own family had left him, in consequence of the Eaton *imbroglio,* I was particularly desirous that he should invite the Judge also, who was then a widower, to reside with him, with which he complied. Knowing the Judge only as the active and open friend of Gen. Jackson, I was not a little struck by the care and

from a similar convention in 1840, by the votes of every member of those bodies. Defeated in 1840, thro' well understood causes, the great majority of the democratic masses rallied for the restoration

circumspection which the latter evinced in every step he took in the matter, but when Judge White declined and I became better acquainted with the personal feeling of both parties, I had no difficulty in understanding what before appeared inexplicable. I had no special claims upon the Judge, but it cost him a great effort to separate from the General, who admonished him, as well as his wife (after his second marriage), in his usual unreserved and emphatic way, of the consequences of the step he was about to take. But Mr. Bell, of Tennessee, chosen Speaker of the House over Mr. Polk, by the votes of the opposition and of democratic members disaffected towards the Jackson administration, and Mr. Webster, by his attentions particularly to a member of the Judge's family as well as to him, overcame his scruples.

I have always believed that if I had possessed a tithe of the skill in subtle management and of the spirit of intrigue, so liberally charged upon me by my opponents, and upon the strength of which they gave me the title of "magician," I could have turned aside the opposition which sprang from that source without much difficulty. Mr. Speaker Bell, tho' not one of Judge White's closest friends, doubtless controlled his action in the matter by force of superior capacity and knowledge. He had a passion for political intrigue and occupied at the moment a position of difficulty and hazard from the circumstances attending his elevation to the chair. I received frequent hints of a desire on his part to hold a confidential conversation with me and was one day invited to dine with a mutual friend well disposed to his advancement; informed (before hand) that the Speaker would be the only other gentleman invited, I expected that the subject of the Presidential election would be introduced and could easily imagine the shape of the suggestions that would be made. Bell and Polk were at the head of rival interests in Tennessee, and the treatment they might respectively expect to receive from the new administration, if I should be elected, was a matter of interest to both. After the ladies retired, the subject was, as I had foreseen, introduced, but a severe toothache compelled me to decline the conversation and to retire almost immediately. We separated with the significant expression, by the Speaker, of a hope that I might not have a tooth-ache when we should meet again. This occurred shortly after the commencement of the session of Congress of 1834-5. Some days thereafter, and on the last day of December, when Mr. Adams delivered before Congress, his address on the Life and Character of Lafayette, another attempt to converse upon the matter was made. The Senate repairing to the Representative Chamber, I, as the presiding officer of that body, was of course placed by the side of the Speaker. He introduced the subject by an expression of his regret that the republican party was to be divided by the nomination of Judge White and the satisfaction he would derive from an amicable adjustment of the matter, and proceeded to say that such progress had been made and such a point reached as made it indispensable that whatever was to be done to arrest it should be done immediately. Determined from the beginning to make no explanations as to the course I would pursue if elected, in regard to personal interests, I put a civil end to the conversation by a few general remarks in regard to the duty that the friends of Judge White owed to the republican cause and my convictions that they could not so far forget it, as well as their interest, as to disregard both by the course indicated, and closed with an observation on the speech which was being delivered in front of us.

Struck by the peculiarity of the time and occasion selected by the Speaker for this communication I turned with greater interest to the correspondence between Judge White and the Tennessee delegation (Mr. Bell being one of them), soon after published, and found that it was only *on the previous evening* that the delegation had obtained his consent to the use of his name and that there was therefore great reason for the urgency manifested, arising from the necessity for speedy action.

It was immediately afterwards announced in the Tennessee newspaper, which was regarded as the Judge's organ, that his name would not be withdrawn, and the sequel is known. His resignation as Senator and final retirement from public life, conscious of the extent to which he had been deceived and used, and sick of politics, followed immediately upon the result of the election.

When his old colleague, Mr. Grundy, reached Washington, I inquired after the Judge and was answered by that facetious and worthy man as follows : " You ask me how he spends his time ! I will tell you :—he sits all the day long in the chimney corner, spitting tobacco juice by the gallon, cursing everything and everybody, except his Creator,— but *thinking* devilish hard of Him ! " *Note by Van Buren.*

of their overthrown principles, by the instrumentality of my re-elevation to ° the Presidency. More than three fourths of the States instructed their delegates either in express terms, or thro' unmistakable avowals of their preferences, to vote for my nomination. Their wishes were, however, defeated at the Baltimore Convention by the intrigues of politicians of which a brief notice will be taken at the proper place.

The unqualified resolutions of respect and confidence adopted with entire unanimity, by both branches of the Legislature of New York, on my resignation of the office of Governor, with the feelings of personal regard manifested by the citizens of Albany, without distinction of parties, was the first *let up* in party violence that I had ever experienced. These exhibitions of friendly and liberal sentiments, coming, to a considerable extent from men between whom and myself there had been, for about a quarter of a century, a ceaseless partisan contest, always more or less acrimonious, affected me deeply—I need not say, most agreeably; not solely on my individual account but on account also of the evidence they presented that there lies at the bottom of our party divisions a mass of kind and generous feelings, on all sides, waiting only fit occasions for their display.

On my way out of the city I paid my last visit to the venerable John Taylor, then supposed to be on his death-bed; a sad anticipation which was soon realized. Gov. Taylor was no ordinary man. From a comparatively obscure condition in life he had by his own unaided efforts raised himself to a position of much influence in the Government, and to the first rank in society. From the beginning a devoted personal and political friend of George Clinton he nevertheless cultivated friendly and social relations with General Schuyler, General Hamilton and many other distinguished federalists, and there were, for many years, few private tables at which leading and eminent men of opposing politics were more frequently assembled than at his—none certainly at which a generous and elegant hospitality was more liberally dispensed, a gratification in which an ample estate, acquired by his own industry and without reproach, enabled him freely to indulge himself.

On my first entrance upon public life he heard me with great kindness, and altho' we had been occasionally at issue in the State legislature and sometimes quite warmly, I never had reason to apprehend that those collisions had produced any change in his personal feelings towards me. The most important as well as the most exciting occasion on which we came in conflict related to the course we respectively pursued in regard to Gov. De Witt Clinton.

° MS. III, p. 5.

He opposed, as has been related, the election of that gentleman for the Presidency in 1812. In doing so it must now be admitted that he acted a wiser part than I did, and I have before referred to the apparent asperity with which, on that occasion, he resented my course in the State Caucus. But, as I have also mentioned, his disposition towards Governor Clinton was subsequently entirely changed, and when the latter became finally separated from the republican party, Gov. Taylor's long indulged partiality for the Clintons proved too strong to prevent him from adopting the same course. From that period to the day of his death we were opposed to each other in politics, but there never was a time when my feelings towards him were not of the kindest character and if I could ever have doubted his cordial reciprocation of them such doubts would have been effectually removed by our last interview.

Apprised of my intention to call on him he had caused himself to be supported in a sitting position and was attended only by his adopted daughter, Mrs. Cooper, one of the very best of women.° Taking my hand, at first, in both of his own and retaining his hold by one until I left, with every sign of regard, he referred briefly and impressively to his own hopeless condition and to the extreme improbability of our ever meeting again in life, and then spoke, earnestly and feelingly, of our past relations, of the length of time during which we had acted together in the service of the State, of the occasions on which we had taken different views of the public interest and of the momentary excitements they had produced, dwelt upon the respect and kindness I had extended to him at all times, and assured me in very gratifying words of the favorable opinions he had formed of my character. He then adverted to the subject of the journey upon which I had started, the new duties upon which I was about to enter, and in flattering terms, to results which might be anticipated from them if my future course was as discreet as the past had appeared to him to have been, and, with the expression of a sincere wish that my future life might be a happy one and that my political career might be crowned with complete success, he bade me a final and affectionate farewell.

I need not say how cordially I reciprocated the assurances of respect and regard with which the dying patriot honored me, nor will I attempt to describe the satisfaction I derived from the circumstance that my residence at Albany, theretofore so stormy and harassing, had been closed by an interview which, in every respect save that it was destined to be the last, was so truly gratifying.

My health had been reduced by the pressure of business to a state which rendered travelling painful, and the irksomeness of my jour-

---

° MS. III, p. 10.

AUTOBIOGRAPHY OF MARTIN VAN BUREN.   229

ney was not a little aggravated by the accounts which I received from friends whom I met on my way of the condition of things at Washington. Mr. Woodbury arrived at New York after I had retired for the night, and knowing that I was to leave early in the morning, he obtained permission to see me in my bed-chamber. His enumeration of the friends who were dissatisfied with the formation of the Cabinet, and the dispositions they had indicated, was rendered more imposing by my knowledge of his usual discretion in speaking of such things. Yet whilst I placed much confidence in his good sense and regard to truth, I was well apprised of the extent of his disappointment in not having been himself selected for the Cabinet, as he, perhaps, ought to have been, and was therefore inclined to make liberal deductions from his description on account of the natural effects of such a condition of mind upon the views of most men. At Philadelphia I had a long and gloomy interview with Mr. and Mrs. Livingston also just from Washington. Mr. Livingston's situation was, in one respect, the reverse of Woodbury's, as he held in his pocket President Jackson's unconditional offer of the mission to France—the only place he desired to occupy. Yet their description of the unpromising state of things at the White House was notwithstanding still more emphasized than the first, especially in regard to matters which were peculiarly within the range of female cognisance and which, tho' not of the highest, are still of considerable importance. On probing the sources of their somewhat dismal forebodings to the bottom, I was gratified to discover that Mr. Livingston's confidence in the strong sense, perfect purity and unconquerable firmness of the President, which I had all along regarded as the promising features of his character with reference to his new position, had not suffered any abatement. He was as well satisfied as he ever had been that no man or set of men could ever lead the General to do an unworthy action, and that his willingness to hear and respect counsel from those who might be better instructed than himself, in respect to particular points, might under all circumstances be relied on. An apprehension, founded on the assumption that an influence was exerted over the President which would, in the natural course of things, in respect to the social phases of the Presidential Mansion, lead to degradation and contempt in the eyes of foreigners and of good society in general, was found to be the principal source of their fears. They informed me at the same time of the offer of the Mission to France and of their confident expectation that Mr. Livingston would be able to accept it. It was therefore only necessary to refer to the probability that they would be the persons most exposed to annoyances at a foreign court, from any scandal that might obtain circulation upon that point, to lead me to the inference that their description was an exaggerated one,

made such to induce me to take early and effective steps to prevent
or to remedy the evils they apprehended.

Thus far were those intelligent and estimable people from foreseeing what soon became obvious to qualified observers, that President Jackson's receptions at the Presidential Mansion would certainly not be considered inferior, either in the cost or brilliancy of
his entertainments or in the grace and dignity with which his guests
were received, as well by himself as by the female members of his
family, or in the genuine hospitality which they dispensed, to those
of any of his most distinguished predecessors.

But my strongest "pose" was reserved for my arrival at New
Castle. As our boat approached the wharf at that place I recognized among the crowd, as I expected to do, my particular friend
Mr. McLane, with disappointment and deep mortification stamped
upon every line of his intelligent countenance. His personal anticipations in regard to the composition of the Cabinet had been higher
and, as he and his friends supposed, better founded than those of Mr.
Woodbury. He took my arm as I stepped on shore and proposed
that we should walk on in advance of the stagecoach, which was
sufficiently delayed to give us a tramp, not a little fatiguing to me
in my state of health, but which gave him a fair opportunity to
relieve his mind, so far as that could be done by "unpacking his
heart with words." He took the *parole* at once and kept it until
the coach overtook us. In the course of his excited harangue, for
such it literally was, he described, in the earnest and energetic manner usual with him when deeply moved, the degraded condition to
which he thought the administration already reduced thro' the advice of the evil counsellors by whom General Jackson was surrounded, and in conclusion referred to a letter that he had written
to me at Albany immediately after the selection of the Cabinet.
In that letter, after saying that such a Cabinet required no comment
and that he could not see how it could command public confidence,
and raising a series of objections to the official arrangement, he submitted to my reflections whether the interests of my friends and of
the Country required of me the sacrifice of assisting in an attempt to
repair its defects and to give strength to the administration, or
whether I should not rather remain in my elevated position in the
State of New York and leave these strange occurrences to run their
course. As I had already resigned the office of Governor, to which
he referred in his letter, he now spoke, with obvious hesitation, in
respect to my throwing up that of Secretary of State, not recommending such a course specifically but giving most emphatic assurances of the indispensable necessity of great changes in the existing
organization of the Government as the only way by which that
step could be avoided without subjecting myself to great discredit.

There were unfortunately many others who had been prominent and active in the support of General Jackson's election scarcely less dissatisfied with the Cabinet selections. The best known and most influential politicians of this description in Virginia and in South Carolina very generally shared in that feeling; and what made this matter more embarrassing to myself was the fact that they constituted a class with whom my relations both personal and political had been the closest, who passed as my zealous friends and who had been from the beginning and to a man, in favor of my being placed at the head of the new Cabinet. General Hamilton, of South Carolina, a very prominent man amongst them, told my friend Cambreleng, as he informed me by letter before I left Albany, that " if I went into the Cabinet I would cut my throat." There was probably not one of these malcontents more disappointed than myself by the composition of the administration. I had been, perhaps, at too great a distance to be conveniently consulted on the subject ° by the President elect, if he had been that way disposed, but my attention had been throughout directed to other quarters. Except Mr. Ingham, the new Secretary of the Treasury, I had not heard that either of the successful gentlemen had been proposed for the Cabinet before I received the news of their selection. It was besides not in my power to regard some of them, though deficient neither in character nor in social or general respectability, as well adapted to a satisfactory performance of the duties to which they had been appointed. Thus situated I could not allow any considerations not involving a sacrifice of personal honor to prevent my acceptance of the President's invitation, and I continued my progress to the seat of Government with the same determination with which I had left Albany, that of contributing all in my power to secure the success of the administration.

It was after dark when I reached Washington and the coach had barely arrived at the hotel before it was surrouned by a crowd of applicants for office whose cases had been deferred until the Cabinet should be full. They followed me into and filled my room, where, from a sofa on which my health compelled me to lie, I informed them that it was my intention to pay my respects to the President within an hour, until the expiration of which time I would listen patiently to any thing they desired to say. They proceeded accordingly to communicate their respective wishes, and when it became necessary to close the interview I informed them that I would carefully examine the papers in such cases as belonged to my department and would endeavor to do justice to their applications, but that I was indisposed to see persons who desired appointments seeking them in

---

° MS. III, p. 15.

person at the seat of Government and disinclined to report in favor of such as did not leave their cases to the justice of the President and go home.

A solitary lamp in the vestibule and a single candle in the President's office gave no promise of the cordiality with which I was, notwithstanding, greeted by General Jackson on my visit to the White House. I found no one with him except his intimate friend Major Lewis. His health was poor, and his spirits depressed as well by his recent bereavement of his wife as by the trials of personal and political friendship which he had been obliged to encounter in the organization of his Cabinet. This was our first meeting as political friends and it was certainly a peculiar feature in that interview and no insignificant illustration of his nature that he received with most affectionate eagerness, at the very threshold of his administration, the individual destined to occupy the first place in his confidence, of whose character his only opportunities to learn anything by personal observation had been presented during periods of active political hostility.

He soon noticed my exhaustion from sickness and travel and, considerately postponing all business to an appointed hour of the next day, recommended me to my bed.

From that night to the day of his death the relations, sometimes official, always political and personal, were inviolably maintained between that noble old man and myself, the cordial and confidential character of which can never have been surpassed among public men. The history of those associations I propose to relate and to accompany it with an unreserved publication of our entire correspondence. But before entering upon this work it may be useful that I should give a succinct account of our personal and political intercourse from the commencement of our acquaintance to the time of his elevation to the Presidency.

I was presented to General Jackson for the first time, at Washington in the winter of 1815–16, whilst on a visit to that city, to which place he had been called by the exciting contest that grew out of his Seminole campaign. Partaking of the extraordinary interest which he inspired wherever he went I sought an introduction to him at the very moment of his departure for Tennessee, and did not see him again until I met him, in 1823, on the floor of the Senate of the United States, of which body he had become a member. Although we agreed better in our fundamental opinions and principles than I did with many with whom I was acting, it so happened that we had taken different sides on occasions of an exciting character. He visited New York at a period when the contest between Gov. DeWitt Clinton and a majority of the republican party of that

State stood at fever-heat, and having been invited to a public dinner by the Tammany Society, which constituted one of the leading interests in opposition to Mr. Clinton, he gave a toast, when called upon, highly complimentary to that gentleman. We were of course very much stirred up at being thus snubbed, as we considered it, by the gallant General,—more so doubtless than the occasion called for. He not only was no politician, but was, at that time, openly and zealously advocating the mitigation if not the entire suppression of party divisions amongst us. It may be very well doubted whether he made himself at all acquainted with the nature or extent of the controversy in which he seemed to take a part. We invited him as a meritorious Chief who had rendered the Country great service, we could not think him capable of offering an insult to his entertainers, we could well afford to allow the right of opinion in its fullest latitude, and there was, it must now be confessed, enough in the character and public services of Mr. Clinton to justify the General's admiration and respect, even admitting the imputation of political infidelity which we preferred against him to have been well founded. The General was, moreover, in those days, as I have just intimated, an advocate of Mr. Monroe's amalgamation policy, which we, on the other hand, regarded as the gross delusion which it proved to be,—an opinion in which Jackson, before the end of his first Presidential term, not only cordially concurred but was inclined at times to carry too far in the opposite direction.

He made his appearance in the Senate in the double character of one of the Senators from Tennessee and her candidate for the office of President of the United States, and among those who opposed his election to the latter place there was scarcely one more actively and zealously employed than myself; an opposition which extended alike to Mr. Adams and to himself and which was neither relaxed nor intermitted until the final settlement of the question by the House of Representatives. But these differences did not produce the slightest trace of ill blood between us. Our personal intercourse from the day we met in the Senate to the end of the severe Presidential canvass of 1824, was, on the contrary uniformly kind and courteous, altho' circumstances occurred which, unexplained, were well calculated to put his self-control at least for the moment, to severe tests.

In November 1816, after Mr. Monroe's elevation to the Presidency had become certain, General Jackson wrote a friendly letter to him in respect to the formation of his Cabinet.[1]

---

[1] See note to p. 198 *ante.*

In that letter he said:—" Every thing depends upon the selection of your ministry. Now is the time to exterminate that monster called party-spirit." Whatever may then have been the real state of Mr. Monroe's feelings in respect to the General's advice, he did not deem its immediate adoption either safe or prudent. He had been elected as the nominee of a party caucus and as the successor of two Presidents in whose support° a similar agency had been employed. To have pursued a course like that recommended to him by General Jackson, under such circumstances, and in the then state of public opinion, could not have failed to prove disastrous to his administration. He therefore wrote to the General an elaborate answer, complimenting his liberality but pointing out the inexpediency of the course he had proposed. In 1821–2, when his first term was about to expire and his re-election for the second had been carried, with only a single electoral vote against him in the whole Country, Mr. Monroe became, as I have elsewhere fully described, ready and anxious to carry into effect the policy recommended to him by the General four years before. The course pursued by his administration to that end was contrary to the general sentiment of the republicans and was met with particular and very marked hostility at two points, as we have seen, to wit: in New York and Pennsylvania; the demonstrations against the President's policy in the former state growing out of the appointment of a postmaster at Albany and of the nomination of Irish,[1] an out and out federalist, for the office of Marshal of the Western District of Pennsylvania, in the latter.

Both of the Pennsylvania Senators remonstrated earnestly with Mr. Monroe against this nomination on the express ground that it was made in the execution of that amalgamation policy to which they and their State were opposed. It was notwithstanding made and they carried the question to the Senate, where it was thoroughly canvassed, and by which body the nomination was rejected by a vote of 26 to 14; the dissentients being, of course, and to a man, republicans. To silence the opposition of Pennsylvania, the President, in the course of his discussions with the Senators from that State, read to them the letter received in 1816 from General Jackson who was already looked upon as a probable candidate for the Presidency and understood to be the favorite of Pennsylvania. Mr. Monroe also, as it subsequently appeared, read the letter to several other members of Congress to remove their objections to the policy he was pursuing. As the letter was shewn to the Pennsylvania Senators, in connection with the performance of their public duties, and in no sense confidentially, they both spoke of the sub-

---

° MS. III, p. 20.   [1] William B. Irish.

ject without reserve. The interest of the public in the matter of course increased with the improvement of the General's prospects of success and the affair soon got into the newspapers and caused a great sensation, particularly in the Western District of Pennsylvania, which was the stronghold and headquarters of the democratic party of that State and already much excited by it. The Crawford newspapers circulated far and near the charge that Jackson had written such a letter. The papers which supported Jackson, well aware that, if written, it could not be successfully defended in that State, denied that the General had written or that Mr. Monroe had received any letter of the kind.

Messrs. Lowrie and Findley,[1] the Senators, were called out from all parts of the State. Findlay, who was in favor of Jackson, refused to say what he knew whilst Lowrie, who was a Crawford man, although he had taken no steps towards a publication of the facts, stated them publicly and truly. George Krehmer, the ever active friend of Gen. Jackson, applied to Mr. Monroe for information and he authorized him to say that it was false that the General had ever written to him such a letter as Krehmer described. Gen. Jackson substantially authorized Krehmer to say the same thing, declaring at the same time that he had reserved no copy of the letter and spoke only from memory. These denials were literally well founded because Krehmer's description of the letter was materially variant from the letter itself.

A protracted correspondence ensued, the parties to which were the President, his son-in-law, Mr. Hay, Gen. Jackson and Mr. Lowrie. The latter removed the technical grounds upon which these denials were founded by setting forth the contents of the letter according to his recollection of them and as he had declared them to be and called, in respectful terms, upon Mr. Monroe to publish Gen. Jackson's letter, a demand which he thought himself entitled to make as it had been shewn to him to influence his course in the performance of a public duty and without reserve. Mr. Monroe refused to explain. Lowrie was thus brought in collision, upon a question of veracity, with two of the most powerful men in the Country, and the Jackson newspapers, as well as those in favor of other candidates, regarding Crawford as the strongest rival of their respective favorites and desiring therefore to reduce his strength, attacked him [Lowrie] with much violence. My opportunities to become acquainted with his [Lowrie] character were very ample and I never met with a more upright and virtuous man in the course of my life.

Whilst the affair was in this condition, Mr. Lowrie's mail was one morning laid upon his desk, by one of the pages of the Senate, at a

---

[1] Walter Lowrie and William Findlay.

moment when my attention happened to be directed towards him. Sitting next to him I perceived that, on opening one of his letters, he turned very pale. To my enquiry as to the cause he replied quickly " See this!", and on examining the letter we found, to our amazement, that it enclosed a copy of Mr. Monroe's reply to the letter from Gen. Jackson which the former had shewn to himself and Findlay. The copy was partly in Mr. Monroe's handwriting and the residue in that of his son-in-law, Mr. Hay, who had published several violent attacks upon Lowrie. It sustained everything that had been said by the latter and was accompanied by a brief anonymous note to the effect that the writer had been induced to send it to him by seeing the injustice which he was suffering.

Struck by the delicacy of the affair in all its aspects and by a sense of the extent to which the possession of such a paper, in the absence of a satisfactory explanation as to the manner in which it had come to Mr. Lowrie's hands, might be made to increase his embarrassments, I held the letter in my hand and beckoned to Mr. Macon to come to my seat. He did so immediately when I informed him of its contents, that I had seen Mr. Lowrie receive and open it, that he had immediately placed the enclosure in my hands and that Mr. Lowrie and myself asked the favor of him to take the papers into his possession, to authorize Mr. Lowrie to state publicly that they were in his keeping and to refer those who desired to see them to him for that purpose. Of the character of that venerable and just man, whose fame was and is co-extensive with our Country and whom all who knew him honored and esteemed for his exemplary purity, I have already spoken. There was perhaps no feature more marked in his long and creditable life than his freedom from the personal contentions to which public men are so often exposed. Pursuing the even tenor of his way he seldom meddled in other men's affairs or became a party to their quarrels, but on this occasion, and without hesitation he replied,—" Yes! yes! Give them to me. Lowrie is an honest young man—he has had great injustice done him. Give me the papers and I will stand by him be the consequences what they may." I gave him the letter, which had upon it the Richmond, Va., post mark, and which with its enclosures, he placed in the inner pocket of his coat, buttoning it up tightly as he walked away to his seat.

Lowrie immediately apprised Mr. Monroe by a note that he was in possession of a copy of his reply to Gen. Jackson's letter and of the manner in which it had come into his hands. He avowed his intention to keep it as a protection against the charges which had been made against him, to a considerable extent with Mr. Monroe's co-operation, and urged him again to relieve him from the painful dilemma in which he was placed, by the publication of Jackson's letter; a document which Mr. Monroe had dedicated to public use by employing it as an excuse for his official course, to which act and its subsequent denial the difficulties in which Lowrie had been involved were fairly attributable. He also sent his friends Judge Baldwin and Speaker Stevenson[1] to the President to ascertain whether he had received his note and what he intended to do in the premises. Mr. Monroe's reply on both occasions was simply that he had not decided to take any further steps in the matter. °By this new phase of the controversy in which Lowrie had heretofore had the worst in consequence of the weight and power of his opponents, the tables were turned against them. His friends justified his retention of the letter on the ground of its necessity to his defense in a matter in which it was now evident to all that he was the injured party and no proceedings could have been instituted to compel its surrender which would not disclose its contents. Nor was the dissatisfaction of General Jackson with the course that had been pursued, which had been obvious from the beginning, at all diminished by the turn it had now taken. When he gave the advice in question he was Commander-in-Chief of the Army, with a soldier's antipathy to party politics and not regarding himself, in all probability, as within the range of Presidential candidates. When, several years after it was written, the use was made of his letter which produced all this evil, he was very likely to become one and was actually nominated by his State a few months afterwards, and his strongest support was believed to be in Pennsylvania, where the doctrines he was charged with advancing were especially unacceptable, quite as much so as in any State in the Union, and where from the circumstances of the case the knowledge of their having been so advanced was in a fair way to be brought to every man's door. Besides the great and well understood change in his position, he may have entertained a different opinion upon the point, as was certainly the case afterwards. All these things were open to Mr. Monroe's observation and reflection and it is difficult to believe that General Jackson was otherwise than dissatisfied that the President should have overlooked or disregarded them, when, after the lapse of years and without even asking his consent, he employed the advice given him in the way and under the circumstances, I have described.

Doubtless in other respects the course that the matter had taken was very galling to the General. He hated concealments. There was no trait in his character more obvious to others or more proudly and justly asserted by himself than his fearlessness in declaring

---

[1] Henry Baldwin of Connecticut and Andrew Stevenson. ° MS. III, p. 25.

his opinions and his readiness to bear any responsibility attaching
to the avowal of them. With the knowledge that I now have of
him, in that respect, I can well understand the mortification he
endured from seeming to be privy and consenting to an evasion
in regard to his opinions, and the correspondence between him and
Mr. Monroe plainly discloses the existence of this chagrin.

Mr. Krehmer once more stepped forward and addressed him on
the subject. In the General's reply, which was throughout respectful to Lowrie, after saying that his correspondence with Mr. Monroe
was private and confidential, although denying the version of his
letter which he erroneously understood Mr. Lowrie to have given
to it, he broke through the entanglements into which he had suffered himself to be drawn by a species of special pleading foreign
to his nature and habits by admitting that his advice to Mr. Monroe
had been to select for his Cabinet " men of probity and talents without regard to party." This was the substance of the advice contained in his letter to the President now expressed with more caution
and in a way well calculated to make favorable impressions on the
minds of large portions of the People.

Having thus relieved himself from the quibbles that had been
resorted to in his behalf by inferior minds, he said, " My opinions
and sentiments such as they have been written or expressed, at any
time, each and every one are at all times welcome to. In public
or in private letters I but breathe the sentiments I feel and which
my judgment sanctions, and no disposition will ever be entertained
by me either to disguise or suppress them."

He also informed Mr. Krehmer that Mr. Monroe had placed all
his letters, at his own instance, in the hands of Major Eaton, with
a view to their immediate publication. They were published and
everything alleged by Mr. Lowrie in regard to the contents of the
one read to him was fully sustained by the letter itself, and his
course was not only fully vindicated before the Country but left
impressions on the minds of his brother Senators which sought and
soon found an opportunity for their gratification by his election to
the profitable and honorable office of Secretary of the Senate. This
place he held for many years during the most exciting periods in
our political history and discharged its duties with credit to himself
and to the satisfaction of every member of the body; at least I
never heard the slightest complaint, from any source, of his official
conduct and I have no doubt that he might have continued in the
position, if he had desired it, to the present day. It was in reference to him that John Randolph uttered the witty paradox, which
contained an undisputed truth, " that altho' he could neither read
nor write he was *the best clerk* that any public body was ever

favored with!" His reading was certainly not of the best and his penmanship egregious, but there was in him beside punctuality, industry and order, a personal amiability which won the hearts, and a firm integrity and sound sense which commanded the respect and confidence of all the Senators.

His seat, while Senator, was, as I have said, next to mine and that of General Jackson directly before us. Altho' well advised of the extent to which Mr. Lowrie had been sustained and counselled by me thro' the trying positions in which he had been placed, the General seldom took his seat in the morning, especially whilst the matters of which I have been speaking were in progress, without exchanging friendly salutations and shaking hands with both of us. His respect for Lowrie was doubtless increased by the fact that the latter called upon him the moment the affair was made public, gave him an account of the contents of the letter read to him by Mr. Monroe, as they afterwards appeared, justified himself in speaking of the matter as he had done, but denied having had any agency in bringing the matter into the newspapers. The General was pleased with his candor and obvious sincerity and assured him that he should never object to let the letter speak for itself by its publication.

I had good reasons to know that he cherished feelings of warm regard towards Mr. Lowrie to the last and, at the time, I was well satisfied that the whole transaction, so far from exciting his prejudices against either impressed him most favorably towards both of us.

Gen. Jackson's position in respect to the Tariff of 1824, acted upon on the eve of the Presidential election, was an embarrassing one. Pennsylvania, a strong tariff State, had been among the first to embrace his cause and she had done so with great zeal and power. A still larger portion of his strength was supposed to lie in the Southern and South Western States, which were all anti-tariff. He entered Congress with a general bias in favor of protection but with several reservations, the most prominent among which was a desire to limit Legislative encouragement to articles necessary to the defence of the Country in time of War. Altho' averse to the prostitution of a question so deeply affecting the interests of the Country by using it for mere partisan purposes, he was, at the same time, unwilling to submit quietly to such an application of it by his enemies to his own prejudice. His military career, peculiar and difficult as was its character, had given him a spirit of watchfulness in regard to the movements of his enemies which was revived by the perplexing situation in which he found himself between Pennsylvania, his Northern head-quarters, and the anti-tariff States of the South and stimulated into action by the obvious and persevering efforts of his opponents to prejudice him, thro' that channel, in the estimation of both. In this dilemma, and following his natural and always strong impulses to defeat the machinations of his enemies, he assumed a position in regard to it more equivocal than any he had ever occupied on any public question, if not the only one in his career to which such an epithet could have been applied with any shew of reason. He declared himself in favor of a "judicious tariff"—an avowal that was no sooner published than Mr. Clay attempted to scandalize it, for its ambiguity, by a characteristic shrug of his shoulders, a toss of his head and the counter-declaration— "well, by——, I am in favor of an *in*judicious tariff!"

The Tariff Bill of 1824, as it came from the House and was reported by the Senate Committee of Manufactures, contained a clause imposing a duty of 4½ cents on every square yard of cotton bagging imported into the United States—a provision understood to have been specially designed to favor large establishments for the manufacture of that° article at Lexington, Kentucky. This provision was particularly obnoxious to the cotton growing States of Georgia, North and South Carolina, Alabama, Mississippi and Tennessee, upon whose votes the General's supporters relied with confidence and the People of which, were among his most zealous friends. The numerous supporters of Mr. Calhoun in those States, between whom and those of Mr. Clay—including the respective Chiefs—there existed, at that time, the most bitter animosity, personal as well as political, united with the friends and supporters of Mr. Crawford not only in opposing the entire bill but in denouncing this part of it with special vehemance. They characterized it as a tribute extorted from the cotton growing states to enrich Mr. Clay's Kentucky pets, and the fact that those were the principal if not the only manufacturers of cotton bagging in the United States gave great force to their charges. These circumstances adding the force of personal and partisan prejudices to a fixed hostility to the policy of protection raised their oppugnancy to this particlar branch of it to feverheat and led to frequent and earnest remonstrances against the support that they feared General Jackson intended to give to it. They often called him from his seat, and as that was directly in front of mine and mine on the outside row, not a few of their conferences unavoidably took place in my hearing.

The division of the Senate upon the Bill was known to be a very close one and great pains were taken by its more zealous friends to impress its supporters with a sense of the danger of losing it if material amendments were permitted to pass that body. The General so understood the matter and had made up his mind

° MS. III, p. 30.

to go for the Bill, as it stood, notwithstanding his repugnance to the cotton-bagging duty and the anxious wish of so many of his friends that he and his colleague, Major Eaton, should cause its rejection by their votes, which they had it in their power to do.

When the cotton-bagging clause was reached Mr. Macon moved to strike out altogether and when the ayes and noes were taken upon that motion I, who had until that moment in obedience to the wishes of my State, voted for the other parts of the Bill, answered in the affirmative, in consequence of which the vote on striking out stood, ayes 23, noes 24; the General and his colleague both voting with the majority. Perceiving at a glance that my course threw the responsibility of the retention of the clause upon his own vote, he turned around and under evident excitement exclaimed—" You give way, Sir! " I replied, " No, Sir, I have been from the beginning opposed to this clause and informed Gov. Dickerson, when he reported the Bill, that I should vote against it unless the duty was greatly reduced. Subsequent reflection led me to regard this provision as an exceedingly exceptionable one and I finally determined to oppose it in any shape, and so informed the Governor." Before I had time to finish what I intended to say he stopped me and earnestly asked my pardon for meddling in a matter with which he had no right to interfere, declared that however great might be his disappointment at my vote, which had drawn from him, under the impulse of the moment, the remark he had made, he ought not to have forgotten that that vote was my own and that he, at all events, had no right to call it in question; and he pressed me, with much earnestness, to say that I was satisfied with his apology, which I did.

The Senate almost immediately adjourned and the excitement caused by the affair was even greater than could have been anticipated. The discontent of some among the offended friends of the General soon found a vent. As my candidate for the Presidency, Mr. Crawford was a citizen of a cotton growing State they saw, in the transaction, a plan to weaken their candidate and to strengthen our own, his most formidable competitor, in those localities, and I soon discovered, to my mortification, that a few of the friends of Mr. Crawford had not been backward in countenancing that idea by their encomiums upon the adroitness of the movement. I had not been, however, actuated by any such motive or by any other feeling than one of disgust at the nakedness and extravagance of the proposed *bonus* to Companies which had been formed to make money, which were without just claims to so large a share of Legislative favor, but which there was every reason to believe were at the time in the receipt of very liberal profits.

So far was I from wishing to encrease Gen. Jackson's embarrassments, of much of which I had been an involuntary witness, that I had been on the contrary, so favorably impressed by his noble bearing in that very matter and by the promptitude and good feeling with which he atoned for his abrupt address to me, by his whole conduct during the exciting scenes of the Lowrie correspondence, and by his general bearing towards me, an undeviating opponent in the Presidential canvass, that my first impulse, on perceiving the excitement that had sprung up, was a desire to aid in relieving him. In this state of mind I approached him, on his appearance in the Senate, on the following morning, referred to the proceedings of the previous day and to the construction placed upon them by some of his friends and, to my great mortification, sanctioned, at least to some extent, by a few of mine, admitted that under existing circumstances, I ought not to be surprised by such interpretations on the part of zealous and excited politicians, but assured him that they were nevertheless entirely unfounded. I then stated to him, more fully than I was permitted to do on the previous day the extent and character of my objections to the duty, reminded him that after the Bill was reported to the Senate Mr. Macon, after so close a vote, would undoubtedly renew his motion which would bring the question up again after the expiration of a week or two, that I would not be disappointed if other members by that time took the same view of the matter that I had done and that I sincerely hoped that he would be of the number.

As I anticipated the motion was thus renewed after the Bill had been reported to the Senate from the Committee of the Whole; [John] Holmes, of Maine, changed his vote, as did also Gen. Jackson, and the clause was stricken out by a vote of 25 to 22. Gov. Dickerson, the Chairman of the sub-Committee, made the greatest efforts to restore it, but with no other effert than to induce Mayor Eaton[1] the General's colleague, who had made a speech in favor of the clause, to vote against it also. The ferment among the General's cotton-growing friends subsided, and the subject passed from the public mind.

Of the failure to elect a President and the choice by the House of Representatives at the next session of Congress I have already spoken. Gen. Jackson resigned his seat in the Senate at its close and retired to the Hermitage, where he awaited, with calmness and dignity, the judgment of the People upon the conduct of the House of Representatives. Nothing transpired during the session to change or affect our relations either personal or political save the natural tho' silent influence of a common defeat to increase mutual good will and sympathy.

---

[1] John Henry Eaton.

From the day we parted at Washington to the evening on which I waited on him to enter upon the duties of the office to which he had appointed me there had been no personal intercourse between us, nor any correspondence or communication in any form, save a formal letter from him introducing one of his friends, one or two letters to him and the Nashville Committee in reply to calls for my opinion as to the proper course to be pursued in respect to certain points in the canvass,[1] all of which will be found in the correspondence herewith published,[2] his letter of invitation to become a member of his Cabinet and my acceptance of it. The first information he received of my determination to support him, which was early formed, could therefore, as has been elsewhere stated, have been only derived from the newspapers or from the letters of others.

---

[1] A letter of Aug. 8, 1828, from W. B. Lewis asking for political advice is in the Van Bureau Papers, but no letter of this nature from Van Buren is now to be found either in the Van Buren or Jackson Papers.

[2] It was Van Buren's intention to accompany this autobiography with selected letters from his papers an intention he did not carry out.

CHAPTER XXI.

On my arrival at Washington I found a very large number of letters, addressed to me from different parts of the Country by our friends, speaking of the state of public opinion in their respective vicinities in relation to the formation of the Cabinet and subsequent acts of the Administration. ° I will not give a detailed description of their contents which were, without any exception that I can remember, of the most gloomy character. This was perhaps the natural result of the circumstances which attended the beginning of the new Government. A very large majority of the supporters of President Jackson in Congress and of the active politicians who had been drawn to the seat of Government to witness the ceremonies of the Inauguration were deeply dissatisfied with the first steps taken by the President of their choice. In very many instances their discontent was aggravated by private griefs, in more by the disappointment of friends for whose advancement they were solicitous and in not a few by sincere and disinterested sorrow in finding high anticipations dashed to the ground, as they supposed, by the formation of a Cabinet of which as a whole, they could not approve. This influential mass embracing a large portion of the respectability and talents of our party, in returning to their respective States spread the opinion formed at Washington broadcast throughout the Country. The views they took of the matter and the opinions they had formed unhappily, to a great and influential extent, flowed into ears prepared, not to say, predisposed, to credit them. General Jackson was not the choice of the politicians, as a body, of any considerable portion of the States. Those of them who had enlisted in the support of his competitors Crawford, Clay, Calhoun, for a season, and Adams, at the previous election, during that excited canvass had worked their minds into the strongest convictions of the truth of the impressions they had at the first imbibed of his unfitness for the place. These had been to a great extent, worn off by the collisions and still greater excitement of the recent election, leaving the subjects of them, however, liable to be more easily carried away by the first adverse current and they constituted the class to take active parts on such occasions who look narrowly into the action of men in power and interfere with their proceedings thro' epistolary and personal remonstrances.

° MS. III, p. 35.

It was doubtless from this class of the President's constituents that these complaints mainly proceeded. The judgment of the masses was still in abeyance.

The duties imposed upon me in respect to these communications were of an extremely delicate and responsible character. Their authors had a right to expect that their views should be submitted to the President whom they had assisted to elect and they could not perhaps have selected a more appropriate channel for that purpose. They told their story "free, offhand" and the remonstrances and advice were not always or indeed generally expressed in terms which excluded the idea of reproach; and the peculiar delicacy of the task of submitting such to the President, by one whose relations with him were of a character I have described mine to have been, was not a little increased by the circumstances that for the most part they came from men with whom I had been closely allied in opposition to General Jackson, at the preceding election. My personal association with him as a political friend was of but a few days standing and tho' cordial on both sides was not, for the reasons I have intimated, at first entirely free from the embarrassments arising from antecedent events. I have moreover alluded to his state of body and mind, ill adapted to exhibit his character and disposition to the best advantage; still every thing that I saw and heard of and from him impressed me in the strongest manner with a conviction of his sincerity, integrity and straightforward truthfulness.

I therefore determined to rely without reservation or hesitancy upon those qualities, to submit in their strongest aspect the adverse views of the course he was pursuing which were entertained by many who had supported his election and to leave our future relations to the judgment he should form upon the whole subject.

With these views I selected from the mass of letters referred to and sent to the President one from Thomas Ritchie, the Editor of the Richmond Enquirer, then regarded, and I doubt not correctly, as my warm personal and political friend, who tho' he had supported General Jackson with much power and effect in the last election, had, with myself, opposed him before and in a manner and under circumstances calculated to excite in him for the moment, strong feelings of dissatisfaction. It was enclosed with a note from myself:

MARTIN VAN BUREN TO THE PRESIDENT [ANDREW JACKSON].

MY DEAR SIR,

On my return from your house last evening, I found the enclosed among some letters which I had not before been able to examine. Upon a careful consideration of its contents I find it to be so evidently written for your perusal as to make it something like a duty on my part to lay it before you; and I do that the more readily from an entire consciousness that you wish to learn all that may be said with decency in respect to your administration by those interested in its success. I have known Mr. Ritchie long and intimately and am well satisfied that there is not a man of purer public spirit in the Country. The disinterestedness of his views with the great ability that has characterized his paper have given it an influence infinitely greater than any other press in the Union. Whatever you may think of the wisdom or justice of the opinions expressed by such a man I am quite sure that they will receive from you a liberal and respectful consideration.

Not being certain, from the great press that is made upon me, that I shall be able to see you today, I have thought proper to enclose it and will receive it again at your perfect leisure.

Yrs. affectionately

March 31st, 1829. M. V. B.[1]

The PRESIDENT.

THOMAS RITCHIE TO M. VAN BUREN.

DEAR SIR,

This is in all probability the last letter I shall have the honor of addressing you for many years to come. Our respective situations, though vastly different from each other, make such a correspondence delicate on both sides. A Secretary of State has his own duties to perform, and so has an Editor however humble he may be. I need not be more explicit, but I cannot reconcile it to myself to remain altogether silent amid the scenes which I have witnessed. You are the only member of the administration with whom I am acquainted. I therefore address myself to you. If there be anything in this letter which you may think it proper to submit to Gen. Jackson you are authorized to lay it before him,—and him only. In truth I would have addressed myself directly to him, but for my anxiety to preserve even the *appearance* of that respect which I sincerely feel for his character and himself.

You, Sir, or perhaps Gen. Jackson, if he should see this letter, may charge the writer with arrogance, impertinence, call it what you will, for intruding my opinion, unasked and unacceptable upon the grave matters of which it proposes to treat. I am content to abide by your severest censures, as I am satisfied with my own motives. This letter is dictated by the most friendly feelings. It is from a sincere desire that you should be possessed of the state of public opinion in this part of the Country that I break thro' all the rules of etiquette.

You know how anxiously I desired the election of General Jackson. My most intimate friends have witnessed the joy which his success inspired. I regarded [it] not simply as the downfall of a party which had corrupted the purity of elections and abused its power for its own little purposes, but as a new epoch in the history of our Country,—as opening a bright prospect of wise and constitutional principles. I need not say, Sir, that I had nothing to gain except as one of ten millions of people. I have nothing to ask,—the administration has nothing to offer which I will accept.

Why this bright prospect is somewhat clouded over within the short space of thirty days I will not enter into a long recapitulation to explain. I pass over the Cabinet. It has disappointed many of the sincerest of the President's friends. In the same proportion, that it dispirited them has it raised the hopes of their enemies. They have already raised the standard of opposition. and a rival, who was abandoning all his views in utter despair, was immediately animated to enter the lists again. I do not speak at random when I make these assertions. The admirable Inaugural Address, however, counteracted these

---

[1] In the Van Buren Papers.

effects ° in some degree. It gave us all additional spirits. But, I speak it with profound regret, the subsequent appointments have thrown a cloud over our friends which it will require some time and great wisdom to dispel. We are sorry to see the personal friends of the President appointed; we lament to see so many of the Editorial Corps favored with the patronage of the Administration. A single case would not have excited so much observation,—but it really looks as if there were a systematic effort to reward Editorial Partizans, which will have the effect of bringing the vaunted Liberty of the Press into a sort of contempt. I make allowance for the situation of these gentlemen. I know most of them are able and qualified. They have fought manfully to put out a corrupt coalition—They have fought with the halter round their necks; and not, as I have done, so much in the country of friends, as of enemies. I allow for all these things, and still the truth cannot be disguised that the press, which shrinks like the sensitive plant from the touch of Executive Power, has been heedlessly handled. Invade the freedom of the press and the freedom of election, by showering patronage too much on Editors of newspapers and on Members of Congress, and the rights of the People themselves are exposed to imminent danger. I know that this was not the *motive* of such appointments; but I argue about *effects:* effects too not to be brought about by *this* administration but by less worthy ones which are to succeed it.

There is some difficulty under all new Administrations to know whom to *put out* and whom to *put in;* and it is the right use of patronage under such circumstances that constitutes one of the most delicate operations of Government. We should suppose that one pretty good rule was for the Chief Magistrate to consider offices not as made for himself, the gratification of his own feelings and the promotion of his own purposes, but as a public trust to be confided to the most worthy. I throw out this suggestion because I have seen too much stress laid upon the personal feelings of the President by some who did not sufficiently estimate the high station which he occupies. There is another thing. I go for reform,—but what is reform? Is it to turn out of office all those who voted against him, or who decently preferred Mr. Adams? Or is it not rather those who are incapable of discharging their duties, the drunken, the ignorant, the embezzler, the man who has abused his official facilities to keep Gen. Jackson out, or who are so wedded to the corruptions of office as to set their faces against all reform? Is it not to abolish all unnecessary offices and to curtail all unnecessary expenses? It surely is not to put out a good and experienced officer because he was a decent friend of J. Q. Adams, *in order* to put in a heated partizan of the election of Gen. Jackson, which partizan chooses to dub himself on that account the friend of Reform. I trust that such a spirit of Reform will not come near to us in Virginia. Should any one be seeking the loaves and fishes of federal office in Virginia I hope the Administration will be very careful *whom* they may put out to serve such an office-seeker. There is no man whom I would touch in this city.

The course of appointments at Washington is calculated to cool and alienate some of our friends. The enemies of the Administration are on the alert. They are availing themselves of all our errors, while we are so situated that we are unable to justify or defend them. You can scarcely conceive the uneasiness which prevails. Will you excuse me for troubling you with the following Extract, which I have received from Washington, from a profound observer of men and things. He is a warm friend of the President—and no Virginian:—

" I can read the history of this Administration more clearly than I did the late one and I was in no respect disappointed in my views respecting its course

---

° MS. III, p. 40.

and termination. Under the profession of Reform changes will be made to the public injury. Let the rule be once known and every man who was not an active partizan of Gen. Jackson will be brought within it. A great number of violent men, alike destitute, I fear, of principle and intelligence, will be thrown into conspicuous positions, in the excitement, and placed in offices of trust. High minded and talented men, in such a result, will, for a time, be thrown into the shade. The contest will be for office and not for principle. This will impair the moral force of our institutions at home and abroad, and may eventuate in their destruction.

" Should the present Administration go down, as I fear it will, and should Clay come into power, *on his system*, I tremble for the Union. A scene of violence, reckless of consequences will then be the order of the day. This is a gloomy picture, and I wish to God I could persuade myself it is too highly colored. I see and understand perfectly all the movements made."

My heart aches as I make this Extract. Sincerely do I trust that its gloomy anticipations may be defeated, and that Gen. Jackson may lay down his power amid the loudest acclamations of a grateful people. I would do anything that was honorable and proper to lead to this result. But I have done.

I beg you to make no answer to this letter. I write in haste and with pain. Perhaps I ought not to write it at all.

I am, Sir, resp'y

THOMAS RITCHIE.[1]

MARCH 27th 1829.

Gen. Jackson's note, returning to me the above letter, it will be seen bears date on the same day with my communication to him and was as follows:

PRESIDENT JACKSON TO M. VAN BUREN.[1]

I have read the enclosed letter with attention and if the facts adverted to would warrant the conclusion the objections would be well founded.

There has been as yet no important case of removal except that of General Harrison; and I am sure if Mr. Ritchie has read the instructions given to our Ministers, who were sent to Panama, he must think the recall of General Harrison not only a prudent measure but one which the interest of the Country makes indispensably necessary. I have referred to the case of Gen. Harrison only, because I cannot suppose Mr. Ritchie has any allusion to the auditors and comptrollers, who were dismissed not so much on account of their politics as for the want of moral honesty.

The gentleman who has been selected to supply the place of Gen'l Harrison is, I believe, as well qualified, if not better, than any other who would have undertaken the mission to that Country.

I would advise the answering of Mr. Ritchie's letter; and in the most delicate manner to put him on his guard with respect to letter writers from Washington. The letter he has extracted from, instead of being from my *friend* must be from some disappoined office hunter—one who merely professes to be my friend, or perhaps from a friend of Mr. Clay in disguise.

How could this letter writer know what changes were to be made? How can he pretend to *foretell*, without knowing who are to be appointed, that the changes will be injurious to the public interest?—You may assure Mr. Ritchie that his Washington correspondent knows nothing of what will be the course of the President on appointments, or he would have known

---

[1] In the Van Buren Papers.

that the President has not nor will he ever make an appointment but with a view to the public good and the security of the fiscal concerns of the nation. He never has, nor will he appoint a personal friend to office unless by such appointment the public will be faithfully served. I cannot suppose Mr. Ritchie would have me proscribe my friends merely because they are so. If my personal friends are qualified and patriotic why should I not be permitted to bestow a *few* offices on them? For my own part I can see no well founded objections to it. In my Cabinet it is well known that there is but one man with whom I have had an intimate and particular acquaintance, tho' they are all my friends in whom I have the greatest confidence. But even if it were as Mr. Ritchie supposes, I have only followed the examples of my illustrious predecessors, Washington and Jefferson. They took from their own State bosom friends and placed them in the Cabinet. Not only this but Gen'l Washington went even farther,—besides placing two of his friends from Virginia near him, he brought into his Cabinet Gen'l Hamilton with whom, if possible, he was upon more intimate terms that I am with any member of my Cabinet.

I have drawn your attention to these facts because I apprehend that our friend Mr. Ritchie ° had not reflected upon the subject or he would not have suffered himself to be so easily alarmed. I have, I assure you, none of those fears and forebodings which appear to disturb the repose of Mr. Ritchie and his Washington correspondent. I repeat, it would be well for you to write Mr. Ritchie and endeavour to remove his apprehensions of difficulty and danger. Say to him before he condemns the Tree he ought to wait and see its fruit. The people expect reform, they shall not be disappointed; but it must be *judiciously* done and upon *principle*.

Yours respectfully

A. JACKSON
March 31st 1829

Mr. VAN BUREN.

In pursuance of the President's suggestion I wrote to Mr. Ritchie as follows:—

M. VAN BUREN TO THOMAS RITCHIE.

Private.

WASHINGTON *April 1, 1829.*

DEAR SIR,

I am constrained by my respect for your opinions and esteem for your personal character to disregard the delicate intimation at the close of your letter, so far at least as to acknowledge its receipt and to say a few words as to its contents and the direction I have given it.

Owing to the great number of letters I found here at my arrival requiring my attention yours did not fall under my observation until Monday evening. After a careful examination of its contents I believed it was due as well to the President as to yourself to submit it to his perusal, which was done on Tuesday morning. He read it with the best feelings and, on returning it to me, entered into a full explanation of the points to which you refer, with the utmost deference to the opinions you have advanced and respect for their author.

I express his sentiments when I say that it is at all times most agreeable to him to learn the candid opinions in relation to its course of those who take as I know you do, an interest in the success of his administration, and

---

° MS. III, p. 45.

to explain, as far as time and circumstances will permit, the principles by which every public act is regulated.

Disclaiming all reserve with those whom he respects, it would be perfectly agreeable to him that you should be fully apprised of the motives and views that have actuated him in making the appointments to which you refer, and it will give me much pleasure should you visit this city (which I sincerely hope you may be able to do) to make you acquainted with both, under a sure conviction that you will admit the purity of the former if you cannot fully concur in the justness of the latter.

Your own good sense will satisfy you of the impracticability of avoiding mistakes or giving any thing like universal satisfaction in the discharge of that portion of the Executive duties which relates to appointments, particularly under existing circumstances. It is not in the wit of man to do so. I have been here but a short time and cannot of my own knowledge say anything as to past measures, but I have seen enough to satisfy me that no man ever entered upon the duties of the Chief Magistrate of this or any other Country with greater purity of purpose or a more entire devotion to the honor of the Government and the welfare of the Country than did the present incumbent, and I shall be grossly deceived if in the sequel, that is not the opinion of the great body of the American People.

Hoping soon to have the pleasure of seeing you I have only to ask that the contents of this as well as the fact that it has been written will be confined to your own bosom, and to assure you of my great respect and regard.[1]

If to these and such as these disturbing and discouraging matters be added the obstacles that were thrown into his path by means of the Eaton embroglio,—a private and personal matter which only acquired political consequence by its adaptation to the gratification of resentments, springing out of the formation of the Cabinet, and, as was supposed, to the elevation or depression of individuals in high positions,—we will be able to estimate justly the adverse influences which surrounded President Jackson when he entered upon his official duties.

Having as military commander abstained from frequent councils of war, because he thought they were too apt to be used to screen the General from a proper and often most salutary responsibility, he carried something of the same feeling into his action as President. His disinclination to Cabinet councils, springing in part from this consideration was doubtless greatly strengthened by the circumstance that he foresaw, at an early day, the division that soon after broke out among his constitutional advisors, from the source to which I have alluded, and he fixed his course in the way he deemed best adapted to neutralize its effects. But whatever may have been his reasons the fact was that for a long time at least his practice was to have interviews with the heads of departments separately as often as was necessary to the proper discharge of the business entrusted to them and to ask the opinions of the other members also separately when he desired them upon questions not belonging to ,

---

[1] Draft in the Van Buren Papers.

their departments. One of the New York newspapers, friendly to him, whose Editor had visited Washington in mid-summer, said, and I have no reason to doubt, correctly, that down to that period not a single Cabinet meeting had been had for the dispatch of business.

Soon after my arrival I met him [the President] to talk over the general concerns of the State Department. The question that first presented itself for consideration was the condition of our representation abroad, the expediency of changes, the extent to which it was desirable to carry them and the persons to be appointed. As soon as these points were broached he volunteered to say that he had committed a great mistake in respect to portions of them for which he thought it was his duty to apologize,—that as he had selected me to manage that branch of our national concerns I ought to have been consulted in respect to the changes to be made and the selection of the ministers,—that instead of this, induced by considerations which he stated and which were, tho' not consistent, as he admitted, with the proper transaction of business, creditable to his heart, he had disposed of the two most important Missions by offering that to England to Mr. Tazewell [1] and the French Mission to Mr. Livingston. [2] Having been apprised by Mr. Livingston himself of these steps I was of course prepared to give my views in respect to them, and admitting, as I did cheerfully, that there were no two gentlemen in the circle of his friends better entitled to such a compliment as he had paid them or in whose behalf my personal feelings would, on suitable occasions, be more cordially enlisted, I yet felt bound to say that, having regard to the character of the business to be attended to at those courts, viz: the settlement of the long pending and greatly complicated questions between us and England in respect to the West India Trade and the still older and scarcely less difficult and tedious subject of our claims upon France, I had not been able to satisfy myself that he had been fortunate in his selections. I assigned my reasons for that opinion, at length, not, it is scarcely necessary to say, urging anything against the public or private worth or general capacity of either, but insisting that the public service in those respects would be, in all probability, more successful if those Missions had been entrusted to active young men whose reputation as Statesmen, unlike those of Livingston and Tazewell, were yet to be established, who would seize upon those questions which had so often baffled the capacities of old diplomatists with the spirit and vigour of youth and who would be sufficiently ambitious to encounter and resist the rebuffs to which, on such oft debated points, they must

---

[1] Littleton W. Tazewell.   [2] Edward Livingston.

expect to be exposed and to submit to the drudgery thro' which final success could alone be hoped for.

He listened to me with marked attention and, when I had finished, said, with much feeling, that his own subsequent reflection had caused misgivings in respect to the adaptation of the gentlemen he had selected for the particular concerns with which they were to be charged and that the views I had expressed convinced him entirely that his course, tho' well meant, had been an unwise one, adding that nothing could afford him more satisfaction than to be able to recall the offers he had made if he could do so in a way ° perfectly consistent with what was due to his own honor and to the feelings of the gentlemen to whom he had tendered them, which we were agreed could not be done. But as his offers had neither been accepted nor refused, tho' considerable time had elapsed since they had been made, the prominence of the subjects referred to in the public mind and the desire that would naturally be felt by the parties particularly interested and by the friends of the Administration to see prompt and effective measures adopted to remedy what the latter had regarded as failures on the part of our predecessors, suggested the propriety of writing to those gentlemen assigning the reasons for speedy action and inviting them to give definite answers upon the point of acceptance and to be ready, if they accepted, to start upon their respective missions as early as the first of August then next, which would leave them four months for preparation. To this he cordially assented and I promised to prepare the letters for his inspection.

The missions in respect to which changes were resolved upon at that interview were those to England, France and Spain. For the last he invited me to suggest a name. I proposed that of Mr. Woodbury,[1] which he promptly accepted. He had served with him in the Senate and as no member of the Cabinet had been taken from New England he considered his location fortunate. I wrote to Mr. Woodbury on the spot.[2]

In my letter I expressed a confident belief that " in the present state of things his talents (of which no one had a higher opinion than myself) would enable him to render essential service to the Country and acquire great credit to himself and that I was authorized to say that the President embraced with pleasure, this, the earliest opportunity which circumstances had allowed him; to manifest the high sense he entertained of his public services and of his (Mr. Woodbury's) claims upon his personal respect and esteem."

Two weeks had not elapsed since I had parted from Mr. Woodbury, at New York, at midnight, with evidences, both ocular and oral, of his serious disappointment, and feeling that the President had made me the happy instrument of a good act in authorizing the offer to him of so honorable a mission I looked with much complacency for the receipt of his answer, not doubting it would show that the wounded spirit had been healed, in some degree, at least, thro' my agency.

It came, but not in the gratifying form I had anticipated, rather as a damper upon my feelings. He was very anxious to do what he could to "furnish the President with any influence in his power towards the successful accomplishment of the policy of his administration, as thus far developed, and to obviate misapprehensions, prejudices" &c; but it was doubtful whether he would be able to accept the mission, and he wanted information on certain named points before he could decide. These related principally to the business to be transacted in Spain—the time to elapse before he would have to start on his Mission—when his salary would commence if he accepted and how long he would be expected to remain abroad.

Without changing our opinions in respect to the strong points in Mr. Woodbury's character or his capacity to make himself useful in the public service, this answer occasioned both to the President and myself no little surprise and disappointment. We could not help seeing that the President's prompt offer, and the flattering terms in which it had been conveyed, instead of being received as proof of our respect and esteem for him had filled Mr. Woodbury with exaggerated notions of our estimate of the importance to the administration that he should be conciliated. Yet this was all a mistake. He was one of the few prominent New England men who had withstood the sectional current in favor of Mr. Adams and remained with us thro' the election, for which reason, strengthened by the fact that the Eastern States were not represented in the Cabinet, I was desirous, sensible of his undoubted capacity, that he should receive an early proof of the favor and confidence of the Executive; but there could not possibly have been a greater error than the supposition that, in the matter of appointments, President Jackson was ever influenced by any consideration like that here suggested. The conciliation of individuals formed the smallest, perhaps too small a part of his policy. His strength lay with the masses and he knew it. He first, and, at least in all public questions, always tried to be right and when he felt that he was so he apprehended little—sometimes perhaps too little—from the opposition of prominent and powerful men; and it must now be admitted that he seldom over-estimated the strength he derived from the confidence and favor of the people and his consequent ability to cope with his political opponents.

Mr. Woodbury's letter was the first answer to the President's offer of important public employment after the organization of his Cabinet and it doubtless served to put him a little upon his mettle. It besides presented a good opportunity for a brief exposé of the course which he intended to pursue in similar cases. I have only the rough draft of my reply before me which I insert, as it furnishes from its confidential character, reliable evidence of the principles upon which the President acted in the discharge of his official duties.

To LEVI WOODBURY.

Private.

MY DEAR SIR,

If you accept the President will expect you to leave the Country as soon as a due regard to your private affairs will allow, so that you are not detained beyond the first of August. Delay in the departure and dispatch in the return of our Foreign Ministers was a vice of the late administration which we condemned then and must not practice now. The President will therefore expect that the Ministers appointed by him shall proceed upon their missions in a reasonable time and regulate the period of their return by the public interest and not by their pleasure or personal convenience. If good cause exists for an early return leave will of course be given but in the absence of special reasons a return in a shorter period than four years will not be anticipated.

The President regards the Mission to Spain as the second in point of importance in the present condition of our foreign relations, and testifies that conviction by the fact of depriving himself of your services in your present highly honorable and responsible situation.

Your salary will, in case of acceptance, commence from the time you leave your home including a visit to this city which will be regulated by the period of your departure.

Hoping that your decision will be such as I cannot but think will redound to your honor and advance the interests of the Country

    I am, dear Sir,

        Your friend and obd't serv't [1]

Mr. Woodbury's answer to this avowed his concurrence in the general views it expressed and disclaimed all desire to have principles so clearly conducive to the public interests departed from on his account. He said that if the Mission had been for a specific object likely to be accomplished in a year or two, he would have overcome all objections and accepted the offer, but that his family were inflexibly opposed to accompanying him, that a large majority of his friends were adverse to his leaving the Country for so long a time, if at all, and as the mission was of a general character and must probably last four years, or longer, he was constrained with great reluctance to decline it. To put him entirely at his ease upon the subject, by direction of the President, I informed him that his letter had been submitted to the latter who found nothing in the reasons assigned otherwise than satisfactory—that he regarded the considerations upon which the declension had been placed as proper to be taken into view and to control the decision, and that it was a satisfaction to the President to know that one consequence of his

---

[1] Written in April, 1829.

disappoinment would be to save to the councils of the nation the advantages of Mr. Woodbury's talents and experience.[1]

In a subsequent letter,[2] based on the preceding one, Mr. Woodbury assured the President of his entire willingness to fill any situation under the Government which would not, like the Mission to Spain, require so long ° an absence from his family, and accompanied that announcement with a gloomy account of the disordered condition of our own party and of the extraordinary activity with which the opposition had already entered on the canvass for the next Presidential election; talked of resigning his seat in the Senate and of retiring from public life, &c., &c, upon all of which Gen. Jackson, in returning his letters to me, remarked in a note "that he inferred that Mr. Woodbury over rated the value of the aid that Mr. Adams would be able to bring to Mr. Clay at the next Presidential election and was more alarmed than the facts would warrant; that we had only to continue the course we have commenced, take principle for our guide and public good our end, and the people will sustain us."

In this brief note and in that relating to Ritchie's letter are to be discovered the secret of the General's extraordinary popularity. Such an abiding trust in the integrity of the people and in their fidelity to those who are faithful to them, accompanied by a readiness to spend and to be spent in their service, a willingness at all times to sacrifice ease and comfort and if necessary to hazard his life for their safety could not escape their knowledge or fail to secure their love and gratitude. Since his character had become known to them by a long series of self sacrificing acts they had not doubted that a solicitude for their welfare most ardent and of never failing disinterestedness was deeply seated in his heart and ever present to his mind. Nor was it surprising that this faith and these dispositions constituted such marked features in his character. They were natural results of peculiar circumstances in his condition. No public man was ever so highly elevated of whom it could be said with more truth that he was one of the people. They were his blood relations —the only blood relations he had in this or, as far as is yet known, in any Country. No one stood nearer to him in that great natural tie than another. The remarkable success which crowned his efforts in their service had inspired him with a firm belief that to labour for the good of the masses was a special mission assigned to him by his Creator and no man was ever better disposed to work in his vocation in season and out of season. It is not surprising that with these convictions and dispositions he should have been so potent with a sagacious and just people.

---

[1] May 3, 1829, Van Buren Papers.   [2] May 18, 1829, ibid.   ° MS. III, p. 55.

I have not introduced these particulars by way of blame or still less of disparagement but to give an inside view of the actions of public men—a view which generally differs materially from that which is seen by the public. The sequel of this work will shew how much there was in Mr. Woodbury's career deserving of the respect and approbation of his Countrymen and of the support which both Gen. Jackson and myself gave to him to the very close of our public lives, notwithstanding striking peculiarities, I might almost say obliquities, in his political course.

Mr. Tazewell, altho' willing to represent his State in the National Legislature, appeared to me to be as free from the love of office as any man with whom I was associated in public life. He came to the seat of Government very soon after my arrival and I think before I wrote to him on the subject of the Mission to England which had been tendered to him by the President. He was he said unwilling to accept it unless he could satisfy himself that by doing so he would have it in his power to render his Country some signal service. Upon that point at least he seemed to carry his heart in his hand, and left no room for misconstruction or doubt as to his sincerity. He had taken as Senator an active part in the proceedings of Congress on the subject of the West India Trade, but his hopes of a successful negotiation in respect to it were not sanguine. In this state of mind his purpose in coming to Washington was to ascertain whether it was at all probable that he would be able to exert an influence in behalf of the repeal or modification of the corn laws, and to place the question of his acceptance upon the result of that enquiry. He announced that determination to the President and myself but we could not with truth give him any encouragement upon the point and told him so without reserve. Being well acquainted with the British Minister at Washington, Sir Charles R. Vaughan, and appreciating the sincerity and frankness of his character, he expressed a desire to see and consult with him upon it to which we saw no objections. He carried, I think, a letter from me expressive of his desire and of the President's approbation of the proposed interview, but Sir Charles expressed so confidently his conviction of the utter hopelessness of the proposed attempt that Mr. Tazewell returned and declined the Mission.

I remember well how much pleasure and relief, amid our cares and vexations we experienced from the candid, unselfish and public spirited disposition shewn by him in these interviews. At the next session of Congress Mr. Tazewell embarked, or, I might perhaps with truth say, was drawn by his personal and political associations into a violent opposition to the Treaty with the Sublime

Porte for the navigation of the Black Sea by American vessels—the occasion of the first overt act of Mr. Calhoun's opposition to the Administration of President Jackson. In this I, having conducted the negotiation, thought him wrong and it was well understood that his State, although interposing no specific complaint, did not approve of his course; but whatever may have been the degree of credit or discredit due to his conduct on the latter occasion I have never forgotten his rare and admirable bearing on that to which I have first referred, and I take much pleasure in making this record of the transaction to which it related.

Satisfied that he had been too hasty in respect to the appointments to England and France, General Jackson informed me that, it it should become necessary to make new selections, he would expect me to name the men and that, having confidence in my judgment, it was more than probable that he would adopt them.

Mr. Berrien, who had been appointed Attorney General, was, at the moment, in Georgia arranging his private affairs preparatory to his removal to the seat of Government. Assuming that he would prefer the place of Minister to England the President authorized me to offer him an exchange of places and, on the assumption that he would certainly consent to it, to offer the Attorney Generalship to Mr. McLane, which was done without waiting for Mr. Berrien's answer. Mr. McLane's reply addressed to me in an unofficial letter, did not come up to my anticipation, but the President was predisposed to regard it in the most favorable light and I was too partial to him to scan his faults. He confessed that he had not his own free consent to accept the place and did so reluctantly, regarding it as a sacrifice to the interests of his large family (which did not leave him at liberty to be fastidious, or to consult his own inclinations) and to those of the cause and of his friends; adding that "if he could have supposed the President intended to make any immediate provision for him he could have suggested one much more desirable to himself and probably equally so for him and all others. He thought moreover that he (the President) had purchased the change in the office of Attorney General at too great a price."

° Fortunately, as we supposed, for the gratification of our friend McLane, the Attorney General decided to remain where he was, and not doubting that it was the English Mission to which the former referred as the place that would have been more desirable to himself and the arrangement probably equally satisfactory to all others, I forthwith presented his name to the President who authorized me

---

° MS. III, p. 60.

to offer it to him. But we were destined to further disappointment. From Mr. McLane's answer, addressed to me, as before unofficially, it appeared that my letter had "embarrassed him;" that when he wrote me *the day before* accepting the office of Attorney General "he was not altogether without his fears that Mr. Berrien might not assent to the change for what was so desirable to *us* and on which account principally he had decided as he did, i. e. to be with me in the Cabinet, and for that very reason the change might not be agreeable to him." To this it was added, among other things, that he hoped that his letter to the President however would shew his disposition to consult his own and the honor of the administration, and thus "preserve my (his) chance for what I will frankly tell you would make me happier than any other honor—the Bench." Meantime, that chance not being impaired, the Mission to England, he thought might be turned to even greater advantage, &c; that considering moreover the impropriety of exposing *you* (me) and the President to many rejected offers as to this Mission, at this period of the administration and understanding from your (my) letter that your (my) individual views are in favor of this determination I will accept the Mission to England * * * "I must trust to your friendship and sagacity to keep me in the mind of the President and to give such a direction to this affair as may ultimately end best for us all."

Upon the suggestion of my esteemed and noble hearted friend, Capt. Jack Nicolson, of the Navy, I proposed the name of Washington Irving, who was then in England, for the place of Secretary of Legation to the English Mission to the President and on obtaining his assent I wrote to his brother Judge Irving [1] for his opinion whether it would probably be acceptable, and receiving a favorable answer, the appointment was forthwith made.

If Mr. Livingston manifested less indifference to the acquisition of his place than Mr. Tazewell it was not because he estimated more highly the distinction or craved the emoluments of office. The enjoyment of official pomp and circumstance is, *quoad* the United States, an Eastern or New England feeling and is still fostered there by the ceremonies and forms incident to public authority. My friend Woodbury, tho' too sagacious to waste much of his earthly substance on account of it, yet took great satisfaction in its indulgence when attainable without too much pecuniary sacrifice, and Webster's passion for it was of a still stronger type. The latter was never more at home or in gayer spirit than when playing the potentate within the circle and to the extent of his official possessions. The Southern people were remarkably free from

---

[1] John Treat Irving.

this weakness nor was there ever much of it in the Middle States. Regarding Webster and Woodbury, from the North, and Marshall and Tazewell, from the South, as examples of the extent of it in their respective sections they represented in this respect antipodes whom it would be difficult to imagine belonging to the same Country and reared under the same Government.

Tazewell, altho' well educated and, in the best sense of the term, a gentleman, would not have been called a literary man, and I am sure he derived more social enjoyment from his games at quoits with Chief Justice Marshall, Gen. Wickham,[1] Dr. Brockenborough[2] and others like them at Richmond,° or from dinners of sheeps-head with his unceremonious but well bred friends and associates at Norfolk, than he could promise himself abroad. To Mr. Livingston nothing could be offered more agreeable than the opportunity and facility for the cultivation of letters and the society of the highest living authorities in art and science at Paris as the fruition of long cherished anticipations of that character. Mrs. Livingston was French by birth and education and possessed withal superior accomplishments and qualifications for the station to which she seemed destined. Besides these circumstances the French Mission had long been a source of honorable pride in his family, having been the highest official distinction enjoyed by his distinguished brother Chancellor Livingston, one of the Committee which reported the Declaration of Independence; in after times it attracted to his own to distinguish it from a worthy connexion of the same name the *sobriquet* of *French Edward.*

But altho' he did not lack inducements, worthy to be taken into consideration in making up his own opinion, there were others entitled to more influence with the President. He had become satisfied that altho' no appointment could be made that in respect to his individual feelings it would give him more pleasure to make and perhaps none that would add more dignity to the Mission, the selection might not prove to have been a fortunate one in view of the particular subject to be acted upon and which he was very desirous to adjust.

I opened a correspondence with Mr. Livington upon the subjects of his acceptance of the Mission and the period of his departure which resulted in his declension on account of the state of his private affairs which required his presence in the United States to a later period than any to which his departure could, in his own opinion, be properly deferred. Subsequent transactions, to be hereafter referred to, would be sufficient to shew, if proof of the fact could be thought necessary, that the result in no degree affected the friendly relations which had long existed between him, the President and my-

---

[1] John Wickham.   [2] Dr. William ? Brockenborough   ° MS. III, p. 65.

self. His decision to decline was, on the contrary, conveyed to the President in a letter which both in matter and manner were highly honorable to him.[1]

By the invitation of the President I suggested a name for the vacant mission—that of William C. Rives, of Virginia, to which he readily agreed, and Mr. Rives promptly accepted the offer. Mr. Livingston's letter to the President having been received by the morning mail from the North I wrote to Mr. Rives by the Southern mail on the same day. On the following morning Mr. Livingston presented himself at my office and thinking it possible that he came to withdraw his declension I informed him at once and in suitable terms of what had been done on the previous day. Nothing appeared during his short stay to confirm or disprove that suggestion, but I have always been of the opinion that such had been his intention.

The President selected from several names presented for the Mission to Spain, which had been declined by Mr. Woodbury, that of Gov. Van Ness,[2] of Vermont, and he was commissioned accordingly. Mr. Van Ness was a man of rare natural endowments and occupied a position among the friends of the National Administration in New England which entitled him to its favorable consideration. My relations with his family had been for years of an unfriendly character but I acquiesced cheerfully in his selection. The appointments of Mr. Preble[3] to the Netherlands, Mr. Randolph[4] to Russia, and several Chargés to other Countries having been agreed upon subsequently, I entered upon a very full examination of the condition of the public business at the different points to which new Ministers were sent, the actual state and past history of unfinished negotiations and the collection of materials for new instructions. Upon this work was bestowed between two and three of the most laborious months of my whole life. Other matters, of course, appertaining to the Department of State, occupied portions of my attention. Communications between the President and Foreign Ministers had been postponed till my arrival and I was grieved to learn from a friendly and well informed source that impressions adverse to the former had been made upon most of the members of the Diplomatic Corps. Naturally inclined, from causes that need not be stated, to side with the party least imbued with the democratic spirit of the Country, the members of that body have been always predisposed to approach with distrust any Chief Magistrate elevated to power by that influence. The character of the canvass which resulted in the election of Gen. Jackson and the

[1] Livingston to Jackson, May 3, 1829, in the Van Buren Papers.
[2] Cornelius Peter Van Ness.
[3] William Pitt Preble.
[4] John Randolph, of Roanoke.

unprecedented extent to which the feelings of the masses of the People had been enlisted in his favor had added much strength to this bias. Apprehensions arising from that and kindred sources, stimulated by the gossips of the Capital, a class to whose reports diplomatists are always ready to listen, had, I found, grown to a sort of panic. An idea of the nature and prevalence of this feeling may be formed by recurring to the interview between Mr. and Mrs. Livingston and myself at Philadelphia. If persons of their intelligence so well acquainted with Gen. Jackson, understanding the many admirable and strong traits in his character and withal sincerely solicitous for his success, could imbibe such gloomy views of the state of affairs at the seat of Government, in respect to points in which the Foreign Ministers took great interest, what must have been those of the Ministers themselves, entertaining in advance the apprehensions to which I have alluded.

I made it my business, without delay, to see Baron Huygens, the Minister from Holland, with whom as a brother Dutchman I had previously established very friendly relations, and Sir Charles R. Vaughan, the British Envoy, with whom I had been for some time also upon intimate and cordial terms, and to do what I could to remove the unjust impressions of which I have spoken, and I met with a degree of success which the elevated character of both had given me good reason to anticipate. I next invited the Diplomatic Corps, by direction of the President, to meet me in a body, at the Executive Mansion with a view to their presentation and on the evening before the day appointed for that purpose I sent the following note

To THE PRESIDENT.

DEAR SIR

In conversation last evening with Mr. Huygens he made a suggestion which I think deserves consideration. I mentioned to him, as I had before done to Sir Charles Vaughan, that as the only object of the introduction tomorrow was to relieve them and yourself from the embarrassments resulting from the very irregular interviews which had previously taken place, it could not be necessary to have anything like formal addresses. To this both assented and Mr. Huygens added that an impression had been made in Europe of an unfavorable character in respect to your dispositions in respect to our foreign relations; that they (the Diplomatic Corps) had already seen sufficient to relieve whatever apprehensions might have existed upon that point and were strongly disposed by their reports to do all in their power to effect the same result at their respective courts; that the invitation for to morrow was very proper in itself and had been well received and that if you should choose to submit a few observations to them of a general character and advancing only the same sentiments as those contained in your inaugural address, it would, he thought, enable them to do great good at home.

I submit to you whether avoiding anything like a set speech, and without designing it for any other publication than would be given to it by the Ministers, in their reports, and by common fame, you might not say to them, with advantage, that the sentiments you expressed in your inaugural address in regard to the foreign relations of the Country you now repeat to them; that your opinion now is and always has been that the true interests of this Country would always be best consulted by preserving the relations of peace with all the world, and an intercourse founded upon principles of fair reciprocity; that you entered upon the trust committed to you without foreign prejudices or predilections and with personal feelings of the most friendly character towards every nation with whom we have intercourse, and that it should be your endeavour as it was your sincere desire to promote the° interests of your own Country, without doing injustice to the rights of others, by the most frank, friendly and sincere negotiations.

I shall have the pleasure of seeing you either this evening or in the morning.

Yours truly

SUNDAY MORNING

April 5th, 1829.

The attendance of the Ministers was full and after they had been individually presented to the President he made them a brief address, expressing substantially the ideas which had been suggested, which, delivered in the General's invariably happy and impressive manner was received with the highest satisfaction and a copy having been furnished to each, at their request, was forthwith forwarded to their respective governments. The introduction was followed by invitations to dinner and an entertainment, to say the least of it, not inferior to those to which they had been accustomed, on similar occasions, anywhere. The simple yet kindly old-school manners of the host with the amicable assurances of his address and the unexceptionable quality of his banquet made the most favorable impressions upon the guests which they took no pains to conceal, and thus the anxieties of these gentlemen were completely relieved and their prejudices materially softened by the most approved diplomatic machinery.

Notwithstanding these auspicious signs of improvement in one branch of the public service, circumstances soon occurred in another by which my own continuance in the Cabinet was, for a brief period, involved in difficulty and doubt.

The President made it a rule of his administration from which he very rarely departed, to bring all questions in respect to which he had reason to anticipate opposition from his Cabinet, to a speedy decision,—a practice, founded in good sense and an accurate knowledge of human nature, which served to prevent the heart-burnings and excitement which such differences in opinion, when often discussed and long kept on foot, seldom fail to engender. He had doubtless, from a very early period, decided to appoint Samuel Swartwout Collector of the Port of New York, and, without anything having passed between us upon the subject, seemed to have

° MS. III, p. 70.

expected opposition from me, certainly, and possibly from the Secretary of the Treasury. He waited no longer than was made necessary by his indispensable attention to other important points which arose upon the complete organization of his Cabinet before that matter was brought forward and first broached to me in the following note:

April 20th, 1829.

DR. SIR

I have this morning sent to Mr. Ingham[1] the papers in relation to the New York Customs, requesting him after he examines them to hand them to you. Will you also have the goodness to look at them and give me your opinion in writing on the relative merits of the several applicants specifying at the same time the offices to which you would appoint them, and how far the principles we have adopted would justify dismissals from office in that Port? I wish now to act promptly on a subject which has a good deal worried me.

In addition to the papers sent Mr. Ingham this morning I have a few more confidential letters, for the most part in favor of Mr. Swartwout. The two Senators from New York, also, verbally recommended Mr. Swartwout.

I am, very respectfully Yrs &c

ANDREW JACKSON

Mr. VAN BUREN.

Although the General referred to the appointments in the Custom House generally, that of Collector was the bone of contention by which he had been worried. Upon examining the documents sent me I found the President's files as was usually the case on similar occasions, overburthened with recommendations in favor of Swartwout's appointment from persons too many of whom would have been bad advisers under any circumstances and had no right to speak for the friends of the administration in the City, and not a few of whom had opposed us in the election, with scarcely a communication from those who were best entitled to be heard from on the subject.

After consulting with the Secretary of the Treasury I wrote to our friends in New York apprising them of the danger of Swartwout's appointment unless they forthwith presented to the President unequivocal evidence of the sense of the city and advising that the Chamber of Commerce should be applied to for an expression of their opinion, not doubting that they would, notwithstanding their general political opposition to the administration, step forward, in a case of such magnitude and endeavour to prevent the great evil which I thought the appointment of Swartwout would be. I wrote to our Senators Dudley and Sanford,[2] to know whether they had recommended the act and received the fullest assurances from them that the President had been deceived upon that point. Having taken

---

[1] Samuel D. Ingram.   [2] Charles E. Dudley and Nathan Sanford.

these steps to secure an interference from the proper quarters, I prepared an opinion, in compliance with the President's invitation, which filled several sheets, stating unreservedly the objections to the appointment of Swartwout and to the character of the recommendations in his case, and suggesting the names of John Ferguson or Saul Alley for the office in question.

The following is an extract from my written opinion:—

I have known Mr. Swartwout for many years although not intimately. I have always regarded him as a generous, warm-hearted, and high-spirited man, influenced by kind feelings to his friends and have consequently never entertained any other than friendly feelings towards him personally. Politically he has never been and is not now in a situation to make his opinions the cause of prejudice or solicitude with me. It is my clear and decided opinion (and a firmer or better grounded conviction I never entertained in my life) that the appointment of Mr. Swartwout to the office of Collector of the Port of New York would not be in accordance with public sentiment, the interests of the Country or to the credit of the administration. Deeply impressed with the peculiar importance of this appointment and anxious fully to discharge the duty imposed upon me by your request, and by the relation in which I stand to you, I feel it my duty to add that his selection would in my judgment be a measure that would in the end be deeply lamented by every sincere and intelligent friend of your administration throughout the Union.[1]

This opinion was dated April 23rd, and delivered to the President on the next morning.

The Secretary of the Treasury informed me that he had prepared an opinion, coming to the same result, but as he did not seem disposed to compare notes with me I did not press him to do so, and I never saw the views he presented of the subject. During the evening of the day on which our opinions had been delivered I received the following notes:

FROM THE PRESIDENT.

April 24th, 1829.

DR SIR,

I have looked over your views and expositions as to the appointments in the Customs of New York with great attention and care, and, with the best lights afforded to my judgment, have settled in the determination to place Mr. Samuel Swartwout in the office of Collector. It will be matter of regret to me if our friends in New York shall complain of the selection, but from the strong and highly respectable recommendations presented in his favor I cannot suspect that any greater dissatisfaction will be produced than would be towards almost any other who might be selected; perfect and entire unanimity in appointments is not to be expected.

Respecting Mr. Swartwout all agree, and many have spoken, that he is a warm hearted, zealous and generous man, strictly honest and correct in all his dealings and conduct; none have impugned his ° integrity or honor. He is reputed to be poor, but as an honest man is " the noblest work of God," I cannot recognise this as an objection to any man. Mr. Jefferson's rule " is he honest— is he capable," I have always admired. This being the case of Mr. Swartwout,

---

[1] In the Van Buren Papers, April 23, 1829.   ° MS. III, p. 75.

from his recommendations, and it appearing that he can give the necessary security required of him, I have thought proper to appoint him.

Your friend

ANDREW JACKSON

Mr. VAN BUREN.

Respecting the appointment at Nashville (Attorney) I shall leave that to you; fair reciprocity is always right, and as I have given you, in your State, a Collector, I leave you, in mine, to give us an Attorney; asking nothing more than that you will give us as qualified a man. I have directed all the recommendations to be sent you for the applicants for this office.

Yours, &c

ANDREW JACKSON

April 24th 1829

To the SEC'Y OF STATE

These notes were accompanied by another informing me that he had appointed my friend, James A. Hamilton, District Attorney for the Southern District of New York. The President was well warranted in assuming that I was friendly to Mr. Hamilton and took an interest in his welfare. He carried a letter from me to Gen. Jackson when he went to New Orleans in his company, as a representative of the Tammany Society, to attend a celebration of the successful result of the Presidential election, and, after my appointment, I had also suggested his name to the President as Acting Secretary of State, during the interval previous to my arrival at Washington. But he was mistaken in supposing that I wished Mr. Hamilton to have or would have recommended him for the appointment conferred upon him. I could not have done so with justice to my political friends in New York and the appointee was himself too well satisfied of this to broach the subject to me, if he was advised of what was intended, of which I know nothing. He was sitting by me when the President's notes were received and they were instantly communicated to him. He said that he had not anticipated his own appointment, or words to that effect, to which I replied that he must be sensible that the difficulties of my position growing out of the appointment of Swartwout, with reference to the feelings of my New York friends, would be materially increased by what had been done; he admitted that such might be the case but added nothing further and I did not think that I had a right to say more. If I had received the slightest intimation that such a step was in contemplation my dissent would have been promptly expressed, altho' not for reasons founded on a want of integrity or capacity on his part. The General had doubtless been induced to believe either from the facts to which I have alluded, or thro' representations of Hamilton's friends, that his appointment would go far to reconcile me to that of Swartwout. I did not think, as I have said, that I had a right, under the circumstances, to ask him to decline, but so far as appearances could speak, he was not left in doubt in respect to my mortification at the whole transaction.

I had been from the beginning aware of the strong preference which Swartwout's apparently chivalrous character and engaging manners had excited in the breast of the President, but I had not anticipated nor was I at all prepared to witness its influence in so grave a form. The result came upon me at a moment when my health was feeble and my spirits depressed, and, tho' I had resisted all the reasonings that had been given to me, since my appointment, by men whose friendship I did not in the least doubt, my mind was not at ease in regard to my position. I took my hat and walked the streets of Washington until a late hour of the night deliberating whether I ought not to adopt the advice I had received and to resign a post surrounded by such embarrassments, but I returned to my lodgings and retired to my bed with my views in respect to the path of duty painfully unsettled. I need scarcely say that it was not by the possible consequences of a single appointment, important as that undoubtedly was, that I was induced to raise the question which I canvassed with so much earnestness. The evils I apprehended from a step of that character might, after all, not occur, or might be limited in extent, but the feeling which so deeply disturbed me arose from an apprehension, excited by what had just occurred that my dissatisfied friends might prove to have been right in their belief that persons who could never possess my confidence had acquired an influence over the President's mind which would force me to an ultimate resignation if they retained it.

But the first impressions of the morning, always to me the clearest and the best, presented the subject in a light which, tho' not divesting it of a few painful features, indicated the right way with reasonable distinctness. I was satisfied that in deciding upon the effect which this act of the President ought to have upon my own course I could not properly go beyond the motives by which I believed him to have been actuated. If I could think for a moment that he had made the appointment with impressions of Swartwout's character similar to my own my instant withdrawal was a matter of duty, but if on the other hand I felt authorized to assume that he had acted in good faith, under a sincere conviction that those impressions on my part were unfounded, and that whilst he gratified his personal predilections, he at the same time consulted well the public interest, I could not make his act the ground of resignation without pretending to rights which I did not possess. He was alone responsible for it and had extended to me all the consideration due to my position by asking and respectfully considering my advice. To have claimed more might well have been thought an encroachment on his Constitutional rights. A perseverance on his part in acts of the same nature to an extent sufficient to shew, beyond reasonable doubt, a radical and incurable defect in his character, would change the state of the question, but as matters stood my first duty was to try to prevent a state of things so greatly to be regretted and there was certainly much in the way the act in question had been performed to encourage me in making such an effort.

There were moreover certain other considerations of much weight in favor of the course I decided to pursue. I could not help feeling that my position was a peculiar one and that there were responsibilities attached to it of a character widely different from those which ordinarily attach to occupants of public stations, to explain which I must take the risk of exposing myself to the charge of excessive vanity—about the only reproach which my political enemies had never laid at my door. No man ever attained to eminence in our Country who was more exclusively the artificer of his own fortunes than was General Jackson, or whose unsurpassed personal popularity was founded to a greater extent upon the confidence of the People in the integrity of his motives and in the value of his disinterested services, unaided by extraneous or adventitious circumstances. In respect to practical good sense, sound and ripe judgment, knowledge of human nature, indomitable and incorruptible spirit and general capacity for business a large majority of the People of the United States relied upon him with the greatest confidence and with entire justice. But of his experience in executive duties like those which appertain to the office of President and of his habitual self control, a matter of vital importance in that high station, many of his warmest supporters were not without lively apprehensions—a portion anxiously distrustful. Hence arose a general solicitude on the part of his friends that he should have nearest to him in his Cabinet one to whose qualifications and discretion, in those respects, they might trust. The gratification of this desire was looked for, as the result proved, with unusual unanimity, in my appointment as Secretary of State, whether rightly or not is a question° which, in this view of the subject, it is not necessary to consider. Accordingly the result of the election was no sooner known than there arose, spontaneously throughout the Country, without respect to sections or cliques, a call upon the new President from those who had raised him to power for that appointment. To that expression there was no avowed exception. I have heretofore quoted Gen. Jackson's published declaration that he considered my name to have been placed before him for the place to which he called me by the united voice of the politi-

---

° MS. III, p. 80.

cal party by which he had himself been elected—a declaration often repeated by him in conversation and in letters as well while the formation of the Cabinet was in progress as subsequently. Thus holding my post my reflections satisfied me that I was not at liberty to withdraw from it without farther efforts to realize the wishes of those who had given me this gratifying proof of their confidence.

Under these impressions I decided to remain and only asked the consent of the President that I should inform my friends in New York that the appointment of Swartwout had been made against my earnest remonstrance and that of Hamilton without my knowledge or desire. This he promptly gave in a letter which stated the facts exactly and which he advised me to send to my friend Mr. Cambreleng with permission to shew it to whom he pleased. Swartwout succeded in making himself a popular Collector and the President made occasional good-natured allusions to the apprehensions I had exhibited on the occasion of his appointment, speaking of the matter as the greatest of the few mistakes he had known me to make. After I had resigned the office of Secretary of State and whilst we waited for the carriage in which he was about to accompany me a part of the way to Baltimore he placed in my hand my protest against Swartwout's appointment saying that it was a document which would not read well hereafter when it is considered how great was the error on which it was founded and begging me to take it and destroy it, or to permit him to do so. Perceiving the kind feeling in which the proceeding originated, I replied that I could not consent to its destruction, that I was free to confess that appearances favored his opinion but that the affair was not ended nor my apprehensions removed; that, however, if he would permit me, I would endorse upon it my sense of the kind motives which induced him to return it and that I accepted it because I could not deny the gratification which I knew he took in doing what he considered a favor to his friends. I wrote the endorsement in the carriage, read it to him and he laughed at my obstinacy.[a]

The sad catastrophe which followed is well known. The subject was never afterwards referred to between us. Even during my visit

---

[a] That my strong apprehensions were not confined to myself abundantly appears from Mr. Cambreleng's reply to my letter notifying him of Swartwout's appointment, from which I extract the concluding paragraph :—

NEW YORK 28 April 1829

MY DEAR SIR,

*   *   *   *   *   *   *

I congratulate you that the appointments for New York are at an end—and now mark me—if our Collector is not a defaulter in four years, I'll swallow the Treasury if it was all coined in coppers.

Most sincerely Yours
C. C. CAMBRELENG.[1]

Honble M. VAN BUREN

[1] In the Van Buren Papers.

to the Hermitage in 1842 when most of the transactions of that and still earlier periods interesting to himself were brought into review in the course of our familiar and to me deeply interesting conversations this matter was studiously avoided. He did not refer to it and I was too sensible of the extent of his disappointment and mortification to do so myself.

At the hazard of being thought to descend to matters too unimportant I recur to the day after my arrival at Washington to mention an incident which happened at that time. I do so because it goes to show how little either the abuse that had been heaped on both himself and Mrs. Jackson, to whom he was devotedly attached, or the rupture of personal and political friendships caused by the selection of his Cabinet, or the peculiar views of those by whom he was surrounded and by whom he was supposed to be unduly influenced, or all of them combined had weakened those just and honourable sentiments with which his nature was thoroughly imbued and which never failed to show themselves when occasion offered. His defeated competitor removed from the White House to Commodore Porter's place, on Meridian Hill, where he resided for some time. Up to the time of my arrival no one connected with the new administration, which had then been organized some six weeks, had called upon Mr. Adams. On examining into the cause of this omission I found that it was considered due to the feelings of the President which had been deeply wounded by an attack on Mrs. Jackson that had appeared in the Washington Journal, a newspaper extensively regarded as under the influence of Mr. Adams. Not believing that Gen. Jackson desired such a course to be pursued, and satisfied as to what my own should be, I apprised him of my intention to pay my respects to the ex-President, to which he instantly replied that he was glad to hear it. He said that the treatment which he had too much reason to think he had received from Mr. Adams was of such a character that he did not feel himself at liberty to overlook it or he would long before have called upon him himself, but this was his personal matter and his friends would best consult his own wishes when they left its treatment to him alone. It was his desire, he said, that those associated with him in the Government should treat Mr. Adams with the respect that was due to him and he was happy to find that I was about to set them so good an example. The beneficial effects shed upon the new relations which had been established between the President and myself by this magnanimous course on his part may well be imagined.

I made my call and was very cordially received by Mr. Adams, and I subsequently sent to him, from time to time, the despatches relating to unfinished negotiations in the results of which he expressed particular interest, with such of the foreign *newspapers* as he desired to read. When I left him he said he would give me a hint that I might find useful which was that no secrets could be kept in the State Department, but that on the contrary the foreign Ministers were always certain in one way or another to get information of any negotiation going on there in which their Governments felt an interest.

The first negotiation we instituted was one with the Sublime Porte for the establishment of commercial relations between Turkey and the United States, and the admission of American vessels to the navigation of the Black Sea. Apprehensive that other powers might interfere to our prejudice I availed myself of Mr. Adams' hint and kept all the papers at my private rooms while the matter was in progress. The negotiation was entirely successful and I embraced an early opportunity to advise Mr. Adams of the proceeding and the result, both of which he highly commended.

Encouraged by the General's remarks, I made a serious effort to re-establish friendly relations between him and Mr. Adams, and for a season with good prospect of success. Believing that the former would be entirely safe in assuming that Mr. Adams had no previous knowledge of the attack upon Mrs. Jackson, which had so much offended him, I urged that it was his business as the victor to make friendly advances and that moreover such was the course which the public would expect from his character. The injury of which he complained was one in regard to which he proved to be more implacable than was the case as to any to which he had been subjected. I finally prevailed upon him notwithstanding to promise me that he would on some fitting occasion speak to Mr. Adams and offer him his hand. The funeral of Doddridge, a member of Congress from Virginia, which I thought Mr. Adams by his partiality for the late member, would attend struck me as likely to present an appropriate opportunity. For some reason I was not able to be present myself but I made it my business to remind the General, before he started, of his engagement which he promised to fulfil. Calling afterwards to ascertain the result he told me, with obvious sincerity but with a smile which I confessed to be irrepressible when I heard his report, that he had approached Mr. Adams with a *bona fide* intention to offer him his hand, but that the "old gentleman," as he called him, "observing the movement, had assumed so ° *pugnacious* a look that *he was afraid he would* strike him if he came nearer!" I had no difficulty in explaining Mr. Adams' looks in a way to keep my proposition open for further consideration. Sometime afterwards the General, Major Donelson[1] and myself were sitting at the dinner table, after the ladies had retired, when one of us, perceiving a copy of a Congressional

---

° MS. III, p. 85.   [1] Andrew Jackson Donelson.

document on the mentelpiece, took it up and found it to be a report made by Adams as Chairman of the Committee on Agriculture. As the weather was unpropitious for walking and they were neither of them wine-bibbers, I proposed that the Major should read the report which he accordingly entered upon. To my amazement the brochure proved to be, under that cover, a labored, unjust and violent attack upon the President and his administration. For a while he listened with composure, occasionally interposing an expression of pity that the author should have nourished such violent antipathies at his time of life, but the charges became hotter and hotter and more and more unjust, his patience became exhausted and he said, with considerable vehemence, "Stop! Major, I will hear no more of it!"— and then, after a moment's pause, he turned to me, with a perfectly composed countenance, and added, "I hope, my dear Sir, that you are satisfied that it will be best to give up the project you have so much at heart."

I sincerely regretted that I was compelled to abandon the idea of reconciliation between these gentlemen as is many personal qualities, they were formed to like each other and were warm friends during the General's Seminole difficulties—perhaps the most trying period of his public life. Whatever differences of opinion may have existed in regard to the propriety of his [Adams] appearance in the House of Representatives or to the course he pursued there, no liberal mind can fail to admire the spirit and indomitable firmness with which he maintained opinions which he, doubtless, conscientiously believed to be right altho' they were not always in harmony with those of the House. On more than one of these occasions he presented a full length portrait of "the old man eloquent" not often exhibited to that body. One of those stirring and unpremeditated outbursts will be long remembered. The occasion was a proposition to give the President power to enforce our claims for indemnity against France. Mr. Webster had wound up a violent attack in the Senate upon the proposition by saying that he would not consent to give the power asked for by President Jackson even if our quasi-enemy were thundering at our doors! Mr. Adams, with kindled eyes and tremulous frame, closed an eloquent and forcible defense of the proposition with a hearty denunciation of the unpatriotic avowal which had been made in the other house and with the declaration, at the top of his piercing voice, that the man who was capable of uttering such a sentiment had but one step more to take, and that was to meet the enemy at the door and to join him! The excited feeling of the House broke forth, for the first time in either Hall of our national Legislature, in a general clapping of hands.

Mr. Adams' general personal demeanour was not prepossessing. He was on the contrary quite awkward, but he possessed one accomplishment for which those who had only seen his grave and unamiable looking countenance of the morning and in public could scarcely have given him credit,—he was, in a small and agreeable party, one of the most entertaining table companions of his day. Whilst the Presidential question was pending in the House of Representatives, I was, one day, somewhat surprised to receive an invitation from George Sullivan, of Boston, then temporarily residing at Washington, to meet Mr. Adams and a small party at dinner. On mentioning the circumstances to my friend, Forsyth,[1] he told me that Sullivan was electioneering for Mr. Adams, in a quiet way, by thus bringing him under the observation of gentlemen who had imbibed personal prejudices against him. He then informed me of Mr. Adams's proficiency in that accomplishment to which I have just referred and of which I was not before aware. I was not able to avail myself of Mr. Sullivan's invitation, but, in after days, I remembered the circumstance, and, as frequently as I felt myself at liberty to do so, especially during my occupation of the White House, I invited Mr. Adams to small round-table dinners and always derived unqualified delight from his society and valuable information from his conversation.

But it is time to return from this long digression. Dismissing from my mind, as far as possible, the feelings of mortification and regret which had been caused by the great mistake the President had unwittingly committed in the appointment of Swartwout, I devoted myself to the preparation of instructions for the Ministers to be sent to England, France, Spain and the Netherlands, besides others of minor grades.

The negotiation with England, in respect to the trade between the United States and her West India and North American Colonies, by the previous administration had not only been brought to an adverse close but had reached that result thro' much irritation on both sides. That with France to obtain indemnity for spoliations upon our commerce was in a condition apparently as hopeless after having been discussed *ad nauseam* under successive administrations. With such difficult and grave matters in the front ground, a thorough review not only of the original transactions out of which existing questions had arisen but of the several steps which had been taken by the parties towards their adjustment became indispensable. By such a course only could I hope to raise points sufficiently new and fresh, either in fact or in the manner of presenting them, to revive interest that had become dormant or to induce them to re-open questions which our adversaries affected to regard as settled.

---

[1] John Forsyth of Georgia.

My labours upon this branch of my official duties were thus spoken of in a contemporary publication:—

Our unadjusted foreign relations have been placed in a fair train of settlement. The labor and devotion to the public service by which this has been accomplished are not much known beyond the circle of the State Department. The Secretary has been employed for weeks in succession, from morning till sundown, in preparing dispatches and fitting out missions, involving the most important interests of the Country. Frequently time has been snatched from the night to accomplish these works in time for the departure of the foreign Ministers. Since last March, four Ministers have been furnished with instructions involving much labor and unweary research in the preparation. Two of these missions were particularly important; Mr. McLane, sent to England, and Mr. Rives commissioned to France. In addition to these foreign missions to England, France, Spain, and Colombia, we learn that Mr. Preble, Minister to the Netherlands, has just arrived at Washington preparatory to his departure for that Country. This Mission involves interests of great importance to the state of Maine. The settlement of the North-east Boundary question, which has been placed before the King of the Netherlands for his arbitration is now in a fair way of reaching a termination. In a short time a functionary will be sent out to Peru; and others perhaps to the other South American governments. Before the commencement of the next session of Congress, the Secretary of State will have accomplished an immense quantity of public business, &c, &c, &c.[1]

The results of these labours were without reserve communicated to Congress and thus subjected to the scrutiny and animadversions of able and violent, not to say reckless opponents, anxious almost without precedent, for the overthrow of the administration and scarcely less so to interpose obstacles in my path.

I am not aware that the construction or matter of those voluminous instructions have ever been unfavorably criticised with the single exception of that portion of one of them which was selected as a pretence for the rejection of my nomination as Minister to England. * * *[2]

---

[1] Niles Register, Vol. 37, p. 172.
[2] Three and a half pages of the MSS. have been cut out at this point.

CHAPTER XXII.

The Ministers to England and France were despatched as early as July and in the same public vessel. They arrived at the Courts to which they were respectively accredited early in September and entered upon the performance of their duties promptly and with a degree of energy, industry and perseverance which was expected from capable young men, covetous of fame and who felt that their success in undertakings of such magnitude, which had long baffled the efforts of numerous predecessors, could not fail to advance their progress towards the great goal—the Presidency—towards which their aspirations were as keen and perhaps as confidently directed as those of their most ambitious cotemporaries. They each brought to the accomplishment of the tasks assigned to them talents of a high order, with habits of industry not easily broken down and spirits not liable to be discouraged by slight obstacles. Speedy and complete success followed on the part of each in respect to the leading matters which had been committed to his care. Mr. McLane succeeded in bringing to a satisfactory conclusion, within ten months from his presentation to the King, the negotiation in relation to the trade between the United States and the English West India and North American Colonies, a subject which had for many years afforded matter of contention between the two governments and had involved six separate negotiations. By that arrangement our trade was placed on a footing more favorable than any on which it had ever stood and our commerce and navigation in the Colonial ports of Great Britain became entitled to every privilege allowed to other nations. To the propriety of the settlement there was no opposition on the part of the Senate, or in Congress or from any other quarter. Mr. Rives' efforts were equally successful altho' the period of the conclusion of his negotiation was somewhat longer deferred in consequence of a change in the Government of France and other causes.

It would be doing injustice to these gentlemen not to assign a large share of credit for the success of these negotiations to their personal exertions, but it would be doing at least equal injustice in another quarter not to notice the extent to which we were indebted for those results to the character of the new President, to the just and liberal principles which he had, unexpectedly to the Sovereigns of Europe, displayed in the developments of his foreign policy and not a little, perhaps, to a prudent foresight of the consequences

274

of persevering injustice in their dealings with a man of his temperament. The latter idea may be considered strengthened by the fact that indemnity was almost immediately obtained from the King of Denmark for claims of some twenty years standing and long continued intercession on our part without the slightest change of circumstances and by other instances of early success in our foreign affairs.

These prosperous negotiations so soon after its inauguration, doubtless added greatly to the strength and credit of the new administration, but its highest and most enduring honors were won by the wisdom and successful prosecution of its domestic policy. The leading points in that policy were:

First, the removal of the Indians from the vicinity of the white population and their settlement beyond the Mississippi;

Second, to put a stop to the abuses of the powers of the Federal Government in regard to internal improvements and to restrict its action upon the ° subject to measures both useful and constitutional;

Third, to oppose as well the re-incorporation of the existing National Bank, as the establishment of any other equally unauthorized by the Federal Constitution, and to substitute, in lieu of the aid which had been derived from such institution in the management of the fiscal affairs of the Government, an agency which whilst consistent with its authority would promise greater safety and greater success in that branch of the public service; and

Fourth, to arrest as far as possible the abuses that had crept into the legislation of Congress upon the subject of protecting duties and to restore it to the footing upon which it was placed at the commencement of the Government by imposing no duties beyond what was necessary for revenue and by assessing those in a way best adapted to encourage our own labor.

These, tho' not the only, were the most prominent of the domestic objects to which President Jackson, from the first moments of his elevation to power, directed his attention and for the accomplishment of which he sedulously employed the powers with which the People had clothed him. He entered forthwith upon the execution of this programme, kept it constantly in view, and labored to the end for its completion with the energy and perseverance that formed so large a part of his nature. Few men had less reason than himself to complain that his official acts were not fairly appreciated by the great body of the People for whose benefit they were performed. Seldom if ever had he to contend, as is so often the case with public men, with that lurking suspicion, common and perhaps natural to the

---

° MS. III, p. 95.

public mind, that the most zealous and seemingly the most earnest efforts for the public good have their origin in motives of personal ambition or self interest. In the great transactions of his life the masses doubted not that his only end and aim was their welfare and happiness. Even those who dissented from the wisdom of his measures were, with limited exceptions, ever ready to admit that he was honest and meant well.

The almost invariable consequence was a full share of public applause for the advantages he had the good fortune to secure to the Country in the course of his official career. Yet I have always thought and still think that the credit which has been awarded to him for the effective aid he rendered to his Country by his policy in respect to Indian Affairs and by the success with which it was executed has fallen far short of his deserts.

Certainly no other subject was of greater importance than this, whether we regard the extent to which were involved in its treatment either the interests of humanity, our national character and the character of our political institutions, or the peace and prosperity of the Country.

It is not requisite here to enter on the question how far our first encroachments upon the red men may be allowed to shelter themselves under the plea of a struggle between Civilization and Barbarism and to find excuse or palliation in the savage cruelties which characterized the resistance made by the latter to the advance of the former. By the events of the War of 1812 they had been reduced from powerful tribes or nations to absolute and otherwise hopeless dependence upon the clemency and justice of the United States. At the close of Mr. Monroe's administration they numbered some three hundred thousand souls, less than half of whom occupied reservations and other lands within our national boundaries, lying within nineteen different States and Territories. Altho' the most untiring efforts had been made to that end yet all past experience had demonstrated not only that any exertions of the Government to fit them for incorporation with the whites as citizens, thro' instruction and civilization would prove abortive, but that the course which had been pursued, that of buying their lands in detail and thus bringing them in closer contact with the white man, tended to hasten their demoralization and extinction. Under these adverse circumstances the thinking and truly philanthropic minds of our Country were directed to and their hopes for the future centered upon the plan for their removal and permanent establishment upon the most generous terms, on the public domain west of the Mississippi, and beyond the bounds of the States and Territories, for assisting them in forming a suitable Government, and for securing to them ample protection against both domestic feuds and encroachments from without.

To the execution of this policy there were obstacles of the gravest kind; not the least of these being that several of the tribes claimed and exercised the absolute right of self-government within the bounds of the States in which they resided. They founded this claim upon the fact that the U. S. Government at early periods in it's existence had treated with them as with foreign powers and upon the character of the Treaties it had made with them. This claim was actually asserted and enforced only in the States of Georgia, Alabama and Mississippi, but if well founded it was of equal efficacy in all the States in which any of the tribes were situated. These States had all been admitted into the Union with defined boundaries, including the Indians, and the sovereign authority reserved to the States by the Federal Constitution over all within their respective borders had been recognised and guaranteed by the Federal Government; and, to increase the complications of the subject, the latter had also, in some instances, bound itself for valuable considerations to extinguish the Indian titles within the state as soon as that could be done on reasonable terms. It is not necessary to enter upon an examination of the validity of the claim referred to on behalf of the Indians, as neither the Federal Government, nor any Department of it entrusted with its powers ever contemplated a removal of the tribes against their will, or the employment of force against them in any form, other than to subject them to the laws of the several States to the same extent to which other citizens were subjected to them. To do the latter it had solemnly bound itself and it was always quite apparent that no serious attempt could be made by it to sustain the Indians in their claims to the right of self government by the exertion of military power without producing a forcible collision between the General and State authorities which might lead to the destruction of the confederacy and more surely to the extirpation of the Indians.

Mr. Monroe, in his last annual Message, referred to the desirableness of their removal and pointed out, for their location, the territory they now occupy, which was then and has ever since been regarded as particularly well adapted to that purpose, and a little more than a month before the termination of his presidency he sent to Congress a special Message advancing many sound and philanthropic arguments in favor of this policy, accompanied by a full report, from the Secretary of War, of the facts necessary to safe and judicious action by the Legislature. No farther steps were taken towards the execution of the proposed plan and circumstances unhappily soon occurred which threw increased difficulties in its way. The Georgia Indians were divided upon the general question and a large and influential portion of them decided to remain where they were, never to sell any more of their lands to the Government, and to live, for the future, under laws of their own enactment. The representatives of that State, at the close of the same session at which Mr. Monroe's extra-message was sent in, charged, on the floor of Congress, that this state of things had been brought about by the intrigues of the officers of the General Government and openly questioned the good faith of the administration in the matter. These suspicions were doubtless increased and the excitement of the parties in respect to them unduly inflamed by the hostile feelings which had arisen between the Secretary of War (Mr. Calhoun) and his numerous friends in South Carolina, on the one part, and many of the prominent and influential public men of Georgia, on the other; feelings which retained their bitterness for many years and extended their disturbing effects to other portions of the Confederacy.

Such was the untoward condition of this great question when Congress adjourned and the Chief Magistracy of the Country devolved on Mr. Adams. Of his desire to do what he thought best as well for the Indians as for the United States, and, making due allowances for his habitual distrust of the doctrine of State rights, for the States also, there can be no doubt; but there is every reason to believe that the policy of the plan of removal to the west of the Mississippi, of which I have spoken, was, at that time at least, unfavorably regarded by him. In the first three of his four annual messages the subject was not even referred to. The Secretary of War, Gov. Barbour, wrote ° a letter to the Chairman of the Committee on Indian Affairs,[1] in answer to its application for aid and advice upon the general subject, in which he discoursed at length and eloquently upon the depressed condition to which the Indian Tribes had been reduced and the strength of their claims on our justice and generosity, and sketched a plan for their removal pursuant to the suggestions made in Mr. Monroe's message. But no one could read his letter without seeing that its entire drift was, not to promote such removal, but to throw obstacles in the way of anything like an effectual execution of that policy. It nowhere appears that that letter was not sanctioned by Mr. Adams and his Cabinet, and, during the second year of that administration, the Country was seriously threatened, as should have been foreseen, with a hostile collision between the Federal and State authorities upon the subject.

This mode of dealing with the matter, this ominous silence in respect to it on the part of the new President, who had himself

---

° MS. III, p. 100.
[1] Feb. 3, 1826. Amer. State Papers, Indian Affairs, v. 2, No. 231, p. 646.

occupied a position next to Mr. Monroe in the preceding administration, the severe denunciation by the Secretary of War of the
only way in which the Indians could, in all human probability,
be induced to remove, when added to the encouragements to remain
which Mr. Forsyth, who was too wise and too honest to deal in
false surmises on so grave a subject, openly announced on the floor
of Congress that they had received from the under officers of the
late administration, induced, as it was natural to expect from their
influence, large portions of the Indians, sufficiently numerous and
powerful to defeat that policy, to decline all further overtures upon
the subject.

The result was a confederacy, openly formed between the powerful tribes of Creeks and Cherokees, scattered over the states of
Georgia, Alabama and Mississippi, to prevent the sale of any more
lands by the members or officers of their respective tribes, and to
establish themselves permanently within those States.

Other circumstances exasperated the feelings of the parties more
immediately concerned to a height which threatened the peace of
the Country. During the last year of Mr. Monroe's administration
a treaty was made with the Creeks in Georgia, by which their title
to all the lands they occupied within that State was extinguished.
A portion of them believed to have been encouraged by the dispositions manifested toward them on the part of men in power, made
various objections to that treaty and resisted its execution. To
allay these dispositions a new treaty was made, during the first
year of the government of Mr. Adams, by which the former treaty
was declared to be annulled and some two or three hundred acres
of the land released by it were left out of the new treaty. Georgia
was of course greatly dissatisfied with this proceeding, not so much
on account of the value of the land attempted to be given back to
the Indians as because it defeated the policy of their removal from
the State for which she was most solicitous. She insisted that she
possessed a right to the soil and jurisdiction over the lands in the
occupancy of the Indians, subject only to the power of Congress
"to regulate commerce with the Indian tribes that she had a right
to legislate for them in all cases not within that exception; that all
the right to them ever held by the Indians was legally extinguished
by the first treaty; that that extinguishment enured to her benefit
and that the Federal Government could not, without her consent, an-
nul that treaty after it had been fully ratified. The dissenting
Indians contested all these points and claimed that Georgia had no
jurisdiction over them and that they could not be affected by any
acts of her legislation.

The legislature of Georgia passed a law in the form prescribed by her Constitution, directing a survey of all the lands to which the Indian title was extinguished by the first treaty. Learning that the surveyors under the direction of the Governor of the State had entered upon the execution of the duties assigned to them by the law referred to, the Little Prince and other dissenting Chiefs of the Creek Nation sent to the surveyor's camp a manifesto signed by them, ordered the surveyors " not to stretch a chain over their lands " and, upon the attempt of those functionaries to proceed, caused them to be arrested, and communicated the facts to the President with a demand for the protection of the Federal Government against further encroachment of the part of the state of Georgia.

In the year 1802 Congress passed an act to regulate trade and intercourse with the Indian tribes and to preserve peace on the frontiers. It provided that if any citizen or other person, resident in the United States, should make a settlement on lands belonging to any Indian tribe, or should attempt to survey such lands, he or they should forfeit one thousand dollars and be liable to imprisonment for a period not exceeding six months. It furnished several summary and very efficient means of enforcing the penalties for such acts; 1st by civil process to be executed when necessary by the Military power of the United States, in any state of the Union where the offender could be found, and his trial and punishment where found; and 2d, by making it the duty of the military forces of the Federal Government to arrest all persons found on such Indian lands in violation of that act and to deliver them to the Civil authorities of the United States in any one of the three adjoining states for trial and punishment.

The facts submitted to the President by the Creek Chiefs presented several very grave questions for his consideration in the first instance viz: 1st, whether the case was of the character contemplated by the act of 1802, and 2d, whether the claims set up by Georgia were valid and whether there was anything peculiar to the conditions of the Indians which exempted their lands from a liability to the authority of the States that could not be questioned in regard to lands owned by any other of her citizens.

The President took it upon himself to dispose of both of these questions, decided then in favor of the Indians and informed Congress, in a message, that he had no doubt of his authority to use the military force in the case presented to him, but that he had abstained from doing so in the first instance because the surveyors ought not perhaps to be considered as solitary transgressors but as the agents of a sovereign state, who would be sustained, it had been intimated, by her utmost power, and thus a violent collision might have occurred between the authorities of the two Governments if he had immediately used the military resources entrusted to him. But he stated distinctly that, if the laws of the Union remained unaltered, and the state of Georgia persevered in her encroachments upon the Indian territory, " a superadded obligation. even higher than that of human authority, would compel the Executive of the United States to enforce the laws and fulfill the duties of the nation by all the force committed for that purpose to his charge."

He submitted to Congress whether any further legislation was necessary to meet the emergency. None was suggested by him or thought proper or necessary by Congress, but the excitement produced in that body by the Message was intense and the debates were unusually bitter but without any results in the way of legislation. In the Senate the select Committee to whom the Message was referred, composed in part of supporters of the Administration, unanimously reported a simple resolution, "that the President be respectfully requested to continue his exertions to obtain from the Creek Indians a relinquishment of any claims to lands within the state of Georgia," which passed without a dissenting voice. But in the House, where the power of the Administration was far greater, the debate and proceedings were intemperate on both sides. The Committee appointed by the Speaker reported against Georgia on all points and concluded with resolutions to the effect that " it was expedient to obtain a cession of the Indian lands within the limits of Georgia," but that until a cession is procured, the laws of the land as set forth in the Treaty of Washington (the second treaty) ought to be maintained by all necessary constitutional and legal means. This report was made on the last day of the session, too late, of course, to be acted upon, but was ordered to be printed.

The Administration relieved itself before the next session of Congress from all further embarrassments upon that particular branch of the subject, greatly complicated by the President's inconsiderate Message and the ground apparently taken by the House Committee in his support, by another °treaty, extinguishing the Indian title to the residue of the lands embraced in the first treaty and excluded from the second. Treaties providing for their removal to a limited extent were occasionally made with Indians willing to go, but nothing very material was effected. Those who were unwilling were, on the contrary, persevering in their efforts to induce their brethren to remain. The Cherokees, a powerful tribe, composed to

---

° MS. III, p. 105.

a considerable extent of whites, some of them educated and instructed in business affairs, taking the lead in carrying into effect the principles for which they contended, proceeded to the establishment of an Independent Government, framed as they insisted upon republican principles, within the bounds of Georgia, and, at page 198 of the 35th volume of Niles' Register, will be found a Message from the principal Chiefs to the General Council of the Nation, after the manner of the official communications from the President of the United States. In it they recommended to the Council, as the immediate representatives of the People, to send a memorial to Congress advising that body to redeem its obligations to Georgia in some other way than one based on the anticipation of further cessions of land from them.

The conflicts thus occasioned between the state of Georgia and the Cherokees can easily be conceived. These continued down to the Presidential election in which Mr. Adams was defeated. In his last Message he seems to have viewed the matter in a far different light. " When we have had," he says, " the rare good fortune of teaching them (the Indians) the arts of civilization and the doctrines of Christianity we have, unexpectedly found them forming in the midst of ourselves communities claiming to be independent of ours and rivals of sovereignty within the territories of the members of the Union. This state of things requires that a remedy should be provided which, while it shall do justice to those unfortunate children of nature, may secure to the members of our federation the rights of sovereignty and of soil," and for an outline of a project to that effect he recommends to the consideration of Congress the report of the Secretary of War. Turning to that document the reader will find that the Secretary, Peter B. Porter, a sensible, practical man, conversant with the Indian character and with Indian affairs, recommends substantially the policy contended for by those who supported the claims of Georgia, including the subjection of " all who remain to the municipal laws of the State in which they reside."

This Message of Mr. Adams was prepared shortly after the election in which his political fortunes had been wrecked and when whatever hopes or plans he subsequently cherished, he considered his public life as closed. He had, as we have seen strongly committed himself to different views. His friends in the House of Representatives, where they constituted a majority, had sustained those views in an able and animated report, they had converted the subject into a material for political agitation in the Presidential canvass and had found it, at least so far as respected him, unavailing. He now looked upon it with the eyes of a Statesman sincerely desirous to set himself right with the Country and with posterity in regard to a matter which he could not but feel was one of the deepest import, and thus considering it, it was impossible that he should have failed to arrive at right conclusions. He directed his attention to the point of greatest prominence and of greatest hazard—the safety of the Union. There was a plausibility, founded exclusively on the loose character of our dealings with the Indians during the early period of our Government, in the pretension to political power set up by them and on their behalf. He found our system already an *imperium in imperio*, perhaps the most complicated in the World, and of course requiring the utmost care and forebearance in the administration of each, subjected in two of the States to the establishment within their bounds of a third Government claiming sovereign and independent political power, and, not only so, but that we were menaced with the immediate establishment of similar Governments in one or two other States, and exposed, if these succeeded, to the erection of others like them in a dozen more, and in all these cases one branch of the tripartite sovereignty was to be lodged in savages and half-breeds. The question presented to his mind by this state of facts was as to the probability not to say possibility of our existing national confederation being upheld under such a process—a confederation so essential not only to the welfare and happiness of the peoples of the United States but in a very great degree, to the interests of human liberty and the hopes of its considerate friends throughout the world, and to the escape of the Indians themselves from ultimate certain annihilation. Such was the question, stripped of immaterial issues and mystifying verbiage about which no sensible man, looking only to the good of the whole, could it would seem, hesitate for a moment. Mr. Adams was satisfied that the great hazards which environed it ought not to be encountered for the sake of a claim so immature and defective as that of the Indians to self-government, and the language in which he admonished Congress in his last Message of the necessity of a remedy for the great evils with which the Country was threatened was that of an enlightened and patriotic statesman.

Secretary Porter, in the report referred to by Mr. Adams said: "If the policy of colonization be a wise one, and of this I believe no one entertains a doubt, why not shape all our laws and treaties to the attainment of that object, and impart to them an efficiency that will be sure to effect it," and advised that all of the Indians who would not emigrate should be subjected to the municipal laws of the States.

If the President and his Secretary of War had spoken thus at the commencement of his Administration and if he and his Cabinet had done all in their power to shape the laws and treaties of the Government to the promotion of the policy of Colonization, that great work would have been accomplished in their day. But we have seen that they did neither, and it was now too late to secure its success under their auspices. When the Constitution makers of France strove to reconcile the first Napoleon to an abridgment of his immediate power by proposing to confer upon him authority to direct what should be done after his decease he promptly refused the offer for the reason that "a dead man was nothing in respect to power whatever or whoever he may have been when alive." The same may be said of a President whom a few short months will dispossess of his station in obedience to the decree of the People. The sceptre had departed from Mr. Adams when he promulgated the words which I have quoted, the hopes of the supporters of his administration for restoration to power were then already turned to another and their decision to the course they would take upon a question, in respect to which the public mind was so liable to be excited, was for partizan reasons, held in abeyance.

Substantially in the state which I have described, these matters stood until Gen. Jackson, then President elect, became President in fact; a state most unpromising for the colonization policy. He forthwith devoted his utmost efforts to the remedy of this great public evil and no man ever entered upon the execution of an official duty with purer motives, firmer purpose or better qualifications for its performance. It seemed a task providentially reserved for one so admirably fitted for it by the elements of his character and by his past experience.

Except perhaps the single subject of slavery there could not have been one more liable to seizure and appropriation to their own purposes by political and partizan agitators than that now under our consideration. As the Christian religion had been the greatest agent of civilization throughout the world, the Government could not, in attempting to extend its blessings to the Indians, omit to invoke the co-operation of the Christian ministry. Clerical missionaries were accordingly sent among them and the Country from time to time heard of the great success which had attended their labours of love. Clergymen are not over liberal as partners in power over a subject to the management of which their agency is admitted and they soon assumed the principal guardianship of the Indians, holding themselves to protect them against oppression whether it might proceed from individuals or from the Government and authorized to weigh the measures of the latter and to condemn them if they considered them worthy of censure. Accountability to what is sometimes called the *religious community*—a class °
among us easily instigated to meddle in public affairs and seldom free, on such occasions, from a uniform political bias, had thus

---

° MS. III, p. 110.

become one of the responsibilities under which the President acted. The Society of Friends was another large interest which claimed the right to speak and seldom failed to make itself heard, in respect to every movement of the Government that related to the Indians and they too entertained apprehensions in regard to the course to be expected from the "unbridled democracy" of which President Jackson, was in their estimation, the favored leader.

It had become manifest that the removal of the Indians could not be brought about by any measures of which the extension of the laws of the State, with the approbation of the Federal Government, over those who remained, after all proper means had been exhausted to provide for their welfare in a suitable and safe new home, did not form a part. That such measures would be disapproved of by the powerful classes of whom I have spoken was positively certain, and it had therefore become indispensable to their success that their execution should devolve upon a man who was willing, in the performance of his duties, to encounter that opposition—a qualification which had not yet been found in any President after the necessity for such measures had occurred. It was scarcely less necessary that he should be one whom experience had made thoroughly conversant with the Indian character, not only knowing them but being also well known by them as one who would do what be promised, whether it was an act of liberality or of severity and as one who, tho' not disposed to withhold from them any favors that would promote their welfare and that could be extended consistently with the safety of our institutions, would not fail, at the same time, to exert all the means lawfully within his reach to accomplish his object.

Gen. Jackson entered upon the consideration of this important subject at the earliest practicable moment and strove for the accomplishment of his policy as long as there was reason to hope for success, regardless of obstacles which would have discouraged less sanguine minds. For the first time, I believe, since the establishment of the Government, the subject of Indian affairs was specifically noticed in the Inaugural Address. As he [the President] was emphatically a practical man and felt that the matter must constitute one of the leading concerns of his administration he thought the sooner public attention was directed to it the better. Within three weeks after his Inauguration having occasion to send a " talk " to the Creeks, in relation to the murder by some of their people of a white man. he introduced to their consideration the subject of removal. He told them that he had been made President and that he now addressed them as their father and friend. He reminded them that in his talk to them many years before he had spoken of the Country west of the Mississippi as one where alone they could be preserved as a great nation and he now advised them to go there. He assured them, however, that if they chose to remain in Alabama, and to come under the laws of that State, they might rely on his protection, that their lands should be set off to them and their families in fee, and that they should be secured in all the rights and privileges enjoyed by the white people; that his whole course towards them should be stamped with the frankness and sincerity by which his dealings with the tribes had always been distinguished and which a full experience had satisfied him was the most likely to be successful in the end. He next caused the Indians in Georgia and Alabama to be officially informed that the project of establishing independent Governments within the States in which they resided would not be countenanced by the Executive. This notice was, he said, due to them, and would, he hoped, have the effect to nip in the bud the movement in that direction which commenced in Mississippi, and to discourage such undertakings, if they were contemplated, in the other States having Indians within their bounds.

When Congress met he made to that body the most unreserved communication of his views upon the whole subject in his Annual Message. He placed the claims of the Indians upon our consideration and favor on the grounds he thought they deserved to occupy, and avowed his readiness to promote all constitutional and practicable measures for their gratification. He then gave his reasons for holding that their pretensions in respect to the organization of separate governments were unfounded, demonstrated their impracticability, foreshadowed the ruinous results to our confederation that would inevitably result from any attempt to establish such a right in them by the power of the Federal Government, and concluded his explanations with the following equally specific recommendations:—[1]

---

[1] The MS. here directs the inclusion of the following: As a means of effecting this end, I suggest, for your consideration, the propriety of setting apart an ample district West of the Mississippi, and without the limits of any State or Territory, now formed, to be guaranteed to the Indian tribes, as long as they shall occupy it; each tribe having a distinct control over the portion designated for its use. There they may be secured in the enjoyment of governments of their own choice, subject to no other control from the United States than such as may be necessary to preserve peace on the frontier, and between the several tribes. There the benevolent may endeavor to teach them the arts of civilization; and by promoting union and harmony among them, to raise up an interesting commonwealth, destined to perpetuate the race, and to attest the humanity and justice of this Government.

This emigration should be voluntary: for it would be as cruel as unjust to compel the aborigines to abandon the graves of their fathers, and seek a home in a distant land. But they should be distinctly informed that, if they remain within the limits of the States, they must be subject to their laws. In return for their obedience, as individuals, they will, without doubt, be protected in the enjoyment of those possessions which they have improved by their industry. But it seems to me visionary to suppose that, in this state of things, claims can be allowed on tracts of country on which they have neither dwelt nor made improvements, merely because they have seen them from the mountain, or passed them in the chase. Submitting to the laws of the States, and receiving, like other citizens, protection in their persons and property, they will, ere long, become merged in the mass of our population.—Jackson's 1st Annual Message.

With the manly and unequivocal recantation by his predecessor of the erroneous views he had at first entertained, and his virtual adoption of the recommendation of his Secretary of War in favor of the very measure Gen. Jackson now proposed, before him, and considering that the political party from which alone he had any reason to apprehend opposition to his policy had not only brought the previous Administration into being but was yet fresh from a great battle for its continuance in power, it is not surprising that a man of Jackson's training, unversed in the ways of politicians, should have counted upon a general concurrence in the praiseworthy views he had disclosed upon a subject so interesting to humanity and so important to the public interest. But he was soon furnished with ample reasons to convince him that any hopes and anticipations of that character were mere delusions. That party knew, as well as any future event of that nature could be known, of the great contest with him on the Bank question which impended, and eagerly seized the tempting opportunity presented by the Indian difficulties to cripple his Administration in advance. Without suggesting anything of their state in respect to the other branch of the divine injunction, those partisans were certainly not as harmless as doves, and knowing full well that we had not as yet had no President possessed of sufficient moral courage to deal with that subject in the way in which alone it could be wisely treated they were slow to believe that this unfledged Statesman would be able to do so successfully, and they determined not to forego the advantages it seemed to offer.

The first step was the passage of a law clothing the Executive with adequate powers if the Indians consented to remove and the next to obtain their consent to its execution. Without success in the latter openly and fairly obtained, Gen. Jackson did not desire it in the general object however important he considered it to the public welfare.

The Committees on Indian Affairs in both Houses reported a Bill, short, simple and comprehensive and then followed the death struggle for its passage, for such, especially in the House of Representatives, it emphatically was. The Bill authorized the President to cause so much of the territory of the United States, west of the Mississippi, as he might judge necessary to be divided into a suitable number of Districts for the reception of such tribes or nations of Indians as might choose to exchange the lands on which they then resided and to remove there; to exchange such districts with any tribe or nation, then residing within the limits of any State or Territory, with which the United States had existing treaties, and where the lands were owned by the United States or where the latter were bound to the States to extinguish the Indian title; to make compensation to the Indians for their improvements, and to provide all necessary aid for their removal and for their support for one year afterwards, with suitable clauses securing the guarantee and protection of the United States as recommended by the President in his Message.

When this Bill was taken up in the Senate, the body in which the subject was first acted upon, Mr. [Theodore] Frelinghuysen, of New Jersey, moved to add to it the following section:

SEC. 9. That until the said tribes or nations shall choose to remove, as by this act is contemplated, they shall be protected in their present possessions, and in the enjoyment of all their rights of territory and *government*, as heretofore exercised and enjoyed, from all interruptions and encroachments.

The clause attempted to mark the nature and extent of the right of self-government proposed to be reserved to the Indians by assuming as a fact what was denied° that it was a right they had "theretofore exercised and enjoyed." But the design in the use of the phraseology employed was to make the proposition appear less rank than it would if the right intended to be reserved was simply and plainly set forth in the additional section. It was meant, as fully appears from the debate, to test the principle as to the right of the Indians to maintain independent political Governments within the States in which they resided, under the belief that the movement would involve the fate of the colonization policy and, if successful, defeat it, as no one would for a moment believe that the Indians would remove as long as the power of Congress stood pledged to support them in the exercise of that degree of sovereignty.

The *Whig* party (as the opposition was then called) rallied with perfect unanimity in favor of Mr. Frelinghuysen's amendment and against the Bill. A more persevering opposition to a public measure had scarcely ever been made. Few men would now venture to deny that it was a factious opposition waged to promote the interests of party at the expence of the highest interests of the Country, upon grounds which were not tenable and for avowed purposes which were not practicable,—or, if practicable, could only become so thro' the agency of the U. S. Army and the probable destruction of the Confederacy. The subject was discussed with brief intermission, from the 9th to the 26th April, when the additional section, offered by Frelinghuysen, was rejected, every whig Senator voting in favor of it as did also the only Jackson Senator from Pennsylvania, and the Bill passed the Senate by a small majority that Senator finally voting in its favor. The opposition did not expect to defeat it in the Senate. The debate and proceedings in that body having been principally designed for the effect they

° MS. III, p. 115.

might produce on the public mind and, through that source, on the popular branch of Congress. It was to the House of Representatives that they looked as the theatre of triumph and the result shewed that they had very strong grounds for the confidence they entertained of such a result. The majority of what were called Jackson men in that body was sixty five, but it was in a great degree composed of gentlemen who had shortly before professed different politics from the mass of his supporters and thus were not only new in the republican fellowship, but many of them not over well instructed or very deeply imbued in the principles of the party they had joined. This class of the General's friends were peculiarly liable to be influenced by the dread of giving offence to the Quakers and to the religious communities, and were prone to communicate their apprehensions to their new associates. The influence of this feeling was strikingly exhibited in the vote of the delegation from Pennsylvania which, tho' more exposed than others to a Quaker panic, was in other respects more relied upon on account of the very general and very strong attachment of her People to General Jackson who, in a great degree, staked the success of his administration upon this measure. Of her twenty six members (of whom all but one were elected as Jackson men) only six voted for the Bill, three of those subsequently voted against the previous question because it would cut off an amendment, which went to defeat the measure in a round about way, two of them were with difficulty brought to the final vote, and such men as [James] Buchanan and [George G.] Leiper, the latter representing a Quaker district, felt themselves constrained to shoot the pit. The same influences produced similar effects upon the representatives of other States and the result was that after a debate as protracted and excited as any that had ever before taken place in that body, and notwithstanding the large nominal preponderance in favor of the Administration, the measure recommended by the President was carried in the House by a majority of only four on a preliminary vote and of five on its final passage.[1]

Congress had performed its duty by the enactment of the law, and the Constitution as well as his oath of office imposed upon the President the obligation to see to its execution. Another opportunity was thus presented to the opponents of his Administration to shew by their actions that they placed a higher value upon the interests of the Country and the welfare of the Indians than upon party conquests. But unfortunately for those interests and for their own highest good, altho' defeated in respect to the passage of the Bill,

[1] An act to provide for an exchange of lands with the Indians * * * and their removal west of the river Mississippi. Approved, May 28, 1830.

they were too much encouraged by their extraordinary success in making converts in the House of Representatives to heed such considerations. They foresaw as they thought the political advantages of the struggle which had been fomented by their unfounded pretension to culminate in their triumph at the ensuing Presidential election, all unconscious of the utter overthrow of their hopes which was gathering strength in the sober second thoughts of the People. They set every engine in motion to throw obstructions in the way of the President, and received a full measure of cooperation from their usual auxiliaries in great crises, the Press, the Courts of law and, last tho' far from least in power and influence, the Church.

If the question had been one of power simply the President would have soon settled it, but he could not act effectively, nor did he desire to do so, without the consent of the Indians and he was both too wise and too just to take any steps to obtain that consent which the good sense and good feeling of the Country would not finally approve. Those who understood his character soon became satisfied of this, but those who did not hoped to drive him to acts of violence which would destroy his popularity. Hence they blamed every thing he did, and responded to every act of resistance on the part of the Indians and by such measures of co-operation as were suited to the habits of civilized life.

The Cherokees refused to meet the President in Council to negotiate upon the subject of their lands, and answered his invitation by a legislative act denouncing the penalty of death against any one of their nation who should attempt to sell their lands without the assent of the National Council. In their Memorial to Congress, rising in their pretensions, from the encouragement they received, they claimed to be a Sovereign State independent as well of the *Federal Government* as of Georgia, and as such one of their Chiefs undertook to stop the mail on its passage over their lands and resisted the exercise of criminal jurisdiction by that State [Georgia] within their bounds.

Those portions of the Press favoring the pretensions of the Indians to the right of self-govenment were at the same time filled with encomiastic accounts of the prudence of the Cherokees and of their capacity for the discharge of its duties and denunciations of the conduct of Georgia and of the President.

Chief Justice Marshall issued a Citation to the State of Georgia to appear before the Supreme Court, pursuant to a Writ of Error, to shew cause why a judgment of a Superior Court of that State against an individual for murder committed within the bounds of that State, but on Cherokee territory, should not be corrected and speedy justice done to the parties. The citation was communicated to the Legislature by the Governor of Georgia with a declaration that orders from the Supreme Court interfering with the decisions of their State courts in such a matter, would so far as related to the Executive Department, be disregarded and any attempt to enforce them resisted with all the force the laws had placed at his command. Thus were the pacific relations between the Federal Government and one of the States of the Confederacy a second time endangered by high functionaries of the former, but the danger was avoided now, as at the first, by the firmness of the State authorities and an abandonment of their avowed intentions on the part of the former.

Nothing further was done with the Writ of Error, but proceedings to the same end were instituted in a different form. A Bill was filed by Mr. Wirt, in the same Court, in favor of "The Cherokee Nation against the State of Georgia," praying an injunction to restrain that State from executing the laws of the State within the Cherokee territory.

Georgia refused to appear to the Summons or to have anything to do with the proceedings. The hearing was therefore *ex parte*, but the application was notwithstanding argued at great length and, as the newspapers said, with great ability, by Messers. Wirt and Sergeant, of course for the Cherokees. The Suit was brought by them, claiming to be a "Foreign State" under the article of the Federal Constitution, defining the extent of the judicial power of the Federal Government. The Supreme Court held, unanimously, that their claim to be so regarded was manifestly untenable.[1] Thus ruling, there was, of course, an end of the proceeding. As the plaintiffs had no right to appear in that Court in the character they had assumed for the purpose, they had no right to ask its opinion on any point in the case they had presented. But Chief Justice Marshall, who delivered the opinion of a majority of the Court, whilst concurring with the Whole Bench that the Plaintiffs had no right to bring the suit, went on notwithstanding, as he did in the famous case of Marbury and Madison, to deliver an *extra-judicial opinion*, upon one of the material points presented by the case, and declared that "so much of the argument of counsel as was intended to prove the character of the Cherokees *as a State*, as a distinct political Society, separated from others, capable of managing their own affairs, and *governing itself*, has, in the opinion of a majority of the Judges, been completely successful." He intimated also that "the mere question of right to their lands *might perhaps* be decided by the Court in a proper case with proper parties", but as the Bill asked them to do more &c they could not interfere. Not content

---

[1] Cherokee Nation *v.* Georgia, Peters, 5, 1–80.

with this he was pleased to add that " if it was ° true that wrongs had been inflicted on the Cherokee nation, and that still greater were to be apprehended, that was not the tribunal to redress the past or to prevent the future."

Justices Baldwin and Johnson [1] delivered separate opinions, concurring in the only point the Court was competent to decide, but dissenting from all that was *said* beyond. Mr. Peters, the Reporter, *decided to publish the case immediately, separately from the volume in which it would appear in the ordinary course, and to give* (to use his own language) " *Mr. Wirt's great argument in behalf of the Cherokees, which had been taken down by stenographers employed for the purpose!* "

Is it possible for an intelligent mind to doubt that the design of these extraordinary proceedings, as well the extra-judicial decision of the Court as the electioneering pamphlet gotten up by its Reporter, was the same, or that that design was to operate upon the public mind adversely to Georgia and to the President?

The Cherokees, as they well might do, regarded the opinion of the Court, on the great point in controversy between them and Georgia, as expressed in their favor, and contended that the President was bound by it and said so in an Address by their Chiefs and Head Men to the People of the United States, which, with Mr. Peters' Report, was published and scattered over the whole Country.

To sustain this suit it was necessary that two points, independent of its merits, should be decided in their favor: 1st, that the Cherokees were a foreign State, in the sense of the Constitution, and, 2nd, that the Supreme Court was competent so far to exercise the political power as to enjoin the action of a State Government in the highest exercise of its sovereignty. It required an extraordinary stretch of charity to believe that their learned and intelligent counsel could have entertained the slightest confidence in the tenability of either position. The fact that the majority of a Court composed of their political friends, honorable men but cherishing sympathies in favor of the cause in which the great abilities of the counsel were employed as strong as their own, rejected both propositions without hesitation, makes overwhelmingly against the good faith in which the proceedings were instituted. They could not therefore complain that their political opponents, as well as the cool judgment of many who were not politicians, regarded the whole proceedings as fictitious, not to say factious, and designed for political effect; and it was a source of deepest mortification that those who moved in it had, in the course of its prosecution, succeeded in obtaining the indirect countenance and aid of the Court thro' its expression, or, to

---

° MS. III, p. 120.   [1] Henry Baldwin and William Johnson.

speak more correctly, thro' the expression by a majority of its members of an extra-judicial and partizan opinion, than which the diffusion of Peters' report and Wirt's eloquent speech in favor of the "poor Cherokees" (altho' objectionable as attempts to prostitute judicial proceedings to electioneering purposes,) was far less painful.

But the political aid derived from impressions systematically made on the religious community by the continued and deceptive agitation of this matter was still greater. Missionaries had been sent into the Cherokee Country, during the Administration of Mr. Adams, by the American Board of Foreign Missions, who were to some extent regarded as Agents of the Federal Government, and, as such, exempted from the laws of Georgia forbidding white men from residing among the Cherokees without a license from the Governor. These men, partaking of the feelings which actuated their friends at home, and not indisposed to acquire the notoriety of political martyrdom in a political cause, busied themselves in the question of removal. The Governor of Georgia asked for their withdrawal and they were disavowed by the Federal Government as persons in its service, but they nevertheless remained at their posts. They were informed of the law and requested to depart, and, on their refusing to do so, were arrested. Declining all offers of accommodation which involved their leaving the Cherokee territory, they were subjected to the operation of the law under which they were convicted and imprisoned. It is scarcely possible now, when the delusion has passed away, and when all see that the course adopted was the wisest and best for the Indians, to realize the extent to which many of our religious societies were agitated and disturbed by the imprisonment of those missionaries, and there was no doubt that not less than eight or ten thousand voters, in the state of New York alone, were controlled at the succeeding Presidential election in the bestowal of their suffrages by that single consideration. Gen. Jackson and myself were then candidates for the offices of President and Vice-President and I cannot perhaps give a more striking illustration of the force of that excitement than by relating an occurrence which fell under my observation. Passing, previous to the election, thro' the western part of our state, where the pro-Cherokee feeling had been lashed to a great height, I stopped for a night at the residence of a near and very dear relative of my own—a lady of remarkable intelligence and strength of character, and deeply imbued with religious feeling. After I had retired to my room she entered it and after a kind introduction and welcome soon proceeded to a spirited denunciation of our proceedings (for she associated me with the President) towards the Cherokees in general and the Missionaries in particular, with the utmost severity consistent with what was due to her sex and to her respect for myself, neither of which was she capable of overlooking. Well aware of the tenacious grasp with which her opinions, in matters of conscience, were held—a feature of her character doubtless, in some degree, derived from the Hugenotish blood which flowed in her veins,—and thinking the hour unsuitable for the argument, I made but little answer to her charges, and, on leaving the room, she said, yet holding the door in hand, " Uncle! I must say to you that it is my earnest wish that you may lose the election, as I believe that such a result ought to follow such acts!"

When such feelings were in this way produced on such a mind towards a relative for whose welfare she cherished a solicitude as ardent and as sincere as she did for any other human being, her parents having been both, long before, removed from this world and she having neither brother nor sister, it is not difficult to imagine how strong must have been the influence of this subject in other cases.

Many other incidents of this great struggle, not less interesting than those of which I have spoken, crowd upon my recollection, but I do not feel at liberty to extend the space already appropriated to the subject. It was my intention, in particular, to have set forth more fully than I have yet done the admirable bearing and sound statesmanship displayed by Gen. Jackson throughout this period, his sincere and persevering efforts to bring the Cherokees into council, his meetings with the Chickasaw and Choctaw tribes, many of whom had fought by his side in the war of 1812, his renewal to them and to the Creeks of the advice he had given to the latter on the very point under consideration, immediately after the disastrous battle of the Horse Shoe, the restoration of the confidence of the tribes in the sincerity of his friendship for them, his success in prevailing upon them to conform to the policy of the Government by removing to the West, and his influence upon the excited Georgians inducing them to exhibit a mildness and a conciliatory spirit in their acts which became matter of comment and surprise to their and his opponents. But I must forego this design.

The day of election came on, not only under the unfavorable circumstances I have described, but subject to the adverse and impure influences of the Bank question and the excitement produced by the President's *veto*. Gen. Jackson was notwithstanding reelected by an immense majority and the Councils of the nation so far as their members could, under the Constitution, be reached by that election, were replenished to overflowing with sincere friends to his administration. The voice of the People produced what reason, justice, and policy had demanded in vain. Defense, encouragement and support of the Cherokees in their political pretensions were no longer insisted on by the anti-Jackson party. The idea of small Indian sovereignties swayed by savage customs and councils, within the borders of certain states of our confederacy, was exploded. The laws of the States according to the recommendation of Secretary Porter, were shaped without hindrance, to the promotion of the only rational policy—that of removing the Indians beyond the reach of the bad influences inevitable from association and contention with the white men. ° The President, forgetting or overlooking the obstacles that had been thrown in his way, pursued his policy with his accustomed energy and perseverance, and his labors were ultimately crowned with complete success. I say *his labours* for that great work was emphatically the fruit of his own exertions. It was his judgment, his experience, his indomitable vigour and unresting activity that secured success. There was no measure, in the whole course of his administration of which he was more exclusively the author than this. His Secretary of War assisted to the extent of his power, he advised freely with me on all occasions and gave such weight to my advice, relating chiefly to the manner of doing what he thought ought to be done, as he thought it deserved, which was never less but frequently more than it was really entitled to, but his were the mind, hand and spirit that controlled throughout.

Gen. Jackson's success excited as it deserved the admiration and applause of the wise and the good. He has received a large share of the gratitude and praise of the American People for the acts of his life, both in the military and civil service of his Country, but, in my opinion, there were none better entitled to such rewards than those which affected the important subject of which I have spoken. I may have considered it in more detail and at greater length than was necessary, but I have been influenced by views which I thought entitled to much force. The fact that what was done in this matter was more exclusively his own doing than could be said of any other measure of his administration and therefore furnishes a most reliable illustration of his character, and the inadequacy of the credit which these services have as yet received have been already noticed. But there are higher motives for a thorough review of the whole subject. Unlike histories of many great questions which agitated the public mind in their day, the account I have here given of the action of the Government and of political parties relates to one which will, in all probability endure, in many important general features, as long as the Government itself and which must in all that time occupy and interest the minds and feelings of our people; to one, moreover, in respect to which we are, as a nation

---

° MS. III, p. 125.

responsible, *in foro conscientiae*, to the opinions of the great family of nations, as it involves the course we have pursued and shall pursue towards a people comparatively weak, upon whom we were perhaps in the beginning unjustifiable aggressors but of whom, in the progress of time and events, we have become the guardians and, as we hope, the benefactors. It has appeared to me that those to whose care the character and interests of the United States as connected with this subject, may hereafter be committed, cannot fail to be deeply interested in if not materially benefitted by a true account of the views, motives and transactions of their predecessors in regard to it on an occasion so critical as was that which I have reviewed.

CHAPTER XXIII.

The next and scarcely less important subject to which President Jackson gave his attention was that of internal improvements under the authority of the Federal Government. Questions in regard to it had constituted the staple of a very large proportion of the debates in Congress for many years before his accession to the Presidency; indeed, this had been the case, with brief intermissions, since the termination of the War of 1812. A race of younger Statesmen, as has been before intimated, full of talents, commendably ambitious to secure the confidence and not indisposed to enjoy the favors of the People, had assigned to it a prominent position among the blessings with which they promised to improve and adorn the Country.

Mr. Gallatin,[1] in 1808, in obedience to a resolution of the Senate, at the preceding session, offered by Mr. Worthington,[2] of Ohio, made an elaborate report embracing the outlines of a general system of internal improvements, and the subject was again referred to by Mr. Jefferson in his next and last message. Having, in a previous message, declared the necessity of an addition to the enumerated powers of Congress to authorize such works, he now spoke of the disposition of a surplus revenue, the accumulation of which he deemed probable, and asked whether it should be suffered to remain unproductive in our vaults, be reduced, or be "appropriated to the improvements of roads, canals, rivers, education and other great foundations of prosperity and union under the powers we may already possess, or such amendments of the Constitution as might be approved by the States." Mr. Calhoun is entitled to the credit, be that what it may, of having been the first to bring the vexed question of Constitutional power before Congress for its immediate decision. A glance at the then state of the question in respect to the power of Congress over the subject will here be neither out of place nor without interest.

Alexander Hamilton, if not the sole author of the principle of implied powers, stood at the head of those whose doctrines in regard to the construction of the Constitution were considered the most latitudinarian. His opinion in favor of the Bank of the United States and his report on manufactures were the ample fountains from which most if not all of these heresies proceeded. Without their aid he regarded the Constitution as utterly impracticable and

---

[1] Albert Gallatin. [2] Thomas Worthington.

he therefore stretched his fertile imagination to the utmost to render that principle as efficient as possible. Yet he disclaimed in express terms powers in Congress to construct roads and canals, within the States, with or without their consent. If there was ever room for doubt upon that point, which there could not well be after his report on manufactures, it has been fully cleared up by recent developments. By that report he carried the money power of the Government to an extent which did not admit of enlargement, and defined it in terms so felicitously as to satisfy the wildest theorist. Speaking of other powers, the exercise of which would be useful, he gave a marked prominence to that we are considering: " Symptoms of attention to the improvement of inland navigation which had," he said, " lately appeared in some quarters must fill with pleasure any heart warmed with a true zeal for the prosperity of the Country. These examples, it is to be hoped, will stimulate the exertions of *the Government and citizens of every State.* There can certainly be no object more worthy of the cares of the *local administrations*, and it were to be wished *that there was no doubt of the power of the national Government to lend its direct aid on a comprehensive plan*," and he then proceeds to shew why the thing could be better done by the latter.

Such language coming from a man of his known dispositions can receive but one construction, and in his letter to Mr. Dayton,[1] eight years afterwards, in which he drew up a programme of the steps that ought, in his judgment, to be taken by the party in power, he uses the following language: " an article ought to be proposed to be added to the Constitution for empowering Congress to open canals in all cases to which it may be necessary to conduct them thro' two or more States or through the territory of a State and of the United States." This letter, which has now, for the first time, come to light thro' the publication of Hamilton's private papers brings our knowledge of his opinion to the point of absolute certainty. He was not the man to go to the People or the States for additional power if he believed that a claim to that which he desired was at all tenable under the Constitution as it stood.

Mr. Calhoun's Bonus Bill, introduced at the first session after the peace proposed to set apart and pledge the Bank Fund Bonus as a " fund for constructing roads and canals and improving the navigation of water courses in order &c. &c.", and in his introductory speech he treated the question of power as indubitable. Referring to the circumstance that no measure of the kind had been ever before introduced he attributed the omission to the adverse state of the Country in regard to the finances and other causes and regarded

---

[1] Jonathan Dayton, 1799, In Hamilton's Works, edited by John C. Hamilton (N. Y., 1851) v. 6, p. 383.

his, as it in truth was, as a pioneer project. "To perfect the communication from Maine to Louisiana, the connexion of the Lakes with the Hudson River, to connect the great commercial points on the Atlantic, Philadelphia, Baltimore, Washington, Richmond, Charleston and Savannah with the Western States and to perfect the intercourse between the West and New Orleans" were among the objects he contemplated. Even Timothy Pickering, altho' he had no difficulty in finding excuses for supporting Mr. Calhoun's Bill, could not refrain from expressing his dissent from the views the latter had taken of the Constitution, which he thought too latitudinarian:—"he did not admit the latitude ° of construction given by the gentleman from South Carolina to the terms of the Constitution. He had quoted that part of the Constitution which said that Congress had power " to lay and collect taxes, duties, imports and excises "—for what purpose?, in order—" to pay the debts and provide for the common defence and general welfare", and hence the gentleman had inferred that as roads and canals would provide for the common defence and general welfare therefore Congress had power to make roads and canals. If this interpretation of the Constitution be correct then the subsequent enumeration of powers was superfluous, for the terms " to provide for the general welfare" would embrace the following enumerated powers and every other imaginable power the exercise of which would promote the general welfare."

Mr. Clay, then Speaker, congratulated Mr. Calhoun on the honor of having introduced the subject, and his Country on the advantages she could not fail to derive from the measure proposed, and expressed an unequivocal opinion in favor of its constitutionality. The Bill was ably opposed by several and particularly that honest man and pure patriot, Philip P. Barbour, of Virginia, by arguments which Messrs. Clay and Calhoun in vain attempted to refute. It was, notwithstanding, passed by a small majority in the House and a larger in the Senate, after a specious amendment requiring the assent of the States to the expenditure of the money within their respective bounds.

Mr. Madison, ill at ease, I cannot doubt, from having just before given his assent to the re-establishment of a Bank, an act at variance with principles vital to the Constitution, of which he, above all other men, was entitled to the credit of having been their enlightened expounder but which he had felt himself constrained to desert because he thought doubtless honestly, that the abuse of those principles upon that point had acquired too deep and too strong root to be disturbed, promptly interposed his *veto*. He did so perhaps the more readily under an apprehension that this additional encroachment

---

° MS. III, p. 130.

upon the Constitution might have originated in his own forgetfulness of the past. In his *veto* Message, with the chastity and felicity of expression in which he had no equal, he placed the unconstitutionality of the measure and the insufficiency of the veil which had been thrown over its character by the Senate, in the plainest possible points of view. His message deprived the Bill of the majority it had obtained in the House, in which it originated, but it did not convince Clay, Calhoun or Webster, all of whom voted for it notwithstanding the veto. Indeed Mr. Clay was so eager to place himself on record in favor of the abstract proposition of Constitutional power that, altho' not obliged, as Speaker, to vote, there being no tie, he claimed the right to do so in that case. Mr. Calhoun was soon after appointed Secretary of War by Mr. Monroe and retired from Congress. In his first Report in that capacity he [1]

At the first session of the succeeding Congress the subject was again brought forward by a Report from Professor Tucker,[2] Chairman of the Committee on Roads and Canals, a representative of the State of Virginia, tho' not an adherent of her prevailing politics. His Report sustained the constitutionality and expediency of such measures as that which Mr. Madison's veto had defeated and concluded with a Resolution in accordance with the Report. Mr. Clay, in an elaborate and able speech supported the positions he had before taken. This debate also brought more conspicuously into public view William Lowndes, of South Carolina, a man whom from the beginning of his public life, all regarded with much favor. Several distinct resolutions were finally offered by Mr. Lowndes as a substitute for that reported by the Committee. That which claimed the right to appropriate money for the construction of post roads, military and other roads and to make canals and for the improvement of water courses passed by a majority of 15 in 164 votes. Those which asserted a power to construct roads and canals necessary for commerce between the States, to construct canals for military purposes, were severally rejected by small majorities. Other propositions were presented but Mr. Lowndes, observing that the sense of the House had been fully expressed in favor of the right to appropriate money for the construction of roads and canals and had thus removed obstructions to propositions embracing that object, moved to lay the rest of the Report on the table, which motion prevailed.

---

[1] A pencil note here states that space is left "for Calhoun's recommendations of Internal Improvements in his first Report as Secretary of War." Van Buren's recollection is at fault. Calhoun's first report as Secretary of War was very brief and did not discuss this subject. His *last* annual report, December, 1824, dealt with the matter in considerable fullness. For a good general account see Meigs' Life of Calhoun (N. Y., 1917), v. 2, 246–51 and, in the Works of Calhoun, his letter to Henry Clay, Speaker of the House of Representatives, Jan. 14, 1819, Vol. V, pp. 40–54; also *ibid.*, pp. 142–6.

[2] Henry St. George Tucker.

Mr. Lowndes views were throughout characterized by modesty, candour and sincerity which commanded the respect of all and conciliated for their author the esteem of those even who dissented from their correctness. He admitted that public works, such as were referred to, would in all probability be more economically and better constructed when the fruit of individual enterprise, or when made under the authority of the States, but roads and canals had, he said, been objects of attention to Government in all Countries and they were, in his opinion, necessary works of that description that would never be constructed unless by the Federal Government, and sincerely believing that Congress possessed the requisite power he was in favor of having them made under its authority and at the expense of the nation.

He was unhappily obliged to retire from public life at the age of forty one and died, in January, 1823 on his way to Europe in pursuit of health, lamented by all who had known him and having by his honorable, just and distinguished tho' unobtrusive career impressed the public mind with a very general belief that his chances for the Presidency would have been, but for his early death, better than those of any of his cotemporaries.

In respect to the extreme power over the subject of internal improvements—that of construction—this great effort in its behalf resulted in its complete overthrow. Even in respect to the power of appropriation, the movement notwithstanding Mr. Lowndes' attempt to swell the majority beyond its legitimate limits, could scarcely be otherwise regarded than as a defeat or in any the most favourable view, as a barren triumph.

Mr. Monroe, at the same session, re-affirmed, in his annual Message, his adherence to the Virginia doctrines upon the question of the power of Congress to construct roads and canals, and informed that body in advance, very much to the annoyance of Mr. Clay, whose position at the moment was one of quasi-opposition to the Administration, that if they pressed a law for such a purpose he would be constrained to object to its passage. But he did not say or intimate, neither was there any reason to apprehend, nor is it probable that he had changed his views in respect to any other portions of those doctrines. A majority of only fifteen in a representation numbering more than two hundred, with a minority moved by a single and sacred motive—to protect the Constitution—against those who were in great part seeking the advancement of local objects which were in themselves well calculated to engender rivalries and divisions, and with the impending danger of a Presidential veto, offered but slight temptation to efforts for the establishment of a system of internal improvements under the patronage of the Federal Government.

This view is fully sustained by the action of Congress from the period when these proceedings took place. During these four years the establishment of a plan for internal improvements under the authority of the General Government was not advanced a step, nor was the power of appropriation, asserted by the only resolution that was pressed, exerted on a single important occasion. Those who, whilst friendly to such improvements were too solicitous for the preservation of the Constitution in its purity to authorize their construction without constitutional authority, had reason to infer, from the course of events, that their objects would be accomplished by individual enterprise acting under the authority of and aided as far as practicable by the State Governments. But occurrences during the winter of 1822 were well calculated to put and in the sequel did put a very different face upon the matter. The patience of Congress having been exhausted by the perpetual drain upon the Treasury for the repairs of the Cumberland Road, the House of Representatives passed a Bill authorizing [o] the erection of gates upon it and the exaction of tolls from those who used it—the avails to be applied to keeping the Road in good condition. It passed the Senate and was sent to the President for his approval.

Mr. Monroe, committed unqualifiedly by the declarations in his first annual Message expressive of his views, which we have no evidence that he even desired to change, objected to the Bill upon the principles he had avowed in that document, and it was rejected. He accompanied his *veto*-Message with, or rather sent to Congress a day or two afterwards a voluminous essay [1] upon the constitutional question, setting forth the arguments on which the opinion he acted upon was founded and which he had, he said, from time to time, as they occurred to him, reduced to writing. At the conclusion of this exposition he avowed his conversion to the doctrine that Congress possessed, under the Constitution, an unlimited power to appropriate money in aid of the construction of roads and canals when constructed by others. The Virginia doctrine as expounded by Madison's Report upon the Alien and Sedition Laws, and thenceforth constituting a portion of the political creed of the republican party, was that Congress not only had no right to construct such works but that the Constitution did not authorize that body to apply money to any such purpose,—that the power of Congress to appropriate the national revenue was limited to objects which it was authorized to undertake and that the principle which denied the power to construct such works necessarily denied the right to pay for them. Those who wish to read a felicitous exposition of this

---

[o] MS. III, p. 135.   [1] Dec. 2, 1817, on internal improvements.

doctrine will find it in Mr. Philip P. Barbour's speech in the great discussion of 1818.

Mr. Monroe admitted that such was the doctrine of 1798, and that it was founded on views of the Constitution which he had before sustained, but said that he had changed his opinion upon the point, and went into an elaborate argument to shew the soundness of his present theory. The time had been when such a declaration coming from Mr. Monroe would have been received with amazement by his old political associates who yet adhered to the faith which had long received their common support. But antecedent and cotemporaneous passages in his official career had gradually paved the way for such an occurrence and consequently lessened their surprise when it was developed. This took place towards the middle of his second term, after he had received all the electoral votes, save one, of his old political opponents and when he was doing openly all that a man of his habitual prudence and circumspection could be expected to do to promote the amalgamation of parties and the overthrow of that exclusive and towering supremacy which the republican party had for many years maintained in our national councils. A diminished zeal for the support of its pure and self-denying principles was the natural consequence of a diminished, might I not say an extinguished solicitude for its continued ascendency. It was almost inevitable that efforts to destroy the republican organization should lead to the gradual abandonment of the principles it sustained. Other causes contributed to give that direction to his feelings. At the head of his Cabinet stood Mr. John Quincy Adams, the latitudinarianism of whose Constitutional views extended beyond those of any of his cotemporaries, and superior to him in influence tho' inferior in grade was the recognised favorite of its Chief, Mr. Calhoun, who had taken the lead in support of the principle that Congress had power to make roads and canals as well as to pay for them, who had established the right of paternity towards such measures and would assert it wherever they were successful. Neither Mr. Wirt, nor Mr. Southard [1] had ever shewed themselves fastidious in regard to the powers of the Federal Government or prone to dissent from the views of the associates to whom I have referred, and the only Cabinet officer, Mr. Crawford, from whom, on account of his position in other respects, opposition to this great change in the action of the President might have been expected, a sincere and ardent republican, was so far from being a strict constructionist that he had supported the Bill for the extension of the old Bank charter against which Mr. Clay made the great speech of his life.

---

[1] Samuel L. Southard.

But whatever may have been the origin of this change in Mr. Monroe's constitutional views there was no room for question in respect to its extent. The principles of the party in which he had been reared had been commended to his preference not only by the circumstances of his location and the character of his early associates, but by his own habits of circumspection. Honest and considerate in his conduct he was never the slave of momentary impulses but arrived at his conclusions by proverbially slow degrees after long and careful deliberation. Mr. Webster exemplified his dispositions in this respect by an amusing anecdote. It was, he said, the President's habit to write on a slate the names of the candidates for prominent places, and after the lists were completed, to rub out one name every day until only one remained, when the slate, of course, was sent to the proper office to have the commission made out.

Festina lente having thus been the rule of his life, he seemed on the occasion of which we are now writing, to have passed in the twinkling of an eye from one extreme to another. The doctrine set forth in the manifesto that accompanied his veto-Message on the Cumberland Road Bill, in regard to the power of Congress to appropriate the national revenue, embraced all that Alexander Hamilton had ever contended for. In his famous Report upon Manufactures the latter in substance thus defines the power of the Federal Government to raise money:

These three qualifications excepted, (viz: that all duties, imposts and excises shall be uniform throughout the United States, that no direct tax shall be laid unless in proportion to the federal numbers of the different States and that no tax or duty shall be laid on exports) the power to raise money is plenary and indefinite, * * * and there seems to be no room for a doubt that whatever concerns the general interests of learning, of agriculture, of manufactures and of commerce comes within the sphere of the national councils as far as regards an application of money.

Mr. Monroe explained his new position substantially as follows:

It is contended on the one side that as this is a Government of limited powers it has no right to expend money except in the performance of acts authorized by the other specific grants according to a strict construction of their powers; * * * To this construction I was inclined in the more early stage of our Government; but on further reflection and observation my mind has undergone a change for reasons I will frankly unfold.

Then after speaking of the unqualified character of the power to declare war and other powers, he says:

The power to raise money by taxes, duties, imposts and excises is alike unqualified, nor so do I see any check on the exercise of it other than that which applies to the other powers—the responsibility of the representative to his constituents. * * * If we look to the other branch of this power—the appropriation of the money thus raised,—we find that it is not less general and unqualified than the power to raise it.

He proceeds with an endeavour to prove, by a course of reasoning which he would once have himself pronounced more specious than solid, that the framers of the Constitution, as well as those by whom it was adopted, designed that both powers should be unqualified. Few persons will contend that, in respect to the power to raise and expend revenue, Hamilton went one iota farther than Monroe. The language of the former was more graceful and captivating but the latter took especial care that it was not more general or far reaching.

Who, in former days, could have contemplated the possibility that a Virginia President, one of the first members of the old republican party and elected as such, would ever be brought to establish, so far as an act of the Executive branch of the Federal Government was capable of establishing it, one of the most ultra and, in practice, likely to be one of the most dangerous principles ever advocated by Alexander Hamilton, and that the individual thus acting would be James Monroe between whom and Hamilton ° political differences had ripened into personal hostility extending to the brink of personal combat? How strong must have been the influence which could work such a change! The laxness of the times, in respect to political consistency, in a great degree brought about by the agency of Mr. Monroe himself, doubtless had much to do with it, but I have always thought that political rivalry was not without its influence in producing a result so remarkable and so much to be deprecated.

° MS. III, p. 140.

CHAPTER XXIV.

When the Message and the accompanying papers were sent to Congress little had been said of Gen. Jackson in connection with the question of succession to Mr. Monroe and, especially in the early part of the canvass, Mr. Adams' claims were but lightly regarded. In 1817–18 Clay and Calhoun were most prominent among the heirs apparent. Altho' exercising his usual prudence in the matter, Mr. Monroe was notwithstanding well understood to prefer Mr. Calhoun. The general conviction doubtless influenced to some extent Mr. Clay's course towards the Administration. He first threw cold water on the efforts to bring about an amalgamation of parties, and satirized, with considerable severity, in one of his speeches, the attentions received by the President, on a Northern tour, from the old federalists. The Administration in turn for some time gave an equally inhospitable reception to Mr. Clay's endeavours to bring about the recognition of South American Independence; but when, by the progress of events, and the indications of public sentiment, efforts to arrest that measure had become unsafe, it exerted itself to take the matter out of Mr. Clay's hands by means of a virtual recommendation of it by the President himself. I well remember Mr. Calhoun's exulting remark when the Message on this subject and this effect of it were alluded to: " Yes! the fruit has now become ripe and may be safely plucked! " It was in this way that Mr. Clay was, as he supposed, deprived of the credit he hoped to have acquired by his championship of South American Independence. His was not a temperament long to brook hostility open or covert. His deep dissatisfaction with the President's course in announcing in advance in his Annual Message in December 1817, that he could not approve of a Bill authorizing the construction of roads or canals, has been noticed. He spoke of it in his great effort on that occasion as a step which if taken by the Crown would have been regarded in England as a breach of the privileges of Parliament and said that it deserved to be considered here, whatever might have been the President's motive, as an attempt to dictate to Congress. Altho' he treated the President throughout with the respect due to his station he evidently did so at the sacrifice of deeply seated feelings of a different character. When it is recollected that the resolutions asserting the power of Congress on that occasion were rejected by very small majorities he might well attribute their defeat as he did to this out of the way tho' not positively irregular step of the President. The introduction by Mr. Clay's *alter ego*, Mr. Trimble,[1] of the Bill authorizing the establishment of toll-gates on the Cumberland Road may have originated solely, or even chiefly in the impatience of Congress at the expences of that Road and in a natural desire to relieve the Treasury from further appropriations of money to keep it in repair: but I confess that I did not see the movement in that light. To compell Mr. Monroe, with the sanction of his Cabinet, not less than three of whose members were contestants in expectancy for the Presidency, to apply the the general principle to which he had volunteered an avowal at the preceding session, of his continued adherence to the pet public work of the West, or, by omitting to do so, to admit its unsoundness, was a temptation too strong for a man like Mr. Clay to resist. He had been baffled by the Administration in an object in which I have no doubt that his feelings were earnestly engaged and upon his success in which he had made large calculations and his retort could hardly be regarded as a reckless one.

By the provisions of the Bill, which was carried through under the lead of Mr. Trimble,—Mr. Clay having retired for one Congress, but I need not add, having his eye on Washington,—the Administration was driven to the alternative I have described. I am confident that Mr. Monroe and the principal members of his Cabinet so understood the movement. In resisting it Messrs. Adams, Crawford and Calhoun acted as a unit, for altho' in regard to their political aspirations each engineered for himself they were equally opposed to Mr. Clay's pretensions. Nor was there then much difference in the character of their personal relations with him, these not being in either case very cordial; perhaps the least so between Mr. Adams and himself in consequence of their then recent and angry correspondence in regard to occurences at Ghent. The movement was met, as was to have been expected from men of their calibre, by an act of a strong stamp, the extent and bearing of which Mr. Clay can hardly have foreseen. The veto was promptly interposed, and so far the Administration was successful, but by the accompanying Presidential manifesto, Mr. Monroe, changing the opinions of his whole previous life, exposed the national treasury to appropriations to any extent for the construction of roads and canals and internal improvements of every description.

Mr. Clay was not in a situation to take advantage of this remarkable somersault of his opponents, for he at that time permitted no man to go beyond him in latitudinarian constructions of the Constitution. Of this the Administration was well aware, but it forgot that he was not the only or the principal observer of its

---

[1] William A. Trimble, of Ohio.

course. It overlooked the circumstance in the eagerness of the struggle, that there was yet a large segment of the old republican party sufficient to form the nucleus for a subsequent successful rally. which had not been carried away by the "era of good feeling," which tho' perhaps not much surprised, was sorely grieved by an act of such flagrant backsliding on the part of the President of their choice and who saw in it the fulfilment of the forebodings which had been excited by his previous dalliance with the opposition. By the utter loss of the confidence of this class Mr. Monroe and those for whose advancement he was desirous, doubtless sincerely and honestly, sustained a far greater injury than any temporary advantage over Mr. Clay could make good.

The veto was interposed near the close of the session and nothing further was done upon the general subject but the struggle was resumed at the earliest practicable moment.

Mr. Hemphill [1] as Chairman of the Committee on Roads and Canals had, at the same session, reported a Bill to procure plans and surveys preparatory to the establishment of a general system, but it was not acted upon. At the beginning of the next he had that Bill committed to the Committee of the Whole. It was considered, and a motion by Mr. Barbour to strike out the first section, on constitutional grounds, failed under the influence of the veto, and the Bill would have passed but for a new move upon the political chess board that prevented it. The legislation of Congress was obviously upon the point of receiving the direction which was designed to be given to it by Mr. Monroe's *veto* and the accompanying expositions of his new opinions. The policy of the Administration, that of abandoning the power of construction and of confining the agency of the Federal Government to appropriations of money in aid of Works constructed by the States, or by individuals under their authority,—was on the point of triumphing over the policy of Mr. Clay, which went far beyond it, when the Bill was tabled on the motion of Mr. Hardin,[2] of Kentucky, a friend of Mr. Clay, and a motion to take it up afterwards refused by the strong vote of 111 to 42, on which division seven of the nine Kentucky members, all ardent advocates for internal improvements by the General Government, together with several prominent Clayites from the West, and from other parts of the Union, voted against further action upon the subject; and nothing further was done during the session of 1822–3.

In his annual Message, at the next° session, 1823–4, President Monroe came to the aid of the policy which his communication to the previous Congress had been designed to install and which the

---

¹ Joseph Hemphill.   ² Benjamin Hardin.   ° MS. III, p. 145.

closing movement on the subject at the last session seemed destined to check, and reiterated his opinion in favor of the power of Congress, recommending an appropriation for the employment of the requisite number of Engineers to make the necessary preparatory examinations for Canals connecting the Ohio with the Chesapeake and also for connecting the waters of the Ohio with Lake Erie. Mr. Hemphill reported his Bill and it was elaborately discussed. Mr. Clay, who had been re-elected and again chosen Speaker, presented himself at the very threshold of the debate, denied *in toto* the doctrines of the *veto*-Message, insisted that if Congress had not the right to cause those works to be constructed, it had no right to pay for them or to appropriate money in aid of their construction, claimed that the Constitutional question upon that point arose upon this Bill and would be decided by it, &c. &c. Mr. Hemphill, still Chairman of the Committee on Roads and Canals, concurred in the views expressed by Mr. Clay and advocated the passage of the Bill on the same grounds. The discussions were still more elaborate than those of 1818, and drew out the power of the House. That pure and inflexible sentinel on the ramparts of the Constitution, Philip P. Barbour, moved again to strike out the first section of the Bill, on the ground of a want of power in Congress to construct and a consequent want of power to appropriate money for surveys. His motion failed by a vote of 109 to 74, and the Bill was finally passed. Nothing more was done upon the subject at that session, and so the matter stood at the time of the Presidential election of 1824.

Making all reasonable allowance for the possibility that the admitted ardour of my political life may continue to influence my judgment more than I imagine it does, I feel confident that no well balanced mind can review the facts and circumstances to which I have referred,—established as they are by the recorded testimony of the actors themselves—without admitting the justness of my conclusion that the important principle contended for by the advocates of internal improvements by the Federal Government was used by its professed supporters as a political shuttle-cock which they tossed backward or forward according to the feelings and exigencies of the moment. Advancing, receding or standing still, the acts of the parties plainly appear now, when passion has subsided and when their projects have been either abandoned or jostled aside by the march of time and events, to have been controlled by partisan views under cover of loud professions for the public good. Nor can this charge be limited to those of whom we speak. It is a vice inseparable from political conflicts that in a large majority of cases the interests of parties and of those whose public fortunes they desire to advance are consulted before those of the Country. It would perhaps not be going too far to say that the exceptions are only when such a course would so palpably disclose the real motive to the general public as to defeat its purpose or when the direction of affairs falls to the hand of a man who takes particular pride in the adoption of measures commonly considered unpopular when he can satisfy his own mind that he is promoting the public interest.

The People having failed to elect a President, Mr. Adams was raised to the head of the Government by the House of Representatives, and Mr. Clay was placed at the head of his Cabinet. They both held that Congress had power to cause to be constructed and paid for out of the national revenue all such internal improvements as would, in its judgment, be conducive to the common defence and general welfare and we have never had reason to believe there was a single dissentient from that opinion in the new Cabinet. There was therefore no constitutional restraint upon the action of Congress in this matter other than that which might be expected from members of the old republican party who yet adhered to the principles of their predecessors, but who constituted minorities in both branches of the national Legislature. The results of this state of things may well be imagined, especially by all who have had opportunities to observe the facility with which members of Congress come to regard everything that can be carried home from the public treasury as lawful spoil and the zeal with which they struggle to secure the expenditure in their own districts of whatever can be extracted from it. The execution of Hemphill's act, authorizing the President to cause surveys and plans for public works to be made, exhibited a striking view of the character and tendency of this disposition on the part of the representatives and their constituents. So difficult was it for the War Department to satisfy itself for the purpose of discrimination of the real character of distant claims to notice and so pressing the solicitations that every corner of the Country was fast being surveyed preparatory to improvements of some kind, for the most part of a purely local character, and so flagrant did these abuses become that the wisest friends of the system insisted, in its defence, that the law should be so altered as to make a specific act of Congress necessary in each case.

The condition of things at the period of Gen. Jackson's elevation to the Presidency was thus described in one of his annual Messages. Speaking of the claim of power in Congress to make internal improvements within a State, with the right of jurisdiction sufficient for its preservation, he says:

Yet, we all know that notwithstanding these grave objections, this dangerous doctrine was at one time apparently proceeding to its final establishment with fearful rapidity. The desire to embark the Federal Government in works of Internal Improvement prevailed in the highest degree during the first session of the first Congress that I had the honor to meet in my present situation, and when the Bill authorizing a subscription on the part of the United States for stock in the Maysville and Lexington turnpike company passed the two Houses, there had been reported by the Committees on Internal Improvements, Bills containing appropriations for such objects, inclusive of those for the Cumberland Road, and for harbours and light houses, to the amount of about *one hundred and six millions of dollars*. In this amount was included authority to the Secretary of the Treasury to subscribe for the stock of different companies to a great extent and the residue was principally for the direct construction of Roads by this Government. In addition to these projects which had been presented to the two Houses under the sanction and recommendation of their respective Committees on Internal Improvements, there were then still pending before the Committees, and in memorials presented, but not referred, different projects for works of a similar character, the expense of which cannot be estimated with certainty but may have exceeded *one hundred millions* of dollars.[1]

Among the Bills referred to was one to authorize the construction of a road from Buffalo to New Orleans which failed by a majority of only fifteen, and was reconsidered by a majority of eight less than two weeks before the interposition of the veto; besides numerous other cases of corresponding magnitude.

---

[1] Sixth annual message, Dec. 2, 1834.

CHAPTER XXV.

The points in our domestic concerns which at this time occupied the largest share of President Jackson's personal attention were the Bank and the removal of the Indians. The engrossing character of the latter has been already described and that of the former will be exhibited in its turn. Having for several years made the subject of Internal Improvements by the Federal Government my study, apprehensions of the evils their prosecution, as the Constitution stood, might entail upon the Country had become grave, and sincerely believing that the adverse current which had set in that direction might and could only be arrested thro' the General's extraordinary popularity I early and assiduously. pressed the matter upon his consideration. He embraced my suggestions not only with alacrity but with that lively zeal with which he received every proposition which he thought could be made conducive to the public good. I propose to give a succinct account of the steps that proceeded from our conversations; and I will first briefly notice some of the General's characteristic qualities by which their advancement was essentially promoted. It is however far from my intention to attempt a complete portraiture of individual character. I am conscious that such attempts often, not to say generally, manifest the ° ambition of the author to shew his skill in depicting a perfectly good or an absolutely bad character instead of a desire to portray his subject as he really was, and that the picture, when finished is thus a reflection of his imagination rather than a reliable representation of real life. I hope to make the world better acquainted with the true character of Andrew Jackson than it was before, but I design to do this chiefly by correct reports of what he said and did on great occasions.

Although firm to the last degree in the execution of his resolution when once formed, I never knew a man more free from conceit, or one to whom it was to a greater extent a pleasure, as well as a recognized duty, to listen patiently to what might be said to him upon any subject under consideration until the time for action had arrived. Akin to his disposition in this regard was his readiness to acknowledge error whenever an occasion to do so was presented and a willingness to give full credit to his co-actors on important occasions without ever pausing to consider how much of the merit he awarded was at the expense of that due to himself. In this spirit he received

---

° MS. III, p. 150.

the aid of those associated with him in the public service in the preparation of the public documents that were issued under his name, wholly indifferent in regard to the extent to which their participation was known, solicitous only that they should be understood by those to whom they were addressed as a true record of his opinions, his resolutions and his acts. That point secured he cared little either as to the form of words in which they were expressed, or as to the agency through which the particular exposition was concocted.

Neither, I need scarcely say, was he in the habit of talking, much less of boasting of his own achievements. Content with the part he had actually taken in the conduct and solution of any important public question and never having reason to complain of the opinions formed and expressed of his acts by a large majority of his Countrymen he had neither a desire nor a motive to parade his own or to shine in borrowed plumes. I have already spoken of Gen. Jackson's early preference for the self-denying theory and strict-construction doctrines of the old republican school and have also, I believe, noticed the circumstance that when quite a young man and a younger politician he chose rather to expose himself to the odium of recording his name against a vote of confidence in and thanks to Gen. Washington than to suffer himself to be caught in the trap set for him and his republican associates by Fisher Ames and company.[1] The design of that artifice was so to connect an approval of the measures which the federalists in Congress had sustained and which the republicans had opposed with an expression of the favorable sentiments universally entertained towards Gen. Washington and his motives in all things, as to put it out of the power of the latter to stand by their avowed opinions without refusing to concur in that expression. They snapped the cords with which it was thus attempted to fetter them and Gen. Jackson's vote on that occasion was urged against him when he became a candidate for the Presidency, some thirty years after.

But the principle of internal improvements by the Federal Government, so far from being acted upon when he was first in Congress, was, as has been seen, disavowed by the great leader of the administration, and a large share of Gen. Jackson's time was spent in the camp whilst the subject was debated by the rising men of the day from 1816 to 1823, when he re-appeared on the floor of Congress. There was besides a peculiarity in his position at the latter period which, tho' it could not—as nothing could—lead him, to do wrong when it became necessary to act, was nevertheless well calculated to lessen somewhat, for the moment at least, his active participation in this particular branch of legislation. To give to that

---

[1] For an account of this see Parton's Life of Jackson (N. Y., 1860), v. 1, 205–212.

peculiarity the weight to which it was entitled the reader must bear in mind the influence exerted by Pennsylvania in bringing Gen. Jackson forward for the Presidency, an influence which will not I think be over-estimated when it is regarded as having controlled the result; and this consideration deserves to be constantly remembered whilst canvassing the merits of his subsequent course upon several very important points.

Pennsylvania is in every sense of the word a great state and worthy of high respect—great in her material resources and great in the constant industry, the morality and general intelligence of her People. When to the credit she derives from these sources is added that which has naturally accrued from the moderate and sound character of her general course it will be seen how well she has deserved the honor shewn her by her sister States in the title with which they have distinguished her of " the key stone of the arch of the Union."

It is nevertheless true that she has for a long time presented a favorable field for the agitation of political questions which address themselves to special interests in the communities upon which they are pressed. Internal Improvements by the Federal Government, a high protective tariff and a Bank of the United States had, for many years before Gen. Jackson's accession to the Presidency, been regarded as favorite measures with the good people of Pennsylvania. In respect to the first, which is now the subject of our consideration, both of the great Reports of the Committees on Roads and Canals, at the period when it embraced a large share of the attention of Congress, were from Pennsylvanians,—Mr. Wilson [1] and Mr. Hemphill. Yet these measures and the question of the removal of the Indians, which had so strongly excited their misdirected sympathies, were destined to be the principal domestic subjects on which Gen. Jackson's Administration, if he succeeded in the election, was to be employed. With the two last, (the Bank and the Tariff) he had made himself familiar and as to them his course was fixed; and, foreseeing the necessity he would be under upon those points to run counter to the wishes of his Pennsylvanian friends at the very threshhold of his administration, it was natural that a man of his generous temper, and of whose character fidelity to friendship was the crowning grace, should have been desirous to avoid any addition to the issues between himself and his no less generous supporters, as far as that could be avoided without dereliction of duty.

It was under such circumstances, and never having made the constitutional question in relation to the power of Congress over the matter a subject of critical examination, that he voted in

---

[1] Henry Wilson.

1823–4 and 5, in favor of the acts " to provide for the necessary surveys for roads and canals ", and " authorizing a subscription to the
stock of the Chesapeake and Delaware Canal Company " and a few
other propositions of similar import, which votes were vehemently
urged, by his opponents, against his subsequent course.

My *début* in Congress had not been free from a like discrepancy.
The bill providing for the erection of toll-gates on the Cumberland
Road came before us a few months after I had taken my seat in the
Senate of the United States and I gave a silent vote in favor of it.
Mr. Monroe's veto, which would have shed enduring honor on his
name, if he had suffered it to stand alone, brought me to instant and
thorough examination and reflection.   It did not take me long to
satisfy myself that I had acted under a grave mistake and I embraced an early opportunity to acknowledge my error on the floor of
the Senate.   Convinced also of the inexpediency as well as unconstitutionality of the construction of works of internal improvement
under the direct or indirect authority of the Federal Government, so
long as the Constitution remained as it was I became earnestly
solicitous not only to arrest the course of legislation on the subject,
which was then making fearful progress, but to devise some way by
which it could be placed on a better and a safer footing.   My name
will be found recorded against all the Bills which the General voted
for and I believe against every similar proposition subsequent to the
act to erect toll-gates on the Cumberland Road.   I have now carefully examined the Journals of Congress and reviewed my official
acts to the close of my public life, and can, I think, safely challenge
a comparison with the straitest of the strict-construction sect in
regard to° a faithful adherence to the principles of that school, with
the single exception of which I have spoken.   When I recall the
names of the many good and pure men who made themselves honorably conspicuous in the support of those principles, particularly
among the Statesmen of Virginia and North Carolina, I am sensible
of the boldness of this proffer, but even then do not shrink from it.
Not content with steadily voting against all unauthorized measures
of the character referred to, and fearing from what was daily passing before my eyes, that it would not be long in the power of those
who were faith'ful to the principles of the Constitution to arrest or
even to check the torrent of reckless legislation which had set in so
powerfully, I proposed an amendment of the Constitution, the object
of which was to make that lawful which was then illicit and to protect the public interest against abuses by wholesome constitutional
restraints, and which I insert here, with the brief remarks with which
I introduced it:

° MS. III, p. 155.

Mr. Van Buren rose, in pursuance of notice given on Wednesday last, to ask leave to introduce a joint resolution, proposing an amendment to the Constitution of the United States, on the subject of the power of Congress to make roads and canals. He said he was as much opposed as any man to frequent alterations of the form of government under which we live, but he would make no apology for bringing this matter before the Senate, in so imposing a form as that of an amendment to the Constitution. He would now do so, because he was entirely convinced that no one could dispassionately consider the present state of the question, to which his resolution relates, without feeling the imperious necessity of some Constitutional provision on the subject. It was not his intention, at this time, to enter into the discussion of the matter; he would only submit one or two general remarks in relation to it. Of the importance of the question, it was not necessary to speak. Suffice it to say that, in its scope, it embraces the funds of the nation to an unlimited extent, and in its result must affect, as far as the agency of the Federal Government was concerned, the future internal improvement of a great and flourishing country. Is the power to make roads and canals, within the States, now vested in the Federal Government? Individuals, said Mr. V. B., may give their impressions, with their reasons for the various ingenious constructions they put upon the different parts of the Constitution, to make out that this power exists; but all candid men will admit that there are few questions more unsettled. Whilst, in some States, the power is universally conceded, and its exercise loudly required, in others, its existence is as generally denied, and its exercise as ardently resisted. Is there cause to believe that, as the Constitution now stands, a construction will obtain, which will be so far acquiesced in as to be regarded and enforced as one of the established powers of the General Government? He thought there was not. For about twenty years, this subject had been one of constant and earnest discussion. Efforts have at various times been made in Congress to exercise the power in question. They have met sometimes with more, and sometimes with less, favor. Bills, containing the assertion, and directing the exercise of this power, have passed the two Houses, and been returned, with objections, by two successive Presidents, and failed for want of the Constitutional majority. The last Congress and the Executive were arrayed against each other, upon the question, and as far as a recent vote of the other House may be regarded as evidence of the present opinion of Congress, there is every reason to believe that such is now the case.

The Government has now been in operation rising of thirty years; and although the subject has always been a matter of interest, no law clearly embracing the power has ever yet been passed. There is, therefore, but little reason to hope that, without some Constitutional provision, the question will ever be settled. If the General Government has not now the power, Mr. V. B. said that he for one thought that, under suitable restrictions, they ought to have it. As to what those restrictions ought to be, there might, and probably would, be diversity of opinion. But, as to the abstract proposition, that as much of the funds of the nation as could be raised, without oppression, and as are not necessary to the discharge of existing and indispensable demands upon the Government, should be expended upon internal improvements, under restrictions regarding the sovereignty and securing the equal interest of the States, he presumed there would be little difference of opinion. He could not but hope, that those who think the better construction of the Constitution is, that Congress now have the power, would also consent to some amendment. They must, at all events, admit that it is far from being a clear, and certainly not a settled matter. and in view of the danger always attending the exercise of a doubtful right by the Federal Government against the persevering opposition of the several States, they would decide whether, instead of contesting this matter as it has been done for so many years, it would not be more for the interest of the nation, as well as the credit of the Government, to place the matter on well defined ground. There were many strong reasons why he thought this course ought to be pursued, and which, at the proper time, he would take the liberty to urge. For the present, he would simply add that, independent of the collisions of State interests, which this power is more likely than any other to produce, the exercise of it in the present state of the Constitution, and with an Executive whose reading of it should be different from that of the present and the two who last preceded him, could not fail to be grossly unequal among the States; because it is well known that there were some States who have invariably, and who will, as long as they prefer the inviolability of the Constitution to their local interest, continue to oppose the exercise of this power with them. Without, therefore, the ability to prevent, they would be excluded from the benefits of its exercise. The course now proposed had been earnestly recommended to the last Congress by the present Executive, and, when the subject came up for discussion, he would endeavor to show that its adoption was called for by the best interests of the nation.

Leave was then granted, and Mr. Van Buren offered the following resolution, which was read, and passed to a second reading:

" *Resolved, &c.,* That the following amendment of the Constitution of the United States be proposed to the Legislatures of the several States:

" Congress shall have power to make roads and canals; but all money appropriated for this purpose shall be apportioned among the several States according to the last enumeration of their respective numbers, and applied to the making and repairing of roads and canals within the several States, as Congress may direct; but any State may consent to the appropriation by Congress of its quota of such appropriation in the making or repairing of roads and canals, without its own limits; no such road or canal shall, however, be made within any State, without the consent of the Legislature thereof, and all such money shall be so expended under their direction." [1]

In December, 1825, I submitted to the Senate, as a substitute for the previous proposition, the following motion and the remarks that follow:

" *Resolved,* That Congress does not possess the power to make Roads and Canals within the respective States.

__" *Resolved,* That a select committee be appointed, with instructions to prepare and report a Joint Resolution, for an amendment of the Constitution, prescribing and defining the power Congress shall have over the subject of Internal Improvements, and subjecting the same to such restrictions as shall effectually protect the sovereignty of the respective States, and secure to them a just distribution of the benefits resulting from all appropriations made for that purpose."

In introducing these resolutions—

Mr. Van Buren said, that it would be recollected that he had, some days since, given notice of his intention to ask for leave to introduce a joint resolution, proposing an amendment of the Constitution on the subject of the power of Congress over the subject of internal improvements. Upon the suggestion of gentlemen who feel an interest in the subject, and think the principal object can, in that way, be better effected, he had consented so far to change the

---

[1] Jan. 22, 1824.—Annals of Congress, 18th, 1st, Vol. I, p. 134.

course originally contemplated, by substituting resolutions expressive of the sense of the Senate on the Constitution, as it now is, and proposing the appointment of a select committee to report upon the subject, under such instruction as the Senate may think proper to give. Such resolutions he would now take the liberty of submitting. He did not, of course, wish to press their immediate consideration, but would call them up at as early a day as would comport with the state of public business and the ordinary course of proceeding in the Senate. He hoped he would be excused for expressing an earnest wish that the conceded importance of the subject would induce gentlemen to turn their attention to it as soon as they conveniently could, to the end that, when it was taken up, it might be carried to a speedy decision, and not exposed to those unprofitable delays and postponements which had heretofore attended measures of a similar character, and ultimately prevented an expression of the sense of the Senate on their merits. He deceived himself, if there was any matter in which, at this moment, their constituents felt a more intense interest, than the question of the *rightful* and *probable* agency of the General Government in the great work of Internal Improvement. Whilst, in the States, measures of that description had been harmonious in their progress, and, as far as the means of the States would admit of, successful in their results, the condition of things here had been of a very different character. From the first agitation of the subject, the constitutional power of Congress to legislate upon the subject had been a source of unbroken, and, frequently, angry and unpleasant controversy. The time, he said, had never yet been, when all the branches of the Legislative Department were of the same opinion upon the question. Even those who united in the sentiment as to the existence of the power, differed in almost everything else in regard to it. Of its particular source in the Constitution, its extent and attributes, very different views were entertained by its friends. There had not been anything in the experience of the past, nor was there anything in the prospect of the future, on which a reasonable hope could be founded, that this great subject could ever be satisfactorily adjusted by any means short of an appeal to the States. The intimate connexion between the prosperity of the country and works of the description referred to, would always induce efforts to induce the General Government to embark in them, and there was but little reason to believe that its claim of power would ever be abandoned. As little reason was there, in his judgment, to expect that the opposition to it would ever be given up. The principles upon which that opposition is founded; the zeal and fidelity with which it has hitherto been sustained, preclude such an expectation. If this view of the subject was a correct one, and it appeared to him that it was, he respectfully submitted it as a matter of imperious duty, on the part of Congress, to make a determined effort to have the question settled in the only way which can be final—an amendment of the Constitution, prescribing and defining what Congress may, and what they shall not do, with the restrictions under which what is allowed to them shall be done. It appeared to him that not only every interest connected with the subject, but the credit, if not safety, of our enviable political institutions, required that course; for it must be evident to all reflecting men, that the reiterated complaints of constitutional infraction must tend to relax the confidence of the People in the Government, and that such measures as may be undertaken upon the subject must be constantly exposed to peril from the fluctuations of the opinion of successive Legislatures. The subject, he said, had been viewed in this light by some of the best and ablest men the country has produced. As early as 1808, the propriety of an appeal to the States upon the point in question, had been suggested by Mr. Jefferson, in his last message to Congress.

The same course had been recommended by Mr. Madison, and the recommendation repeated by Mr. Monroe.

As yet, no decided effort to effect this great object had been made; he permitted himself to hope that such effort would now be made. It was true, he said, the subject had not been referred to by the present Executive, and the reasons why he had not done so were apparent, from the communications he has made to us. From those, it appeared that the President entertained opinions, as to the power of Congress, which removed all difficulties upon the subject. But Mr. V. B. said that, although that circumstance might possibly diminish, it certainly did not obviate the necessity of now acting upon the subject, as the Senate were not left to conjecture as to the fact, that there existed a discordance of opinion between the Executive and portions, at least— how large time would shew—of the other branches of the Legislative Department. Mr. V. B. said that, entertaining such views upon the subject, he had felt it his duty to bring the subject thus early before the Senate, and when the proper period for discussion arrived, would avail himself of their indulgence to assign his reasons for the course proposed.[1]

These movements excited the attention and received the approbation of Mr. Jefferson and raised for the moment the drooping spirits of many sincere State-rights men. It soon, however, became evident that there was no reasonable hope for their success. It was obvious that the Virginia and Kentucky doctrines of *Ninety Eight* had been too successfully derided and contemned to leave, at that moment the slightest ground of confidence in the adoption of any such proposition. I therefore, after postponing its consideration from year to year in the hope of more favorable indications, suspended further efforts of that nature. But it will be seen that I was not idle, and that my failure was not my fault. I prepared, after much reflection and laborious examination a *brief*[2] for the discussion of the subject, in which I take more pride than in any of my speeches and which, under the sincere tho' too probably mistaken belief that I have not formed a partial estimate of it, I have directed to be published with such of my speeches as those who come after me may deem worthy of so much notice. If the mad schemes of that day should ever be revived those who take a part in defeating them may perhaps find in these notes useful suggestions. They will at all events prove the deep interest that I took in the matter and what follows will shew that in all probability they exerted, altho' in a way very different from the one originally intended for them, a salutary influence upon the great measure of relief to the Country from the evils of spurious legislation upon this great subject.

None but the men who were active and conspicuous in the service of the Federal Government at that day, and of these now few

---

[1] Dec. 20, 1825.—Debates in Congress, 19th, 1st, Vol. II, p. 20.

[2] This brief is not found either in the Van Buren or the Jackson Papers in the Library of Congress.

remain amongst us, can form any adequate opinion of the power and influence which those who had embarked their political fortunes in attempts to commit the General Government irretrievably to the promotion and construction of Internal Improvements, had acquired both in Congress and among the most alert and enterprising portions of the People. The wild spirit of speculation, to whose career our ever growing and ever moving population and our expanded and expanding territory offered the fairest field, became wilder over the prospect before it and the wits of Congressmen were severely tasked in devising and causing to be surveyed and brought forward under captivating disguises the thousand local improvements with which they designed to dazzle and seduce their constituents. It required an extraordinary degree of resolution in a public man to attempt to resist a passion that had become so rampant, but this consideration might stimulate but could not discourage Gen. Jackson so long as he was convinced that the course presented for his consideration was the path of duty. He was unfeignedly grateful to Pennsylvania for what she had done for him, he knew well that upon this question as upon those of the removal of the Indians and of the Bank she had taken a lead in the wrong direction, he was extremely loth to add another to the great points upon which his duty would compel him to throw himself in the way of her gratification, but for all and against all such appeals and motives he promptly opposed the suggestions of right, and the ever present and ever operative sense of an official obligation superior to personal feeling.

He appreciated to their full extent the arguments in support of the inexpediency of the legislation which he was asked to arrest, whilst the Constitution remained unaltered, but preferred to meet the question on constitutional grounds. No Cabinet councils were called: not another member of the Cabinet was consulted before his decision had become irrevocable. It was understood between us that I should keep an eye upon the movements of Congress and bring to his notice the first Bill upon which I might think his interference would be preferable, and that when such a case was presented, we would take up the question of Constitutional power and examine it deliberately and fully.

The Bill authorizing a subscription to the stock of the Maysville, Washington, Paris and Lexington Turnpike-road Company appeared to me to present the looked for occasion. Its local character was incontestably established by the fact that the road commenced and ended in the same State. It had passed the House and could undoubtedly pass the Senate. The road was in Mr. Clay's own State and Mr. Clay was, the General thought—whether rightfully or not is now immaterial,—pressing the measure and the question it involved upon him rather for political effect than for public ends, and it was his preference, in accordance with a sound military axiom to make his enemy's territory the theatre of the war whenever that was practicable.

I brought the subject to the President's notice during one of our daily rides, immediately after the passage of the Bill by the House and proposed to send him on our return the brief of which I have spoken and of which I had before promised him a perusal. I had myself no hesitation in respect to the course that ought to be pursued and spoke of it accordingly. He received my suggestions favorably, appeared sensible of the importance of the proposed step and at parting begged me not to delay sending him the brief—which was done as soon as I got to my house.

Within five days after the passage of the Bill by the House of Representatives I received from him the following note.

(Private.)

MAY 4TH, 1830.

MY DEAR SIR,

I have been engaged to day as long as my head and eyes would permit, poring over the manuscript you handed me; as far as I have been able to decipher it I think it one of the most lucid expositions of the Constitution and historical accounts of the departure by Congress from its true principles that I have ever met with.

It furnishes clear views upon the constitutional powers of Congress. The inability of Congress under the Constitution to apply the funds of the Government to private, not national purposes I never had a doubt of. The Kentucky road bill involves this very power and I think it right boldly to meet it at the threshold. With this object in view I wish to have an interview with you and consult upon this subject that the constitutional points may be arranged to bear upon it with clearness so that the people may fully understand it.

Can I see you this evening or Thursday morning?

Your friend

ANDREW JACKSON

Mr. VAN BUREN.

Those who take the trouble to refer to the manuscript will be able to decide for themselves on the justice of the encomiums bestowed upon it by the President. I returned the following answer with which I have been furnished by Mr. Blair, to whom the General's papers were entrusted by his will.[1]

° TO THE PRESIDENT.

MY DEAR SIR.

I thank you for your favorable opinion of the notes. This matter has for a few days past borne heavily on my mind, and brought it to the precise conclusion stated in your note. Under this impression I had actually commenced throwing my ideas on paper to be submitted to you when I should get through,
y wu

[1] These papers are now in the Library of Congress.   ° MS. III, p.

to seé whether it is not possible to defeat the aim of our adversaries in either respect, viz; whether it be to draw you into the approval of a Bill most emphatically *local*, and thus endeavor to saddle you with the latitudinarian notions upon which the late administration acted, or to compel you to take a stand against internal improvements generally, and thus draw to their aid all those who are interested in the ten thousand schemes which events and the course of the Government for a few past years have engendered. I think I see land, and that it will be in our power to serve the Country and at the same time counteract the machinations of those who mingle their selfish and ambitious views in the matter. We shall have time enough; the Bill has not yet passed the Senate and you have, you know, ten days after that.

I want to see Mr. McDuffie this evening upon the subject of the outfits and may not, therefore, call. I should prefer too to complete first the arrangement of my ideas, and then we can take up the subject more satisfactorily.

Yours truly

M. VAN BUREN

W. *May 4th 1830.*

I requested him some days after to obtain from the Secretary of the Treasury the financial statement which accompanied the *veto-Message*, and received in reply the following spirited note.

PRIVATE.

May 15th, 1830

DEAR SIR,

Your note is received. I am happy that you have been looking at the proceedings of Congress. The appropriations now exceed the available funds in the Treasury, and the estimates always exceed the real amount available. I have just called upon the Secretary of the Treasury for the amount of the estimated available balance on the 1st January 1831.

The people expected reform retrenchment and economy in the administration of this Government. This was the cry from Maine to Louisiana, and instead of these the great object of Congress, *it would seem*, is to make mine one of the most extravagant administrations since the commencement of the Government. This must not be; The Federal Constitution must be obeyed, State-rights preserved, our national debt *must be paid, direct taxes and loans avoided* and the Federal union preserved. These are the objects I have in view, and regardless of all consequences, will carry into effect.

Yr. friend   A. J.

Mr. V. B. *Sec. of State.*

Let me see you this evening or in the morning.

Not one out of twenty of the opposition members believed that President Jackson, notwithstanding his proverbial indifference to the assumption of responsibility, in respect to measures he believed to be right, would venture to veto an act for the internal improvement of the Country in the then state of public opinicn upon the subject and after the votes he had so recently given in favor of such acts. If they had thought otherwise they would not have presented him a Bill so purely local in its character. Apprehensive that they would, when his designs became known to them, change their course in that respect, and avail themselves of the selfish views and unsettled opinions of a sufficient number of those who had been elected as Jackson men to substitute a Bill for a work more national in its pretensions, I was extremely solicitous that nothing should be said upon the subject until it should be too late for such a step, and pressed that point upon the General. It was the only one, I knew, that required to be pressed and it was, moreover, that which I was persuaded would be the most difficult for him. He was entirely unreserved in his public dealings—the People, he thought, should know every thing and "give it to Blair" (or *Blar* as he pronounced it)—was almost always his prompt direction when ever any information was brought to him which affected or might affect the public interest. Apropos of which I was once told by Major Donelson that, in relation to all affairs in which men were alone concerned, the General was inveterately opposed *to secrecy* excepting only when a duel was in the wind, on which occasions he was a "counsellor—most still, most secret and most grave." Indeed we were often alarmed at the exposed manner in which he kept his letters and other private papers on his table, and ventured to remonstrate with him on the subject, assuring him that for ten dollars ———— could induce a very clever but sinister looking mulatto in the President's service to carry them to him over night; to which suggestion the General replied "If ———— will come here he shall have the perusal of them for half the money." An occasion was soon presented on which his habit in this respect involved him in some embarrassment.

Col. Johnson,[1] of Kentucky, was induced by Western members, who had been alarmed by floating rumors, to sound the President and if he found that there existed danger of such a result to remonstrate with him, in their names and his own, against a *veto*. At the moment of his appearance the President and myself were engaged in an examination of the exposé of the state of the Treasury to which I have referred, and alone. After a delay natural to a man possessed as the Colonel was of much real delicacy of feeling and having an awkward commission in hand, he said that he had called at the instance of many friends to have some conversation with the General upon a very delicate subject and was deterred from entering upon it by an apprehension that he might give offense. He was kindly told to dismiss such fears, and assured that as the President reposed unqualified confidence in his friendship he could say nothing on any public matter that would give offense. He then spoke of the rumors in circulation of the feelings of the General's Western friends in regard to the subject of them, of his apprehensions of the uses that Mr. Clay would make of a *veto*, and encouraged by the General's apparent interest,

---

[1] Richard M. Johnson.

and warmed by his own, he extended his open hand and exclaimed "General! If this hand were an anvil on which the sledge hammer of the smith was descending and a fly were to light upon it in time to receive the blow he would not crush it more effectually than you will crush your friends in Kentucky if you veto that Bill!" Gen. Jackson evidently excited by the bold figure and energetic manner of Col. Johnson, rose from his seat and advanced towards the latter, who also quitted his chair, and the following questions and answers succeeded very rapidly: " Sir, have you looked at the condition of the Treasury—at the amount of money that it contains—at the appropriations already made by Congress—at the amount of other unavoidable claims upon it?"— "No! General, I have not! But there has always been money enough to satisfy appropriations and I do not doubt there will be now!"—"Well, I have, and this is the result," (repeating the substance of the Treasury exhibit,) " and you see there is no money to be expended as my friends desire. Now, I stand committed before the Country to pay off the National Debt, at the earliest practicable moment; this pledge I am determined to redeem, and I cannot do this if I consent to encrease it without necessity. Are you willing—are my friends willing to lay taxes to pay for internal improvements?—for be assured I will not borrow a cent except in cases of absolute necessity!"—"No!" replied the Colonel, "that would be worse than a *veto!*"

These emphatic declarations delivered with unusual earnestness and in that peculiarly impressive manner for which he was remarkable when excited quite overcrowed the Colonel who picked up the green bag which he usually carried during the ° session and manifested a disposition to retreat. As he was about to leave I remarked to him that he had evidently made up his mind that the General had determined to veto the Bill at all events, but that when he reflected how much of the President's earnestness was occasioned by his own strong speech and how natural it was for a man to become excited when he has two sets of friends, in whom he has equal confidence, urging him in different directions, he would be less confident in his conclusion. Reminded by this observation that he had suffered the guard which he had imposed on himself to be broken down by the Colonel's *sledge-hammer*, the General told him that he was giving the matter a thorough investigation and that their friends might be assured that he would not make up his mind without loking at every side of it,—that he was obliged to him for what he had said and wished all his friends to speak to him as plainly, &c. &c. The Colonel with his accustomed urbanity deported himself as if reassured and appeared to consider the case not so desperate as he had at first imagined, but his manner was assumed for the purpose of quieting my apprehensions which he perceived and understood. When he returned to the House he replied to the eager enquiries of his Western friends that the General had thanked him and assured him that he would thoroughly examine the subject, but his private opinion decidedly was that nothing less than a voice from Heaven would prevent the old man from vetoing the Bill, and he doubted whether that would!

Still so strong was the impression derived from Gen. Jackson's habit of never concealing his views upon a subject on which his mind was made up, that the incredulity of the members was but slightly removed by the Colonel's report: what he would do in the matter remained an open question to the last. The consequence was that the importunities of his friends were increased, but as the detailed account of Col. Johnson's embassy discouraged direct remonstrances with the President they were addressed to me, and in my efforts to keep both sides quiet by statements of the difficulties with which the subject was environed by reason of the conflicting struggles of the friends of the Administration, I exposed my own course to some suspicion or affected suspicion in the end. The General told me, on my return from England, that one of the charges brought against me by Mr. Calhoun's friends, to justify the rejection of my nomination as Minister, was that I had been opposed to the *veto* and had tried to prevent him from interposing it. He named, in particular, Mr. Carson,[1] of North Carolina, a peppery young man, ardently attached to Mr. Calhoun and, for no other reason that I knew of, very hostile to me, as one who had circulated that report, and said that to silence him, he one day, took up a pamphlet-copy of the *veto*-Message and holding it before him asked him to look at it closely and see whether he could not discover my likeness on every page.

The impression among the General's Western friends, that he would destroy his popularity by a *veto*, was universal and prevailed also extensively among those from the North. The Pennsylvania members generally were rampant in their opposition and most of them voted for the Bill after the *veto* was interposed. Being with him to a very late hour the night before the Message was sent up, he asked me to take an early breakfast with him, as Congress was on the point of breaking up, and would therefore meet at an early hour. In the morning I found our friends, Grundy, Barry, Eaton,[2] and Lewis[3] at the table, wearing countenances to the last degree despond-

---

[1] Samuel P. Carson.
[2] Felix Grundy, William T. Barry, and John H. Eaton.
[3] William B. Lewis.

ing, occasioned, as I well knew, by their convictions of the injurious effects that must result from the step about to be taken. On going up stairs to his office, he leaning on my arm on account of his extreme physical weakness, I observed that our friends were frightened. "Yes," he replied,—"but don't mind that! The thing is here" (placing his hand on the breast-pocket of his coat)" and shall be sent up as soon as Congress convenes."

It was sent up that morning and a scene ensued that baffled all our calculations. If there was any sentiment among our opponents which we knew to be universal, before the reading of the *veto*-Message, it was that it would prove the political death warrant of the Administration and we were prepared to hear denunciations against the violence and destructive effects of the measure and the reckless insult offered to the House by the President in sending it. But no such clamor arose, and the first and principal objection that was made against the Message, when the reading was finished, and which was persevered in to the end, was that it was "an *electioneering document*" sent to Congress for political effect!—and that the "*hand of the magician*" was visible in every line of it!

It was indeed received with unbounded satisfaction by the great body of the disinterested and genuine friends of the Administration throughout the Country. At a public dinner given by the republicans of Norfolk to John Randolph on the occasion of his departure for Russia, the following toast was drunk standing and with cheers three times three:—"The *rejection of the Maysville Road Bill* it falls upon the ears like the music of other days." Some, whose friendship for the Administration, if not completely alienated, had certainly been greatly abated, felt obliged to praise it. Col. Hayne, of South Carolina, at the great Charleston dinner given to inaugurate nullification, and thro' its means to put that Administration to the severest trial that any had ever been exposed to in our Country spoke of the *veto* as "the most auspicious event which had taken place in the history of the Country for years past." I refer but to one other of those acceptable exhibitions of public feeling which pervaded the Union, tho' less imposing in form not less gratifying. Col. Ramsay,[1] one of the Representatives from Pennsylvania, an excitable but honest man and true patriot, irritated almost beyond endurance by the *veto*, followed us from the Capitol to the White House, after the close of the session, and, presuming on the strength of his friendship for the General, fairly upbraided him for his course. The latter bore his reproaches, for such they really were altho' intended only as a remonstrance which he thought allowable in a devoted friend, with a degree of mildness that excited my admiration, begging the dissatisfied representative to say no more upon

---

[1] Robert Ramsay.

the subject until he had seen his constituents and venturing to prophesy that he would find them pleased with the veto. The worthy Pennsylvanian received the intimation as an additional injury and parted from us in an exceedingly bad humor. A short time afterwards, as I was one day approaching the President he held up to me in an exultant manner, a paper which proved to be a letter from our good friend Ramsay in which he announced the confirmation of the General's prediction and acknowledged that, in that case at least, the latter had known his constituents better than he himself had known them.

And yet this measure was but the entering wedge to the course of action by which that powerful combination known as the Internal Improvement party was broken asunder and finally annihilated. I have already given an extract from the President's Message descriptive of its ramifications and extent at the period of the *veto*. The power which a combined influence of that description, addressing itself to the strongest passion of man's nature and wielded by a triumvirate of active and able young statesmen as a means through which to achieve for themselves the glittering prize of the Presidency, operating in conjunction with minor classes of politicians, looking in the same general direction and backed by a little army of cunning contractors, is capable of exerting in communities so excitable as our own, can easily be imagined. The danger in offending and the difficulty of resisting such an influence were equally apparent. The utmost prudence was required in respect to the ground that should be occupied by the President in the first step that he was to take in the prosecution of the great reform that he had in view. His own past course increased the necessity of great circumspection at the start. The votes he had given for the survey-bill and for the appropriation in aid of the Chesapeake and Delaware Canal, with his letter to the Governor of Indiana, written during the canvass and referring to those votes as exponents of his opinions were fresh in the recollections of the People. His name was, in very deed, a tower of strength,° but prudence as well as sound principle dictated that their partiality should not be put to an unreasonable test by the ground he now took, on an occasion of intense interest, in a document which, as we all well knew, would have to pass through the severest scrutiny.

In view of this state of things the *veto*-Message assumed the following positions:—

1st. The construction of Internal Improvements under the authority of the Federal Government was not authorized by the Constitution.

° MS. III, p. 170.

2nd. Altho' the true view of the Constitution in regard to the power of appropriation was probably that taken in Madison's Report concerning the alien and sedition laws, by which it was confined to cases where the particular measure which the appropriation was designed to promote was within the enumerated authorities vested in Congress, yet every Administration of the Government had, in respect to appropriations of money only adopted in practice (several cases of which were mentioned) a more enlarged construction of the power. This course, it was supposed, had been so long and so extensively persisted in as to render it difficult, if not impracticable, to bring the operations of the Government back to the construction first referred to. The Message nowhere admitted that the more enlarged construction which had obtained so strong a foothold, was a true exposition of the Constitution, and it conceded that its restriction against abuse, viz., that the works which might be thus aided should be " of a general, not local—National, not State " character, a disregard of which distinction would of necessity lead to the subversion of the Federal System, was unsafe, arbitrary in its nature and inefficient.

3d. Although he might not feel it to be his duty to interpose the Executive veto against the passage of Bills appropriating money for the construction of such works as were authorized by the States, and were National in their character the President did not wish to be understood as assenting to the expediency of embarking the General Government in a system of that kind at this time; but he could never give his approval to a measure having the character of that under consideration, not being able to regard it in any other light than as a measure of a purely local character; or if it could be considered National no further distinction between the appropriate duties of the General and State Governments need be attempted, for there could be no local interest that might not, under such a construction, be denominated, with equal propriety, National.

His *veto* was placed on that specific ground, and the rest of the Message was principally taken up in discussing the propriety and expediency of deferring all other action upon the subject, even of appropriations for National works until the Public Debt should be paid and amendments of the Constitution adopted by which such appropriation could be protected against the abuses to which they were exposed.

These positions, fairly interpreted, were not inconsistent with the votes which Gen. Jackson had given in the capacity of Senator during the Canvass of 1823–4. The Survey-Bill was in terms limited to roads and canals which the President should deem of *National importance*. Mr. Calhoun's Bonus Bill proposed to set aside a fund for the *construction* of roads and canals, and still both he and Mr. Clay contended that the constitutional question did not arise before the specific bill was presented for the action of Congress. With much more propriety could that be said of the Survey Bill. The appropriation in aid of the Chesapeake and Delaware Canal was sustained on the ground of its being a work of national importance and the Maysville *veto* did not expressly deny the constitutionality of such appropriations. Whether that was one of such a character or not was a question in respect to which, in the absence of constitutional regulation, Gen. Jackson was obliged to exercise his discretion. He did so in that case and voted for the Bill—he did the same thing in the case of the Maysville Road and vetoed it. The propriety of the *veto* was therefore reduced to the single question as to the character of the road—was it national or local?—an issue on which his opponents could not sustain themselves for a moment. He was thus enabled to go to the Country with his views in favor of suspending action even upon works of national importance until the public debt was paid and constitutional amendments obtained, to guard against otherwise unavoidable abuses, unembarrassed by side issues of any description other than that to which I have last referred and upon which his position was absolutely impregnable.

It was the consciousness of the soundness of the positions taken in the *veto*-Message that produced the raving debates in the House when it was first presented to that body, and it was doubtless a similar consciousness that forced Mr. Clay in a speech on the Message delivered at Cincinnati, shortly after its appearance, so far to forget the proprieties of his position to compare the Message to the paper sent by George III, during his insanity, which, tho' it had his name attached to it, could not be said to have spoken his sentiments, and to exclaim that he could not read it without having the name of Talleyrand! Tallyrand! Talleyrand! continually recurring to his mind. He could hardly have been aware of the weight of testimony he bore in the latter exclamation in favor of the Message on the score of talent and power. The reader will judge for himself as to the degree of success with which the views sketched in my note to the President of the 4th of May, before given, were carried out.

A great step had been taken towards removing from Congress an incubus which had for years weighed upon it in the shape of unavailing effort to establish a useful system of internal improvement under its auspices and by its authority. Whilst the time of that body was wasted in unfruitful debates and its capacity for usefulness in the channels designed for its action by the Constitution impaired, every thinking and fair minded man saw that to establish such a system previous amendments to the Constitution were absolutely indispensable. A step in advance had been taken but we knew very well that more was to be done and that other positions must be assumed to make that step available, and we devoted ourselves without delay to a consideration of their character. Neither of us laboring, it is but truth to say it, under vain conceits of our self-sufficiency, I with the approbation of the President, sought the best counsel that the Country afforded by opening a correspondence on the subject with Mr. Madison. In his recent *veto*-Message, the President had given a construction to Mr. Madison's *veto* of Mr. Calhoun's Bonus Bill, of which we thought it fairly suspectible altho' not with absolute certainty of our position. I am free to admit that a floating impression existed in my mind throughout that Mr. Madison might, altho' I could not well see how, disavow that construction. I sincerely wished for such a result and the wish was doubtless father to the thought. I therefore sent him an early copy of the General's *veto*-Message, in a way best calculated to elicit an expression of his views upon the point without asking them. His first note shews the result and as the residue of the correspondence explains the reasons for its continuance I will make no apology for inserting all the letters here. What such a man as Mr. Madison has said upon a subject of so much importance cannot be too carefully preserved and there is clearly no reason for a continuance of the confidence in which his letters were written and which has hitherto been observed.

FROM MR. MADISON.[1]

J. Madison has duly received the copy of the President's Message forwarded by Mr. Van Buren. In returning his thanks for this polite attention, he regrets the necessity of observing that the Message has not rightly conceived the intention of J. M. in his *Veto* in 1817 on the Bill relating to Internal Improvements. It was an object of the Veto to deny to Congress as well as the appropriating power, as the executing and jurisdictional branches of it, and it is believed that this was the general understanding at the time, and has continued to be so, according to the references occasionally made to the document. Whether the language employed duly conveyed the meaning of which J. M. retains the consciousness is a question on which he does not presume ° to judge for others.

Relying on the candor to which these remarks are addressed he tenders to Mr. Van Buren renewed assurances of his high esteem and good wishes.
Montpelier, June 3, 1830.

TO MR. MADISON.

WASHINGTON *June 9th, 1830*

DEAR SIR,

I have shewn your note of the 3rd inst. to the President who requests me to express his regret that he has misconceived your intentions in regard to your veto on the Bill for Internal Improvements in 1817. As far as opportunities

---

[1] Madison's draft is in the Madison Papers in the Library of Congress.
° MS. III, p. 175.

place it in his power to correct the error in informal conversation he will not fail to do so, and should an occasion occur on which a more formal correction would be pertinent it will give him pleasure to make it, if advised that that course would be preferred by you.

Will you excuse me for troubling you again upon this interesting and perplexing subject? I am deeply sensible of the necessity of repose to one of your advanced age and of the claims to its enjoyment which are founded upon your past usefulness, but deriving confidence from your ready acquiescence in my wishes on a former occasion I venture to intrude once more upon your retirement. You have had some experience of the injurious tendency of legislation upon this subject by Congress, but no one can have an idea of the demoralizing effect which for years past it has had upon their proceedings without being on the spot and forming a part of the Government. The President is deeply impressed with the importance of arresting its further progress and very willing to incur whatever responsibility he can properly take upon himself to promote that object. You have seen the ground he has taken and can appreciate fully the position he occupies. It is unnecessary for me to say to you that the matter cannot rest here but that it will be necessary for him to go farther at the next session of Congress.

Among the points which will then come up for consideration will be the following: 1st, the establishment of some rule which shall give the greatest practicable precision to the power of appropriating money for objects of general concern; 2d, a rule for the government of grants for light houses and the improvement of harbors and rivers which will avoid the objects which it is desirable to exclude from the present action of Government and at the same time to do what is imperiously required by a due regard to the general commerce of the Country; 3d, the expediency of refusing all appropriations for internal improvements, (other than those of the character last referred to if they may be so called,) until the national debt is paid, as well on account of the sufficiency of that motive, as to give time for the adoption of some constitutional or other arrangement by which the whole subject may be placed on better grounds,—an arrangement which will never be seriously attempted as long as scattering appropriations are made and the scramble for them thereby encouraged; 4th, the strong objections which exist against subscriptions to the stock of private companies by the United States.

There is no man more willing to hear with patience and to weigh with candor the suggestions of those in whom he has confidence than the President. The relation in which I stand to him will give him the right to be furnished with my views upon these matters and I need not say how much I would be benefitted in forming and fortified in sustaining them by your friendly advice. I ask it in confidence and will receive whatever your leisure and inclination may induce you to say upon the subject under the same obligation.

Wishing to be kindly remembered to Mrs. Madison, I am dear Sir,

Very truly yours,[1]

MADISON TO VAN BUREN.[2]

MONTPELLIER, *July 5, 1830.*

DEAR SIR.—Your letter of June 9th came duly to hand. On the subject of the discrepancy between the construction put by the message of the President on the veto of 1817, and the intention of its author, the President will of course consult his own view of the case. For myself, I am aware that the

---

[1] Van Buren's draft is in the Van Buren Papers, the letter sent is in the Madison Papers.

[2] Copies are in both the Madison and Van Buren Papers.

document must speak for itself, and that that intention can not be substituted for the established rules of interpretation.

The several points on which you desire my ideas are necessarily vague, and the observations on them can not well be otherwise. They are suggested by a respect for your request, rather than by a hope that they can assist the object of it.

"Point 1. The establishment of some rule which shall give the greatest practicable precision to the power of appropriating money to objects of general concern."

The rule must refer, it is presumed, either to the objects of appropriation, or to the apportionment of the money.

A specification of the objects of general concern in terms as definite as may ne, seems to be the rule most applicable; thus Roads simply, if for all the uses of Roads; or Roads, post and military, if limited to those uses; or post roads only, if so limited: thus, Canals, either generally, or for specified uses: so again Education, as limited to a university, or extended to seminaries of other denominations.

As to the apportionment of the money, no rule can exclude Legislative discretion but that of distribution among the States according to their presumed contributions; that is, to their ratio of Representation in Congress. The advantages of this rule are its certainty, and its apparent equity. The objections to it may be that, on one hand, it would increase the comparative agency of the Federal Government, and, on the other that the money might not be expended on objects of general concern; the interests of particular States not happening to coincide with the general interest in relation to improvements within such States.

"2. A rule for the Government of Grants for Light-houses, and the improvement of Harbours and Rivers, which will avoid the objects which it is desirable to exclude from the present action of the Government; and at the same time do what is imperiously required by a regard to the general commerce of the Country."

National grants in these cases seem to admit no possible rule of discrimination, but as the objects may be of a national or local character. The difficulty lies in all cases where the *degree* and not the *nature* of the case, is to govern. In the extremes, the judgment is easily formed; as between removing obstructions in the Mississippi, the highway of commerce for half the nation, and a like operation, giving but little extension to the navigable use of a river, itself of confined use. In the intermediate cases, legislative discretion, and, consequently, legislative errors and partialities are unavoidable. Some controul is attainable in doubtful cases, from preliminary investigations and reports by disinterested and responsible agents.

In defraying the expense of internal improvements, strict justice would require that a part only and not the whole should be borne by the nation. Take for examples the Harbours of New York and New Orleans. However important in a commercial view they may be to the other portions of the Union, the States to which they belong must derive a *peculiar* as well as a *common* advantage from improvements made in them, and could afford therefore to combine with grants from the common treasury, proportional contributions from their own. On this principle it is that the practice has prevailed in the States (as it has done with Congress) of dividing the expense of certain improvements, between the funds of the State, and the contribution of those locally interested in them.

Extravagant and disproportionate expenditures on Harbours, Light-houses and other arrangements on the Seaboard ought certainly to be controuled as much as possible. But it seems not to be sufficiently recollected, that in relation to our *foreign* commerce, the burden and benefit of accommodating and protecting it necessarily go together, and must do so as long and as far as the public revenue continues to be drawn thro' the Customhouse. Whatever gives facility and security to navigation, cheapens imports; and all who consume them wherever residing are alike interested in what has that effect. If they consume they ought as they now do to pay. If they do not consume, they do not pay. The consumer in the most inland State derives the same advantage from the necessary and prudent expenditures for the security of our foreign navigation, as the consumer in a maritime State. Our local expenditures have not of themselves a correspondent operation.

" 3. The expediency of refusing all appropriations for internal improvements (other than those of the character last referred to, if they can be so called) until the national debt is paid; as well on account of the sufficiency of that motive, as to give time for the adoption of some constitutional or other arrangement by which the whole subject may be placed on better grounds; an arrangement which will never be seriously attempted as long as scattering appropriations are made, and the scramble for them thereby encouraged."

The expediency of refusing appropriations, with a view to the previous discharge of the public debt, involves considerations which can be best weighed and compared at the focus of lights on the subject. A distant view like mine can only suggest the remark, too vague to be of value, that a material delay ought not to be incurred for objects not both important and urgent; nor such objects to be neglected in order to avoid an immaterial delay. This is, indeed, but the amount of the exception glanced at in your parenthesis.

The mortifying scenes connected with a surplus revenue are the natural offspring of a surplus; and cannot perhaps be entirely prevented by any plan of appropriation which allows a scope to Legislative discretion. The evil will have a powerful controul in the pervading dislike to taxes even the most indirect. The taxes lately repealed are an index of it. Were the whole revenue expended on internal improvements drawn from direct taxation, there would be danger of too much parsimony rather than too much profusion at the Treasury.

" 4. The strong objections which exist against subscriptions to the stock of private companies by the United States."

The objections are doubtless in many respects strong. Yet cases might present themselves which might not be favored by the State, whilst the concurring agency of an Undertaking Company would be desirable in a national view. There was a time it is said when the State of Delaware, influenced by the profits of a *Portage* between the Delaware and Chesapeake, was unfriendly to the Canal, now forming so important a link of internal communication between the North and the South. Undertakings by private companies carry with them a presumptive evidence of utility, and the private stakes in them, some security for economy in the execution, the want of which is the bane of public undertakings. Still the importunities of private companies cannot be listened to with more caution than prudence requires.

I have, as you know, never considered the powers claimed for Congress over roads and canals, as within the grants of the Constitution. But such improvements being justly ranked among the greatest advantages and best evidences of good government; and having, moreover, with us, the peculiar recommendation of binding the several parts of the Union more firmly together, I have always thought the power ought to be possessed by the common Government; which commands the least unpopular and most productive sources of revenue, and can alone select improvements with an eye to the national good. The States are restricted in their pecuniary resources; and Roads and Canals most important in a national view might not be important to the State or States possessing the domain and the soil; or might even be deemed disadvantageous; and on the most favourable supposition might require a concert of means and regulations among several States not easily effected, nor unlikely to be altogether omitted.

These considerations have pleaded with me in favour of the policy of vesting in Congress an authority over internal improvements. I am sensible at the same time of the magnitude of the trust, as well as of the difficulty of executing it properly and the greater difficulty of executing it satisfactorily.

On a supposition of a due establishment of the power in Congress, one of the modes of using it might be, to apportion a reasonable share of the disposable revenue of the United States among the States to be applied by them to cases of State concern; with a reserved discretion in Congress to effectuate improvements of general concern which the States might not be able or not disposed to provide for.

If Congress do not mean to throw away the rich fund inherited in the public lands, would not the sales of them, after their liberation from the original pledge, be aptly appropriated to objects of internal improvements; and why not also, with a supply of the competent authority, to the removal to better situations of the free black as well as red population, objects confessedly of national importance and desirable to all parties? But I am traveling out of the subject before me.

The date of your letter reminds me of the delay of the answer. The delay has been occasioned by interruptions of my health; and the answer such as it is, is offered in the same confidence in which it was asked.

With great esteem & cordial salutations.

JAMES MADISON.

Mr. VAN BUREN.

FROM MR. MADISON.

MONTPELLIER, Oct. 9, 1830.

DEAR SIR

I rec^d your letter of July 30th ^a in due time but have taken advantage of the permitted delay in answering it. Altho' I have again turned in my thoughts the subjects of your former letter "on which any further remarks from me would be acceptable", I do not find that I can add anything material to what is said either in my letter of July 5th or in preceding ones. The particular cases of local improvements or establishments having immediate relation to external commerce and navigation will continue to produce questions of difficulty, either constitutional, or as to utility or impartiality, which can only be decided according to their respective merits. No general rule, founded on precise definitions, is perhaps possible; none certainly that relates to such cases as those of Light Houses, which must depend on the evidence before the competent authority. In procuring that evidence it will, of course be incumbent on that authority to employ the means and precautions most appropriate.

With regard to the Veto of 1817 I wish it to be understood that I have no particular solicitude; nor can the President be under any obligation to notice the subject, if his construction of the language of the Document be unchanged. My notice of it, when acknowledging the receipt of the Message you politely enclosed to me, was necessary to guard my consistency against an inference from my silence.

---

^a I have not kept a copy, it appears, of my letter of July 30. I must have again referred to the subject of the President's misconstruction of the veto of 1817.

With a regret that I cannot make you a more important communication, I renew the assurances of my great esteem and my cordial salutations.

JAMES MADISON.

Mr. VAN BUREN.

Having carefully observed the course of public opinion and being satisfied that it had settled down decidedly in favor of the policy of postponing all appropriations for works of internal improvement, even for such as might fairly be deemed of a national character until the public debt was paid, as he had suggested in his veto-Message, the President was prepared to take his own position upon that point in his second annual Message in December of the same year.[2] Justice cannot be done to him without accompanying this view of those important transactions with explanations which might, under other circumstances be considered unnecessary. He first took notice of the vote he had given, whilst Senator, in favor of the Chesapeake and Delaware Canal of which he spoke as follows:

In speaking of direct appropriations I mean not to include a practice which has obtained to some extent, and to which I have, in one instance, in a different capacity, given my assent—that of subscribing to the stock of private associations. Positive experience, and a more thorough consideration of the subject, have convinced me of the impropriety as well as inexpediency of such investments. All improvements effected by the funds of the nation for general use should be open to the enjoyment of all our fellow citizens, exempt from the payment of tolls, or any° imposition of that character: The practice of thus mingling the concerns of the Government with those of the States or of individuals is inconsistent with the object of its institution, and highly impolitic. The successful operation of the federal system can only be preserved by confining it to the few and simple but yet important objects for which it was designed. * * * The power which the General Government would acquire within the several States by becoming the principal stockholder in corporations, controlling every canal and each sixty or hundred miles of every important road, and giving a proportionate vote in all their elections, is almost inconceivable and, in my view, dangerous to the liberties of the people.

Having thus acknowledged with characteristic frankness the change which his opinion had undergone on the point referred to, he spoke with the same freedom of the general subject, and said, among other things:

In my objections to the bills authorizing subscriptions to the Maysville and Rockville Road Companies, I expressed my views fully in regard to the power of Congress to construct roads and canals within a State, or to appropriate money for improvements of a local character. I, at the same time, intimated my belief that the right to make appropriations for such as were of a national character had been so generally acted upon and so long acquiesced in by the Federal and State Governments, and the constituents of each, as to justify its exercise on the ground of continued and uninterrupted usage; but that it was nevertheless, highly expedient that appropriations, even of that character, should, with the exception made at the time, be deferred until the national

---

[1] Madison's draft is in the Madison Papers.   [2] 1830.   ° MS. III, p. 180.

debt is paid, and that, in the meanwhile, some general rule for the action of the Government in that respect ought to be established.

These suggestions were not necessary to the decision of the question then before me; and were, I readily admit, intended to awake the attention and draw forth the opinions and observations of our constituents, upon a subject of the highest importance to their interests, and one destined to exert a powerful influence upon the future operations of our political system. I know of no tribunal to which a public man in this Country, in a case of doubt and difficulty, can appeal with greater advantage or more propriety than the judgment of the people; and although I must necessarily, in the discharge of my official duties, be governed by the dictates of my own judgment, I have no desire to conceal my anxious wish to conform, as far as I can, to the views of those for whom I act.

All irregular expressions of public opinion are of necessity attended with some doubt as to their accuracy; but, making full allowance on that account, I can not, I think, deceive myself in believing that the acts referred to, as well as the suggestions which I allowed myself to make, in relation to their bearing upon the future operations of the Government, have been approved by the great body of the people. That those whose immediate pecuniary interests are to be affected by proposed expenditures should shrink from the application of a rule which prefers their more general and remote interests to those which are personal and immediate, is to be expected. But even such objections must, from the nature of our population, be but temporary in their duration; and if it were otherwise our course should be the same; for the time is yet, I hope, far distant when those intrusted with power to be exercised for the good of the whole will consider it either honest or wise, to purchase local favors at the sacrifice of principle and general good.

So understanding public sentiment and thoroughly satisfied that the best interests of our common Country imperiously require that the course which I have recommended in this regard should be adopted, I have, upon the most mature consideration, determined to pursue it.

It is due to candor as well as to my own feelings that I should express the reluctance and anxiety which I must at all times experience in exercising the undoubted right of the Executive to withhold his assent from bills on other grounds than their constitutionality. That this right should not be exercised on slight occasions, all will admit. It is only in matters of deep interest, when the principle involved may be justly regarded as next in importance to infractions of the Constitution itself, that such a step can be expected to meet with the approbation of the people. Such an occasion do I conscientiously believe the present to be. In the discharge of this delicate and highly responsible duty I am sustained by the reflection that the exercise of this power has been deemed consistent with the obligations of official duty by several of my predecessors; and by the persuasion too, that whatever liberal institutions may have to fear from the encroachments of Executive power, which has been every where the cause of so much strife and bloody contention, but little danger is to be apprehended from a precedent by which that authority denies to itself the exercise of powers that bring in their train influence and patronage of great extent; and thus excludes the operation of personal interests, every where the bane of official trust. I derive, too, no small degree of satisfaction from the reflection, that if I have mistaken the interests and wishes of the people, the Constitution affords the means of soon redressing the error, by selecting for the place their favor has bestowed upon me a citizen whose opinions may accord with their own. I trust, in the mean time, the interests of the nation will be saved from prejudice, by a rigid application of that portion of the public funds which might otherwise be applied to different objects to that highest of all our obligations, the payment of the public debt, and an opportunity be afforded for the adoption of some better rule, for the operations of the Government in this matter, than any which has hitherto been acted upon.

After his re-election, and in his sixth annual Message he repeated the views he here expressed and took a final leave of the subject in the following emphatic terms:

So far, at least as it regards this branch of the subject, my best hopes have been realized. Nearly four years have elapsed, and several sessions of Congress have intervened, and no attempt, within my recollection has been made to induce Congress to exercise this power. The application for the construction of roads and canals, which were formerly multiplied upon your files, are no longer presented; and we have good reason to infer that the current of public sentiment has become so decided against the pretension as effectually to discourage its reassertion. So thinking, I derive the greatest satisfaction from the conviction that thus much at least has been secured upon this important and embarrassing subject.

From attempts to appropriate the national funds to objects which are confessedly of a local character we cannot, I trust, have any thing further to apprehend. My views in regard to the expediency of making appropriations for works which are claimed to be of a national character, and prosecuted under State authority, assuming that Congress have the right to do so, were stated in my annual message to Congress in 1830, and also in that containing my objections to the Maysville Road bill.

So thoroughly convinced am I that no such appropriations ought to be made by Congress, until a suitable constitutional provision is made upon the subject, and so essential do I regard the point to the highest interests of our Country, that I could not consider myself as discharging my duty to my constituents in giving the Executive sanction to any bill containing such an appropriation. If the people of the United States desire that the public Treasury shall be resorted to for the means to prosecute such works, they will concur in an amendment to the Constitution, prescribing a rule by which the national character of the works is to be tested, and by which the greatest practicable equality of benefits may be secured to each member of the confederacy. The effects of such a regulation would be most salutary in preventing unprofitable expenditures, in securing our legislation from the pernicious consequences of a scramble for the favors of Government, and in repressing the spirit of discontent which must inevitably arise from an unequal distribution of treasures which belong alike to all.

From this declaration he excepted appropriations for the improvement of our harbors and for the removal of partial and temporary obstructions in our navigable rivers, for the facility and security of our foreign commerce, as standing upon different grounds.

For seven years of General Jackson's administration was the general subject thus banished from the halls of Congress and by my election as his successor that virtual interdict (if it may be so termed) was extended to eleven years. It was in consequence of the steps of which I have spoken that the project of a system of Internal

Improvements by the Federal Government was—there is every °reason to believe—forever withdrawn from the action of that Government. Not that any such consequence can be attributed to the opinion or action of any man who may for a season be placed at its head, for no one conversant with human nature or with the course of political events will ever expect with confidence such a result from such causes. The opinion I have expressed is founded on more potent considerations. Every effort in the direction referred to was certainly suspended for eleven years and other fields of exertion in behalf of such works were soon found and occupied. To a people as impulsive as ours eleven years of denial and delay are almost equivalent to an eternal veto, and those who maintained that the passion for Internal Improvements, so rampant at the seat of the Federal Government at the commencement of the Jackson administration, would seek other and constitutional directions for its gratification, if that could be perseveringly denied to it there for even a shorter period, stand justified by the event. All of the works of that character which it was ever hoped might prove safe and useful to the Country, have been made by or under the authority of the State Governments. All motive for enlisting the interference of the National Government for generations to come, has thus been superseded. In the cases of wild and unprofitable or speculative projects, losses, to the extent of many millions, which the Treasury would have sustained if these works had been constructed under Federal authority, have fallen with a weight diminished by the vigilance inspired by private interest and by State supervision, upon the shoulders of those who expected to make money by them, instead of emptying the national ¢offers, to be recruited by taxes collected from the mass of the people who would have derived no exclusive advantages from their success.

We have had two administrations of the Federal Government whose politics were of the Governmental-improvement stamp, but none of the old projects have been brought forward—resolutions in favour of Internal Improvements have been dropped from the partisan platforms of the party that suported those administrations. The theory and the practice—except as to cases not involved in the general question—are both exploded as regards the action of the Federal Government and the signal advantages which the Country has reaped from this result so far as they have not been now refered to will be elsewhere noticed.

° MS. III, p. 185.

CHAPTER XXVI.

I have once or twice incidentally mentioned, an affair, under the name of the Eaton-imbroglio, which, tho' in no proper sense political, exerted perhaps a more injurious influence upon the management of public affairs than could be ascribed to any of the disturbing questions of the excited period of which I write. Breaking out at the very commencement of the administration, kept alive by feelings of the bitterest character and soon directed to the acomplishment of political as well as personal objects it maintained for two years a foothold at the seat of the Federal Government, a plague to social intercourse, destructive in many instances of private friendship, deranging public business and for a season, at least, disparaging the character of the Government. Except perhaps the disreputable scenes that were witnessed in England, occasioned by the quarrel between George IV and his unfortunate Queen, there has not been seen in modern times so relentless and so reckless a foray upon all those interests as that to which I refer. There, as here, time has somewhat effaced the remembrance of scenes which, as a general rule, are never so well treated as when they are delivered over to its devouring tooth. That this should be the common fate of transactions which reflect no credit on the living or the dead is certainly desirable, but the gratification of such a wish is subject at all times to well settled and unavoidable restrictions. History asserts her right—always within the limitations of truth and decency—to make the follies, vices, and crimes of an epoch, as well as its virtues and meritorious achievements subservient to her high calling, which is to warn succeding generations as well as to attract them by examples; and individuals who defend themselves against attempted implication in transactions which she must condemn or their friends who recognise the duty of protecting their memories when they can no longer speak for themselves, have at all times a right to probe such affairs to their most secret depths in the pursuit of their objects.

Most gladly would I pass this subject without notice if the circumstances under which I write would permit me to do so. Altho' drawn against my will into the very focus of the excitement and from first to last exposed to its fury, I at no time regarded it with any other feelings than those of pain and disgust; pain produced by daily witnessing the anguish it caused to the President and disgust at the uses made of a private matter as to which the general community should have been left to the uninterrupted maintenance of its rights and to the performance of its own duties. But standing in the relation of closest friendship to General Jackson whilst he lived, and revering his memory I cannot be insensible to the unfavourable inferences and surmises which would inevitably follow, if whilst professing to give a faithful account of his administration, I were to pass over in silence an affair of which the immediate effect was to break up his family circle, which in its consequences contributed largely to the dissolution of his Cabinet, and for the part he took in which he was arraigned before his constituents with much formality but with undisguised rancor. Reasons against such a course thus urgent in his case, have become imperative in regard to myself. Not only was my responsibility for what was done in the matter held by my opponents to be at least co-extensive with that of the President, but in addition to attacks thro' the public press and on the floor of the Senate, which were visited upon both of us, a resolution was offered to the latter body by Mr. Holmes, a Senator from the State of Maine, for the appointment of a Committee to examine into my conduct in the premises with authority to send for persons and to compel the introduction of papers. It is true that the Senator offering it soon abandoned his resolution for reasons the utter frivolousness of which afforded abundant evidence of the unworthy motives by which he had been governed in its introduction—a demonstration quite unnecessary to convince me, who had wintered and summered with him and well understood the stuff of which he was made, that such was its real origin and character. But his resolution stands upon the record and would if there were no other reasons effectually preclude me from omitting, in a sketch of my own life and times, a faithful account of my course in the matter and as much of the conduct of others as may be necessary to make that entirely intelligible. This I shall endeavour to do with proper respect to every consideration entitled to it and bearing upon the subject.

The dissatisfaction caused by Gen. Jackson's Cabinet arrangements has been already referred to. This discontent was not confined to a particular class, neither was it in all cases, occasioned by precisely the same causes. Major Eaton was the son of a highly respectable lady of Tennessee, a widow at the time of which I write, much esteemed by Gen. Jackson, and her son also had strongly ingratiated himself in his regard and was the author, I think, of the first formal history of the General's life. Major Lewis, Eaton's brother-in-law, had long been an intimate personal friend of the General, came with him to Washington and was for many years an inmate of his family. The cast of the Cabinet carried a suspicion to the minds of many of General Jackson's Tennessee friends, including a majority of the representatives of that State in Congress, that Eaton and Lewis had exerted a preponderating influence in its construction. Their *amor proprius* was offended by this as they thought it evinced an undeserved preference, and jealousies and enmities accordingly sprang up among his supporters in Tennessee many of which were never healed. Major Donelson, a nephew of Mrs. Jackson, whose wife was also her neice, and who had been from his infancy a member of the General's family—a man moreover of much more ability than he had credit for—partook largely of this feeling. The seeds of dissatisfaction with and opposition to the first act of the President were thus extensively and deeply sown not only in his own State but in his immediate household.

There was another, perhaps I should say a higher class—a class at all events moved by higher considerations and looking to graver objects—which shared freely in the prevailing discontent. When these latter came to canvass the materials of which the new Cabinet was composed and the circumstances under which it was formed they thought they saw in them the evidence of a design on the part of ° the President-elect to counteract Presidential aspirations which his popularity had caused to be suspended, but the realization of which at the end of his first term, was confidently anticipated.

The hostile feelings towards the new Cabinet, at its start, entertained by these branches of malcontents were, in variously modified forms, extended to the President himself and, in the sequel, especially to the individual whose advancement was supposed—how correctly will be hereafter seen—to have been the main object in its formation. It was not long before they found vent and thro' the same channel. Major Eaton,[1] the new Secretary of War had married a young widow[2] of much beauty and considerable smartness in respect to whose relations with himself before marriage, and whilst she was the wife of another, there had been unfavourable reports. A question was on that account raised as to her fitness for the social position otherwise due to the wife of a member of the Cabinet, her unworthiness alleged, with various degrees of publicity, and her exclusion from fashionable society insisted on. The President whilst willing and at all times avowedly ready to open the door to the severest scrutiny as to the facts, but confiding in her innocence with a sincerity that no man doubted, resented these doings, with the spirit and resolution natural to him on all occasions, but especially when feeling called upon to defend his friends. An issue was in this way and thus early formed between him and respectable, numerous and very powerful portions of his supporters which, independently of any question as to the wisdom, justice or propriety of the ground assumed on either side, could not possibly

---

° MS. III, p. 190.
[1] John H. Eaton.
[2] Margaret [Peggy] O'Neale, widow of Purser J. B. Timberlake, U. S. N.

fail to generate ill-will and speedily to sever the amicable relátions which had until that time existed between them.

Congress was fortunately upon the eve of its adjournment when this struggle commenced, and the President, the new Cabinet, the officers of Government and the good people of Washington, or, perhaps more correctly speaking, the fashionable society of Washington, with temporary visitors to the seat of Government,—not an inconsiderable number at the commencement of a new administration—were the principal persons, before whom and by whom the question of Mrs. Eaton's eligibility was in the first instance discussed and acted upon. Reaching Washington some two months after the controversy had commenced, and my appointment having in no degree contributed to its occurrence, I was entirely uncommitted on my arrival, but finding the traces of the feud too plain not to be intelligible, in walks which it was my duty to frequent, and too disturbing in their character to be disregarded, I felt the necessity of deciding upon the course I ought to take in respect to it without unnecessary delay. After looking at the matter in every aspect in which I thought it deserved to be considered I decided, for reasons not now necessary to assign, to make no distinction in my demeanour towards, or in my intercourse with the families of the gentlemen whom the President had, with the approbation of the Senate, selected as my Cabinet associates, but to treat all with respect and kindness and not to allow myself, by my own acts, to be mixed up in such a quarrel. That others would do the latter office for me I thought not improbable but that I could not help; I could only take care, and that I resolved upon, that they should have no good grounds for their impeachments. A very eligible opportunity was soon presented to make my intentions understood by Major Eaton and his particular friends. An office-holder under the new régime, of no mean degree, a clever fellow, in both the Yankee and the English sense of that word, who by his own *bonhommie* and the social popularity of his amiable family, by his generous tho' unostentatious hospitality, it is fair to add by his qualifications for his official duties and last, tho' not least, by his facile politics has succeeded in retaining his place (with a single and short interruption) for the thirty years that have passed since that day, paid me an early and somewhat significant visit. He sided warmly with the lady and with her husband and their friends and proceeded to enlighten me on the state of the controversy, with full descriptions of the sayings and doings on both sides of it. When he had freely unbosomed himself and well nigh exhausted his budget of news I asked him, with unusual seriousness to listen attentively to what I had to say to him. This, with evident surprise, but politely and kindly he agreed to do. I then remarked in substance that it had been my good fortune to be absent when the disturbance to which he alluded was first developed, that I was therefore in a better condition to control my feelings and actions in regard to it than most of my associates in the Government; that I sorely regretted its existence not only on account of its tendency to destroy the pleasures of social intercourse between many of us, but in view of what was far more important, its inevitable effect to mar the success and security of the administration; that I knew nothing, nor had I heard of anything which would, in my opinion, require on my part the line of conduct that was pursued (as I was informed) by others in respect to Mrs. Eaton; that so long as I continued to view the matter in that light I would treat the Secretary of War and his family with the same respect and cordiality that I manifested towards the other members of the Cabinet and their families; that I should always stand ready to do anything in my power to allay and if possible eradicate the bad spirit that unhappily prevailed, but that I did not want to hear what was said and done in the matter and finally I desired that he should understand me as preferring not to talk about it.

My visitor was clearly disappointed by the character of my observations and seemed to think, altho' this idea was expressed obscurely and with becoming respect, that I evinced a degree of lukewarmness, in the matter, quite unexpected and perhaps not justified by the circumstances, or else a want of confidence in him. Understanding fully what was passing in his mind I first endeavoured to disabuse him of any suspicion of that kind by avowing the favourable opinion I sincerely entertained of him personally, and then remarked that there were occasions when a man should reserve the exclusive right of judging in relation to his proper course and conduct, that the one now the subject of our conversation was of that nature, in my opinion, so far as I was at all concerned, and that my conclusions in regard to it were such as I thought due to my own self-respect and to my official position. A man of the world and of good sense himself, he appeared, as I thought, inclined to change his impressions and left me in good humor.

I soon found, although nothing was said to me about it, that he had communicated our conversation to the Secretary of War and his immediate friends and especially to the President, from whose manner of treating the subject, whenever it was introduced in my presence, I inferred with pleasure his approbation of the course I had marked out for myself.

The female members of the President's family were Mrs. Donelson, the wife of his private Secretary, and her cousin, Miss Easton, both nieces of Mrs. Jackson and both excellent and highly esteemed ladies. Unaffected and graceful in manners, amiable and purely feminine in disposition and character, and bright and self possessed in conversation, they were fair representatives of the ladies of Kentucky and Tennessee. Both alas! are now no more. On an occasion when the name of Mrs. Eaton was accidentally and harmlessly introduced, and which was shortly after my interview above described, Mrs. Donelson, in the presence of her cousin, expressed her surprise that whilst almost every tongue in the city was canvassing that lady's merits and demerits she had never heard me say anything upon the subject, a remark the tone of which rather than the substance conveyed, tho' gently, a complaint of my reserve. I was under an engagement which called me away and had only time to assure her that my silence had not arisen from an unwillingness to talk with them upon the subject and that with her permission I would do so upon the first favorable occasion. She took me at my word and we fixed the time when I was to call upon them for that purpose. When we met I was happy to be immediately relieved from the embarrassment that seemed inseparable from the ° parties to and the nature of our discussion, by a statement from Mrs. Donelson of the grounds on which she justified the course she was pursuing, which was a marked one and decidedly adverse to the lady in question. She spoke of her as possessing a bad temper and a meddlesome disposition and said that the latter had been so much increased by her husband's elevation as to make her society too disagreeable to be endured. She did not allude to any rumored imputations upon her fame; she might not have believed them, she might have omitted to notice them from motives of delicacy, or she might have thought allusion to them unnecessary on account of the sufficiency of those which she frankly acknowledged. Whether influenced by the one or the other motive I had no desire to inquire but took the matter up on the grounds on which she had placed it. For the sake of the discussion only, I agreed, after a moment's reflection, to admit that she was right in her views of Mrs. Eaton's character and disposition and proceeded to impress upon her that although her reasons would excuse her from cultivating a close intimacy with that lady they neither required nor would justify her, having regard to her position as the female head of her Uncle's family, to decline her society to the extent to which she had gone, and to caution her against being controlled in her course by persons whom she esteemed, and who were entitled to her respect and regard, but whose opinions upon that particular subject as I thought—indeed, as I was certain—were unduly influenced. It is unnecessary to recapitulate my arguments; they were, in some respects, to her at least, of a more serious character than any that she had previously allowed to be taken into her consideration; they related to the situation of her Uncle, whom she dearly loved, to the difficulties he had to contend with in the performance of his public duties, to the value he placed upon the peace and harmony of his family and the misery he suffered in seeing them destroyed by an affair in respect to which she certainly knew that he acted a sincere part, and to the extent to which her course sanctioned imputations of a graver character both upon the lady in question and upon himself for sustaining her, which were used by his enemies to injure him; &c. &c. Before I had concluded Miss Easton who had sought to hide her emotions by gradually withdrawing herself from sight in the embrasure of the window, sobbed aloud, and I preceived that Mrs. Donelson besides being deeply agitated was also offended by my allusions to the probability that she had been unduly influenced by others upon such a subject. I rose from my seat, begging her to excuse whatever I might, under the excitement of the moment, have said to hurt her feelings, but perfectly satisfied that they were too far committed to be reached by anything I could urge, and I asked her permission to drop the subject. To this she assented, acknowledging that she had been momentarily ruffled by some of my remarks but assuring me that she was not offended with me.

Our conference did not produce the slightest change in our subsequent relations. I stood, upon her invitation, as one of the sponsors in baptism of her daughter, and her bearing towards me continued respectful and kind to the day of her lamented death.

I became convinced that Mrs. Donelson's earnest feelings on this occasion and in reference to this affair were less the effects of anything that she had heard or believed than of natural sympathy with her husband who was deeply interested in the quarrel—differing widely in opinion and feeling from his Uncle, the President. As evidence of his great excitement at this time he afterwards told me that his dislike to me during the progress of these transactions had become so strong that "he could have drowned me with a drop of water." The relations between the General and his family grew every day more complicated and embarrassed until Major Donelson and his family quitted the White House and returned to Tennessee and his place as private Secretary was supplied by the appointment of Mr. N. P. Trist.

It is a fact worthy of notice that altho' I was well acquainted with Major Donelson's views and sentiments in respect to the Eaton matters and his temporary leaning towards Mr. Calhoun and his friends I never suspected him of having entertained feelings of personal hostility towards myself until I received from him the letter which follows, many years afterwards and heard from his own lips the explanations of its import which I have given above. Desiring to offer some proof of my great respect and sincere esteem to the General at parting and having the opinion of the Major's talents which I have already expressed, I decided, soon after my election to offer the latter a place in my Cabinet, and apprised them both of that intention. But having consulted a discreet and disinterested friend from the same quarter of the Union in respect to the opinion likely to be formed there of the propriety of such a step I was led to doubt its expediency. My friend doubted neither the Major's capacity nor his integrity but thought that the appointment would cause a surprise on the part of the public and would be regarded as an advancement disproportioned to the stations he had before occupied. I suggested the doubt to the General (who had not asked the appointment) and found that the same idea had passed through his own mind, but that he had not felt himself at liberty, under the circumstances, to suggest it. I immediately wrote to the Major that I had changed my mind, giving frankly the reason for it, and received in reply the following manly letter which, it will be seen, refers to the state of his feelings towards me during the first term of the General's Presidency, of which also, he afterwards spoke to me, as I have mentioned.

FROM MAJOR DONELSON.

NASHVILLE, *February 21st 1837*

DEAR SIR,

Your letter post marked the 8th inst. has just reached me. I shall set out in an hour or two for Washington under the hope of joining the General before he leaves the city and with the intention of accompanying him to the Hermitage if I can be of service to him.

I am grateful for the kindness manifested in your letter and no one can be more sensible than I am that the views it expresses respecting the policy of my being placed in a responsible situation near you are correct. So strong were my convictions on this subject that I thought it my duty some eight or ten days ago to write such a letter to the General as would induce you, even if the judgment of mutual friends had created any doubt in your mind, to come to the decision which has been adopted.

I cannot value too highly your friendship. It is the reward of a long acquaintance manifesting much forbearance and generosity on your part. I went to Washington full of misconception of your character and deeply biassed by many of the circumstances that attended the first four years of General Jackson's canvass for the Presidency.[a] It will be my endeavour to make some amends for the injustice done you by doing all I can in my humble sphere to make your true character known to those who are willing to credit me. If in no other respect I may in this do some good to the Republican cause by adding to the number of those who will judge your administration impartially.

Although I am about to start to Washington I prefer to send this letter by

---

[a] This is a slip of the pen. The intended reference was to the first four years of the General's Presidency.

the same stage, imperfect as it is as an expression of my grateful feelings
towards you, to risking the chances of my not being able to see you before the
4th of March.

Remember me kindly to your sons and believe me sincerely

Your friend,

A. J. DONELSON

The nature of the personal feelings which the state of things
I have described was calculated to engender among those connected
with the Government and residing at Washington may be easily
inferred. All were more or less affected by it and it was under
its adverse influences that we worked through the spring, summer
and the first months of the autumn. Those feelings grew every
day more and more bitter because they were to a great degree
smothered as no opportunity was presented for their open indulgence on the part of the leading officials. The entertainment given
to the Diplomatic Corps in the spring was a dinner-party of gentlemen ° only and passed off without embarrassment. A Cabinet dinner, to which the ladies of the families of the members who composed it would have to be invited was not even spoken of in my
hearing before the month of November. That subject was then introduced by the President in one of our rides, which, when the weather
permitted, were almost of daily occurrence and gradually length-
ened as presenting the best opportunities for consultation left to us
by the press of visitors and other preoccupations. He had, he said,
been led to postpone his Cabinet dinners to so late a period by an
undefined apprehension that the violent feelings of the members on
both sides of the social problem out of which our difficulties had
arisen, and of which he had not been suffered to remain ignorant,
might lead to unavoidable acts on his part with which he thought
it would be more difficult for an Administration to deal in its infancy, than after it had been some time under way and been
allowed opportunities to advance itself in the favor of the people.
Public business, he remarked, must always be attended to when the
occasion for its performance arises, but with matters of ceremony,
like that under consideration, he thought a greater latitude was
allowable. As the session of Congress was however near at hand,
when this matter should not rest undisposed of he thought the
sooner it was entered upon the better.

I had entertained similar apprehensions and had therefore omitted
to allude to the subject in our familar conversations—embracing,
from time to time, almost every other subject. But I never expected
an outbreak upon the President's invitation, believing rather that the
public explanations of the stand which I did not doubt was con-

---

° MS. III, p. 200.

templated by a portion of the Cabinet would be reserved for mine, which would naturally follow. I expressed that opinion to him with much confidence and it was decided that his invitations should be forthwith sent out.

There were no absentees at the President's Cabinet dinner, and no very marked exhibitions of bad feeling in any quarter, but there were nevertheless sufficient indications of its existence to destroy the festive character of the occasion and to make it transparently a formal and hollow ceremony. The President escorted the wife of the Secretary of the Treasury to the table and I gave my arm to Mrs. Donelson. The disposition of the others I have forgotten, but I will remember the care with which the arrangement of the parties was made. The general was as usual courteous and affable altho' suffering much from bad health and more from mortification at what was passing before his eyes. My young friend and partner for the entertainment summoned up spirits enough to call my attention chiefly by glances, to the signs of the hour and following the movements of our host, we left the table with the ladies after which the company dispersed sooner than usual. I had intended to spend a few moments with the President after they were gone but soon perceived that the return he had received for all his sacrifices of old friendships and his unhesitating confrontal of enemies in the formation of the Cabinet which had just left him had overcome his feelings, and commending him to his pillow I also took my leave.

The display I had witnessed would have been sufficient to put me on my guard in respect to my own contemplated entertainment if that had been needed. But without such warning I understood too well the motives which pointed to that occasion as one best adapted for a kind of semi-official notification of the rule by which some of my associates intended to be governed, to fail of circumspection in my movements. That they would decline my invitation I had no doubt, but whether in so doing, they would only assert and exercise their own rights without offense to me, or whether they would go farther could only be known by the sequel. It was my business to be prepared for either contingency.

According to the established forms of society in Washington it would have been my office as host to give the highest position and the most marked attention to the wife of the Secretary of the Treasury, if no ladies were present except those of members of the Cabinet. Mrs. Ingham was an excellent and estimable person, but excitable and especially stirred up upon the vexed question which agitated the official and social circles of the Federal Capital. I was entirely willing to pay all the honors due to herself and to her position. [I was nevertheless quite confident that she would decline, and I was not disposed to make the vacancy occasioned by that event conspicuous by filling it with a lady of inferior rank.][1] But Mrs. Randolph, the widow of Gov. Thomas Mann Randolph, of Virginia, and the only surviving child of President Jefferson, in all respects one of the worthiest women of America, was then residing at Washington, a lady with whom and with her family consisting of an unmarried daughter and of Mr. and Mrs. N. P. Trist, the latter also her daughter, my relations were cordial and intimate. I waited upon her in person, informed her of my intention to invite the Cabinet to dine with me and of my desire to combine with that official ceremony an act of respect towards her which had been already too long delayed and requested her to name the day if she was willing to do me the honor to attend.

She cheerfully agreed to my proposition, the day was fixed and the invitation extended to all the members of her family. I need scarcely say at least to those acquainted with the ways of Washington, that it would have been quite impossible to prevent this proceeding on my part from becoming known without any agency of hers to the other invited guests who were thus apprised of my intention to give the precedence to Mrs. Randolph. As my dinner party was to be what in common parlance is called a ladies' dinner I was desirous that there should be no lack of ladies and anticipating further declensions I invited several military gentlemen and their wives, who all attended. I was obliged to omit my highly esteemed and amiable friend the Commander in Chief,[2] because Mrs. M. (who was his second wife) had made herself—more to his amusement than annoyance, for he took such things lightly-- a conspicuous party to the war which raged around us; but I remember well the presence of the veterans, Hull and Chauncey and of Commodore Warrington[3] and of the wives of all three who were among the most agreeable as they were also the leading members of the society of Washington.

Never having been very careful or orderly in securing even my important papers and having especially exposed them by frequent changes of residence to be lost or mislaid, it is a curious instance of the accidental escape of such trifles from destruction that I have still in my possession the answers of the Secretary of the Navy and of the Attorney General to my invitation on this occasion. I suppose that they were originally kept in anticipation of a rupture of some sort in our relations. They lie before me as I write—recalling the minutiæ of the scenes and events, great and small, of thirty years ago, which I am describing.

---

[1] Words in brackets were stricken out in the MS.
[2] Maj.-Gen. Alexander Macomb.
[3] Isaac Hull, Isaac Chauncey, and Lewis Warrington.

Mr. Branch [1] writes that he "will avail himself of the honor of dining with Mr. Van Buren" on &c. but that he is requested to say in behalf of Mrs. Branch and the young ladies that "circumstances unnecessary to detail will deprive them of the pleasure" &c. Mr. Berrien presents his respects but pleads a "conditional engagement to leave the city" for his own declension and "her state of health" for that of his daughter. According to the best of my recollection Mr. Ingham [2] accepted for himself, and Mrs. Ingham certainly declined. The other two members of the Cabinet, Major Eaton and Mr. Barry,[3] brought apologies from their wives, who were faithful allies and who it appeared had also resolved to remain behind their batteries. Thus it resulted that at the second Cabinet dinner of the season to which all the ladies of the family of its members were invited not one of them "assisted", and the party being freed from any kind of embarrassment their joy was unconfined. Mrs. Randolph especially manifested the greatest gratification, to the satisfaction of all my guests who reverenced her almost as much as I did; to come quite up to that mark required a more intimate knowledge of her admirable qualities than they had enjoyed opportunities to acquire.

It may as well be said here as anywhere that neither in their answers to my successive invitations, nor in their angry correspondence with others nor in their excited appeals to the public, all of which I have now taken the trouble to re-peruse, did Messrs. Ingham and Berrien impute to me a blameable act or motive in respect to these transactions, although the latter papers were written under very excited feelings. These facts speak a language that cannot be misunderstood as to the sense in which they felt obliged to regard my whole demeanour in the affair now under consideration,[o] and are more than sufficient to repel any unfavorable inferences that can be drawn from the introduction of a resolution of enquiry by a proverbially indecorous Senator—a resolution which even he abandoned. Of Gov. Branch's course I am not quite so certain. On the evening before my resignation and that of Major Eaton were published, but when the facts were known, and indeed, after he had himself resigned, the President and myself were invited to attend the wedding of his daughter. He [Branch] took me apart, spoke of our resignations, acknowledged that he had been at first somewhat annoyed but was now entirely reconciled to the proceeding as the necessary result of causes which we could not control, and encouraged me to hope that the whole matter would settle down as

---

[1] John Branch.   [3] William T. Barry.
[2] Samuel D. Ingham.   [o] MS. III, p. 205.

quietly as all the letters of resignation and acceptance gave the public a right to expect. From that day to the present I have never seen him save once and for a moment. I heard, from time to time, of his making violent speeches against me and others, but I never saw them nor had I any desire to see them. I believed him to be an honest man and knew him to be in general influenced by just and generous impulses, but made of inflammable materials which were easily ignited by others; indeed, but a few days after our meeting and conversation referred to I heard that he had been thus excited. I knew, however, that he would say and do what was right when his feelings were sobered down, and in the course of time they arrived at that condition, he " conquered his prejudices " against President Jackson, paid a brief visit to the White House during his second term, when I saw him for a few moments and exchanged respectful and kind salutations with him. Major Donelson, whose brother had married his daughter, informed me afterwards that the Governor had expressed to him the mortification he had experienced in being treated with so much urbanity by a man of whom he had said so many hard things. I begged the Major to assure him that he need give himself no uneasiness on that head because I had never read his speeches and certainly would not think of doing so now.

Determined to go thro' with the matter in hand, so far as I was myself concerned, and to have done with it, I sent out invitations shortly after my Cabinet dinner and after Congress had assembled, for a large evening party. With some modifications my official associates held to their previous course, and to add fuel to the flame a communication appeared in the *Washington Journal* newspaper, over the signature of " Tarquin," (!) charging me with an attempt, in conjunction with Sir Charles Vaughan, the British Minister, to force a person upon the society of Washington who was not entitled to its privileges and calling upon those who had been invited to resent the outrage by refusing to be present. The circles of Washington however quite naturally declined to be instructed in the proprieties and moralities of social intercourse by a " Tarquin " and no party of the season was attended more numerously or enjoyed more hilariously.

Suffering at the time from ill-health and much exhausted by the reception I availed myself of the moment when the attention of my guests was attracted by the commencement of dancing to retire to a sofa in a lower room for rest. I had not been there long before a friend entered and said, in a jocular tone, "Are you here, Sir!—You ought to be above if you wish to prevent a fight! ", and answered my look of enquiry by the information that Mrs. Eaton and Mrs. M. had jostled each other, doubtless accidentally, in the crowd, and that the collision had provoked manifestations of mutual resentment sufficiently marked to attract attention and to excite general remark. I received his story as a jest, which it probably was in a measure, and begged him to see fair play in my behalf and to leave me to my repose.

I have described more particularly than they would appear to deserve these two entertainments, but for a brief season they obtained much consequence as incidents of a campaign in which social, political and personal feuds were so mixed up that all of them were more or less affected by every movement, and the gossips had looked forward to the arrangement of my parties as the occasion and the field for a general engagement. When they were over it was found that they had not materially contributed to the development of hostilities, and I confess that I experienced all the complacency naturally inspired by the consciousness of having passed unscathed thro' an ordeal as difficult and as severe as could be devised by a conspiracy of excited women and infuriated partisans. But the outbreak was not long delayed. At a ball given by the Russian Minister, Baron Krudener, in the absence of Mrs. Ingham, led Mrs. Eaton to supper, as ranking next to her, and Madame Huygens, the wife of the Dutch Envoy, was assigned to the Secretary of War. Madame Huygens was reported to have been highly offended by the arrangement and to have declared that she would retaliate by giving a party to which Mrs. Eaton should not be invited and that her example would be followed by Messrs. Ingham, Branch and Berrien. Major Eaton was a man of moderate intellectual capacities, but justly distinguished for the kindness, generosity and unobtrusiveness of his disposition and demeanour. If he had done the wrong before his marriage which was imputed to him, as to which I knew and sought to know nothing, he had also done all that a man could do to remedy the evil and there was no reason even to suspect that the life of the lady after marriage was not, in that respect at least, free from reproach. A reverend gentleman had indeed carried rumors to the President to the effect that her conduct had been exceptionable on a visit to the Northern cities. The General insisted that his informer should go immediately and sift the stories thoroughly, assuring him that if his report sustained them by reliable facts no one would have reason to complain of his own course in the matter. The mission was accepted, the Cabinet, except Major Eaton was called together in the evening to hear the report but it was found to amount to nothing.

A man of the temperament I have ascribed to Eaton was likely, under any circumstances, to have warm and sympathizing friends. The number in his case, was of course greatly increased by the patronage at his disposal and by the favour with which he was regarded by the President. These pressed upon the latter the Major's grievances with much earnestness and their appeals found favorable responses in his own breast. The alleged threat of Madame Huygens and the three parties which certainly followed—whether she actually threatened them or not—supplied ample and stirring materials for such complaints. The President sent for me at an early hour one morning and I went to him before breakfast. I found him deeply moved by communications that had been made to him on the previous evening. His eyes were blood-shot and his appearance in other respects indicated that he had passed a sleepless night, as he indeed admitted had been literally the case. He was however unexcited in manner. The stories so often told of his violent and furious style on occasions of great anger or deep feeling, so far as my observation extended, had no other foundation than this that when he thought he could in that way best influence anybody to do his duty—of which I have given some instances and shall give others—he would assume an earnestness and an emphasis much beyond what he really felt. To me he always appeared most calm when he felt most intensely. On the occasion of his very narrow escape from assassination, at the funeral of Warren R. Davis, I followed him to the White House, immediately after the rites of burial were concluded, and found him sitting with one of Major Donelson's children on his lap and conversing with General Scott, himself apparently the least disturbed person in the room.

He presented, with deliberation and clearness, the reasons which led him to regard the proceedings to which I have referred as an attack upon himself designed to be made effectual thro' a combination between members of his Cabinet and the wife of one of the Foreign Ministers, and stated, in the same manner, the course which he thought it would become him to pursue, which was—if his views should prove to be well founded to dismiss his own Ministers and to send Mr. Huygens his passports.

His immediate object was to attend to the latter, and to that end he had sent for me to obtain my counsel and co-operation. My personal relations with Chevalier and Madame Huygens were of a friendly and indeed intimate character. I had no reason to doubt that she felt hurt as was represented, by the occurrences at Baron Krudener's, but deemed it quite unlikely that she would have given expression to her feelings in the way which had been reported to the President. If, however, the information of the latter was correct, I could not for a moment doubt the propriety of the course he suggested, in that direction, and declared this opinion to him without hesitation.

As soon as I reached my office I informed Chevalier Huygens by note that I desired to see him on business, and that as it would also be necessary to communicate with Madame Huygens I would call at his house at a named hour. For reasons, not necessary to be stated, they anticipated the object of my visit and received me with their usual kindness. After declining their invitation to the pipe and schiedam, notwithstanding the appropriateness of these preliminaries to a Dutch negotiation,° I stated explicitly that the President disclaimed all right or desire to meddle with their social relations or with the question of whom they invited or whom they omitted to invite to their house, but that declarations had been attributed to Madame Huygens and communicated to the President which went beyond the exercise of the rights which belonged to them, and I described the impressions which the possibility of the correctness of his information had made upon his mind. Madame Huygens assured me solemnly that she had never used the expressions attributed to her or any of similar import—that she had been too long connected with diplomatic life, and understood too well what belonged to her position, to meddle in such matters and that she had only pursued the path I conceded to her without advising with others or troubling herself about their course. The Chevalier united earnestly in the views she expressed, and avowed his conviction of the accuracy of her recollections, and my mission was thus satisfactorily concluded. As we had no desire to pursue the enquiry further I reported the result to the President who received the information with unaffected pleasure for he sympathized heartily with the respect and regard I entertained for the Dutch Minister and his estimable family.

As the matter in some sense bore on our relations with a Foreign Government I thought it desirable that I should possess some evidence of the statement upon which I had proceeded, and so wrote to the President from whom I received immediately the following reply:

FROM THE PRESIDENT.
(Private.)

MY DEAR SIR

Your note was rec'd, of this evening, when I had company, and so soon as they have left me I have hastened to reply—The story is this—Shortly after the party at Baron Krudener's it was stated that Madame H. was piqued at something that took place there and said she would give a party and would shew society that she did not recognize Mrs. E. as a fit associate and would not invite her to it. The Heads of the Departments, say the gossips, would follow suit and Mrs. E. and the Major would be put out of society. This came to the ears of some members of Congress, and the attempt *thus*, by a Foreign Minister's family, to put out of society the family of a

---

° MS. III, p. 210.

member of my Cabinet was thought to be such an attack upon me, who had invited this member to come into it, that it aroused their feelings and the communication was made to me. The three parties that followed, given by the three Heads of Departments, were well calculated to give credit to the story of a combination headed by Madame H. to put Major Eaton and his family out of society and thereby to assail my character for inviting him into it. These are the tales and I am happy Madame H. has stated they are not true as far as she is concerned. *This is the substance.*

Yrs.
ANDREW JACKSON.

JAN'Y 24TH 1830.

It was probably on the following day—certainly before the 27th of that month, that I had, at his instance, a conference with the President upon the subject of the relations between him and the members of his Cabinet and the effect upon them of the matters related. Nothing was then done upon the subject, but a year and a half later and after the war had broken out between him and the portion of his Cabinet with whose course he had been offended, and I had left Washington and was awaiting the sailing of the packet from New York, he applied to me for my recollections of this branch of the general subject. I retained a copy of so much of my letter as related to it, which was never published, but will now be given at the proper place. According to my then recollection it appears that he showed me, at that interview, a paper containing the basis of a communication which he intended to address to those gentlemen and that I expressed the opinion that he did not by it sufficiently guard himself against the imputation of entertaining a desire to control the domestic and social intercourse of their families and advised a personal interview with them for which a paper more carefully constructed might be prepared and shewn to them in preference to a formal correspondence; that he disclaimed any such intention or desire and agreed not only to such a modification of the paper but also to the substitution of a personal interview for a letter. I added that such a paper as I recommended may have been prepared by me on the spot from the materials before me, to be copied by him and reserved for the use contemplated—the course which I am quite confident was pursued. He then informed me that he had held some conversation on the subject with Col. Richard M. Johnson who was very desirious of an interview with the gentlemen alluded to before any communication was made to them on his part in the hope of being able to quiet existing difficulties. Knowing the Colonel's character and disposition perfectly and that with proved and undoubted courage he united qualities admirably adapted to the office of peace-maker, but that from his unsuspicious temperament he was not always as guarded in conversation as might be desirable in such a case,

I begged the General, if he consented to his interference in the matter, to be careful that he should be fully possessed of his views, and suggested the propriety of reading to him, before he entered upon the business, the paper already prepared, and that the character in which he acted should also be clearly understood.

The Colonel had his conferences with Messrs. Ingham, Branch and Berrien, and the President his interview with them in which he spoke to them of the alleged combination and attempt to drive Major Eaton from the Cabinet and I always supposed that he shewed them the paper referred to, but whether he did or did not do this they were all satisfied that he did not claim any such right as that which was described in it, and altho' the principal matter remained substantially on the footing on which it stood before, those gentlemen remained in the Cabinet a year and a half longer. During that period the Eaton affair was eclipsed in importance and soon divested of any agency in mischief or disturbance by two occurrences—Mr. Calhoun's *pronunciamento* and, some two or three months later, the resignations of Major Eaton and myself, drawing after them the resignations of all the members of the Cabinet except 'Postmaster General Barry. The latter, altho' he adhered throughout to his friends, the Eatons, pursued the tenor of his way so unobtrusively and noiselessly as to give no offense to the other parties to the quarrel.

The outbreak between the President and the gentlemen who had formed a part of his Cabinet assumed a very violent character after I left Washington. Those who have the curiosity to look into the matter will find that the dissolution of the Cabinet had been to all appearance, amicably accomplished. There was some little demur on the parts of the Secretaries of the Treasury and Navy to sending in their resignations, but in the end the correspondence, on its face imported a friendly settlement. All were to remain at their posts until their successors were appointed and their official business placed in the state in which they desired to leave it. The resignations, except Mr. Berrien's, who was absent till June, were in April, and the final retirement of the Cabinet was delayed until June. With the single exception of a few enigmatical givings-out by the Secretary of the Navy as to the existence of a "malign influence" everything seemed to be going on to a favorable issue. The hopes of those who felt an interest in the character of the Government and thought that it had been prejudiced by the quarrel, and of those who desired the success of General Jackson's administration began to revive. It was believed that the functions of Government were no longer to be performed in an atmosphere tainted by private scandal, and that the State was relieved from the defiling clutch of the gossips. In this condition of things I left Washington, but had scarcely reached my own State when the disease with which the Capital had so long labored broke out afresh and with redoubled fury. It is not easy to determine precisely who was most to blame for this new outbreak. It is certain that the fault was not altogether on either side. The *U. S. Telegraph* newspaper, referred to the course pursued by the families of the three Cabinet Ministers towards the family of Major Eaton in an offensive way. This was indefensible and proved to be very mischievous. The Major, claiming to hold those gentlemen in some sense responsible for the course of the *Telegraph* in that matter, published an article in the *Globe*, obviously designed to bring Mr. Branch, who had left the city, to a fight. Eaton also copied the article from the *Telegraph*, in which ° the course said to have been pursued by their families was described as that of the gentlemen themselves, and sending the extract to Messrs. Ingham and Berrien, called upon them to avow or disavow its contents. His notes and extracts were in terms the same, and both admitted of no other construction than that the proceedings were intended as preliminary to a duel with each in certain events. This was also wrong. He had no right to hold them responsible for the publication in question and the assumption of such a responsibility was plainly a pretence thro' which to revive with them, in another form, a quarrel from which he had suffered much and to which he saw there was to be no end. Mr. Berrien answered his note on the basis of the article, as explained in an issue subsequent to the original publication, and by which its application was limited to the course of the families of members of the Cabinet, disclaimed his responsibility in explicit terms, but wisely decided to make a reply to the Major's alleged grievance. He did this coolly and admirably and in a way which obliged Eaton, whose good nature never entirely deserted him, to enter a *nolle prosequi* as respected the Attorney General, without the slightest sacrifice of character or dignity on the part of either.

Mr. Ingham, unhappily in a great rage, for which he certainly thought he had abundant cause, adopted the extract in the shape given to it originally and as it was sent to him, and replied to Eaton's demand that the latter " must be not a little deranged " to call upon him to disavow what all the inhabitants of Washington knew, and perhaps half the people of the United States believed to be true to wit: that *he* had refused to associate with his (Major Eaton's) family. A challenge was the consequence, and, that not being accepted, preparations for a personal assault followed. Amidst demonstrations offensive and defensive connected with such an operation the time arrived which the ex-Secretary of the Treasury had fixed upor. for his departure from Washington, and after having as he thought sufficiently exposed himself in the streets, accompanied by the gallant Col. Towson, a friend or two and his son, the latter and himself, armed, he left the city.

If no blood was spilled—which is somewhat remarkable in a quarrel upon so exciting a subject and kept on foot for two years— a sufficient quantity of ink certainly was shed upon the subject. The *Telegraph* charged the President with having seventeen months previously thro' a distinguished member of Congress, required the members of his Cabinet to associate with Mrs. Eaton, at least so far as to invite her to their large parties, on pain of dismissal. This was presented as a great abuse of office, as it certainly would have been. The *Globe* denied this charge, stigmatized it as a calumny and defied its author to the proof. No attempt to establish it being made the latter went further and declared that the member of Congress referred to was admitted to be Col. Richard M. Johnson, a man of proverbial benevolence, great bravery and undoubted veracity, that the Colonel denied the truth of the charge in the fullest manner, and that Mr. Berrien had, in his correspondence with Major Eaton, admitted the falsity of the charge. This brought out Mr. Berrien, who, after some parleying in respect to a promise he had made to Col. Johnson (who was at his home in Kentucky) to wait until an opportunity could be afforded to all the parties to compare recollections before publications were °made, if any should be found necessary, denied the admission. Mr. Blair rejoined by setting forth the following declaration of Mr. Berrien to Major Eaton when speaking of his interview with the President in January 1830:—"In the interview to which I was invited by the President, some few days afterwards, I frankly exposed to him my views on the subject, and he disclaimed any disposition to press such a requisition." This Mr. Blair construed into an admission such as he had claimed in the *Globe*. Mr. Berrien, in answer, insisted "that a disclaimer of an intention *to press* a requisition was a wholly different thing from a denial of ever having made it," and here the correspondence between these parties, in which there had been a good deal of sharp shooting, terminated. But Messrs. Berrien, Ingham, Branch and Eaton all came out with impassioned and elaborate appeals to the public upon this question. The alacrity and zeal with which the authors of the charge entered upon its support and the labor and formality given to those quasi-State papers, denote the confident expectation of overthrowing the President by its influence. Mr. Berrien in his voluminous publication—embracing the correspondence between himself and Major Eaton, his and Mr.

° MS. Book IV, p. 1.

Ingham's letters to Col. Johnson and Mr. Ingham's statement made from notes taken at the time,—spoke of the subject as one " of awakening interest to all." They affirmed that Col. Johnson came to them as from the President and representing his views and that he required, in his behalf, that they should invite Mrs. Eaton to their large parties on pain of dismissal. They denied that the President had shown them the paper of which I have spoken and which had been brought before the public by Mr. Blair, upon the authority of the President, who declared then that he had read it to them or made them acquainted with its contents, but Mr. Berrien stated that he did not question the *intention* of the President to have shewn this paper to him nor his belief that he did so, and they admitted that he had waived, in Mr. Berrien's language, had not " pressed," the requisition of which they charged that Col. Johnson had been the bearer, but understood this as a change of position brought about through the intervention of his Tennessee friends.

Col. Johnson met-these charges and statements by two letters addressed to Messrs. Ingham and Berrien, separately, in reply to the letters they had written before their appeals to the public. His letters were published in the *National Intelligencer*, newspaper; and the following is a brief extract from that to Mr. Berrien:—

OAKLAND, (KY.) *July 20th, 1831.*

DEAR SIR:

Your favor of the 7th instant has been received. I find that you understood me to say that the President would at least expect the invitation of Mrs. Eaton when you gave large and general parties. The President never did, directly or indirectly, express or intimate such an expectation. He informed me that he had been induced to believe that a part of his Cabinet had entered into a combination to drive Maj. Eaton from it, by excluding him and his family from society; that he had been also informed that the successive parties to which you allude was a link in the chain; that attempts had been made even upon foreign ministers to exclude Maj. Eaton from their parties; and such a state of things gave him great distress; that he was determined at all hazards to have harmony in his Cabinet. He then read a paper containing the principles upon which he intended to act. In my conversation with you I referred to this paper. No doubt it is now in existence. It disclaimed all intentions, on the part of the President, to regulate in any manner whatever, the private or social intercourse of the members of his Cabinet. As a mutual friend I called upon you, and as a peacemaker, my object was to make the above communication in the most delicate manner possible. During our conversation, in the anxiety of my heart to serve my friend and my Country, it was I alone, upon my own responsibility, who made the suggestion or proposition or rather enquiry whether you could not, at those large and promiscuous parties, invite Maj. Eaton and his family. From the total social non-intercourse of the members of the Cabinet the want of harmony was inferred, more than from any other circumstance; and my desire was to remedy that evil by the suggestion or inquiry which I made. It would have been an absolute unqualified and total misrepresentation of his views if I had represented the President as making any such demand.

From Col. Johnson's letter to Mr. Ingham I extract as follows:—

BLUE SPRINGS, *July 31, 1831.*

DEAR SIR—

Yours of the 16th instant was this day received, accompanied by a statement which, it seems, you have prepared for the public, purporting to contain separate conversations, with the President and myself, relative to an allegation made in the public journals that General Jackson had authorized a member of Congress to require of Messrs. Berrien, Branch, and yourself, and your families, to associate with Major Eaton, and his family under the penalty of being dismissed from office. You refer to two articles in *the Globe* to justify your appeal to the public, previously to receiving my answer, in which it appeared that I had denied the above allegation, if it had any allusion to me. After the publication of this·accusation against General Jackson, I received a letter from a friend, intimating that I was the member of Congress to whom allusion was made, and requested to know if I had ever made such a communication. In my answer I confined myself to the specific accusation thus publicly made against the President, and which is attributable to yourself, and most unequivocally denied that General Jackson ever made such a requisition through me, and as positively denied having ever made such a statement to you. On the contrary I asserted and now repeat, I did inform you, in each and every interview that the President disclaimed any right or intention to interfere in any manner whatever with the regulation of your private or social intercourse.

Thus in a matter in which I was engaged to serve you, and other friends, in a matter of a delicate and highly confidential nature, and in which I succeeded, unexpectedly I found myself presented in the public journals as a witness impeaching one of those friends, and ascribing to him declarations which he never made; and placed in that attitude by you, self respect and self defence called upon me to correct that erroneous statement. I cannot, therefore, agree with you, that I did in any degree change my view of the subject in considering it improper in any of the parties to come before the public without the opportunity of comparing our different recollections. But if you feel under any obligations of a personal or political character to come before the public previously, you will find me as ready as yourself to meet any responsibility or difficulty which such a course may produce. I now come to the material point in controversy—whether Gen. Jackson, through me, required of you to invite Major Eaton and his family to your large parties. This suggestion was made upon my own responsibility, with an anxious desire more effectually to reconcile the then existing difficulties. But Gen. Jackson never did make such a requisition, in any manner whatever, directly or indirectly, nor did I ever intimate to you that he had made— such a demand. The complaint made by Gen. Jackson against this part of his Cabinet was specific, that he had been informed, and was induced to believe, that they were using their influence to have Major Eaton and his family excluded from all respectable circles, for the purpose of degrading ° him, and thus drive him from office; and that the attempt had been made even upon the foreign ministers, and in one case had produced the desired effect. He proposed no mode of accommodation or satisfaction, but declared expressly that if such was the fact he would dismiss them from office. He then read to me a paper containing the principles upon which he intended to act; which disclaimed the right to interfere with the social relations of his Cabinet.

° MS. IV, p. 5.

Such was the issue between the President and the three ex-Secretaries, and such were their respective allegations and proof. It was never pretended that the requisition referred to had ever been made upon them by the President in person or thro' any other channel than Col. Johnson. In the only conversation they had had with him upon the subject, seventeen months before they resigned, they say he did not press it—he says he disclaimed it in the most unequivocal terms. Col. Johnson's statement is the only evidence that was introduced and notwithstanding the formality and confidence with which this grave accusation had been brought forward and the zeal with which it was supported by the entire opposition of the Country, the public judgment was so clear and so decided that in the General's canvass for re-election, which took place the very next year, when everything else was raked up, it was never alluded to.

A few words more in respect to myself. Whilst at New York and on the eve of sailing for England I received a letter from the President inquiring as to my recollections upon this branch of the general subject, which I gave him in a letter, dated August 14th, 1831, the whole of which together with the letter to which it was a reply, will be found in the Correspondence.[1]

My statement was never published as the President, I was happy to find, adopted the advice I gave him.

The following extract embraces what relates to the present matter:

I will in the first place answer your queries in regard to the interview between Messrs. Ingham, Branch & Berrien & yourself upon the subject of their course towards Mr. & Mrs. Eaton. Neither with those gentlemen, nor with Colonel Johnson have I had any conversation, confidential or otherwise, upon that subject. I recollect your sending for me one morning & that when I arrived I found you sensibly affected by an impression which had been made upon your mind that Messrs. Ingham, Branch & Berrien were taking measures in concert to exclude Mrs. Eaton from the society of Washington. You stated to me in a general way the grounds upon which that impression was founded, referring to several successive parties which had been given by those gentlemen, & to information which had been given to you by others without warning them, and declared that you felt it to be your duty & had made up your mind to interfere in a prompt & efficacious manner & put an end to the proceedings of which you complained. You then shewed me a paper which, according to my recollections, was in the form of a letter addressed to those gentlemen, expressive of your views & feelings on the subject.

I do not remember to have seen that letter since & cannot undertake to state with certainty its form or contents. In one respect, however, I can, from the circumstance I am about to state, speak with more precision. I recollect that upon reading the paper, it appeared to me that the manner in which you expressed yourself might be construed into an attempt on your part to control those gentlemen in their personal associations, which I believed to be foreign

---

[1] Jackson's letter of Aug. 8, 1831, and **Van Buren's autograph signed reply**, Aug. 14, are in the Van Buren Papers.

to your wishes, and under that impression I suggested to you the propriety of being altogether explicit upon that point. You at once disclaimed such a wish & expressed a readiness so to modify the paper as to disavow any such intention, and to confine your complaint in terms to the supposed concert on the part of those gentlemen to effect the object referred to, a course of conduct which you regarded as not only unjust towards Mr. & Mrs. Eaton, but as being a direct attack upon yourself for continuing in your Cabinet a gentleman towards whose family such steps could be deemed justifiable. Expressions to that effect were introduced in the paper which were I thought sufficient to prevent misapprehensions with regard to your views. It is my impression that I took the further liberty of suggesting to you the propriety of substituting a personal interview & a frank & free communication of your sentiments in preference to a formal correspondence upon the subject, adding that you might in that case also have the grounds you intended to take previously stated in writing, that there might be less room for misapprehension upon a point which we both regarded as one of great delicacy.

I left you, according to my best recollection, either positively decided or at least strongly inclined to adopt that course. It may be that the paper was drawn up whilst I was with you & that my observations were founded upon your declarations as to what you intended to say,—but my best recollection is as I have stated. Since that time I have not seen the paper referred to, nor have I, my dear Sir, the slightest recollection that the subject was at any time afterwards made matter of observation between us. It is quite natural to suppose that such may have been the case, but I have, before as well as since the receipt of your letter, thought much upon the subject & I cannot call to mind anything that passed between us in regard to your interviews with Messrs. Ingham, Branch & Berrien, after they had taken place. It may well be that you informed me of what had transpired at them—but if you did it has certainly escaped my recollection; and my belief is that the matter being, as you hoped, finally disposed of & influenced by a wish, which you have always manifested, not to press the general subject unnecessarily upon my attention, you thought it best to drop it altogether.

I do not pretend to be accurate as to words but believe that I am right as to the substance of what I have stated. It is quite possible that I may have forgotten some things & that I am mistaken in others; & under the pressure of public duties in which I was then engaged it would not be strange if it were so; but I give it to you as I have it—wishing only to be excused for the confused manner in which it is done, & which the circumstances under which I write render almost unavoidable.

One word more upon this subject. The anxiety of your friends that you should not suffer yourself to be drawn into a newspaper controversy upon it is intense & universal. They regard it as incompatible with your station & uncalled for by anything that has appeared. The time may come when you can with propriety say upon the subject what you may deem necessary, and the discussion of the question, whether your statement or that of the other parties, in regard to the paper having been shown to them, is correct, may with entire safety be deferred to that period. That is not the question at issue—but a mere circumstance; that question is whether you did or did not attempt to regulate & control their private and social intercourse, & upon that point how does the case stand? Neither of the gentlemen assert that you either made such an attempt in your personal interviews with them or either of them, or that you admitted that you had done so through Col. Johnson,—and he, the only person who can speak to the point, acquits you in the most solemn and emphatic manner of any such act or design. Can a reasonable & enlightened community require more? I think not.

The sequel of Major Eaton's career presented an instructive commentary on the past and fully justified the opinion I had formed in regard to the effect of my resignation in commending him to the favor of those by whom he and his had been so unsparingly condemned. His lax political notions, for they could scarcely ever be said to have risen to the dignity of opinions, with his easy dispositions in respect to most things, were well calculated to expose him to the sinister intrigues of a class of habitual hangers-on at the seat of Government, whose business it is to practice upon the credulity of public functionaries and to serve, in their way, an administration or a party which will countenance, patronize or employ them; of course they prefer the party which uses the most money and which is most tolerant of politicians of easy virtue. When the Democratic party is in power and its representative at the head of the government is a democrat in fact as well as in name, acting always in the spirit of its simple, just and abstemious precepts that the world is governed too much, and that the benefits and burdens of °necessary Government should be distributed equally and impartially, doctrines favored by farmers and mechanics, who constitute a vast majority of the party,—when he duly appreciates his proud position as the Chief Magistrate of a Government founded on public virtue, whose duty it is to suppress indirections of every description, a wall of separation has always stood between this class and the administration. Such was emphatically the case at the time of which we are speaking. President Jackson's well understood principles and the struggle in which he was engaged with the Bank and with other selfish and corrupt interests in the Country served to range that political brotherhood unanimously on the side of the opposition to his administration. Their attention was forthwith directed towards Major Eaton, backed by the arts and appliances which they so well understand, to seduce him from the relations in which he had before stood towards his party and friends. Their first movement in this direction was to cause him to be appointed President of the Ohio and Chesapeake Canal Company. This appointment was the more easily obtained in consequence of the desire of the Company to obtain assistance from the Federal Government and their hope of deriving increased facilities to that end by the installation of a personal friend of the President at the head of their board of directors. But the ground taken by General Jackson in regard to the agency of the Federal Government in the promotion of internal improvement, which be-

°MS. IV, p. 10.

came in the end an immovable position upon the subject, soon cut off all expectations of that nature..

Major Eaton was not a man of business in any department. The qualities neither of his head nor of his heart were such as to give value to his superintendence of a concern like that which had been committed to his charge. Another place was therefore sought for by his friends—new and old. The extreme sympathy at one time felt in his position and fate and in those of his family by General Jackson had doubtless been considerably weakened, but the wane of his fortunes was a sufficient motive with the General to befriend him, and he, without hesitation, nominated Eaton to the Senate for the office of Governor of Florida; and that body, in which the opposition had then a majority of ten—the same which rejected the nomination of the accomplished and upright Taney, as Secretary of the Treasury, by a vote of 28 to 18, and that of Andrew Stevenson, as Minister·to England,—promptly and without division confirmed the nomination.

Was it possible that gentlemen who sincerely thought Mrs. Eaton unfit for the society of Washington could deem it proper to place her at the head of that of one of our territories—certainly not the least polished or moral of our communities! Two years afterwards Eaton's name is again sent to the Senate to represent the Country abroad as Envoy Extraordinary & Minister Plenipotentiary at the Court of Spain and in the circles of Madrid and again confirmed by the Senate, without a division—a Senate of which Messrs. Clay, Calhoun and Webster were members. Are not these striking commentaries upon the hue and cry that was raised against this couple when they were the supposed favorites of Gen. Jackson, and suspected of favoring my elevation to the Presidency, whose fate it was after all to bear the brunt of their hostility?

I found Major Eaton in possession of the Spanish Mission when I became President, in 1837, and concluding that the interests of the Country might be promoted by a change I decided to recall him in 183—, but, desiring to give as unexceptionable a form to the proceeding as possible I directed the Secretary of State to reply to an unanswered application for leave to return by giving the permission asked for, and by requesting the Minister to fix the period when it would be convenient for him to leave his post to the end that I might prepare to supply his place. He asked that the period might be left to his discretion, which was declined, and he returned forthwith. He paid me a visit soon after his return and reported himself to me as a recalled Minister. I asked whether his description of his position was precisely correct, and he said at once that he had no purpose in view in thus expressing himself—that it was my right and duty to recall him if I thought the public interest would be thereby advanced, and that he had neither the right nor the disposition to complain of the steps I had taken to that end—whether they should be considered a recall or permission to return on his own application. But he had, he said, suffered a grievance of no ordinary character of which he had good reason to complain. An order had issued, as he stated, from the State Department, purporting to be by my direction, by which he had been deprived of the right always enjoyed by our Ministers, to draw at their discretion upon our bankers at London, without specific authority from the Department, for any sums to which they believed themselves entitled from the Government, subject to a settlement of their accounts under its authority. Of this he complained that he had been suddenly deprived, by which a stigma had been attached to his credit, and thro' which he might have been exposed to serious embarrassments. I admitted that the order had been issued by my direction—that its necessity had been shown by the fact that one of his predecessors, who was named to him, had overdrawn his account to an extent which would make a suit at law necessary to recover the excess,—that the order was general and equally applicable to all our Ministers abroad, and I insisted that it was proper in itself as their convenience could be easily provided for by seasonable applications to the Department of State, and that the only fault was the omission on the part of Mr. Forsyth to apprise him that the order was a general one founded on general principles and not on any distrust of him, and that the necessity of its observance had been pointed out by experience.

With these explanations and accompanying assurances of my entire confidence in his integrity he seemed satisfied. I have doubtless seen him since (altho' I have no recollection of the occasion) but I have never conversed with him, with this exception, or with Mrs. Eaton, since their return from Spain. His tendency politically had been for many years in the direction of the opposition, into whose ranks he gradually fell, and his new associations led to acts and declarations on his part which entirely alienated from him the friendship of Gen. Jackson, who silently closed the troublesome relations that had existed between them by turning to the wall the face of his portrait, which hung in the drawing room at the Hermitage.

CHAPTER XXVII.

The following announcement in the *"National Intelligencer—* "On Wednesday last a subscription was handed about for signature in the House of Representatives, by the messengers of the House, which ran thus: *"Proposals for publishing, by subscription, by Duff Green, a correspondence between Gen. Andrew Jackson and John C. Calhoun, President and Vice President of the United States, on the subject of the course of the latter in the deliberations of the Cabinet of Mr. Monroe, on the occurrences in the Seminole War. 52 pages; price six dollars a hundred"*—heralded the approach of the quarrel which broke out in 1831 between Calhoun, Jackson, Crawford and others and which produced unparalleled excitement in the public mind.

Professing to act strictly on the defensive, Mr. Calhoun solemnly invoked the protection of his constituents, the People of the United States, against the injustice which he claimed to have suffered from the impeachment by President Jackson of his official acts in one of the most important occasions of his life. By the same appeal he called for their indignant condemnation of a plot which he undertook to lay bare and which he said had been devised for his destruction by William H. Crawford, and others acting thro' him, and which he regarded as a part of the same movement. Gen. Jackson was in terms excluded from an intentional participation in the plot, and Mr. Crawford's agency, tho' alleged to have been great, was, on account of his misfortunes and physical infirmity, referred to more in sorrow than in anger. The whole affair was presented by Mr. Calhoun as "a political manoeuvre, in which the design was that he (Gen. Jackson) should be the instrument, and himself (Calhoun) the victim, but in which the real actors were carefully concealed by an artful movement," and against these he professed to direct his greatest resentments.

The " real actors " thus spoken of were not named, but such views were presented of the transactions complained of as to leave no doubt, and it was intended to leave none, that he referred to me not only as a principal " actor " in it but as the individual for whose benefit the plot had been devised.

Of this *exposé* and of the transactions which it professes to describe it becomes my duty to speak in so far as they may be supposed to have had a bearing upon my own acts. The questions put at issue between Gen. Jackson and Mr. Calhoun as to what Mr. Calhoun's course in respect to the General, in Mr. Monroe's Cabinet, really was, and whether it was justifiable or otherwise, were discussed, in part, in the life time of the parties. In his last letter to Mr. Calhoun, of the correspondence here referred to, the General said, " In your and Mr. Crawford's dispute I have no interest whatever, but it may become necessary hereafter, when I shall have more leisure and the documents at hand, to place the subject in its proper light, to notice the historical facts and references in your communication,—which will give a very different view to the subject * * * Understanding you now no further communication with you is necessary." He left behind him an " exposition " of the whole affair, a document of considerable length and great power, which, with a brief statement of the circumstances under which it is there published, will be found in *Benton's Thirty Year's View*, vol. 1, p. 169. My own case stands upon a different footing. The " Card " published by me a few days after the appearance of Mr. Calhoun's appeal is the only publication from me upon the subject heretofore; pursuing in that instance the course which I have always preferred, that of living down calumnies unsupported by proof, instead of attempting to write them down. Altho' not aware that I have, upon the whole, suffered from its adoption on that occasion, it is, of course, palpable that a sketch of my life would be incomplete if ° it included no more extended notice of a subject on which I was widely and violently assailed than I chose to take of it when the phrensy and prejudices of the hour were unfavorable to its candid and dispassionate examination.

I pass by the letter from Mr. Crawford to Mr. Balch [1] of the 14th December, 1827, advising opposition to Mr. Calhoun's election as Vice President, as solely intended to bring into view the fact that Mr. Cambreleng [2] and myself, in our trip to the South, in the spring of that year, visited Mr. Crawford at his home in Georgia. That letter was certainly not necessary to establish the fact that hostile relations then existed between Calhoun and Crawford, for that was a matter known to the whole Country and equally notorious were the efforts of the latter to prevent the support of the former on the same ticket with Gen. Jackson; still less could it be of use to implicate me in Crawford's opposition to Calhoun, as my *support* of him, was, wherever I was myself known, as notorious as the fact of his election and to none was it better known than to himself and by none more highly appreciated. It was not referred to for the purpose of injuring Mr. Crawford, for all desire to do so, as well as everything of that character, is again and again disclaimed, and Mr. Crawford

---

° MS. IV, p. 15.   [1] Alfred Balch of Nashville.   [2] Churchill C. Cambreleng.

is treated as a man *hors de combat*. But to make me chiefly responsible for all the grievances complained of, for what was done as well by Mr. Crawford, who is brought forward as the first, altho' not the principal actor in the drama, as by all the minor performers, my visit to him, at that time, at his remote residence in Georgia, was a circumstance too portentous to be overlooked in the preparation of an impeachment which was, of necessity, to be made of shreds and patches. Recollecting the fact of his opposing the support of Mr. Calhoun at that time, I have referred to Mr. Crawford's letters and find one, which if not necessary for any other purpose, will shew that I held the same language to Mr. Calhoun's enemies in Georgia and South Carolina that I held at home. In this letter, dated Dec. 21st, 1827, a week after his letter to Balch, he says: "Soon after you left Gen. Williams—(Gen. David R. Williams, of South Carolina, one of the most distinguished men of that State, but an early and consistent opponent of Mr. Calhoun,)—last spring, I received a letter from him thanking me for my supposed influence in procuring him the pleasure of a visit from you. In that letter he expresses much pleasure with the visit, but he expressed regret that you appeared to him disposed to let Mr. Calhoun remain in his present position." Of that, not disposition only but determination, so far as related to my own action, Mr. Crawford was himself also explicitly and definitely informed by me in reply to a letter from him urging me to support Mr. Macon, of North Carolina.

The following narrative will, I think, present a fair view of the remainder of the case upon which Mr. Calhoun predicated his grave charges. In respect to facts there is little room for mistake, as they are principally derived from original papers published at the time; for motives we must rely on the declarations of the parties tested by natural inferences from acknowledged facts.

James A. Hamilton, Esq. of New York, at the time my personal and political friend, was appointed by the Tammany Society one of the Delegates to represent that Society at the celebration of the Eighth of January in New Orleans, at which Gen. Jackson was to be present. He accompanied the General and his suite to that city, and informs us that on their way down there was much conversation among them in respect to the charges which had been made at the preceding election against the General and which were or might be revived in the canvass then in progress; and amongst other matters, as to the course pursued against him by Mr. Crawford, in Mr. Monroe's Cabinet, on the question of Gen. Jackson's conduct in the Seminole War, and on the proposition supposed to have been then made to arrest him. Mr. Hamilton says that an attack upon the General, upon that point, was anticipated and as it was understood that he intended to pass thro' Georgia on his return and to visit Mr. Crawford he either was asked by Major Lewis or he offered to ascertain truly what passed in the Cabinet on the occasion and upon the point referred to, and to inform him (Lewis) of the result. The motives for this step, he says, were to enable the General's friends to repel the attack if made, " but, above all, if possible, to produce a perfect reconciliation between those gentlemen (Jackson and Crawford) and their friends."

Finding it inconvenient, on reaching Georgia, to visit Mr. Crawford, he wrote to Mr. Forsyth, asking him to obtain the desired information and to send it to him at New York. He kept no copy of this letter, but it was subsequently produced and published by Mr. Forsyth. As this was the opening movement in the supposed conspiracy it deserves a more particular notice. After mentioning his intention to have paid Mr. Crawford a visit and his regret at not having been able to do so, he said:

> I wish you would ascertain from him and communicate to me *whether the propriety or necessity for arresting or trying Gen. Jackson was ever presented as a question for the deliberation of Mr. Monroe's Cabinet.* I understand Mr. Southard (who was a member of the Cabinet) *in his suppressed correspondence* has asserted that to have been the fact. I want the information, not to be used, but in order that I may in the event of a publication, which may come from a high quarter, know where to look for information on this subject. Of course nothing would be published without the consent of Mr. Crawford and yourself.

This was the whole letter.

No question was asked in regard to what Mr. Crawford had done or what Mr. Calhoun had done and none which was calculated to draw out a comparison between their respective acts. It would not have been an easy matter, it strikes me, to have framed a letter which would, on its face, have been more in harmony with a *bona fide* prosecution of the professed object of the enquiry, viz: to enable the friends of Gen. Jackson to repel an attack on him by Mr. Southard charging that he had stood in the attitude described before Mr. Monroe's Cabinet and had been, perhaps, suffered to escape thro' the forbearance of its members. Mr. Hamilton took Washington on his way home and staid for a day or two at the same house with Mr. Calhoun, and being anxious to obtain the information he had thus far failed to get from Mr. Crawford, he requested an interview with the former at which he asked him "whether, at any meeting of Mr. Monroe's Cabinet, the propriety of arresting Gen. Jackson for anything done by him during the Seminole war had been discussed." Mr. Calhoun replied " Never!—such a measure was never thought of, much less discussed. The only point before the Cabinet was the answer to be given to the Spanish Government." On being further asked whether he desired that his answer should be regarded as confidential he said that he did not. Mr. Hamilton says that at that time he had not the slightest knowledge of the course Mr. Calhoun had considered it his duty to pursue in the Cabinet on the occasion referred to, and that his impressions received from the conversations of which he had spoken were that Mr. Calhoun had been in favor of, and Mr. Crawford adverse to Gen. Jackson. The perfect similarity in substance, and bearing, of the question put to Mr. Calhoun to that proposed to Mr. Crawford, through Mr. Forsyth, cannot fail to be perceived.

Hamilton left Washington on the following morning and on the 19th of February, 1828, being the second day after his arrival at New York, he wrote a letter to Major Lewis of which the following was given as an extract—the letter having been tendered but never called for or produced:

"I did not see Mr. Crawford, as I intended to do, because his residence was seventy miles out of my way; but the Vice President (Mr. Calhoun), who, you know, was the member of the Cabinet best acquainted with the subject, told me Gen. Jackson's arrest was never thought of, much less discussed." To this letter he received a reply from Major Lewis in which he said—"I regret that you did not see Mr. Crawford. I was desirous you should see him and converse with him on the subject of his former misunderstanding with the General. I have every reason to believe that the information given to you by Calhoun is correct, for Mr. Monroe assured me, nearly nine years ago, such was the fact. It follows then that Mr. Crawford must have been vilely slandered by those whose object was to fan a flame their interest required should not be extinguished." All still in harmony with the professed objects of the enquiry, viz; to be able to repel the charge referred to, if made, and to conciliate still further the friends of Mr. Crawford who, where they were most numerous, in Virginia, North and South Carolina and New York, had already taken ground in favor of Gen. Jackson. Believing that the information might become useful at Nashville where almost every day produced a new charge against the General, Hamilton, on the 25th of February, wrote to Mr. Calhoun, setting forth what had passed at their interview, as I° have already stated it, telling him that he was thus particular in seeking to obtain his confirmation of it to enable him to confirm Major Lewis, a confidential friend of Gen. Jackson, of its truth; not with a view to enable him to make a publication on the subject but to be prepared to repel an apprehended attack founded on events connected with the Seminole campaign. On the 28th of February he received a letter from Mr. Forsyth, in reply to the one he had addressed to him from Savannah, in which Mr. F. informed him that Mr. Crawford had been a few hours on the previous day at Milledgeville, the place of Mr. Forsyth's residence, that he had conversed with him on the subject referred to in Hamilton's letter, and was authorized to say—"that at a meeting of Mr. Monroe's Cabinet to discuss the course to be pursued towards Spain, in consequence of Gen. Jackson's proceedings in Florida during the Seminole War, Mr. Calhoun, the Secretary of the War Department, submitted to and urged upon the President the propriety of arresting and trying Gen. Jackson: that Mr. Calhoun had previously communicated to Mr. Crawford his intention to present the question to Mr. Monroe; an intention Mr. Crawford approved" (Mr. Crawford subsequently corrected this statement by saying that Mr. Forsyth had misunderstood him— that Mr. Calhoun's proposition in the Cabinet was that Gen. Jackson should be punished in some form or reprimanded in some form, he was not positively certain which: as Mr. Calhoun did not propose to arrest Gen. Jackson he felt confident that he could not have made use of that expression in his conversation with Mr. Forsyth.

After the receipt of Mr. Forsyth's letter he (Hamilton) received Mr. Calhoun's reply to his letter of the 25th of February. This reply was dated March 29th and said that as Mr. Hamilton had not, at the time of their interview, stated the object of his enquiry he had supposed it was designed only to meet mere general rumour falsely put out to influence the result of the Presidential election; that his answer had been predicated on such an assumption, was intended to meet assertions unsupported by any name in the same general manner without name and to be limited, even with that view, to a denial of what was falsely stated to have occurred on that occasion. Mr. Calhoun then repeated Hamilton's object as stated in his letter of the 25th of February, and said that he had, under that aspect of the subject, deliberately considered how far he could, with propriety, speak of the proceedings of the Cabinet at all and had come to the conclusion that a duty of a very high and delicate character imposed silence upon him; that entertaining such views he declined the introduction of his name in any shape as connected with what passed in the Cabinet on the occasion referred to. To this Hamilton answered on the 10th of March, that Mr. Calhoun's reasoning as to the confidence which ought to be observed in regard to occurrences in the Cabinet was clear and conclusive, and that he had written to Major Lewis, that day, that his (Mr. Calhoun's) name should not be used in any manner with the denial, should a publication be called for, which he did not believe to be the case,—adding that *the subject had derived increasing interest from a communication he had received since he had written to Mr. Calhoun.* This brought a reply from Mr. Calhoun in which he said that it had appeared to him desirable, on several accounts, that if an attack on Gen. Jackson was meditated, in the manner supposed, he (Mr. Calhoun) should be put in possession of the facts from which it was inferred: that his knowledge of the facts might enable him to ascertain from what quarter the blow might be expected and to take measures to parry it: that if he (Hamilton) should concur in that view and felt himself at liberty to communicate what he knew it might ultimately prove serviceable to the cause and should be received in strict confidence. Hamilton replied, on the 26th March, that he regretted to say that he did not feel himself at liberty to disclose what he knew of the matter referred to in Mr. Calhoun's letter, that the information he had received was not declared to be confidential, nor was it necessarily so, yet, as it was communicated to him only because he could be instrumental in obtaining the means of resistance, having done so he felt that he ought to consider himself as no longer in possession of it. Having in good faith pursued thus far the business he had undertaken to perform and which, I am confident, had no other aims than those which were professed, Hamilton's eyes were opened by the contents of Forsyth's letter and by the abrupt closing of the door to further disclosures by Mr. Calhoun, upon a subject in respect to which he had before been so ready to speak and so unreserved in his answers, to the depth of the waters into which he was plunging and the stirring character of the investigation he had entered upon and to an appreciation of the troubles to which he might expose himself by a wish to make himself useful to a cause in which he had become suddenly conspicuous and perhaps somewhat by a passion, not uncommon with young men, to take part in important and exciting public transactions in which the prominent actors are the most distinguished men of their day; and he decided to draw off. Hence his ready acquiescence in Mr. Calhoun's reasons against the propriety of answering a question which he had just before put to Mr. Crawford, standing precisely in the same situation, and his instructions to Major Lewis not to use Mr. Calhoun's name in any form touching the matter. His steps were well directed to the end he now aimed at, if we except the intimation to Mr. Calhoun that he was in possession of a further communication which had given to the whole matter a deeper interest, which produced in the latter an anxiety to learn the character of that communication; his decision to disentangle himself was a wise one and if he had acted upon it from the spring of 1828 till the autumn of 1829, during which period Mr. Forsyth's letter remained on his own files and was not, as he says, shown to any body, he would have saved himself much anxiety and his friends much trouble.

In the fall of the latter year, however, eighteen months after Forsyth's letter had been written and when the subject had substantially passed from the minds of all who had taken a part in it, he read that letter to Major Lewis at his own house in New York. But even this step would in all probability have produced no disturbing results had the principal parties remained in their original position towards each other which was very far from the case, the friendly relations which had existed between Gen. Jackson and Mr. Calhoun having been by that time seriously impaired through the agency of the Eaton imbroglio, and giving place soon after to open hostility. It was not probably until the latter period that Lewis, who sympathized in the General's feelings throughout, informed him of the contents of Forsyth's letter, and this was, I verily believe, the first reliable information he had ever received as to Mr. Calhoun's precise course in Mr. Monroe's Cabinet in regard to his conduct in Florida—a subject on which the General's feelings were always keenly sensitive. He had never before even suspected that that course had been hostile to him. Hamilton says that he became acquainted with the contents of the letter but does not say how. My statement that it was communicated by Major Lewis is an inference only, but I have no doubt that it is a just one, and that the Major would, without hesitation, confirm it. Of course, General Jackson demanded to see the letter. He would have done so if he and Mr. Calhoun had remained friends, and was less likely to omit it under their hostile relations. This was in the month of May, 1830, more than two years after the proceedings of which we have been speaking had taken place and until that time I had never received the slightest intimation, from any source, of their occurrence. It was after Gen. Jackson had demanded a sight of Forsyth's letter that Hamilton for the first time gave me a general statement of its contents as the ground of a request for my advice in regard to the answer he should make to the General's application. I instantly decided to have nothing to do with the affair and declined to express my opinion upon the question he submitted to me. He then applied to Mr. Forsyth to give to the President directly the information that he (Forsyth) had communicated to him in the letter referred to. Mr. Forsyth was not a friend of Mr. Calhoun—none of Mr. Crawford's friends in Georgia stood in that relation towards him; the feuds between the chiefs had been of too long standing and too bitter to admit of very friendly feelings between their respective adherents; but he was a man of truth and honor unquestioned by Mr. Calhoun or by any other. This is his account, given in February, 1831, of what passed in respect to Hamilton's application:

A word or two of explanation, in the further agency I have had in this affair, is justly due to Mr. Crawford. I heard nothing of my correspondence with Major Hamilton, and the subject was scarcely thought of until during last winter that gentleman came to the Senate Chamber, and requested me to give to the President, if not improper in my judgment, the information I had given to him. I asked him if he ° had not my letter. He answered that he had. I then said Mr. Crawford spoke to me and speaks to everybody of this affair, with the same indifference that he does of every other incident in his political life. I am sure he does not care what you do with the letter. You may give the President a copy of it. Major Hamilton declined doing so from a motive of delicacy. He stated that he had conversed, or corresponded, I do not recollect which, with Mr. Calhoun on this subject, and that the statements of Mr. Crawford and Mr. Calhoun did not agree. He was, therefore, unwilling to interfere, further than to comply with the President's wish in asking of me the information. On this statement I was determined not to give the information without Mr. Crawford's express assent. The information was no longer a matter of indifference, and I did not choose to give it to the President without apprising Mr. Crawford that he and Mr. Calhoun differed in their account of the transaction and without submitting to him my statement of our conversation for correction, if it was, in any respect, erroneous. I obtained for that purpose, and enclosed to him a copy of my letter to Major Hamilton. His answer is before the public. I found, to my surprise, that I had erred in repeating what he had said, and to avoid the possibility of any other mistake, I deemed it safest to send to the President a copy of my letter to Major Hamilton and Mr. Crawford's letter to me. In making this communication, from respect to the personal delicacy of Major Hamilton, his name was kept out of view.

On the 12ᵗʰ May 1830, Mr. Forsyth delivered to the President both of the letters spoken of by him, viz: that from him to Mr. Hamilton of the 8ᵗʰ Feb. 1828, and that to him from Mr. Crawford, of the 30ᵗʰ April, 1830, containing Mr. C's account of what was done in Mr. Monroe's Cabinet in respect to Gen. Jackson's conduct in the Seminole War, and which was given in Mr. Calhoun's appeal. This letter was on the following day sent by Gen. Jackson to Mr. Calhoun, inclosed with the following:[1]

MAY 13, 1830.

SIR:

That frankness which I trust has always characterized me through life towards those with whom I have been in the habit of friendship, induces me to lay before you the enclosed copy of a letter from William H. Crawford Esq., which was placed in my hands on yesterday. The submission you will perceive is authorized by the writer. The statements & facts it presents being so different from what I had heretofore understood to be correct, requires that it should be brought to your consideration. They are different from your letter to Governor Bibb, of the 13th. May, 1818, where you state " General Jackson is vested with full power to conduct the war in the manner he may judge best," and different too from your letter to me at that time which breathed throughout a spirit of approbation & friendship, & particularly the one in which you say, " I have the honor to acknowledge the receipt of your letter of the 20th. ultimo, and to acquaint you with the entire approbation of the President of all the

---

° MS. IV, p. 25.
[1] Calhoun's answer dated May 13, 1830, is in the Jackson Papers.

measures you have adopted to terminate the rupture with the Indians." My object in making this communication is to announce to you the great surprise which is felt & to learn of you whether it be possible that the information given is correct; whether it can be under all the circumstances of which you & I are both informed, that any attempt seriously to affect me was moved & sustained by you in the cabinet council, when, as is known to you, I was but executing the *wishes* of the Government, and clothed with the authority "to conduct the war in the manner I might judge best."

You can, if you please, take a copy; the one enclosed you will please return to me.

I am, Sir, very respectfully, your humble servant,

ANDREW JACKSON.

The Hon. J. C. CALHOUN.

The enquiry and the only enquiry made of Mr. Calhoun by this letter was whether any attempt seriously to affect Gen. Jackson was moved and sustained by him in the Cabinet council of Mr. Monroe. If the General had stopped here the course pursued by Mr. Calhoun in reply might well have been regarded as an uncalled for extension of the matter in controversy, designed as was alleged by Mr. Crawford, to get rid of a fact which he could not frankly and distinctly deny by attempting to prove a negative by argument. But the letter went further and claimed that the acts referred to were justified by instruction received from the War Department, at the head of which Mr. Calhoun then stood, and approved by the President. Mr. Calhoun was thus invited if not necessarily called to the consideration and discussion of so much of the acts of the War Department and the President as was claimed by Gen. Jackson to have conferred upon him authority to capture and hold for a season the Spanish Posts in Florida if he should think it necessary to the protection of the frontier and of our people against the inroads of Indians. He at least considered such to be the position in which he was placed by the General's letter, and undertook in an elaborate reply, covering many sheets, extracts included, to prove that the General's orders did not authorize the occupation by him of St. Marks and Pensacola, taking in those respects the ground that had always been taken by Crawford, his friends, and the opposition in Congress, and also that the General had, at the time, been fully informed that such were his views of the matter. He answered the General's specific enquiry in the following terms:—

As Secretary of War I was more immediately connected with questions whether you had transcended your orders, and, if so, what course ought to be pursued. I was of the impression that you had exceeded your orders and had acted on your own responsibility; but I neither questioned your patriotism nor your motives. Believing that, where orders were transcended, investigation, as a matter of course, ought to follow, as due in justice to the government and the officer, unless there be strong reasons to the contrary, I came to the meeting under the impression that the usual course ought to be pursued in this case, which I supported by presenting fully and freely all the arguments that occurred to me.[1]

This altho' rendered a little less harsh by the language employed amounted, in substance, to an admission of the correctness of Mr. Crawford's statement—as punishment of some sort would, in the usual course, follow conviction. Crawford said, "Mr. Calhoun's proposition in the Cabinet was that Gen. Jackson should be punished in some form, or reprimanded in some form, I am not positively certain which." The General's question was therefore answered, and was, doubtless, intended to be understood as answered affirmatively. Mr. Calhoun's reply was, I think, sent to the President on the evening before the adjournment of Congress, in May, 1830. The first I saw of it was on the day of the adjournment. After my return from the Capitol with the President and the other members of the Cabinet, who are usually in attendance on the last day of the session, Major Lewis came to my house and laid upon the table at which I was sitting a file of papers, saying "There is Calhoun's letter. The General begs you to read the papers attentively and when you have had time to do so he will be glad to see and advise with you upon the subject." Hamilton having, as I have stated, apprised me of the general bearing of the correspondence, I required no time to reflect upon my answer to this application. I told the Major that I was quite sure the General would not have sent the papers to me if he had reflected on the impropriety of my taking a part in any controversy between himself and Mr. Calhoun and on its liability to misinterpretation, and apprising him of the answer I had given to Hamilton, requested him to take them back and to report what I had said to the General. He did so, and the General embraced an early opportunity to assure me that I was altogether right, and apologized very earnestly for what he called his "carelessness" in the matter. He sent a brief reply to Mr. Calhoun, of which I have given the substance in the introduction to this review, but which I did not see, neither was I apprised of its contents until the appearance of Mr. Calhoun's pamphlet.[2]

There the matter rested until the next winter. The gossips of Washington got hold of the fact that there had been a correspondence and some of the newspapers gave loose and contradictory accounts of its contents. Mr. Calhoun did not arrive at Washington until some weeks of the following session of Congress had elapsed. Attempts were subsequently made (and perhaps before) by gentle-

---

[1] This letter, dated May 29, 1830, an A. L. S. of Calhoun's, is 48 pp. long. It is in the Jackson Papers.

[2] Correspondence between Gen. Andrew Jackson and John C. Calhoun * * * on the subject of the course of the latter, in the cabinet of Mr. Monroe, on the occurrences in the Seminole War. Washn. Printed by D. Green, 1831. A copy is in the Library of Congress.

men who claimed to be friends of both the President and Vice President to bring about a reconciliation between them. Mr. Samuel Swartwout was particularly active in that direction. Gen. Jackson apprised me of those efforts and I advised him, earnestly and sincerely, to consent to any amicable arrangement of the subject that would be consistent with his honor. I was° sitting with him, one day, in one of the rooms of the White House which had been appropriated as a studio by his friend Col. Earle, who was painting his portrait, when a servant announced that Mr. Swartwout was in his office and requested to see him for a moment. He went out and, on his return, told me that the whole affair was settled. He gave me the substance of the terms, but my recollection upon the subject is not distinct enough to justify me in undertaking to state them. I expressed my gratification at the result. He did not appear entirely satisfied with what he had agreed to, but said the matter was done with and he would think no more about it.

The adjustment of the whole affair, was for several days publicly spoken of. Information of the fact was communicated to persons out of the city and I received letters in which the pacification was spoken of as undisputed. But Mr. Calhoun's publication appeared notwithstanding. No explanation of the failure of the negotiation has, to my knowledge, been given on either side. Two attempts were subsequently made—the last immediately before Mr. Calhoun's 'appeal' appeared—to give that paper a character and to have it published in a way which would be satisfactory to Gen. Jackson and to prevent him from replying to or taking any notice of its contents. Col. Richard M. Johnson and Senator Grundy, recognised and warm friends of Mr. Calhoun, as they were also of Gen. Jackson's called (as he now informs me) on Mr. F. P. Blair, with whom they enjoyed a cordial intimacy, and whose feelings were then personally favorable to Mr. Calhoun, and made a labored effort to persuade him to publish it in the *Globe* with comments indicating that it was neither in fact, nor in intention an attack upon Gen. Jackson. He resisted their solicitations to the end, insisting that the paper could not be so qualified as to avoid a rupture with the General which must be the ruin of Mr. Calhoun. Mr. Blair does not now recollect whether any, or, if any, what communications took place between him and General Jackson in respect to the proposition, or whether, indeed, he was permitted to talk to him on the subject. Failing in this overture a negotiation of the same character was instituted by Mr. Grundy with Major Eaton, whose interest in a general pacification need not be enlarged upon.

° MS. IV, p. 30.

Its character and results are fully set forth in the following publication:—

[From "the Globe" of March 26, 1831.]

[We have been favored with the following communication from the Secretary of War, which will show the groundlessness of the intimation conveyed by a late *Telegraph* (newspaper) that the intimate friends of Gen. Jackson, if not the General himself, were satisfied with Mr. Calhoun's address, &c., before it appeared in public.]

Recently it had been stated in the U. S. Telegraph, that the appeal of Mr. Calhoun to the public, previous to its publication, had been submitted to and approved by a confidential friend of the President. The allusion is to myself. I perceive not the force of the argument which would make this circumstance to operate beneficially or otherwise; but as it has been mentioned, I take occasion to present the agency particularly that I had in this business, and how and why it was occasioned.

Previous to the publication being made I received a request from Mr. Grundy to see me. I afforded him the interview he sought. He informed me the Vice President had concluded certainly to make publication of the correspondence; and that his (Mr. Grundy's) great anxiety was that the appeal intended to accompany it should be so framed as that the President might not feel himself called upon, by any thing it should contain, to offer a reply. If the President should adopt this course he entertained the opinion that the matter would soon pass away, and every thing of party excitement be avoided. Such was the nature of our conversation and I readily accorded with him in his frank desire.

Mr. Grundy expressed the opinion that it would be in his power to obtain the assent of the Vice President to show me the remarks which Mr. Calhoun intended to present to the public. Shortly after dark the next evening I went to his lodgings. Arriving, I was told by the servant at the door that Mr. Grundy was not at home but had gone to Mr. Ingham's. I directed him to go there and say that I wished to see him. He soon returned, and shortly afterwards Mr. Grundy came in, and we sat down together, and alone, in his bed room.

He observed it had been permitted to him to show me the paper of which he had before spoken; and after some cursory remarks, such as he thought it would now do, and that I would, as he read it, note any exception which I might consider exceptionable, proceeded to read it. Whenever a remark occurred which I thought calculated to excite, or which, by possibility, might be misconceived, I offered suggestions agreeably to the invitation which Mr. Grundy had tendered; of all which he made notes. I kept none myself and hence cannot say that all were adopted. I do not doubt about it however, as Mr. Grundy afterwards informed me that they had been adopted.

Having read through the appeal, Mr. Grundy observed, " Well, if the suggestions and illustrations we have made, shall be approved, do you think the President will feel himself called upon to reply, or to notice, himself, any thing that the appeal contains?" My answer was, I thought not, and my anxious desire was that he would not; but without doubt the newspapers would take hold of and canvass the matter, and to what a course of that kind in the end might lead, time only could determine.

We were about to separate when Mr. Grundy observed,—"Will you see Gen. Jackson and explain to him what has taken place? I will see Mr. Calhoun, and if the course we have taken be approved you shall be informed." But I did not communicate the subject to the President. because, upon reflection, I thought it improper to do so. From Mr. Grundy I received a note the next day, stating that all was right, which I understood to mean that the suggestions offered had been adopted.

The evening preceding the day when the correspondence made its appearance, a printed copy was enclosed to me, with a request that I would submit that too to the President. This also I declined to do.

Ill health has prevented me from making this communication earlier.

That the accuracy of this statement was assented to by Mr. Grundy necessarily results from the relation in which they both stood towards Gen. Jackson and from the facts that Mr. Grundy was on the spot at the time it was made and that he did not question it. It is further confirmed by the declaration of Mr. Ingham, in his address to the President, of July 26, 1831, that "the preface to the correspondence" (which was the 'appeal') "had been previously revised by the President's particular friend, and every expression which he thought might be personally offensive to the President had been erased at the suggestion of that friend." Mr. Grundy, having informed Major Eaton the next day, by note, "that all was right" by which the latter understood that the suggestions offered had been adopted, and hearing nothing to the contrary, inferred, of course, that the Major had carried into effect the arrangement made between them and that the General had assented to it.

This inference, which no steps on the part of Eaton counteracted, was confirmed by the circumstance that a copy of the pamphlet was sent to him the evening before it was issued to the public to be laid before the President, so that the latter might read it before it came out, of which also Eaton took notice. He does not say who sent it, but it is not to be supposed that it would have been so sent without the approbation of Mr. Calhoun, or under any other impression than that the arrangement had been found satisfactory and acceptable to Gen. Jackson. That the 'appeal' was ushered to the people under a full belief that such was the real state of the case it is impossible to doubt, and conversant as I was with the then condition of things as affecting that point I can very well conceive that, but for that mistake, and the publication which was its first consequence, Mr. Calhoun might have been raised to the Presidency. If the terms of the settlement, which fell through in his hands, were of the character described by Mr. Calhoun's confidential and most efficient friend, in the address already referred to, (and of that I can now say nothing with certainty) viz: that the correspondence was to be destroyed, that Mr. Calhoun was to leave his card for the President; to be invited to his table and no further notice was to be taken of the controversy, every thing would have tended, in all probability, to that result. It was a strong feature in Gen. Jackson's nature that an interest in the welfare, and a desire to be instrumental in promoting it, of those with whom he had been at variance quickly sprung up in his breast upon an amicable adjustment of differences. My own feelings at that time in respect to the succession, of which I will speak more particularly hereafter, would have interposed no obstacles to Mr. Calhoun's advancement if that had become the wish of our party. On finding, as he would have found ° that I had no more to do with the proceedings of which he complained than the man in the moon, the friendly relations that had arisen between us before the election would have been restored and I see no good reason to doubt that the end which I have intimated would have resulted. But unfounded jealousy and consequent ill will towards myself, with bad advisers, decreed otherwise.

The direct consequence of the success of the Grundy and Eaton arrangement would have been to throw the brunt of the war—where it was, from a very early period, if not from the first conception of the 'plot,' intended that it should fall ultimately,—on my shoulders. No man of sense, familiar with the characters and events of that day, can read Mr. Calhoun's 'appeal,' and its supplements, without perceiving the two principal objects of its construction—viz: self exculpation in the matter of his course in Mr. Monroe's Cabinet towards Gen. Jackson—now for the first time made known to the latter—and the implication of myself in a plot from which I could not escape and for really engaging in which I would have deserved the political destruction prepared for me. Altho' my name was carefully and with some manifest labour kept out of both the 'appeal' and its addenda, yet the fact of its being aimed at me was conveyed without the possibility of failure to the apprehension of the political reader. When speculation had been suffered to work upon it for a season the Editor of the *Telegraph*, with well painted horror, disclosed the secret (!) as to the intended application of the reference to "concealed actors." In the copy of the letter from Mr. Crawford to Mr. Forsyth, which was sent by the latter to the President, and by him enclosed to Mr. Calhoun, blank spaces were in two or three instances substituted, for a name, (as Mr. ———,) which substitution was subsequently explained, thus by Mr. Forsyth, as heretofore quoted,— "from respect to the personal delicacy of Major Hamilton his name was kept out of view." But the eagerness and energy with which Mr. Calhoun, under the influence of his passions, seized upon these luckless blanks would have been amusing, if the distortions of a really great mind could be thus ever regarded. He referred to Mr. Crawford's letter sent to him by Gen. Jackson as "a copy with important

---

° MS. IV, p. 35.

blanks" demanded by what rule of justice he was deprived of evidence material to his defense—of a statement of the conversation and correspondence of the two individuals whose names are in blank ";— " Why not" said he " inform me who they are? Their testimony might be highly important, and even their *names alone* (so italicised in the original) might throw much light on this mysterious affair." Again " this whole affair is a political manoeuvre in which the design is that you (Gen. Jackson) should be the instrument and myself the victim, but in which the real actors are carefully concealed by an artful movement; a naked copy, with the names referred to in blank, affords slender means of detection, * * * the names which are in blank might of themselves through their political associations point directly to the contrivers of this scheme." Apparently for the purpose of preventing my escape from the full force of his onset under cover of a divided responsibility for the ' plot,' he proceeds to separate this " blow " from that " meditated " by Hamilton's application in 1828, in which he did not then suspect me of participation. He says— " several indications forewarned me long since that a blow was meditated against me: *I will not say from the quarter from which this comes;* but in relation to this subject, more than two years since, I had a correspondence with " &c.[1] describing his correspondence with Hamilton.

The mysterious blanks were at once, and to the great disappointment of those who expected, not to say hoped, differently, explained by Mr. Forsyth as referring in each instance to the same person, viz: to Mr. Hamilton, of whose agency in the matter Mr. Calhoun was fully aware.

Was it uncharitable to attribute to this anxiety to implicate and consequently to destroy me politically the failure of the accommodation between the two highest officers of the Government generally supposed to have been successfully negotiated by Swartwout, and the substitution of a mode of bringing the matter before the Country which might accomplish both results?

Before I go further I must say a word, in justice to my own feelings, in relation to the parts taken in this affair by Col. Johnson and Mr. Grundy. Johnson was the friend of the human race and all who needed his services in any honorable way could have them. In rendering them thus readily and thus liberally it sometimes happened that in serving one he unintentionally injured another—a not uncommon fate of such a disposition. He was an old friend of Mr. Calhoun, not only willing but anxious to serve him. From my knowledge of him I am quite confident that the idea of the injurious effect which

---

[1] This and the preceding quotations are from Calhoun's letter of May 29, 1830, in the Jackson Papers.

his success in the proposed arrangement with Mr. Blair might have upon me never occurred to him. I cannot in candour say as much for Grundy. He had too strong a taste for political manœuvreing—within allowable boundaries—and was too experienced a tactician to have failed in seeing the bearing of the whole thing. My intercourse with him before this period had been in comparison with Mr. Calhoun's very limited. He was several years later a member of my 'Cabinet and I became much attached to him. He was a man of liberal and just feelings and quite devoted where he took a liking. He and Mr. Calhoun served together in Congress during the War of 1812 and formed with each other friendly relations which were, I believe, never entirely obliterated notwithstanding the confidential position in which he was subsequently placed in respect to Gen. Jackson and the enmity that arose between the latter and Mr. Calhoun. One of the most amusing scenes I witnessed in the Senate, during my long service in that body, was produced by Mr. Clay's attempting to implicate Mr. Grundy in Mr. Calhoun's nullification scheme. The bantering vivacity and persistency of the arraignment, with the earnestness and vigour of the defense, and the invincible good nature of the parties called out frequent bursts of applause and laughter. The accused described with his finger an imaginary line between himself and Mr. Calhoun, who sat quite near him, declared in the strongest terms his warm regard for that gentleman, referred with satisfaction to the many political battles they had fought, side by side, against the federalists during the war, then, pointing to the line of nullification as he had indicated it, admitted that he had some times been found near it but affirmed with great solemnity and obvious sincerity that he had never in a single instance passed it, and challenged Mr. Clay to produce a particle of proof to the contrary. This position he very successfully sustained to the end of the debate to the great entertainment and amusement of the Senate, not excepting Mr. Calhoun himself.

Mr. Grundy was also unreservedly loyal to the friendship he professed for Gen. Jackson. He knew very little, at that time, as I have said, of me but I do not believe that his feelings towards me were ever positively unfriendly and the general amiability of his disposition (which extended to all his acquaintances except his colleague Judge White,[1] whom he cordially disliked, chiefly because he had good reason to know that the Judge disliked him) would have inclined him, I doubt not, to draw us all out of the quarrel if he could; as that however would have defeated the main purpose he was not permitted to do it and hence his efforts were confined naturally to the side of his two old friends and he left me to the buffetings of the storm which he saw approaching.

---

[1] Hugh Lawson White.

It has been by such considerations, with the knowledge I subsequently acquired of his fondness for the strategical branch of political warfare, to which I may again have occasion to refer, that my feelings in regard to his agency in the present matter have been controlled.

Admitting the truth of every thing said in Mr. Calhoun's pamphlet of 52 pages about Gen. Jackson and himself in regard to the question in dispute between them there was nothing that would or should have impaired the confidence of the American people in the General's patriotism or integrity. Mr. Calhoun admitted in the correspondence that he had never questioned either. The General had passed through an active campaign before Congress and having fought his battles over again before that body in respect to the same matters had come out of the contest confirmed in full possession of the favor and confidence of the people. His case was strengthened by that very correspondence in bringing, for the first time, to the knowledge of the Country the ° facts that he had written a private letter to President Monroe telling him that if the Administration appreciated as he did the indispensable necessity of occupying temporarily the Spanish posts and wished him to take them without positive instructions, they had only to give a hint to some confidential member of Congress—(say " Johnny Ray ") [Rhea] and the General would take possession of them on his own responsibility, and that no answer had ever been returned to that letter, thereby leaving him a fair excuse at least for regarding the silence of the President as furnishing the suggested hint. What the General had done, whether within the line of his instructions or not, had been done to protect the lives of our people against the savages led on by renegades from all nations who were indirectly, at least, fostered and encouraged from the places upon which he had seized. All admitted the purity of his motives and a majority of his countrymen were satisfied that the high necessity of his act was sufficiently apparent to justify the exercise of the authority with which he had been clothed and of the power he held. Upon the same overruling principle of the safety of the people, he confessedly exceeded his instructions at New Orleans, and by his conduct on that occasion not only closed the War of 1812 in a blaze of glory, but attracted to himself the attention and support of the people for the elevated civil position to which he succeeded.

Gen. Jackson's personal inducements to fight his Seminole campaign still another time in the newspapers were very slight, but thinking that he saw in the whole proceeding a design to strike down a man whom he knew to be innocent and who was moreover

---

° MS. IV, p. 40.

his intimate friend and constitutional adviser he indignantly refused to sanction the arrangement that had been been devised, and
to suffer that assault to be made over his shoulders. My situation
was however very different. The offence charged against me was
in every respect a heinous one. If I could so far have forgotten
what was due to my position and to my own honour as to have
revived that old and forgotten affair for the purpose of producing
a quarrel between the President and Vice President, who had never
quarrelled about it before, in the hope of thereby promoting my
own political advancement, there was scarcely a depth of public
scorn and reproach to which I would not have richly deserved to
sink. It would have been difficult to conceive of a case better calculated to excite the unmeasured condemnation of all good citizens.
The welfare of the people, the character of the Government, so far
as that depends upon the conduct of its highest officials, and the
peace of mind of an old and care worn public servant, yet bearing
on his shoulders the gravest responsibilities of the State, with many
other scarcely less important interests would all have suffered outrage through such an intrigue on my part.

That the main object of the publication was to fasten that offence
upon me was clearly indicated by the ' appeal,' was the public understanding of the matter and shortly after it was published ceased to
be denied in any quarter. The developments of time have furnished
specific proof of this design. Col. Benton in his work already frequently referred to, describing the origin of the "*Globe*" newspaper
makes the following statement:[a]

At a Presidential levee in the winter of 1830–31, Mr. Duff Green, Editor of
the "*Telegraph*", newspaper, addressed a person then and now a respectable
resident of Washington city (Mr. J. M. Duncanson) and invited him to call
at his house, as he had something to say to him which would require a confidential interview. The call was made and the object of the interview disclosed, which was nothing less than to engage his (Mr. Duncanson's) assistance
in the execution of a scheme in relation to the next presidential election, in
which Gen. Jackson should be prevented from becoming a candidate for re-
election and Mr. Calhoun should be brought forward in his place. He informed
Mr. Duncanson that a rupture was impending between Gen. Jackson and Mr.
Calhoun; that a correspondence had taken place between them, brought about,
(as he alleged) by the intrigues of Mr. Van Buren; that the correspondence
was then in print, but its publication delayed until certain arrangements could
be made; that the democratic papers at the most prominent points in the
States were to be first secured; and men well known to the people as democrats, but in the exclusive interest of Mr. Calhoun, placed in charge of them
as editors; that as soon as the arrangements were complete the *Telegraph*
would startle the Country with the announcement of the difficulty (between
Gen. Jackson and Mr. Calhoun) and the motive for it; and that all the secured
presses, taking their cue from the *Telegraph* would take sides with Mr. Calhoun, and cry out at the same time; and the storm would seem to be so uni-

---

[a] Benton's Thirty Years' View; vol. 1, p. 129.

versal, and the indignation against Mr. Van Buren would appear to be so great that even Gen. Jackson's popularity would be unable to save him.

Mr. Duncanson was invited to assist by taking charge of the Kentucky *Argus* and, notwithstanding flattering inducements, declined, and subsequently caused Gen. Jackson to be informed of the overture who thereupon took measures to establish the *Globe*.

The effects produced were certainly, for a short period in fair proportion to the odious nature of the charge, the artful disguises which had been thrown over the transactions out of which it was constructed, and the machinery so cunningly devised to help it to do its work. To show the nature and extent of those effects I content myself with the insertion here of a single letter selected from the numerous anxious communications I received on the subject. It proceeded from the capital of a State lying comparatively near the seat of the Federal Government—a State which always bestowed more earnest and busy attention upon national questions than was given by any of her sister States and which, I may add, then at least exerted a greater influence than any others, upon the general sentiment of the Country. Mr. Ritchie possessed my unlimited confidence, and had been encouraged to communicate his opinions upon all public subjects in which I was concerned without reserve—a privilege which he exercised, on stirring occasions, in its broadest latitude.

This letter bears the following endorsement: "*received on the day that my Card appeared and after its appearance*" The letter and the Card passed each other that day on the Richmond *route*.

DEAR SIR,

You know me too well to suppose that I would intrude upon your valuable time without some strong reason. I have always treated you with frankness, and I think it due to you to address you in the same spirit on the present occasion. I will address you as I candidly did Mr. Crawford in 1824, when, without being personally acquainted with him, I requested a particular friend to visit Washington specially, with a confidential letter, to request an explanation upon a point of fact, in which he might be supposed to be deeply compromitted. He met the matter with the utmost possible frankness—explained all the circumstances, and removed every doubt and apprehension.

But to the point at once;—I refer to Mr. Calhoun's Correspondence. It is in vain for him to disclaim any "allusion to one particular individual"—*he does intend you,* and so every man who reads the publication will suspect. I will go further. The prompt declaration of the President has not been sufficient to clear you from the imputation. Many do believe it who were your friends and his. One of your mutual friends at Washington (who is in the President's confidence, I know) assured me, three weeks ago, that he knew all the circumstances and that you had had no agency at all in this affair. My friend Campbell, to whom I wrote six or seven weeks ago *upon this very point,* with the privilege of showing my letter to the President and to yourself informed me in reply that you had no hand in it. I know not whether he showed you my letter. I really wish he had. But this information is not in such a shape as to be given to the Public, and it wants your own stamp to make it more decisive.

I need not inform you that this matter is the subject of universal conversation among us. Many of our friends have expressed their doubts and fears, some, very vehemently: and a forcible article is° already put into my hands, by a warm friend of the administration, explaining the attitude in which he thinks this Correspondence places yourself.

Discussion is inevitable. It struck me from the first and I am now more strongly satisfied of it. Will you then excuse me for asking your attention to the subject—for asking frankly whether you were concerned or consulted in bringing up this difference between the President and Vice President, and, moreover, for suggesting that you * should take the same public course which the Vice President has taken—now that *he* has taken it—and make it clear to the Nation that his allusions to *you* are without foundation. All the evidence, which my Correspondent at Washington wrote me was in the possession of your friends, ought to be at once and fully produced,—every atom of it, with the most perfect and unblenching frankness. It is due to yourself and I am confident, to the Administration.

I address you Sir, without any circumlocution or intermediation. But if you have no objection I would take it as a favor that you show my letter to Gen. Jackson. I address you, too, with the sincerest wishes that you may be able to demolish every doubt, every apprehension, every political enemy. I trust that the thing may be made out as clear as a ray of light from Heaven. It has been my gratification to write you more agreeable letters, but never one that was dictated in a franker or more friendly spirit.

I am, dear Sir, Resp^y yours,

THOS. RITCHIE,
Richmond, Feb. 21, 1831.

As soon as all the persons of this drama had come forward—Mr. Calhoun with his pamphlet, Gen. Jackson with a few authorized statements in the *Globe*, and Messrs. Crawford, Forsyth, and Hamilton with their letters and explanations, I published this Card:

[From the U. States Telegraph, Feb. 26.]

MR. VAN BUREN TO THE EDITOR OF THE TELEGRAPH.

Mr. Van Buren transmits the enclosed to the Editor of the United States' Telegraph for insertion in his paper of tomorrow.

February 25th, 1831.

Mr. Van Buren desires us, in relation to the correspondence between the Vice President and various other persons which has recently appeared, to make the following statement in his behalf.

He observes that an impression is attempted to be made upon the public mind that certain applications by James A. Hamilton, Esq., of New York, to Mr. Forsythe, the one in February 1828, and the other last winter, and a similar one to the Vice-President, for information in regard to certain Cabinet transac-

---

° MS. IV, p. 45.

* I correct my expressions. I would not have you rush into the newspapers, if some person, who is conversant with all the facts, would frankly come forth with all the exculpatory evidence, in the calmest but most ingenuous terms.

tions during the administration of Mr. Monroe and which are referred to by the latter gentleman, were so made by Mr. Van Buren's advice or procurement. Leaving the motives and objects of those applications to those who may deem it necessary to notice them, Mr. Van Buren avers that they and each of them were not only made without agency of any description on his part, but also without his knowledge; and that he has at no period taken any part in the matters connected with them.—He desires us further to say that every assertion, or insinuation, which has for its object to impute to him any participation in attempts, supposed to have been made in the years 1827 and 1828 to prejudice the Vice President in the good opinion of Gen. Jackson, or at any time, is alike unfounded and unjust. He had no motive or desire to create such an impression, and neither took, advised nor countenanced, directly or indirectly, any steps to effect that object. For the correctness of these declarations he appeals, with a confidence which defies contradiction, to all who have been actors in the admitted transactions referred to, or who possess any knowledge on the subject.

Washington, Feb. 25, 1831.

I have known few more striking instances in public life of a strong current of prejudice and suspicion arrested not only, but turned back upon those who started it, by an exposition so simple and so brief. Its effects were no less visible in their faces than in their conduct, and beyond the reckless invectives of the *Telegraph* no serious efforts were made further to uphold the plot. Many of my friends, roused from the stupor into which the apparent difficulties of the time had thrown them, urged me to go on and sustain my denial by the use of documents, some of which were then in my possession, and by the direct testimony of every person who had been named as principals or agents and who were all ready and anxious to come forward. Hamilton, as will be seen by his letter to Lewis, was somewhat miffed that he was not called upon to exculpate me. Gen. Jackson could not forbear, years afterwards, when he heard of the reconciliation between Mr. Calhoun and myself, to send me a not only unsolicited but entirely unexpected letter testifying to my innocence,[1] of which he was, of all others, the best informed because he was the man whom I was charged with attempting to prejudice and inflame against Mr. Calhoun. Two or three of these papers are inserted here, * * * but at the time I refused to go a step beyond my Card. I opposed to the charges and insinuations of my enemies a defiant contradiction and a character which, tho' long and vilely traduced, had never been successfully impeached. Before these the 'plot' exploded, aided as they were by the utter unsoundness of the materials out of which it was constructed which became more and more manifest to the apprehensions of men as the excitement subsided.

The preliminary steps, relied upon as evidence of its original concoction and design, occurred in the years 1827 and 1828; the year pre-

---

[1] 1840, July 31. In the Van Buren Papers.

ceding the Presidential election in which Gen. Jackson was chosen, and the year of that election. The immediate object of the plotting was (it was said) to obtain evidence that Mr. Calhoun had acted an unfriendly part in Mr. Monroe's Cabinet towards the General touching his conduct in the Seminole war. This would have been proof of ill will on the part of Mr. Calhoun of which it was conceded the General had never been informed and of the existence of which he never even suspected. *Cui bono*—such an operation?[1]

The friends of Mr. Crawford, who had supported him at the previous election, were, in Virginia, in New York, indeed in most of the States, save perhaps somewhat less cordially in Georgia, rallying to the support of Gen. Jackson, on the same ticket with whom, as candidate for the Vice Presidency, and bound to the support of that ticket by interest and I doubt not by feeling also, stood Mr. Calhoun. The ascertainment of any fact which might place the relations between Mr. Crawford and Gen. Jackson upon a more cordial footing and by that means stimulate the comparatively sluggish support of the Georgians, an object avowed by the so called 'conspirators' and discussed on the trip to New Orleans, would have been a sensible movement. But what could be said or thought of an attempt to ferret out a fact which would have then inevitably produced, as it did produce when it came to light, hostility perhaps outbreak between Gen. Jackson and Mr. Calhoun and a dismemberment of the ticket? Would not Lewis and Hamilton and their advisers, if they had any, have deserved to be called mad men if they conceived or entered upon such a scheme? Suppose, for the sake of meeting every ground of suspicion or of imputation that their object was to obtain information to be used at some distant day, after the election, to bring about the desired alienation between their candidates—would they then have gone directly to Mr. Calhoun and thus putting him on the track of their machinations have addressed to him the question the prosecution of which was to bring to light the evidence of his hostility to Jackson on a certain occasion, the precise question put to Crawford and then not yet answered? Would they not rather have waited for the desired information which Mr. Crawford's well known enmity to Mr. Calhoun authorized them to expect speedily from him? No! The notion of a design " to extract from him, if possible, some hasty and unguarded expression respecting the course of the Cabinet on the Seminole question," by which he might be " entangled "· will be found, on looking at the facts as afterwards stated by Mr. Calhoun in his 'appeal' unsustained by a single circumstance or feature of the case, and the simple solution of the matter is doubtless this:—Mr.

---

[1] A good presentation of this affair will be found in Bassett's Life of Andrew Jackson, (N. Y., 1911) chap. xxiv, vol. 2, p. 497 *et seq.*

Calhoun's reflections satisfied him that in the account which he had given to Hamilton of the proceedings in the Cabinet he had made a mistake which, if published, would in all probability render necessary a further and unreserved disclosure of those proceedings in their integrity, like that which, in the sequel, he felt himself constrained ° to give in his ' appeal.' The certain consequence of such a step would have been, as he could not doubt, to involve him then in a quarrel with Gen. Jackson, as it did involve him when it was afterwards taken by the publication of the ' appeal.' This he was for obvious reasons anxious to avoid—for which purpose the only resource (if any existed) was the interdiction of the publication of what he had already said and the refusal to add further disclosures, on the ground of the sanctity due to Cabinet proceedings. By this course the revelation of the disturbing proceedings would, at the worst, be left to chance, and if Hamilton, after it had slept for two years, had not shown Forsyth's letter to Lewis manifestly as a matter of curiosity, that revelation might never have been made.

This was the construction ultimately placed by most disinterested and fair minds upon all the assertions and inuendoes, statements and counterstatements in the case, and the conviction became general that what plotting there was had been directed by other hands and aimed at the destruction of a different individual. In all my subsequent political contests the charge of concocting and engineering that famous conspiracy was never revived against me, unless the vague and remote allusions on the occasion of the rejection of my nomination as Minister to England—when the use of the charge was in keeping with its original object, may be considered such a revival.

I did not see any of the papers contained in Mr. Calhoun's pamphlet before its public appearance in February 1831, but had, in the way I have described, received general impressions in respect to their contents. Our intercourse, consequently, became daily more and more formal and ceased altogether after I had read that work. From that time until the extra-session of Congress in September 1837, a period of between six and seven years, our relations were those of undisguised hostility. At that session he supported the principle and the recommendations of my Message to Congress openly, ably, and without reserve. This was no holiday determination, promising recreation and ease. The doctrines to the support of which he thus committed himself unavoidably involved him in the internecine war with the Money-Power of the Country—a power by which he had been as well in the early as in the later periods of his political career, not a little petted—and he encountered the hazards and toils of that struggle upon the official invitation of a President with whom he was not

---

° MS. IV, p. 50.

and had not been for nearly seven years upon speaking terms. I appreciated and expressed, on all fitting occasions, my respect for and admiration of his noble bearing. But it could work no change in our personal relations, until the gulf which he had created, as has been described, between us should be bridged by a satisfactory concession of the injustice which had been done to me. No one understood better than he or was more sensible of the propriety of my course in avoiding the slightest advance towards a personal reconciliation. Altho' prepared in his feelings to take the first step in that direction himself he deferred doing so for more than two years for reasons which he assigned on the floor of the Senate in reply to Mr. Clay's insinuations upon the subject which shall be hereafter noticed. At the session of 1839–'40, soon after my Message had been sent in, William H. Roane, one of the Senators from Virginia and a worthy son of Spencer Roane, Jefferson's confidential and devoted friend, asked an interview for the special purpose of conversing with me upon the subject of the existing personal relations between Mr. Calhoun and myself. The substance of his communication was that on their way to Washington Mr. Calhoun had told him that he thought the time had arrived to put an end to the non-intercourse which had so long existed between us and that he had outlived his prejudices against me and was ready to make proper advances to that end,—that agreeing in politics and engaged as we both were in the support of a great public question such a course, in respect to our personal relations, was in his judgment demanded by public considerations of an imperative character,—that altho' he did not expect to find anything in it to change his views he would prefer to see my forthcoming Message before any step was taken in the matter, but after that he wished Mr. Roane, if not otherwise instructed, to communicate to me what had passed between them, and if the course referred to was agreeable to me, he and Mr. Roane would make me a friendly visit, and, in that way, accomplish the object in view, and he thought this would be best done without referring to the past. I accepted the proposition with unaffected cordiality, and named the time at which I would receive them. They called and as we shook hands, Mr. Calhoun, in a few well chosen terms, repeated what he had said to Mr. Roane, which, being replied to in the same spirit, was succeeded by general conversation upon the topics of the day.

Mr. Calhoun's separation from the party at the head of which stood Clay and Webster after having so long acted with them in opposition to Gen. Jackson's Administration, excited their ill-will, as is usual in such cases. He was fiercely attacked for his course by Mr. Clay on two occasions. The first was in February 1838, when the Independent Treasury Bill passed the Senate, and the next in December 1839, when the personal reconcilation between Mr. Calhoun and myself became publicly known. The debates on both occasions have been carefully and impartially reported by Col. Benton in the second volume of his *Thirty Year's View*, and are unusually interesting, the lines of attack and defence extending to the entire political lives of both Senators and exhibiting on both sides thorough preparation and extraordinary ability.

On the first occasion the previous personal relations between Mr. Calhoun and myself had been harshly commented upon, as respected the former, at the very threshhold of the debate but the reconciliation had not then taken place. When that became public Mr. Clay forthwith lugged it into the discussions of the Senate.

Mr. Calhoun brought forward a Bill authorizing the cession of certain portions of the public lands, which he had introduced before any of the occurrences here referred to, notwithstanding which fact, Mr. Clay enquired of him whether the measure now brought forward was favored by the Administration and based the enquiry upon the rumored change which had recently taken place in the personal relations that had so long existed between the Senator and the President. This was followed by a succession of thrustings and parryings upon various points, spirited, and not wanting in an undertone of bitterness. After some protesting against the indecorum of Mr. Clay's course in dragging his personal relations before the Senate, Mr. Calhoun felt himself constrained by his persevering personality to enter into an explanation of what had taken place between us so far as that had any public bearing, and it is due to him that I should give it in his own words.

I will assure the senator, if there were pledges in his case, there were none in mine. I have terminated my long-suspended personal intercourse with the President, without the slightest pledge, understanding, or compromise, on either side. I would be the last to receive or exact such. The transition from their former to their present personal relation was easy and natural, requiring nothing of the kind. It gives me pleasure to say, thus openly, that I have approved of all the leading measures of the President, since he took the Executive chair, simply because they accord with the principles and policy on which I have long acted, and often openly avowed. The change, then, in our personal relations, had simply followed that of our political. Nor was it made suddenly, as the senator charges. So far from it, more than two years have elapsed since I gave a decided support to the leading measure of the Executive, and on which almost all others since have turned. This long interval was permitted to pass, in order that his acts might give assurance whether there was a coincidence between our political views as to the principles on which the government should be administered, before our personal relations should be changed. I deemed it due to both thus long to delay the change, among other reasons to discountenance such idle rumors as the senator alludes to. That his political course might be judged (said Mr. Calhoun) by the object he had in view, and not the suspicion and jealousy of his political

opponents, he would repeat what he had said, at the last session, was his
object. It is, said he, to obliterate all those measures which had originated
in the national consolidation school of politics, and especially the senator's
famous American system, which he believed to be hostile to the constitution
and the genius of our political system, and the real source of all the disorders and dangers to which the country was, or had been, subject. This done,
he was for giving the government a fresh departure, in the direction in which
Jefferson and his associates would give it, were they now alive and at the helm.
He stood where he had always stood, on the old State rights ground. His
change of personal relation, which gave so much concern to the senator, so
far from involving any change in his principles or doctrines, grew out of
them.[1]

° The declaration of Mr. Calhoun that he was induced to sustain
my Administration, then in the third year of its existence, the
course of which he had minutely watched under the influence of
extreme prejudice, by his desire to co-operate in a system of measures designed and well calculated " to obliterate all measures which
had originated in the National Consolidation school of politics,"
which he believed to be " the real source of all the disorders and
dangers to which the Country was or had been subject," and " to
give the Government a fresh departure in the direction in which
Jefferson and his associates would give were they now alive and
at the helm," was certainly a compliment of great value coming
from such a source. My motives in settling and promoting its
course could not have been more ably or truly delineated. Nor was
the same debate wanting in a marked expression of personal respect
from Mr. Clay towards myself even whilst he censured Mr. Calhoun
for supporting my policy. At the very commencement of his arraignment of that gentleman for his desertion of the Whig party,
after repeating some violent speeches about me which he charged
upon him, he thus spoke for himself:

Who, Mr. President, are the most conspicuous of those who perseveringly
pressed this bill upon Congress and the American people? Its drawer is the
distinguished gentleman in the white house not far off (Mr. Van Buren); its
indorser is the distinguished senator from South Carolina, here present. What
the drawer thinks of the indorser, his cautious reserve and stifled enmity
prevent us from knowing. But the frankness of the indorser has not left us
in the same ignorance with respect to his opinion of the drawer. He has often
expressed it upon the floor of the Senate. On an occasion not very distant,
denying him any of the noble qualities of the royal beast of the forest, he
attributed to him those which belong to the most crafty, most skulking and
the meanest of the quadruped tribe. Mr. President, it is due to myself to say,
that I do not altogether share with the senator from South Carolina in this
opinion of the President of the United States. I have always found him, in
his manners and deportment, civil, courteous and gentlemanly; and he dispenses,
in the noble mansion which he now occupies, one worthy the residence of the

---

[1] Extract from Calhoun's speech. 1838, in the debate between Clay and Calhoun.
Benton's Thirty Years' View, 2, 120.
° MS. IV, p. 55.

chief magistrate of a great people, a generous and liberal hospitality. An acquaintance with him of more than twenty years' duration has inspired me with a respect for the man, although, I regret to be compelled to say, I detest the magistrate.[1]

The word 'detest' expressed without doubt the Speaker's disapprobation of my official conduct with exaggerated emphasis as an offset, for the gratification of his followers, to the personal compliment; which latter seems indeed a bold and hazardous exploit when one recalls the descriptions of the desperate wickedness of my political designs with which Mr. Clay and his associate orators had long labored to excite the Country. It is apparent that he felt the political necessity of taking back with one hand what he bestowed liberally and genially with the other.

I invited Mr. Calhoun to my table and he and his family frequently broke bread with me, our intercourse at once assuming a friendly and familiar footing. I felt that he had made me the *amende honorable* in the face of the Country and in a way wholly free from exception. The prejudices I had naturally imbibed against him on account of previous transactions were as effectually wiped from my mind as if they had never existed. He supported my Administration during the residue of my term and his State gave its vote in favor of my reelection—that being the first time in twelve years that she had voted for the Democratic candidate. Withdrawn from Washington by the loss of the election I never saw Mr. Calhoun again, but nothing occurred to give a character to our personal relations different from that which we had ourselves given to them, until the time approached for the designation of the Democratic candidate for President for the election of 1844.

It was perhaps not surprising that Mr. Calhoun should, under the circumstances I have narrated, not only have thought himself entitled to the nomination but have also thought that I ought not to permit my name to be brought forward in opposition to him. He was slightly my senior in age and altho' not earlier in the political field had much sooner become conspicuous in Federal politics than myself and had been twenty years before supported for the Presidency by a respectable section of the party. If for a season at variance with a majority of its members, he had returned to its support at a critical period and was then in full communion, and had, what I assumed to have been, his own sense become the sense of our political friends generally, I would not have felt disposed to interpose obstacles in the way of its gratification. Indeed I do not hesitate to say that I should very decidedly have preferred his nomination to that which was finally made. But whilst nobody

---

[1] Extract from Clay's speech, 1838, in the debate between Clay and Calhoun. Benton's Thirty Years' View, 2, 101.

then thought of the latter save as a busy applicant for the second, few evinced a preference for Mr. Calhoun's nomination for the first place. It turned out, on the contrary, that the mass of the party—certainly two thirds and probably three fourths of its members—considering that they had, in 1840, with absolute unanimity, approved the principles upon which I had administered the Government, and had, with equal accord, nominated me for re-election, and that I had been defeated almost without reference to the soundness or unsoundness of those principles but thro' the instrumentalities and debauncheries of a political Saturnalia, in which reason and justice had been derided, deemed it due to the honor of their cause that the reproach of that defeat should be effaced, when they had recovered their ascendancy in the popular vote, under an organization similar to that which had been subjected to it, and that this desirable object required my nomination. In their avowals of that opinion personal preferences appear to have had little weight. They were the expression of the conviction of a great party in respect to what was due to its own character and important to its future usefulness and such a decision was entitled to respect and acquiescence on the part of the minority. I had no right to withhold my consent to the action by which it proposed to effect that object when satisfied that its course had been determined upon fairly and its wishes unmistakably pronounced. A letter was addressed to me at an early period in the canvass by Mr. Henry Horn, a distinguished democrat from Pennsylvania, calling for my decision of that very question. My answer was, and it could have been no other, that, whilst I would take no steps to promote my own nomination, I would not deny the use of my name to the Democratic party if it was required. This answer was published.[1]

Mr. Calhoun was opposed to my renomination, and at once took the field to defeat it. The first intimation I had of his determination was derived through a family affair and was not on that account less convincing to my mind. In the winter of 1842 I visited the South and was engaged to pass a few weeks at the residence of Col. Singleton, in South Carolina; that gentleman being the father-in-law of my eldest son and standing in the same relation to Mr. McDuffie, the early and abiding friend of Mr. Calhoun. On the invitation of Col. Singleton, Mr. McDuffie, who had, in letters written to me for that purpose, applauded the course of my Administration in the strongest terms, agreed, long before I left home, to meet me on the occasion of my visit, but he did not come altho'

---

[1] Horn's letter of 1841, Nov. 13, and Van Buren's reply, Nov. 26, are in the Van Buren Papers. The reply was printed in the *Nashville Union*, 1842, Feb. 6.

expected from day to day and his non-arrival gave rise to much disappointment and to various conjectures as to its cause. I did not think proper to enlighten my worthy host, altho' I well understood the circumstance to be an evidence of Mr. Calhoun's determination, and however I might and did deprecate a new rupture in that quarter I could only regret it. Mr. Calhoun's friends in Charleston, in addition to many other acts of unaffected personal kindness, united with some gentlemen who were politically well disposed towards me, independently of his views, in inviting me to a public dinner which I declined, in conformity with my invariable practice. He continued his opposition in various ways, one of which will necessarily be referred to in speaking of another matter, until my name was withdrawn from the National Convention when his friends, who had until that time attended it as spectators, had their names entered as delegates from South Carolina and took part in its action.

Whilst it would be idle to deny that the agreeable feelings excited by the reconciliation which had succeeded to many years of enmity, between Mr. Calhoun and myself, were somewhat blunted by these transactions I still do myself the justice to say that they were not eradicated. I could not with justice impute to him much blame, after his long and, having regard to what is considered the *ultima Thule* of political life, adverse career, for wishing to prevent a nomination the defeat of which ° might enure to his own advancement, and I knew of no steps taken by him to promote his wishes the employment of which would not, as the world goes, have been deemed allowable. I saw therefore no cause of personal hostility in his course neither was any such feeling engendered in my breast, although, from 1844 to the period of his death, there was no intercourse between us.

This whole affair was perhaps as satisfactorily disposed of as could be expected among eager and excited politicians. All that remains to be done in respect to it and to kindred matters of a common origin, such as nullification and the rejection of my nomination as Minister to England, none of which would, in all probability, have ever arisen, certainly not at that time, but for the Eaton *imbroglio*, and in most of which Mr. Calhoun was a prominent actor, is that the facts in respect to them should be well ascertained and correctly recorded.

° MS. IV, p. 60.

CHAPTER XXVIII.

These transactions and questions possess an interest beyond the actors in them and the times in which they arose. That of which I am now writing was a political quarrel between the highest officers of the Republic in which, altho' an attempt was made on one side to make its injurious consequences fall on an humbler head, the principals appeared in proper person, and it involved a review of the conduct of a public war in respect to acts of grave importance affecting the rights and, as it was supposed, the honor of a third Power. Another—South Carolina nullification—brought to the test the construction of the Federal Constitution upon a point vital to the existence of the Government and from the desperation of the contest to which it gave birth exposed the Federal Union to greater peril than any which it has at any other time encountered. The next was an attempt by a controlling part of one of the great branches of the Federal Government to humiliate and degrade its representative at one of the first Courts in Europe, performing his official duties in the presence of similar representatives from all the civilized States of the world—to do this upon pretences which not only were discountenanced, as will be seen, so far as was allowable, by the Government to which he was accredited and condemned by all just and liberal foreigners whose attention was directed to them, but were denounced by a majority of the People of the United States, by whom the intended victim was raised to the first place in the Government whilst the authors of the attempt were ever afterwards excluded from their confidence when they acted in their highest function of selecting the Chief Magistrate of the Republic.

These things occurred in the face of the world. They belong to history and those who from time to time are moved to carry forward the work of history will pay their respects to them whether the actors or their representatives do so or not. We have seen in our day that the power of truth and the progress of liberal ideas have broken down the barriers behind which it was the custom to keep hidden the secrets of States and Statesmen, and have established the rule that they shall at proper times, and having regard to the feelings of the actors, be brought into view, and that accordingly the private papers of our public men, which were deemed to possess any interest, have been unreservedly given to the public. When these sheets see the light, if they ever do so, the time will have arrived for the application of these principles to the transactions of which

I am speaking, without ground of complaint on the part of any. Altho' my narrative combines the disadvantages of being told by a party interested in the scenes I describe, with the advantages of having been a contemporary and eye witness, I aim only to do justice on all sides under the guidance of the first and fundamental law of history as declared by Cicero, that "it should neither dare to say anything that is false, nor fear to say anything that is true."

The "Plot" having exploded, the *brochure* got up by the Congressional printer (Duff Green) and hawked about by Congressional messengers, lay on public and private tables a *Caput mortuum* exciting little feeling other than pity for the weakness in which it was engendered. I might be pardoned a momentary feeling of exaltation when I saw my bitter and remorseless enemies struggling in the toils which they had prepared for my destruction; I certainly had reason to rejoice that so fitting an opportunity had been presented to place my conduct—such as it really had been on an occasion which might have offered strong temptations to an intriguing politician—fairly before the Country and to contrast it with the untiring machinations against me. This was a point of peculiar importance, as the efforts to fasten impressions upon the popular mind of a capacity and disposition on my part for political intrigue had met with a greater degree of success than had attended other calumnious assaults upon my character, and to have the falsity of charges of this description so satisfactorily demonstrated at a moment when those impressions were upon the point of doing me the greatest harm was both useful and gratifying.

Nor was the prospect of the personal and political advantages to be derived from my continuance in office without allurements. The Eaton affair, which had been the plague spot of Administration during two years past, had lost its interest or suffered eclipse, and offered no further embarrassment which might not be ended, if it became expedient, by sending the immediate parties on a foreign mission, as was afterwards done, and the so considered refractory members of the Cabinet might have been left in possession of the pageantry of their official positions so long as they did not, by complicity with its enemies, obstruct the course of the Administration, or they might have been dismissed, without the slightest disturbance, when they did so.

There seemed, indeed, no insurmountable obstacle so far as related to the Executive branch of the Government to the further prosecution of the idea to which I have before referred as one which had taken full possession of my thoughts from the time I became thoroughly acquainted with Gen. Jackson's qualities and with his power over the public mind, namely, to essay how far the political capital thus furnished—the greater, all things considered, than had been possessed by any previous Administration—might be successfully employed in the acquisition of public advantages which, under less potential auspices I would have justly regarded as hopeless. Nevertheless the interval between the publication of Mr. Calhoun's Correspondence and 'appeal' and my resignation of the office of Secretary of State was clouded by doubt and anxiety in regard to my future course. Through the transactions of which I have spoken and the strong emotions excited by them in the breast of Gen. Jackson my position had become, in the phrase of the day, that of heir apparent to the succession. I needed no more than my experience for the past two years, confirmed by that of Messrs. Adams and Clay, to satisfy me of the great evils to which an Administration was exposed whose chief Cabinet officer occupied that position. They were of a nature impossible to escape the eyes of any but the foolhardy and blindly ambitious. It was not safe to found hopes of exemption from them on the examples of success in such situations furnished by the earlier periods of the Government. In those days the selection of candidates was confined to comparatively few individuals and the republican party was not the theatre for Presidential intrigues upon any thing like the same scale as that since in vogue. No degree of abstinence or discretion on the part of the Minister plausibly suspected of aiming at the succession could protect an Administration thus encumbered from the assaults to which he would inevitably expose it. Whether he availed himself of his position to intrigue for his advancement or not he would be charged with doing so by thousands who would believe him guilty of it and by other thousands in the ranks of the supporters of the Administration who would think themselves interested in spreading such a belief. Thus the design of working for my own elevation at the expiration of Gen. Jackson's first term was freely imputed to me whilst I solemnly affirm that I had been a steady advocate of his re-election and was exerting myself at the time to put down movements that were attempted in my behalf.

Near the close of the first year of the Administration, in reply to some givings out in my favor by Major Noah, of the *New York Courier and Enquirer*—an editor proverbially imprudent and who in the sequel became worse—the *Telegraph* stated as follows: " We KNOW that no one is more opposed to the agitation of that question [that of the succession] than Mr. Van Buren, and that he permits no fit opportunity of discountenancing and discouraging it to pass by ·unimproved." Without enquiry into the motives of this apparently friendly statement, the course of events makes it proper to say that it was made before the establishment of the "*Globe*" and before matters were ripe for an attack on me—perhaps before such a step was contemplated, It was at all events, at a time when the editor of the *Telegraph* hazarded nothing in ° saying about me what he honestly believed to be true, but no sooner had war been declared in form by Mr. Calhoun than my desire to precipitate the question in regard to the succession and my intrigues to secure my own elevation at the end of Gen. Jackson's first term were his daily themes. When I come to speak of my first nomination for the Presidency I will have occasion to refer to circumstances which will place my entire course upon this subject beyond the reach of cavil. Altho' it was not in his power to lay his hand upon a shred or semblance of evidence to show that my conduct upon the point in question had varied in the slightest degree, yet his views of his own interests having changed and the period having arrived for the development of projects which had been for some time in preparation, the absence and indeed non-existence of proof made no difference and I knew that it would make no difference in future either with him or with the affiliated presses of which he spoke to Mr. Duncanson, or with the opposition press in general. That was the vantage ground from which the attacks of all were to be made to the end of the war, which if the general should be re-elected and should live so long, was to last for a period of six years; a ground the strength and efficacy of which were likely to be constantly increased during that interval by the addition of new aspirants to the Presidency from our own ranks and to be brought to bear upon Congress, the press, the people and wherever else such aspirants might hope to discover recruits. In my cordial aversion to being made the cause of such a warfare upon the Administration of that honest old man who had devoted the remnant of his life and strength to the public service and upon the interests of the Country committed to his charge, the idea originated of resigning the high office to which I had been appointed. My inquietude was doubtless increased sensibly by the reflection that I had been the object of similar assaults before I came to Washington, and that I had hoped by the change in my field of action to throw off the hounds by whom personal character is hunted down. I was for many years, while in the service of my state persistently charged with influencing the action of the appointing power for my own advancement when I was thoroughly conscious that there was not one among my cotemporaries who estimated as lightly as I did the advantages of such appliances, or who was more disinclined by taste and by judgment than myself to meddle in them. Such incessant defamation added to the thousand vexations to which official station is otherwise exposed wore upon my health and spirits to an extent which would now be deemed incredible by such of my associates as judged only

---

° MS. IV, p. 65.

from what they saw of me in public, but which nevertheless made
me at times heartily sick of public life; so much so that I often
determined, during successive winters, to throw up the offices I held,
in the spring and to confine my future exertions to my profession.
These resolutions as they were from time to time formed were the
subject of discussions in my family and occasionally communicated
to my friends; the latter however did not believe in them, and I
had perhaps no right to expect them to do so as, thro' causes more
easily appreciated than described, I myself had so often contra-
dicted my professions by my action when the time arrived for
carrying them into effect. They were notwithstanding always sincere. Of the frequent occasions on which I was thus 'seriously
inclined' one occurs to my recollection as I write to which I will
refer. Whilst holding the offices of State Senator and Attorney
General, I was one afternoon about to return to Albany from
Schenectady whither I had been called by business. I found Colonel
Aaron Burr at the hotel enquiring for a conveyance to Albany and
as I travelled in my own carriage I offered him a seat. The period
was after his return from Europe and when his fortunes were at
their lowest ebb. Our drive occupied us till a late hour of the evening during which I was entertained much by his free, caustic and
characteristic observations. Whilst sounding me in regard to my
political expectations, of which he was pleased to say complimentary things, I surprised him by the remark that I thought of giving
up politics and of devoting myself to my profession and that with
that view I meant to resign my place in the Senate in the ensuing
spring. He was curious to know my reasons and I gave them in the
spirit I have here indicated. After a brief reflection he answered,
"Sir! you have gone too far to retreat. The only alternative left
to you is to kick or to be kicked, and as you are not fool enough
to prefer the latter you will not resign!"

CHAPTER XXIX.

My career in State politics had been in general successful and in the end signally such. After competing for a quarter of a century, the greater part of the time as the undisputed leader of my party in my County and State, with such men as De Witt Clinton, Ambrose Spencer, Abraham Van Vechten, William W. and William P. Van Ness, Elisha Williams, Thomas P. Grosvenor, Thomas J. Oakley, John Duer, Chancellor Jones, David B. Ogden, Harry Croswell, Solomon Southwick and William Colden, *mutatis mutandis*, I left the service of the State for that of the Federal Government with my friends in full and almost unquestioned possession of the State Government in all its branches, at peace with each other and overflowing with kindly feelings towards myself, and not without hope that I might in the sequel by good conduct be able to realize similar results in the enlarged sphere of action to which I was called. I soon found, however, that in respect to the practicability of carrying into effect the best intentions there was a peculiar difference between the two systems, which young Statesmen will do well to bear in mind. Whilst the public functionary connected with the State Government acts almost under the eyes of and in constant intercourse with those who are the judges of his actions and consequently has full opportunity to enable them to appreciate his motives, under the General Government the actions of the official are, with very few exceptions, to be passed upon by men a vast majority of whom can have no personal knowledge on the subject and who must weigh his conduct at a distance and decide from report. Having learned to estimate at its true value this important distinction and convinced by experience and observation of the aggravated effects which it promised to long continued harping upon the old theme, even false as it was, I felt that my success was at least doubtful. It should be borne in mind that in the days when this conclusion was arrived at respect was yet maintained for the obligation of Government to preserve the purity of the elective franchise, or as declared by President Jackson in his Inaugural address, to eschew " bringing the patronage of the Government into conflict with the freedom of elections." My apprehensions might well be derided at the present time when the contrary practices are indulged in by all parties with a license that contemns both right and decency and which threatens, if not seasonably arrested, to subvert our institutions.

Having accepted a high and responsible official trust, I was duly conscious that I was not at liberty to permit personal considerations to control my course in resigning it, and I certainly did not design to do so. The success of Gen. Jackson's Administration and his own tranquillity and comfort were to be promoted, in my judgment, by that step, nevertheless views and considerations of self obtruded themselves in all my deliberations in regard to it; it was not possible to exclude them altogether and to say how far I was influenced by them would require a greater proficiency in self-knowledge than I pretend to. They at all events mitigated the sacrifice involved in the course on which I decided when stimulated afresh by the plots, intrigues and calumnies by which I had been for two years surrounded, I recurred to my often formed and often abandoned resolution to retire from the political field.

This is as full and as correct a view as it is, at this late day, in my power to give of the opinions and feelings under which I resigned the office of Secretary of State, a step which, from its being at the time entirely unexpected, produced much excitement, which my opponents found or affected to find impossible to comprehend, and which my friends did me the honor to regret. It has seemed to me, under present circumstances, proper to give it, whether it may be deemed of a nature to attract approval or disapproval, to qualify, or to confirm the opinion heretofore formed of my conduct on the occasion.

The only inmate of my household at the time, besides the servants, was my son Colonel Van Buren, to° whom alone I confided my intention and who after hearing my reasons, unhesitatingly concurred in them, notwithstanding the professional and social advantages which he derived from my official position and residence and which surrounded him with strong inducements to regret the step I was about to take. A fit occasion to break the matter to the President was only waited for and that I looked to find during one of our frequent rides. Several however occurred and passed by without my having had the heart to broach the subject and as I returned from each with the business undisposed of I was received with a good humoured laugh at my expense by my son. My hesitation arose exclusively from my apprehension, I may say consciousness of the pain the communication would give to the General. On one occasion we were overtaken by a severe thunder storm which compelled us to take shelter in a small tavern near the race course, and to remain there several hours. His spirits were on that day much depressed and on our way out he spoke feelingly of the condition to which he had been reduced in his domestic establishment, Major

Donelson and the ladies and children, of whom he was exceedingly fond, having, some time before, fled to Tennessee to avoid the Eaton malaria, leaving Major Lewis his only companion in the Presidential Mansion. I have scarcely ever known a man who placed a higher value upon the enjoyments of the family circle or who suffered more from interruptions of harmony in his own; feelings which are more striking in view of the fact I have mentioned before that not a drop of his own blood flowed in the veins of a single member of it. But they were generally the near relatives of a wife whose memory he revered. Observing his unusual seriousness I said little to him during our detention and spent much of the time in an adjoining room conversing with an intelligent farmer of the neighbourhood who had been driven to the same shelter by the storm. When the rain ceased we remounted, and, as the weather was still lowering, soon took to a brisk canter. We had not gone far when his horse slipped on the wet road and threatened to fall or to throw his rider. I was near enough to seize the bridle and thus to assist him in regaining his footing. As he recovered his seat, the General exclaimed quickly " You have possibly saved my life, Sir !" I said that I did not regard the danger he had escaped in so grave a light, yet congratulated myself on the service whatever might have been its degree, to which he answered in broken and half audible sentences which I understood to import that he was not certain whether his escape from death, if it was one, was, under existing circumstances, worthy of much congratulation. Neither the incidents of this day nor the General's frame of mind invited me to make the communication which I still kept in store for him.

We subsequently started earlier than usual and with charming weather bent our course up the Potomac river. After passing Georgetown I missed one of my gloves and begging him to go on returned to look for it. On remounting after finding it, and putting my horse to a gallop to overtake my companion I resolved that I would break the subject of my resignation to him forthwith. We were just turning from the Potomac road towards Tenally Town and he was expressing a more cheerful and sanguine view of our prospects of relief from domestic broils, saying, with confidence that " we should soon have peace in Israel," when I replied " No! General, there is but one thing can give you peace." He asked quickly "What is that, Sir ? " to which I answered—" My resignation ! " Thirty years have passed since that day and still I recall to mind the start and the earnest look with which he received the words as vividly as if the scene had occurred yesterday. " Never, Sir ! " he said solemnly, " even you know little of Andrew Jackson if you suppose him capable of consenting to such a humiliation of his friend by his enemies:"

I was myself not a little confused by the warmth and vehemence of his exclamation, but after a few moments of silence to recompose my thoughts I returned to the subject. His expressions applied, as it was natural they should in the first instance, to the personal aspect and bearing of the suggestion. The idea presented to his mind was that of sacrificing his friend to appease the clamor of his enemies than which nothing could be more revolting to his feelings. I therefore hastened to say that my faith in the extent and sincerity of his friendship had no limits—that I knew as well as I knew anything that he would sooner endure any degree of personal or official injustice and persecution than consent to my leaving the Cabinet for any object or for any reasons save such as were by the obligations of honor and of patriotism made binding upon both of us; that he would immediately perceive that our personal feelings and interests were not worthy of consideration, under the circumstances in which we found ourselves, when compared with the greater question of what we both and especially what, from the higher character of the trusts he had assumed, he owed to the Country and to the people whose agents we were. Undoubtedly there were many and important points to be calmly and carefully reviewed before we could hope to arrive at a correct conclusion on the main question, and I assured him that I had not ventured to disturb his feelings by the suggestion I had made without having long and anxiously considered it in every possible aspect and that, if he would give me a patient hearing, I thought I could satisfy him that the course I had pointed to was perhaps the only safe one open to us. He agreed to hear me but in a manner and in terms affording small encouragement as to the success of my argument. I proceeded for four hours, giving place only to brief interrogations from him, to present in detail the reasons upon which my suggestion was founded, extending to a careful and, as far as I was able, a clear review of the public interests and of our own duties and feelings involved in the matter. In the course of it we passed without notice the Tenally Town gate, always before the limit of our rides in that direction, and did not reach home until long after our usual dinner hour. He heard me throughout not only with patience but with deep interest. In returning he asked me what were my own views, as to the future, if he should accept my resignation. I replied that I would return to the practice of my profession, but he instantly declared that such a result, or any that would be matter of triumph to our enemies would be an insuperable objection with him whatever might be his conclusion on the views of the principal question which I had presented to him and by which he confessed that his first impressions had been weakened. In this connection the English Mission was spoken of as probably the best means of carrying out his wishes if he should persist in them, and either then or subsequently I brought to his notice my understanding of the acceptance of that appointment as a virtual abandonment of any expectation or hope my friends might otherwise entertain on the subject of my accession to the Presidency. I begged him not to speak of my proposed resignation to any person, not excepting Lewis and Eaton, as it would be very undesirable to have it known, in case of failure, that such a wish had been entertained. He took my hand, at parting, and said that I had given him much to think of and that I must come over after dinner and discuss the subject again deliberately.

I had an engagement for the evening but promised to see him in the morning. When I called at the White House, on the following day my mind was not free from serious misgivings. The President had from the ingenuousness of his nature seemed to yield to the obvious force of the truth as I had spread it before him, but his concessions had been so evidently against his inclinations that I feared they would not be found to have kept their ground thro' the watches of the night. I had no sooner entered his room than I saw a confirmation of my apprehensions in the usual signs of a sleepness night, and on my expressing a hope that the propriety of my suggestion the previous day had been strengthened in his opinion by subsequent reflection he regarded me with an expression of countenance not indeed indicative of anger or excitement but on the contrary unusually formal and passionless, and said " Mr. Van Buren, I have made it a rule thro' life never to throw obstacles in the way of any man who, for reasons satisfactory to himself, desires to leave me, and I shall not make your case an exception." Without giving him time to say more, I rose from my chair and standing directly before him replied in substance that the matter had taken the turn I most feared and the apprehension of which had so often deterred me from broaching it; that he had allowed himself under the excitements and embarrassments of the moment to suspect that I was influenced by anticipations of the failure of his Administration and by a wish to escape in season from the consequences; that in this he had wronged my disposition and entirely misconceived my motives; ° that I had never felt wish more strongly than I wished then that I had a window in my breast through which he might read my inmost thoughts, but as that was vain and as words on such an occasion would have little value I could only oppose my actions to his distrust. " Now, Sir!" I concluded, " Come what may, I shall not leave your Cabinet until you shall say, of your own motion, and without reference to any supposed interests or feelings of mine,

° MS. IV, p. 75.

that you are satisfied that it is best for us to part. I shall not only stay with you, but, feeling that I have now performed my whole duty in this particular, I shall stay with pleasure and perform with alacrity whatever it may become proper for me to do." He seized my hand, and exclaimed "You must forgive me, my friend, I have been too hasty in my conclusions—I know I have—say no more about it now, but come back at one o'clock—we will take another long ride and talk again in a better and calmer state of mind." I found him with his usual punctuality already mounted at the hour appointed. We went again over the whole subject—he taking the parol and I contenting myself with full answers to his inquiries but pressing nothing. On our return he asked my permission to consult with Post Master General Barry to which I agreed adding a similar consent in respect to Major Eaton and Lewis. On the following day he told me that they had considered the matter together and had all come to the conclusion that I was right; that they were to be with him in the evening and he wished me to join them. Before leaving home I ordered supper to be prepared intending to bring them back with me, and after an hour or two with the President we adjourned to my house. Up to this time the idea of Eaton's resignation had not been thought of by any one as far as I knew or had reason to believe. It was a consummation devoutly to be wished but one I would have assumed to be hopeless and for that reason, I suppose, had never given it a moment's entertainment, and such would have continued to be the case if my attention had not been called to it by himself. Moreover I never doubted, as I have elsewhere said and as the result proved, that my resignation would disarm hostility to him and would thus answer every necessary purpose. On the way to my house the Secretary of War suddenly stopped us and addressed us nearly in these words: "Gentlemen, this is all wrong! Here we have a Cabinet so remarkable that it has required all of the General's force of character to carry it along—there is but one man in it who is entirely fit for his place, and we are about consenting that he should leave it!" Eaton's open hearted disposition and blunt style left no doubt that he said exactly what he thought, but the only answer he received was a loud laugh from the rest of the party. After getting within doors he recurred to the matter and asked "Why should you resign? I am the man about whom all the trouble has been made and therefore the one who ought to resign." His remarks again passed without particular notice, as the subject in that view of it was not free from delicacy.

At supper, however, he spoke of it again and, appearing somewhat hurt that his previous observation had not produced a response from either of us, said that he was so well satisfied that he was the person who ought to resign, if any one, that he would do so in any event. I then excused myself for having omitted to notice his previous intimations on the ground that as his resignation had not been spoken of or thought of before, I had regarded his remark as a matter of civility to myself, but it being now evident that he was in earnest I said he must permit me to ask, whilst knowing that he would do in the business what he thought proper, what Mrs. Eaton would think of such a movement as he proposed. He answered promptly that he knew she would highly approve of it. We then discussed the President's probable disposition in regard to it, and it was upon my suggestion, arranged that we should meet again at supper, at my house, the next evening and that Major Eaton should in the mean time talk the matter over with his wife and report to us. His report fully confirmed his statement and it was forthwith agreed that we should both resign with General Jackson's consent, which was obtained on the following day. Eaton's resignation was dated before mine because he preferred to have it so, but this is a correct narrative of the entire proceedings. I promised the President to accept the English Mission if I did not after consulting with my friends, give him satisfactory reasons for declining it, and among my correspondence will be found some letters from them upon the subject. In my letter of resignation[1] I placed the step upon the grounds herein set forth, saying in effect that the difficulties and embarrassments which I described could in no way be gotten rid of save by my resignation, or disfranchisement—that was by declaring, in a manner to obtain belief and to secure compliance, that I would under no circumstances accept the office of President, declarations which, all other considerations apart, I did not think it becoming in me to make:—a statement which my opponents affected to find difficult to comprehend.

Some time after our resignations were published—according to my recollection just before my departure from Washington and long enough after her husband's relinquishment of office to make her sensible of the change in her position, the President and myself having extended our walk as far as the residence of Mrs. Eaton, paid her a visit. Our reception was to the last degree formal and cold, and what greatly surprised me was that the larger share of the chilling ingredient in her manner and conversation fell to the General. Since my first acquaintance with her there had been no time when such a change towards myself would have very much astonished me. We staid only long enough to enable us to judge whether this exhibition

---

[1] Apr. 11, 1831, autograph draft is in the Van Buren Papers. Jackson's acceptance of the resignation, dated Apr. 12 is also in the Van Buren Papers.

was that of a passing freak or a matured sentiment, and after we had fairly quitted the house, I said to my companion—"There has been some mistake here." His only reply was "It is strange" with a shrug. As the topic was obviously not attractive it was dropped, but I was satisfied that our brief interview had been sufficient to convince him that in his past anxiety on her account he had at least overrated her own sensibilities.

DATE DUE
